# Leadership in Supply Management

ANNA E. FLYNN, PH.D.

Published by: Institute for Supply Management, Inc.™
Paul Novak, CPSM, C.P.M., A.P.P., Chief Executive Officer


P.O. Box 22160, Tempe, AZ 85285 USA
www.ism.ws



ISBN: 978-0-9815770-0-5

# Introduction

Institute for Supply Management™ became the name for our association on January 1, 2001. The name was changed in recognition of the shifting role that you play in your profession. That role is not just about purchasing any more and has not been for many years.

The knowledge required to be a successful supply management professional has broadened more quickly than any of us might have predicted. Many factors caused this change, but none were more important than your willingness and ability to take on an expanded role.

ISM's new qualification, which will be launched in 2008, recognizes the expanded body of knowledge that you are expected to master. The Certified Professional in Supply Management (CPSM) is a qualification through which you demonstrate your mastery of the body of knowledge and commitment to the profession.

This three-book series represents a compendium of the broad knowledge of our profession. While these books don't represent all there is to know about our profession, they serve to open the door to the complete body of knowledge.

ISM is committed to the development and communication of this body of knowledge. These books, along with the resources that membership in ISM offers, will help you expand your knowledge and skills throughout your career.

*Paul Novak,* CPSM, C.P.M., A.P.P.
CEO
Institute for Supply Management™

# ISM — Your Source for Supply Management Resources

Institute for Supply Management, Inc.™ (ISM) has served the supply management profession since 1915. As the first and largest supply management institute in the world, ISM works with affiliated associations to continually keep its members well informed and trained on the latest trends and developments in the field. ISM's membership base includes more than 40,000 individual supply management professionals. A not-for-profit institute, ISM provides opportunities for the promotion of the profession and the expansion of professional skills and knowledge.

The information available from ISM is extensive. One of the greatest resources is the ISM Web site, www.ism.ws. In addition to general information, this expansive site features a vast database of supply management information, including a list of general supply management references as well as an extensive article database, listings of available products and seminars, periodicals, contact information for ISM affiliate organizations worldwide and links to other related Web sites. The *members only* online Career Center is a valuable resource for both individuals seeking jobs and organizations recruiting prospective employees.

The monthly Manufacturing and Non-Manufacturing *Report On Business*®, including the PMI for the manufacturing survey and the NMI for the non-manufacturing survey, continues to be one of the key economic indicators available today. ISM members receive this valuable report in the pages of *Inside Supply Management*® magazine. *Inside Supply Management*®, a monthly magazine (available to members only), is the authoritative resource for supply management executives, focusing on leadership strategies and trends.

The A.T. Kearney Center for Strategic Supply Leadership at ISM (CSSL) is an exclusive organization where today's and tomorrow's forward-thinking senior supply executives convene for thought leadership and a view into solutions and opportunities for the next two to four years.

Founded in 2004, the Center emerged because of a gap identified by today's senior leaders. The Center is committed to exploring the future two-year to four-year supply management horizon and translating it into robust, strategic development programs designed for executives.

The Center serves as a catalyst for new thought in the field of supply management. It is dedicated to closing the gap between the growing expectations of CEOs and the results delivered by their organizations' supply partners.

ISM also publishes the *Journal of Supply Chain Management,* a one-of-a-kind publication for supply management scholars. Authored exclusively by highly recognized scholars in supply-chain management, this quarterly subscription publication offers up-to-date research and thought-provoking studies.

Members also enjoy discounts on a wide variety of educational products and services, along with reduced enrollment fees for educational seminars and conferences.

For supply management professionals interested in a professional qualification, ISM administers the Certified Professional in Supply Management (CPSM) program. ISM members receive discounts on test preparation materials, study books and materials and examination fees.

To provide a forum for educational enhancement and networking, ISM sponsors the Annual International Supply Management Conference. The annual conference, which attracts more than 2,000 participants worldwide, provides a unique opportunity for members and nonmembers alike to learn from each other and share success strategies.

To learn more about ISM and the many ways it can help you advance your career or to join online, visit ISM at www.ism.ws. To apply for membership by telephone, call ISM customer service at 800/888-6276 (United States and Canada only) or +1 480/752-6276, extension 401.

## ISM PROFESSIONAL SERIES

**Foundation of Supply Management**
Joseph R. Carter, DBA, CPSM, C.P.M.
Thomas Y. Choi, Ph.D.

**Effective Supply Management Performance**
Darin L. Matthews, CPPO, C.P.M.
Linda L. Stanley, Ph.D.

**Leadership in Supply Management**
Anna E. Flynn, Ph.D.

# Series Overview

In recent years, the supply management profession has begun to mature. No longer looked at as just "purchasing" or "procurement," supply management is viewed today as an integrative process that spans many disciplines and activities, providing both internal and external linkages across the supply chain. Today, ISM defines supply management as:

> *The identification, acquisition, access, positioning and management of resources and related capabilities that an organization needs or potentially needs in the attainment of its strategic objectives.*
>
> *Supply management includes the following components: disposition/ investment recovery, distribution, inventory control, logistics, manufacturing supervision, materials management, packaging, product/service development, strategic sourcing, procurement/purchasing, quality, receiving, transportation/traffic/shipping and warehousing.*

This definition cuts across industry sectors, global economies, private and public organizations and types of purchases. It covers both the day-to-day issues faced by supply management professionals and the strategic issues that shape supply management's structure and its influence in the organization.

In keeping with the spirit of the new, broader definition of supply management, Institute for Supply Management™ has broadened the scope of its new qualification to fit the latest demands on supply management professionals. This three-book series was designed to specifically address the issues of concern to supply management professionals today. These books help professionals better understand the potential scope and concerns within supply management. These books also are designed to support the new Certified Professional in Supply Management (CPSM) examination and professional credentials.

The three books are organized around the three examinations of the CPSM as follows:

1. *Foundation of Supply Management*
2. *Effective Supply Management Performance*
3. *Leadership in Supply Management*

These three books all support the strategic supply management process across various industries, cultures and types of purchases. The strategic supply management process is illustrated in the following Figure I-1:

**Figure I-1 Strategic Supply Management Process**

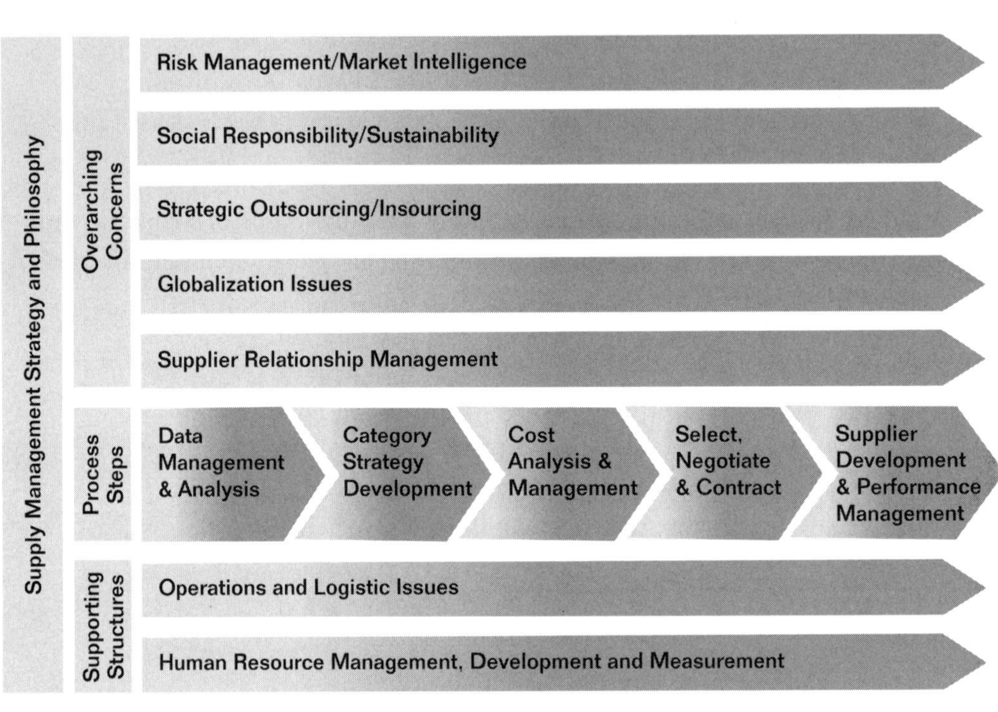


On the far left of the figure is the vertical box, "Supply Management Strategy and Philosophy." This is the way that supply management is viewed by the organization and the way that supply management views itself. It embodies the culture of the supply management organization as it works to support the objectives of the larger organization.

At the top of the figure, the small vertical box "Overarching Concerns" deals with five major issues that supply management professionals face today: Risk Management, Social Responsibility, Strategic Outsourcing, Globalization Issues and Supplier Relationship Management. Supply management professionals must consider all five major issues in their strategic decision-making. While supplier relationship management has long been recognized as important by most progressive organizations, the other four issues have taken on a new importance in recent years. Because of their overarching nature, these issues are touched on in each of the three books in a variety of ways. More specifically, supply management professionals must ask the following questions:

1. What risks might we face and how can we plan for these risks?

2. How does the decision we are making fit with the organization's social responsibility objectives?

3. Is outsourcing an option for this particular decision? How would this affect the answers to these other questions?

4. Are there global solutions available, and how does the source of supply fit with the market in which we are selling? This may be particularly relevant for purchased services.

5. What type of relationship do we want to have with our supplier(s) for this item and why?

Within supply management, some basic "Process Steps" must occur, as illustrated in the middle of the figure. Virtually all organizations have a model for the execution of the supply management process that includes all these activities, although they may be divided into a different number of steps. The process begins with a thorough analysis of internal and external data to better understand the threats and opportunities in the internal and external environment. Next, specific strategies are developed for the particular purchase category and tactics for developing those strategies are identified. Closely related to this, the organization engages in a cost analysis of the item, looking for ways to better manage and reduce costs. It then narrows down the choice of suppliers through data analysis and bidding, negotiates and develops the contract. Finally, ongoing supplier measurement and management occurs, and may include supplier development efforts to improve supplier performance.

To support these activities, a supply management professional must work closely with other supply management professionals responsible for operations and logistics, as well as have an excellent system in place for managing and developing the organization's most valuable resource, its people. These are the "Supporting Structures" for supply management.

Volume 1, *Foundation of Supply Management,* deals with several of the more traditional areas of concern for supply management, yet looks at these issues from a leading-edge perspective. This volume covers data analysis, budgeting, cost management, including cost-price analysis and total cost of ownership analysis, and leasing arrangements. This book also provides an in-depth view of sourcing, negotiating and contracting with suppliers. Taken as a whole, these chapters provide an excellent perspective on the process steps associated with strategic sourcing. The final third of the book focuses on three of the overarching concerns of supply management: supplier relationship management, social and legal responsibility and international issues, including global sourcing, logistics and exchange rate and countertrade issues. This book is a critical read for those who might be relatively new to supply management, those who have not had a formal education in supply management and anyone who wants to stay abreast of the latest practices in supply management.

Volume 2, *Effective Supply Management Performance,* focuses on many of the operational issues that are part of a successful supply management performance. The latest surveys show that supply management professionals are responsible for a majority of the components of supply management; many of these are detailed in the definition of supply management provided previously. These are new areas of interaction for many supply management professionals. Volume 2 provides coverage of many operational issues such as project management, new product and service development, forecasting, warehousing, materials handling, logistics and international transportation, asset and inventory management and quality. These all provide supporting structures for supply management. The book closes with an in-depth discussion of supplier performance management and metrics and information systems as key ways to integrate knowledge within and across organizations. This book is a must-read for anyone newly assigned to operations-oriented issues or who supervises or manages transportation, logistics or inventory management personnel as part of his or her supply management responsibilities.

Volume 3, *Leadership in Supply Management,* focuses on many of the human resources issues that supply management professionals face. The first half of the book, "Creating a Shared Vision," explores management issues within the supply organization, such as managing and leading, developing shared values and setting direction, creating alignment and creating commitment for the supply organization's shared vision. These chapters deal with issues such as various leadership styles, developing strategies, aligning with internal and external stakeholders, team building and managing conflict. These are critical supporting structures for supply management. The second half of the book, "Managing Complexity," focuses on risk management and mitigation, developing business plans and linking these to the strategic sourcing process, including outsourcing, developing and staffing the supply management organization, providing rewards and professional development for supply management and executing the strategic sourcing process. This section includes a look at issues related to the overarching concerns of supply management, the process steps of supply management and the supporting structures. Taken as a whole, it deals with human resources and strategic issues of management that all supply management functions face.

This book should be read by anyone who manages the supply management function or who is involved in the supply management strategy setting and planning process.

It has been a privilege to be involved in this important project, supporting the continued growth and recognition of the supply management profession. It has been challenging for all of those involved to capture the vast amount of material represented in these three volumes. The extensive practical and theoretical knowledge and expertise of the excellent group of authors will provide the reader with both a broad and deep perspective of the topics covered here. I hope you find these books both interesting and valuable as you study for the new CPSM examination or simply work on enhancing your own knowledge of supply management.

Lisa Ellram, Ph.D.
C.P.M., A.P.P., CMA
Series Editor

Lisa M. Ellram, Ph.D., C.P.M., is chair of the department of management at Colorado State University's College of Business. Ellram joined the CSU College of Business as Allen Professor of Business in 2006. Prior to that, she was the John and Barbara Bebbling Professor of Business at Arizona State University's W.P. Carey School of Business. Dr. Ellram earned her undergraduate degree and her MBA from the University of Minnesota. She earned her master's and doctorate from The Ohio State University. She is a certified management accountant.

Dr. Ellram is an award-winning educator and prolific publisher, and has spoken to audiences throughout the world. She has garnered sizeable grants for research in areas including strategic cost management, outsourcing, total cost modeling and supply chain sustainability. Dr. Ellram is a member of the Institute for Supply Management™ (ISM) and a member of the editorial review board for *Inside Supply Management*®. She is currently Editor-in-Chief of the *Journal of Supply Chain Management.*

# Preface

This book is divided into two parts, "Part I: Creating Shared Vision" and "Part II: Managing Complexity." Chapter 1 explores the differences and similarities between *leadership* and *management.* Chapters 2 through 4 focus on the three primary roles of a leader: setting direction, creating alignment and gaining commitment. These aspects of leadership are fundamental to the strategic sourcing process depicted in Figure P-1, and cut across the entire process.

"Vision is a key component of leadership; it is that mental journey from the known to the unknown, creating the future from the montage of current facts, hopes, dreams, risks and opportunities that effective leaders embrace in all walks of life."[1] A shared vision focuses and energizes and inspires commitment from everyone to attain it.

"Part I: Creating Shared Vision" focuses on three aspects of leadership: setting direction, creating alignment and gaining commitment. Chapter 1, "Leading and Managing," discusses the differences and similarities of leadership and management. Chapter 2, "Setting Direction," addresses three components: (1) creating a values-

**Figure P-1 Strategic Supply Management Process**

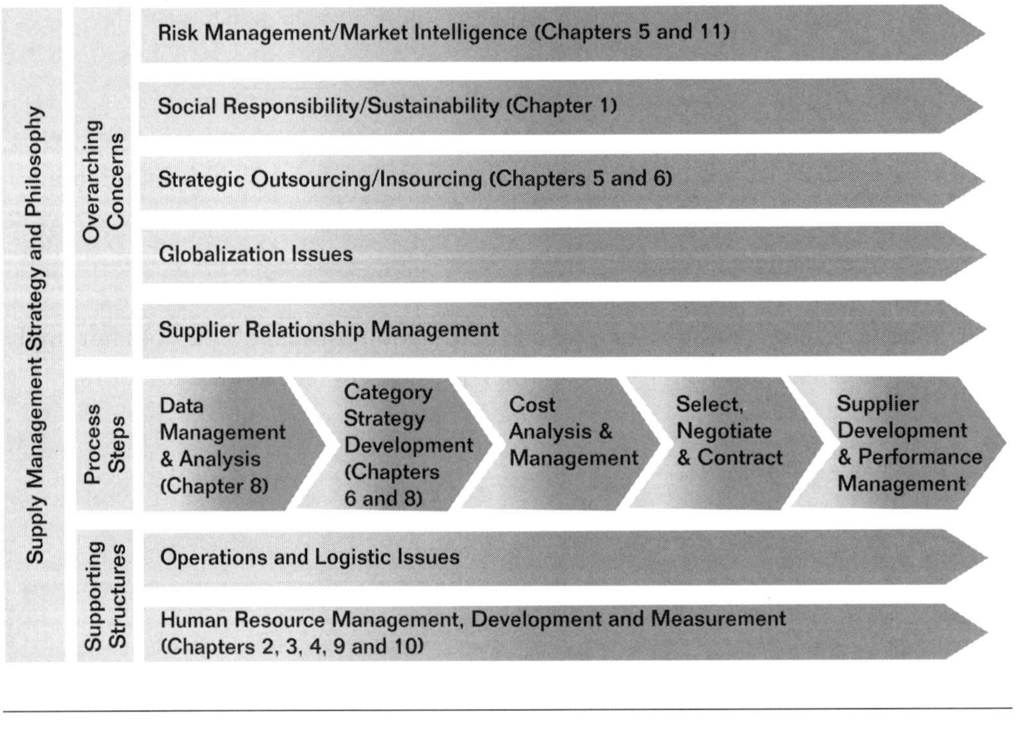

Supply Management Strategy and Philosophy

Overarching Concerns
Risk Management/Market Intelligence (Chapters 5 and 11)
Social Responsibility/Sustainability (Chapter 1)
Strategic Outsourcing/Insourcing (Chapters 5 and 6)
Globalization Issues
Supplier Relationship Management

Process Steps
Data Management & Analysis (Chapter 8)
Category Strategy Development (Chapters 6 and 8)
Cost Analysis & Management
Select, Negotiate & Contract
Supplier Development & Performance Management

Supporting Structures
Operations and Logistic Issues
Human Resource Management, Development and Measurement (Chapters 2, 3, 4, 9 and 10)

based organization, (2) assessing risks and opportunities and (3) developing vision and strategies. Chapter 3, "Creating Alignment," focuses on developing internal and external business partnerships. Chapter 4, "Gaining Commitment: Motivating and Inspiring People," discusses approaches to communicating vision and energizing people to attain that vision.

"Part II: Managing Complexity" focuses on the managerial aspects of planning, organizing, staffing, controlling and problem-solving (budgeting is addressed in *Foundation of Supply Management* (ISM Professional Series)). Planning (and budgeting), which are complementary to the leadership task of setting direction, are addressed in Chapter 5, "Assessing, Mitigating and Managing Supply-Based Risks," and Chapter 6, "Developing Business Plans." These chapters focus on the role of supply professionals in assessing risks from a supply perspective and developing sourcing and supply management plans that align with organizationwide plans. Organizing and staffing, complementary to the leadership task of creating alignment, are addressed in Chapter 7, "Organizing and Building Supply Management Infrastructure," and Chapter 8, "Developing a Strategic Sourcing Process and Adopting Enabling Technology." Chapter 7 addresses the issues around building an effective supply management structure, and Chapter 8 covers the development and implementation of an efficient and effective sourcing process with relevant policies and procedures and performance-enabling systems and technology. Chapter 9, "Staffing the Supply Management Organization," focuses on attracting, retaining and empowering human capital, and Chapter 10, "Developing Supply Management Talent," addresses the ongoing professional development of that talent. Chapter 11, "Measuring the Supply Management Department Performance," addresses the tools and techniques available to measure and manage supply department performance relative to the vision, mission and strategies of the organization. Chapter 12, "Establishing Internal Controls and Ensuring Compliance," covers before-the-fact, during-the-fact and after-the-fact controls and compliance management.

The term *supply leader-manager* is used throughout this text. This does not imply that the same person always fulfills both roles. Rather, this reminds the reader that leadership and management are two different things and both are needed in an organization. Also, while reading this text, remember that organizations need many leaders at many levels just as they typically employ many managers. Leadership potential can and should be recognized and developed to the fullest in each person.

## About the Author

Anna E. Flynn, Ph.D. is the Clinical Associate Professor of Supply Chain Management at Thunderbird School of Global Management.

Prior to working with Thunderbird School of Global Management, Dr. Flynn was a Vice President who provided subject matter and instructional design expertise to the educational product development team at ISM. Before joining ISM, Dr. Flynn was a senior lecturer and director of the undergraduate program in Supply Chain Management (SCM) at Arizona State University where she was instrumental in developing corporate relationships with recruiters. Dr. Flynn also taught *Purchasing and Supply Management* and *Research and Negotiation*. She used purchasing case studies and projects, in which teams analyzed cost and price data and purchasing benchmarking data, and developed and implemented negotiation strategies using techniques such as value analysis, process mapping, and root cause analysis. The SCM Program consistently received the highest ratings from students in the College of Business for teaching, and academic and career advising, areas for which Dr. Flynn was directly responsible.

Dr. Flynn is co-author of the ISM Supply Management Knowledge Series Volume IV, *The Supply Management Leadership Process* (2000), co-author of *Value-Driven Purchasing: Managing the Key Steps in the Acquisition Process* (1995), and co-author of the 13th edition (2006) of *Purchasing and Supply Management* with Michiel R. Leenders, Harold E. Fearon, and P. Fraser Johnson. Dr. Flynn's interest in teaching people to be effective decision-makers led her to conduct her doctoral research on the influence of groups on problem solving in a case-based learning environment. She combines a practical outlook and approach with impressive academic credentials and up-to-date knowledge in the field of purchasing and supply management. Dr. Flynn earned a bachelor's degree in international studies from the University of Notre Dame, an MBA from Arizona State University, and a Ph.D. in learning and instructional technology from Arizona State University.

# Contents

## Chapter 1: Leading and Managing



## Chapter 2: Setting Direction

## Chapter 5: Assessing, Mitigating and Managing Supply-Based Risks



## Chapter 6: Developing Business Plans

## Chapter 8: Developing a Strategic Sourcing Process and Adopting Enabling Technology



## Chapter 9: Staffing the Supply Management Organization

## Chapter 10: Developing Supply Management Talent



## Chapter 11: Measuring the Supply Management Department Performance

CHAPTER

# 1

# Leading and Managing

*The manager asks how and when;*
*the leader asks what and why.* WARREN BENNIS[1]

*Great managers look inward; great leaders*
*look outward.* MARCUS BUCKINGHAM AND CURT COFFMAN[2]

*You've got to think about big things while you're*
*doing small things, so that all the small things go*
*in the right direction.* ALVIN TOFFLER

There are no answers to the *how* and *when* questions until the *what* and *why* questions have been answered. And once the leaders have looked outward to determine what direction the organization should go in and why it is going there, managers are needed to look inward to ensure that the processes, procedures, policies and systems are in place to execute strategies. There is no benefit to managerial-led efficiency if the organization is going in the wrong direction. Doing small things the right way is a waste of time if they do not align with the big things. Therefore, leaders need managers and managers need leaders. Organizations need both.

Warren Bennis drew 12 distinctions between leaders and managers in his 1989 book *On Becoming a Leader:*

1. Managers administer; leaders innovate.
2. Managers ask how and when; leaders ask what and why.
3. Managers focus on systems; leaders focus on people.
4. Managers do things right; leaders do the right things.
5. Managers maintain; leaders develop.

6. Managers rely on control; leaders inspire trust.
7. Managers have a short-term perspective; leaders have a longer-term perspective.
8. Managers accept the status quo; leaders challenge the status quo.
9. Managers have an eye on the bottom line; leaders have an eye on the horizon.
10. Managers imitate; leaders originate.
11. Managers emulate the classic good soldier; leaders are their own person.
12. Managers copy; leaders show originality.[3]

The managerial and/or leadership behaviors a person will be called on to exercise will depend on the needs of the organization. These organizational needs are determined in large part by internal and external complexity and the pace of change. Effective leaders are in greater demand in times of rapid change. Effective managers are in greater demand in highly complex organizations. Both effective leaders and effective managers are in demand when a complex organization requires rapid, dramatic change. Most people would agree the world is experiencing both increasing complexity and rapid change.

If a complex organization needs dramatic and rapid change in how supply is managed, then the supply leader's ability to motivate and inspire people to embrace change may be the most important skill he or she possesses. Likewise, a supply management professional's ability to organize processes, structure, technology and people in alignment with the organization's vision may be his or her most important skill set. According to P. Fraser Johnson and Michiel R. Leenders, perhaps the greatest challenge facing CPOs is dealing with economic, political, social and technological external change compounded by internal change in structure, resources, responsibilities and roles. "Thus, coping and prospering, despite and perhaps because of change, may be the CPO's ultimate test."[4] Ken Newton, former chief procurement officer at Texas Instruments, Inc., (TI), for example, was brought into the company in 1996 "to change drastically the role and responsibilities of TI's procurement and logistics function." He faced the daunting task of transforming a highly decentralized transactionally oriented organization into a "proactive and strategic value-adding function." And he was an outsider in an organization that typically promoted from within.[5]

*Leading* and *managing* are both action words. But the question is, do leaders and managers engage in the same activities or different ones? And can or should these actions be executed by the same person or different people, and how many people can play leadership and management roles in an organization? Additionally, how does the external environment drive the need for leaders and managers in an organization? Also, how does the internal environment shape the roles and responsibilities of its leaders and managers and either enable or disable them in successfully executing these roles? Lastly, how can leaders and managers work in harmony to ensure effective development and execution in the pursuit of an organizational vision?

The first step in answering these questions is to clarify the differences between a leader and a manager. This chapter explores these two concepts more fully and lays the foundation for the remaining chapters. Chapters 2 through 4 focus on the specific actions of leaders and Chapters 5 through 12 address the corresponding actions of managers. All the chapters include organizational examples from different sectors, industries and countries. This chapter is divided into four sections: (1) what is leadership? (2) theories of leadership, (3) what is management? and (4) theories of management.

### CHAPTER OBJECTIVES

- Discuss different theories and perspectives on leadership and management.
- Describe the different roles and tasks of leaders and managers.

## What Is Leadership?

> *To lead people walk behind them.* LAO-TZU, ANCIENT CHINESE PHILOSOPHER[6]

*Leader. Leadership.* These terms are weighted with expectations that all too often are met with disappointment by the leader and his or her followers. Is leadership an art or a science or a little bit of both? Is it a skill that can be learned and developed or is it an inherent trait or attribute of an individual? Can a person develop and exercise his or her leadership ability in any sphere of influence or only in formal positions of power? If an organization possesses leadership that is superior to that of its competitors, will this give it a competitive advantage? Or is leadership about relationships and what occurs between and among people? These are questions that researchers and practitioners have explored for decades with changing perspectives across time and culture.

Leadership has been defined in many ways. The roots to the English words *lead* and *leadership* are found in the Old English word *lithan,* which means "to go," and the ancient root *leith,* which means "to go forth and die," as in battle. Leaders, by this last definition, mobilize one group against another and fight to the death. Leaders were typically authority figures who had leader status by virtue of their position. Recently, the term *leadership* has been prefaced with a descriptor such as ethical, collaborative or transformational. According to the 2006 edition of *Merriam-Webster's Dictionary,* leadership means "to guide on a way, especially by going in advance." This definition does not hint of conflict let alone death, but hints at being at the forefront and guiding people, not commanding them.

The leadership approach reflected in the Chinese philosophical system of Taoism contrasts with this Western image of one person leading a group of followers. Philosopher Lao-tzu is credited with writing the *Tao-te Ching* (*Classic of the Way of Virtue*) more than 2,500 years ago. It contains 81 poems outlining a philosophy that stresses uniting with and yielding to the natural flow of the universe. Diane Dreher, chairman of the English Department at Santa Clara University in Santa Clara, California, and author of *The Tao of Personal Leadership,* points to one of the best-known Tao verses as an example of its relevance to leadership: "With the best of leaders, When the work is done, The project completed, The people all say, 'We did it ourselves.'" According to Dreher, "The Tao leader is someone who can remain centered, be mindful, assess a situation, bring people together, build consensus and discover solutions by drawing on the talents of everyone involved."[7] Lao-tzu wrote that "to become an excellent leader, you have to abandon addiction to praise from above and flattery from below. The excellent leader leads least. He studies the distinctive skills and natural inclinations of both those above and those below, and he directs their attention to accomplish what is required to benefit all. When this has been done, all declare they have been part of a worthwhile purpose."[8]

This Chinese leadership model places high value on managing relationships. According to Lien Siaou-Sze, senior vice president of the Hewlett-Packard Technology Solutions Group in Asia-Pacific and Japan, "Before people will follow willingly and enthusiastically, they must truly believe in the leader. This is based on the leader's core values and the credibility that has been accumulated over time."[9]

The philosopher Confucius stressed the value of the thoughtful man, learning through mistakes while consciously respecting traditions and values. In Geert Hofstede's research on cultural influences in the workplace conducted from 1967–1973 in IBM in 70 countries and subsequent studies up to the present in many countries and occupations, China ranked the highest in terms of "long-term orientation" and lowest on "feelings of individualism."[10] This is reflected in the Chinese cultural tradition of *guan xi,* which stresses the relatedness and connections among individuals and the utmost importance of patience and perseverance. These differences require understanding and adaptation by all parties to work successfully in a multicultural business relationship or team.

In an interview in the *Harvard Business Review,* Zhang Ruimin, chief executive officer of the Haier Group, discussed his evolving leadership style. At present, he believes that Haier employees "need to make decisions for themselves and not to feel they are following me in their work." In explanation, he quoted Lao-tzu, who said, "In the highest antiquity, the people did not know that there were rulers." Ruimin interpreted this to mean that "a leader whose existence is unknown to his subordinates is really the most brilliant one."[11]

Until fairly recently, many Western definitions of leadership focused on a single person and his or her personal qualities or attributes and skills. The goal in colleges, universities and organizations was to identify the qualities or abilities, traits and behaviors of effective leaders and teach people how to exhibit these attributes to improve their leadership effectiveness as a result. According to Warren Bennis, "The most dangerous leadership myth is that leaders are born — that there is a genetic factor to leadership. This myth asserts that people simply either have certain charismatic qualities or not. That's nonsense; in fact, the opposite is true. Leaders are made rather than born."[12] Adherents to this thinking believe that organizations can seek out people with leadership potential and expose them to career experiences designed to develop that potential. With careful selection, nurturing and encouragement, dozens of people can play important leadership roles in a business organization.

The Western focus on the individual leader is changing in many settings. In their book, *The Leadership Challenge: How to Keep Getting Extraordinary Things Done in Organizations,* James M. Kouzes and Barry Z. Posner report that "What we've discovered, and rediscovered, is that leadership isn't the private reserve of a few charismatic men and women. It's a process ordinary people use when they're bringing forth the best from themselves and others. Liberate the leader in everyone, and extraordinary things happen."[13] According to *The McKinsey Quarterly,* organizations need a "cadre of leaders with the right capabilities at the right levels of the organization" to successfully execute strategy. "The leadership cadre typically includes the 3 to 5 percent of employees throughout the organization who can deliver breakthroughs in performance."[14] According to the Whirlpool Corp., for example, "The success of any company begins with its leadership — the men and women responsible for guiding the day-to-day activities of the business as well as identifying future opportunities for growth."[15]

Other definitions of leadership have focused on the leader's sources of power or aspects of the situation to determine how to improve leader effectiveness. Recently, conversations about leadership have been about influencing others by one's actions as well as one's words. According to mediation expert Mark Gerzon, effective leadership can then be viewed as "the ability to *involve others* in the process of *accomplishing a goal* within some larger *system* or environment. That is, a leader leads or influences a collaborator or group of coworkers towards achieving some end in the context of an organization, social community and environment. Leaders, therefore, have the ability to help people and organizations go from where they are to where they could or should be. Leadership is about change, growth and movement."[16]

Carlos Ghosn, for instance, became president and chief operating officer of Nissan Motor Co. after Nissan reported its biggest loss ever. He is credited with returning Nissan to profitability in 12 months. This was especially impressive because Ghosn was chosen by Renault, a French automaker and Nissan's controlling shareholder, to run a Japanese company. In an interview with *The McKinsey Quarterly,* Ghosn said, "I had to make a decision, and a decision has to come from strong inner beliefs. And my strong inner belief was that it was time to totally break with the past ten years of Nissan. At the end, I made a decision to commit my own job if any one of the objectives was not met. It was very important for the credibility of the plan, both internally and externally, to make this kind of commitment so people knew that you are going to be 100 percent behind the Nissan revival plan. The ultimate sacrifice for the top manager is to say, 'I'm putting my job on the line if I don't achieve these targets.' You can't ask a manager for more than this, especially in my position, because I had nothing to do with this [company's problems]. I was not in any way responsible for the situation. On top of this, I was saying, 'I bet my job on this.' So it has a high level of credibility. In a certain way, this limited — not eliminated — the anxiety and the skepticism about the question, 'Are they really going to do this?'"[17]

Warren Bennis also explores the idea of leadership in groups or "Great Groups" as he calls well-known, highly successful groups. Without exception, the leaders:

- Provide direction and meaning,
- Generate and sustain trust in the group and in the leadership,
- Display a bias toward action, risk taking and curiosity and
- Are purveyors of hope.[18]

Joseph Rost, author of *Leadership for the Twenty-First Century,* defines leadership as an influence relationship among leaders and followers who intend to make real changes that reflect their mutual purposes. This definition of leadership is characterized by "collaboration, power-sharing, facilitation and empowerment in a world that is more complex and diverse, mutually shaping and spontaneously changing."[19]

Contemporary definitions most often reject the idea that leadership revolves around the leader's abilities, behaviors, style or charisma. Today, scholars discuss the basic nature of leadership in terms of the "interaction" among the people involved in the process — both leaders and followers. Thus, leadership is not the work of a single person; rather, it can be explained and defined as a "collaborative endeavor" among group members. Therefore, the essence of leadership is not the leader, but the relationship.[20] This approach has relevance to the supply management leader who must collaborate internally with various stakeholder groups and externally with suppliers.

Other terms for leaders who focus on influencing and motivating disparate groups include "cross-boundary leaders" (John W. Gardner), "advocates for the whole" (Peter Senge), "bridging leaders" (Peggy Dulany and the Synergos Institute), "integral leaders" (Ken Wilber) and "third-side leadership" (William Ury). As the Welsh proverb says, "He that would be a leader must be a bridge." The command-and-control leadership style may be less effective in today's fast-changing, highly competitive markets. In its place is leadership that motivates people to want to take the leadership themselves to get from here to there.

For example, at TI, Ken Newton built the supply leadership team at the semiconductor division from the bottom up. He began by enlisting the help of TI insider and Senior Vice President Silicon Technology Development K. Bala to identify high-potential candidates for the purchasing and logistics group. To build the group's technical and wafer production, assembly and test credibility, Newton focused on people with strong technical qualifications and hired all but one person from within TI. Twenty-five full-time commodity procurement teams were created and given specific value targets and bonus opportunities. These teams reported to the Procurement Strategy Leadership Team (PSLT), which was composed of six to eight people from across major user groups worldwide. Goals were aligned with corporate goals.[21]

While Western leadership experts generally have viewed leadership as an individual characteristic until fairly recently, in less individualistic cultures, more emphasis is on the collaborative, communal nature of leadership. "More traditional approaches to leadership often talk about *individual* leaders and their followers, usually within organizations," observes Jacinto Gavino, professor at the Asian Institute of Management in Manila. Like many of his colleagues in Asia, Latin America and Africa, Gavino believes there is an "inordinate emphasis on the self" in the European and North American leadership model. Indeed, in the several dozen in-depth case studies of "bridging leaders" gathered from seven countries, Gavino and his fellow members of the Global Leadership Task Force found that the subjects of their research did not think of themselves as separate individual "leaders" but as part of a leadership "web," "fabric" or "community."[22]

The shift to cross-functional and cross-organization teams in North America and Europe may signify a shifting perspective in Western thinking to more of an effort to incorporate a collaborative view of leadership. As Peter Drucker said, "The leaders who work most effectively, it seems to me, never say 'I.' And that's not because they have trained themselves not to say 'I.' They don't think 'I.' They think 'we'; they think 'team.' They understand their job to be to make the team function. They accept responsibility and don't sidestep it, but 'we' gets the credit. ... This is what creates trust, what enables you to get the task done."[23]

The goals of leaders may also be influenced by culture. For example, University of Michigan Professor C.K. Pralahad says, "The quest is to develop a capitalism that 'puts the individual at the center of the universe,' placing employees and customers first so that they can benefit shareholders."[24] In an article titled, "Karma Capitalism," authors Pete Engardio and Jena McGregor discuss the trend of many senior managers and leaders to refer to and reflect on the teachings of the *Bhagavad Gita* to business.[25] One key message is that enlightened leaders should master any impulses or emotions that cloud sound judgment. Good leaders are selfless, take initiative and focus on their duty rather than obsessing over outcomes or financial gain. "The key point," says Ram Charan, a coach to CEOs such as General Electric (GE) Co.'s Jeffrey R. Immelt, "is to put purpose before self. This is absolutely applicable to corporate leadership today."[26] While many Indian management and leadership theorists emphasize interconnectedness, India is so large and diverse economically and socially that many perspectives influence their work. "We are a fusion society," according to Harvard's Rakesh Khurana. As a result, many Indian management theorists "tend to look at organizations as complex social systems, where culture and reciprocity are important," he says. "You won't hear too many of us say the only legitimate stakeholders in a company are stockholders."[27] What's more, India's extreme poverty imposes a natural pressure on its companies to contribute more to the common good.

While hotly debated in academic circles, Geert Hofstede's "dimensions of culture scales" are one valuable resource for gaining perspective on the cultural influencers on leadership around the world. Through his research he developed five scales: power distance index, individualism, masculinity, uncertainty avoidance and long-term orientation. The power distance index focuses on the degree of equality, or inequality, between people in the country's society. A high score reflects greater inequality and less allowance for upward mobility. Individualism focuses on the degree the society reinforces individual, or collective, achievement and interpersonal relationships. A high score indicates that individuality and individual rights are paramount within the society. Masculinity focuses on the degree the society reinforces, or does not reinforce, the traditional masculine work role model of male achievement, control and power. A high score indicates the country experiences a high degree of gender differentiation. In these cultures, males dominate a significant portion of the society and power structure, with females being controlled by male domination. The uncertainty avoidance index focuses on the level of tolerance for uncertainty and ambiguity within the society. A high score indicates the country has a low tolerance for uncertainty and ambiguity. This creates a rule-oriented society that institutes laws, rules, regulations and controls to reduce the amount of uncertainty. Long-term orientation indicates a society's time perspective and an attitude of persevering, that is, overcoming obstacles with time, if not with will and strength. Values associated with long-term orientation are thrift and perseverance; values associated with short-term orientation are respect for tradition, fulfilling social obligations and protecting one's "face." A long-term orientation is thought to support a strong work ethic where long-term rewards are expected as a result of today's hard work. However, business may take longer to develop in this society, particularly for an "outsider."[28] Supply leaders who are developing globally integrated supply networks must be able to lead people from many cultural backgrounds and orientations.

### What Do Leaders Do?

No matter what style or approach a leader adopts, he or she takes action and performs tasks. What are the tasks or actions of leaders? According to Tom Peters, management consultant, "Leaders focus on the soft stuff. People. Values. Character. Commitment. A cause. All of the stuff that was supposed to be too goo-goo to count in business. Yet, it's the stuff that real leaders take care of first. And forever. That's why leadership is an art, not a science."[29] John Wooden, Hall of Fame basketball coach, echoes this sentiment. "Knowledge alone is not enough to get desired results. You must have the more elusive ability to teach and to motivate. This defines a leader; if you can't teach and you can't motivate, you can't lead."[30]

No matter which definition or theory of leadership, all assume that leaders do something different than managers do. The belief that leadership is about action fits well with those who believe that leadership is all about results. In *The Extraordinary Leader,* John Zenger and Joseph Folkman define leadership as a combination of attributes × results. The attributes of a great leader are those that drive results such as unit profitability, retention statistics, customer satisfaction and employee commitment metrics, as well as those attributes that mean the most to those being led.[31]

In the *Harvard Business Review on Leadership,* Charles M. Farkas and Suzy Wetlaufer describe five approaches to leadership, each with a singular focus: strategy, people, expertise, controls or change. The approach taken depends on the leader's philosophy about how he or she can best add value. Strategy-focused leaders devote the majority of their time to external matters such as customers, competitors, technological advancements and market trends and delegate internal operational activities. People-focused leaders devote their time to managing and developing the organization's talent and to imparting the values, behaviors and attitudes that they believe will lead to success. These leaders delegate strategy development to those close to the markets. Expertise-focused leaders devote their time to the area of expertise that is the source of competitive advantage. Controls-focused leaders devote time to creating, communicating and monitoring internal controls. This is evident in highly regulated industries such as banking. Change-focused leaders devote their time to creating an environment of continual reinvention through communication activities designed to motivate people to embrace change. Each of these five approaches was found to give structure and meaning to the CEO's leadership role and to enable the CEO to deliver "clarity, consistency and commitment."[32]

Each of these approaches might be applied to leadership of a supply management organization depending on the nature and complexity of the business, the degree of change needed in the supply organization and the specific strengths of the supply leader. For example, TI's Newton took a people-focused approach. At Thomson Multimedia (TMM), Charles Dehelly, senior executive vice president of Strategic Business Units, IT, and sourcing from 1998–2002, focused on introducing supply management expertise from the high-tech sector that would make a difference to TMM competitively.[33] He introduced supply practices such as the Product Model Cost Follow-Up Process to track all costs for a particular product to take actions to improve margins and build joint responsibility for product success. He also focused everyone in supply management on measuring their return on capital employed. He was also personally involved in all major supplier initiatives.

Ram Charan identified eight things essential for leadership success:

1. Positioning and repositioning your business by focusing on the central idea that meets customers' needs and makes money
2. Pinpointing patterns of external change ahead of others
3. Leading the social system of your business by shaping the way people work together
4. Judging people by getting to the truth of a person and unleashing his or her natural talents
5. Molding a working team of leaders from a group of high-energy, high-powered, high-ego people
6. Developing goals that balance what the business can become with what it can realistically achieve
7. Setting laser-sharp priorities that become the roadmap for meeting your goals

8. Dealing creatively and positively with societal pressures that go beyond the economic value creation activities of your business[34]

Citing case studies from his consulting practice, Charan identified personal traits of leaders that help or interfere with becoming a true leader:

1. *Ambition.* The drive to accomplish something but not win at all costs.
2. *Tenacity.* The drive to search, persist and follow through, but not too long.
3. *Self-confidence.* The drive to overcome the fear of failure and response, or the need to be liked and use power judiciously but not become arrogant and narcissistic.
4. *Psychological openness.* The ability to be receptive to new and different ideas but not shut down other people.
5. *Realism.* The ability to see what can be accomplished and not gloss over problems or assume the worst.
6. *Appetite for learning.* The ability to grow and improve the eight "know-hows" and not repeat the same mistakes.[35]

The Center for Creative Leadership described the following leader behaviors that help create effective change:

- *Setting a direction.* The supply leader must develop a vision of the future and then define strategies for producing the changes needed to accomplish that vision. Key questions include: Where are we going? What are we going to do? Why are we doing it?
- *Aligning people.* Alignment involves communicating and building teams or coalitions with key stakeholders and making sure everyone understands where the organization is going and is acting cohesively to realize the vision. Key questions include: How can we stay together? How can we work better as a group? How can we improve cooperation?
- *Motivating and inspiring.* The leader generates commitment through the use of encouraging and supportive behaviors that keep people energized in the face of resistance to change. As John Quincy Adams said, "If your actions inspire others to dream more, learn more, do more, and become more, you are a leader." It is the relentless focus on the future and the movement toward that future that sets apart the leader from the follower. Key questions are: How can we develop a shared understanding of our situation? How can our actions be better coordinated?[36]

A number of theories of leadership have been developed to explain leadership effectiveness. These include motivational theories, contingency theories and competency models. These theories are addressed in the following section.

## Theories of Leadership

Prior to the 1980s, leadership development in organizations primarily focused on identifying different leadership *styles* and matching the style to a specific situation. Effective leadership was a function of adjusting one's style and actions to a particular situation to get someone to efficiently accomplish a specific task.

### Motivators of Behavior

David McClelland, the late Harvard psychologist, was a pioneer in research on the motives of leaders and how motives affect leadership behavior. He identified three "social motives" or internal drivers that explain behavior: achievement, affiliation and power.

McClelland's research showed that motives generate needs that generate aspirations that drive behavior. By identifying his or her primary internal driver, a person can assess his or her leadership style and make adjustments to improve leadership performance.[37]

**Achievement-Oriented Leaders.** A leader whose primary motivation is achievement will aspire to improve personal performance and meet or exceed standards of excellence, accomplish something new or plan for his or her long-term career advancement. As a result, the leader may micromanage subordinates, do things himself or herself or set the pace for others to ensure achievement. These leaders may give little positive feedback and few directions or instructions. In high-stress situations, high achievement–oriented leaders may cut corners and focus on goals and outcomes rather on than people.

**Affiliation-Oriented Leaders.** A leader whose primary motivation is affiliation will aspire to establish, maintain or restore close friendly relationships in an effort to be liked and accepted. This person may participate in group activities primarily for social reasons. As a result, the leader may avoid confrontation and avoid giving negative feedback, worry more about people than performance and look for ways to create harmony.

**Power-Oriented Leaders.** A leader whose primary motivation is power will aspire to be strong and to influence others. Power comes in two forms: personalized, where the leader gets his or her strength from controlling others and making them feel weak, or socialized, where the leader gets his or her strength from helping people feel stronger and more capable.

PERSONALIZED POWER. Leaders with a high need for personalized power want to control, persuade or influence people. They take actions to impress people inside and outside the organization and to maintain their reputations, positions or strength. These leaders generate strong emotions, positive or negative, in other people. As a result, the leader may be coercive and ruthless, control or manipulate others, look out for his or her own reputation and interests and focus more on impressing higher-ups (managing up) than on managing subordinates.

SOCIALIZED POWER. Leaders with a high need for socialized power want to help people feel stronger and more capable. They seek to persuade people and empower them. Leaders with a high need for socialized power, like those with personalized power needs, also take actions to impress people inside and outside their organization and to maintain their reputations, positions or strengths. However, their impact on others is more positive. These leaders give help, advice or support and generate strong positive emotions in others. As a result, the leader coaches and teaches, is highly supportive and more democratic and involves others in decision-making. These leaders focus on the team or group rather than on themselves and work through others. They enable others to do the work rather than doing it themselves.

## Six Leadership Styles

The Hay Group in Boston has continued McClelland's work and through its assessment of the motives of more than 40,000 managers and executives, it has identified six distinct leadership styles, each of which is appropriate in certain situations: directive, visionary, affiliative, participative, pacesetting and coaching.[38] Each style is appropriate in specific situations and with stakeholders who are motivated by different drivers. They are discussed in Chapter 3.

**Emotional Intelligence.** The Hay Group and Daniel Goleman have identified competencies that identify individuals with emotional intelligence. Emotional intelligence is defined as "the capacity for recognizing our own feelings and those of others, for motivating ourselves, for managing emotions well in ourselves and in our relationships." The competencies fall into four clusters: self-awareness and self-management (which relate to the individual's capacity for understanding one's own emotions and self-regulating behavior), social awareness (which relates to understanding the what and why of others' feelings and actions) and relationship management (which relates to the individual's ability to get desired results from others and reach personal goals).[39]

## Contingency Model of Leadership Effectiveness

The contingency model focuses on changing the situation, not the leader. Based on research that dates back to the 1950s, the contingency model of leadership effectiveness influenced leadership training programs into the 1980s. This model suggests that leadership effectiveness is contingent on the degree of control the leader has over a situation and the individual's style or typical way that the person interacts with members of the group. This model posits that the leader can improve effectiveness by focusing on changing critical aspects of the situation to enable the leader to better manage the situation, rather than focusing on changing his or her leadership style. The degree to which the leader has control over the tasks, the group and the outcome is referred to as situational control. When a person has the "right" amount of situational control, he or she tends to feel more secure, relaxed and at ease. The right level of situational control affects the leader's behavior and ability to function. A person must first establish the "right" level of situational control for optimal performance and then determine how to engineer or manage the situation to meet that right level.

**Task Motivated or Relationship Motivated.** The contingency model uses an assessment known as the least preferred coworker (LPC) to determine if a person is task motivated or relationship motivated. From this assessment, the leader is then able to determine how he or she is likely to behave if his or her level of situational control is low, moderate or high. A person's LPC score indicates the needs, goals and motivations that a leader will see as most important in various leadership situations. Behavior varies as the situation changes.

**Leadership Situation.** In the contingency theory, a leadership situation is classified by the degree to which it provides the leader with control and influence; the degree to which the leader can predict and determine what his or her group is going to do, and what the outcomes of his or her actions and decisions are going to be; and the degree to which the leader can predict with a high degree of certainty and assurance what will happen when he or she wants something accomplished. Control and influence are determined by (1) leader-member relations, (2) task structure and (3) position power. A high-control situation is one in which the group is loyal, dependable and supportive; the task is clearly spelled out, goals are known and there is a clear and accepted procedure for performing the task; and the leader has formal organizational power with the power to recognize and reward good work or punish poorly performed work. Of the three factors, leader-member relations is the most important, followed by task structure and, lastly, by position power.

## Competency Model of Leadership Effectiveness

The competency model of leadership effectiveness focuses on the attributes of effective leaders. According to *Merriam-Webster's Dictionary,* "an attribute is an abstraction belonging to or characteristic of an entity." An abstraction is a construct by which objects or individuals can be distinguished. Leadership attributes are often referred to as habits, traits, competencies, behaviors, styles, motives, values, skills and character. This movement has identified the knowledge, skills and behaviors that leaders possess.

Warren Bennis, for example, proposes a framework for leading knowledge workers. The leader should have:

- *Technical competence.* Business literacy and a grasp of one's field.
- *Conceptual skill.* A facility for abstract or strategic thinking.
- *Track record.* A history of achieving results.
- *People skills.* An ability to communicate, motivate and delegate.
- *Taste.* An ability to identify and cultivate talent.
- *Judgment.* Making difficult decisions in a short timeframe with imperfect data.
- *Character.* The qualities that define who we are.

Bennis believes that while all these skills are important, in tomorrow's world exemplary leaders will be distinguished by their mastery of the softer side: people skills, taste, judgment and, above all, character.[40]

## Leadership Is All About Results

In their book, *Results-Based Leadership,* Dave Ulrich, Jack Zenger and Norman Smallwood posit that it is organizational capabilities (such as agility or adaptability) and leadership competencies (such as trust, vision and character) that lead to and are connected to results. The formula is: effective leadership = attributes × results. Leaders must demonstrate the appropriate attributes and they must deliver the desired results. Results come in four major areas: employee results (human capital), organization results (learning, innovation), customer results (delight target customers) and investor results (cash flow). The focus is on identifying and developing effective measures of leadership results because what gets measured gets attention and should improve over time. The attributes side of the equation frames the behavior of leaders so that they do not focus on results at all costs or on the "I don't care what you have to do, hit the numbers!" mentality and practice.[41] What is accomplished is important and how it is accomplished is equally important. For example, according to Whirlpool Corp., "Whirlpool Corporation's management team believes in the company's values-based strategy. These executives put the customer at the center of everything they do, encourage innovative thinking, promote teamwork, and value the contributions of their employees."[42]

The Center for Creative Leadership developed a "Model of Leader Competencies" to help leaders see the broad repertoire of knowledge, skills and abilities needed to be effective. According to this model, it makes sense that different types of activities and assignments develop different competencies. The leader's task is to seek out experiences to gain the practice that is needed.[43] Cynthia McCauley, author of *Developmental Assignments: Creating Learning Experiences Without Changing Jobs,* offers guidelines for competency development (see Figure 1-1).

**Figure 1-1 Developing Leadership Competencies**

| BEHAVIOR | ACTIONS |
|---|---|
| **Adaptability** | Choose experiences that force you out of your routine or make you consider perspectives different from your own. |
| **Self-awareness** | Seek experiences in which people more readily give you feedback because you are new to the work or are trying to change or improve a situation. |
| **Managing yourself** | Find chances to set priorities, manage stress and keep balanced amid the pursuit of difficult goals. |
| **Capacity to learn** | Take on experiences that add diversity or require you to work in a completely different setting. |
| **Leadership stature** | Seek out experiences that you are attracted to and excited about taking on. |
| **Drive and purpose** | Find a way to play a key role in seeing that the organization achieves important outcomes. |
| **Ethics and integrity** | Commit to an experience in which having high-trust relationships is essential. |
| **Managing effective teams** | Practice managing a wide variety of teams in a wide variety of contexts. |
| **Building and maintaining relationships** | Choose experiences in which you are working with others to create change. |

| | |
|---|---|
| **Valuing diversity and differences** | Seek out opportunities that expose you to the value of diversity and difference. |
| **Developing others** | Find situations in which you must motivate and develop employees to be successful. |
| **Communicating effectively** | Practice your communication skills with different audiences. |
| **Managing change** | Choose experiences in which you are creating new directions or fixing problems. |
| **Solving problems and making decisions** | Find situations that require addressing ill-defined or recurring problems or making decisions that require broad input from across the organization. |
| **Managing politics and influencing others** | Take chances to work across organizational boundaries, exert influence without hierarchical power or engage in high-visibility work. |
| **Taking risks and innovating** | Search for experiences in which you and others are bringing fresh perspective to a situation or need to find new solutions to problems. |

*Source:* Cynthia McCauley, *Developmental Assignments: Creating Learning Experiences Without Changing Jobs,* Center for Creative Leadership, 2006.

## Transformational Leadership

The mid-1980s saw a shift in focus from "transactional" to "transformational" leadership. Transformational leaders promoted the expression of each individual's potential and helped the individual perform "beyond" the expected outcomes. Transformational leadership focused on vision, change management, motivation to continuous improvement and the key role of trust in promoting true team spirit.

The past decade has seen an extension of transformational leadership through the skills of visionary leadership and metaleadership (leading and developing other leaders). This has led to the emergence of other leadership abilities in relationship to promoting change, realizing core values, recognizing the potential of each individual and developing and empowering people.

In the emerging views of leadership, leaders do not have influence simply because they have positions of power. Rather, leaders are people who are committed to "creating a world to which people want to belong." This commitment demands a special set of models and abilities to effectively and ecologically manifest the visions that guide those committed to change. It involves communicating, interacting and managing relationships within an organization, network or social system to move toward one's highest aspirations. The transformational leader's tasks are outlined in Figure 1-2.

**Figure 1-2 Tasks of the Transformational Leader**

| TASK | ACTIVITIES |
|---|---|
| **Set vision and strategy** | Work in situations that allow you to think about possible future scenarios and craft strategies for aligning people and systems to achieve long-term objectives. |
| **Manage work** | Choose experiences that draw on managerial knowledge and expertise. |
| **Enhance business skills and knowledge** | Find opportunities to be exposed to parts of the business or organization with which you are less familiar. |
| **Understand and navigate the organization** | Seek out ways to operate within broader strategic initiatives, competing priorities and a network of relationships. |

### Pulling Together the Models

According to the contingency model, basically, with the right level of situational control, a leader can be effective in any given situation. The competency model essentially says that if the leader has the right set of attributes, he or she can be effective. Jack Zenger and Joseph Folkman take this a step further and describe the leadership sweet spot where the passions of the leader, the competencies of the leader and the needs of the organization intersect.[44]

The challenge is, of course, to match up people and organizations where a person's mix of competencies and passion fills the needs of the organization. Leadership development initiatives can be directed toward this goal and focused on identifying and strengthening competencies, fueling the individual's passion for the work and matching individuals to the appropriate roles in the organization. This approach recognizes that leaders hold formal or informal leadership positions. The goal is to fully develop the leadership potential of each person within his or her sphere of influence.

Figure 1-3 illustrates the three major roles of the supply leader or leadership team. Each of these tasks is discussed in detail in this book.

Figure 1-3 Major Leadership Roles

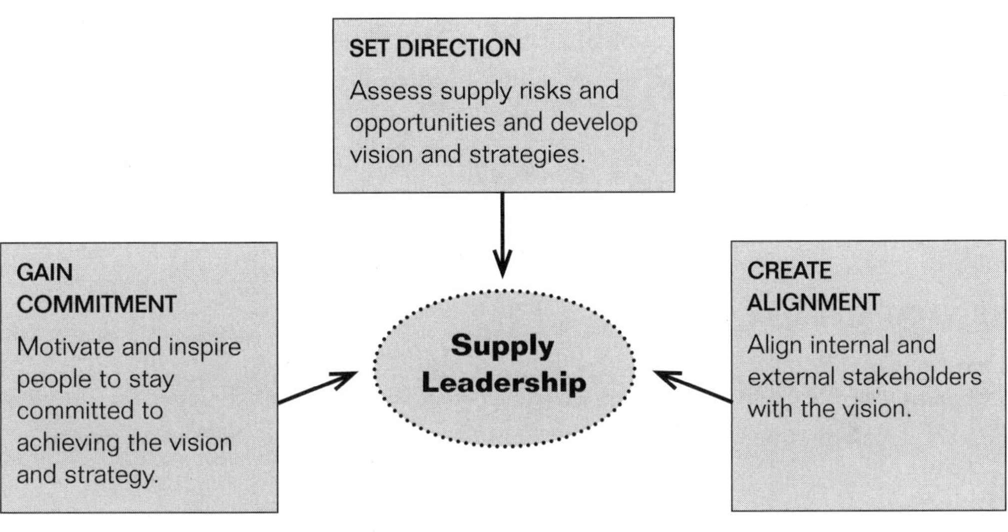


## What Is Management?

> *Management means, in the last analysis, the substitution of thought for brawn and muscle, of knowledge for folkways and superstition, and of cooperation for force. It means the substitution of responsibility for obedience to rank, and of authority of performance for the authority of rank.* PETER DRUCKER[45]

The root to the English word *management* is the Italian word *maneggiare,* the French word *manege* and the Latin *manus,* which mean "to handle," in its original meaning to control a horse. In 1579, the English word was extended to other objects or businesses besides horses. The word *manager* came into use in 1588 and referred to one who manages, and in 1705 this term came to mean specifically "one who conducts a house of business or public institution." According to the 2006 edition of *Merriam-Webster's Dictionary, management* means "1: the act or art of managing: the conducting or supervising of something (as a business); 2: judicious use of means to accomplish an end; and 3: the collective body of those who manage or direct an enterprise." From the earliest of times, managing was associated with handling things. The things that managers "handle" and the tools they use to "handle" things change to fit the times.

Today, we live in an information age where knowledge, knowledge creation and knowledge management is fast becoming the key to competitive advantage. In his book, *Building Wealth: The New Rules for Individuals, Companies, and Nations in a Knowledge-Based Economy,* Lester Thurow says that knowledge will replace natural resources as the asset most critical to economic success.[46] This modern concept is driven in large part by the easy accessibility to vast stores of knowledge brought to us by rapidly advancing technology. The challenges are: (1) how to manage technology, (2) how to manage knowledge workers and (3) how to manage the complexity of a global economy. For a manager, these tasks are ever-present.

### What Do Managers Do?

According to Henry Mintzberg, academic and author, managerial work involves interpersonal roles, informational roles and decisional roles. These roles require skills, namely, developing peer relationships, carrying out negotiations, motivating subordinates, resolving conflicts, establishing networks and disseminating information, making decisions with little or ambiguous information and allocating resources.[47]

Chris Chen described the following management behaviors that keep complex systems in order:

- *Planning and budgeting.* Planning and budgeting behaviors include setting time-phased performance measures, establishing targets and goals, defining detailed steps to accomplish these goals and allocating resources.
- *Organizing and staffing.* These behaviors ensure that the organization has the capacity to carry out goals. They include creating the organizational structure: who reports to whom, who has decision-making authority and how information flows; defining job roles; interviewing and selecting organization members; and monitoring job performance.
- *Providing supervision and problem-solving.* These behaviors include monitoring results versus the plan, identifying deviations or exceptions and solving problems or disputes.[48]

## Theories of Management

The development of management thought and practices can be traced back to early human organizations. It was the Industrial Revolution of the 1800s (the first Industrial Revolution) that catalyzed the movement to find ways to increase efficiency and profits in the new factory environment enabled by power-driven machinery. The appendix at the end of this chapter provides a quick reference for major management theories. The major contribution of each theory provides the thread connecting current management thought and behavior with the origins of these ideas.

Western management thought ruled for many decades in most large, multinational organizations. Then the success of many Japanese companies based on quality and lean thinking infused Japanese management theories into many organizations around the world. The challenge with any culturally based theory is transplanting that theory successfully to a different culture. For example, early adopters of just-in-time or total quality practices in Western organizations often failed miserably because American workers and American management did not approach teams, quality and work in the same way the Japanese did. Likewise, Western ways of managing may not work in other cultures for similar reasons. The emerging Indian-inspired management theory of creating value and creating social justice may not take the same form in organizations around the world. However, the globalization of business and management thought indicates a move toward globalized management theory adapted to fit local cultures, customs and norms. Think global, act local applies. This is especially relevant to any discussion of motivation.

## Motivational Theories[49]

The extent to which a manager is successful in motivating and developing employees depends largely on his or her own skill in creating an operating environment that elicits voluntary dedication and the desire to excel among departmental employees. An effective manager of human capital involves employees in the decision-making processes in an attempt to effect a harmonious blending of individual and departmental objectives.

As a basis for creating such an environment, it is important that a manager understand the basic factors that motivate individuals, as well as the relationship between motivation and ensuing behavioral patterns. Three major schools of thought emerged to explain motivation and its relationship to performance: (1) content theory focuses on the needs of the individual, (2) process theory focuses on the variables that influence and motivate behavior and (3) reinforcement theory focuses on the influence of consequences on behavior.

**Content Theory: Maslow's Hierarchy of Needs.** One of the most well-known and widely accepted content theories was developed by Abraham Maslow. His theory, Maslow's Hierarchy of Needs, holds that the satisfaction of basic human needs, in varying degrees, produces certain somewhat predictable behavior patterns. In Maslow's hierarchy, physiological and security needs are more basic and concrete than other needs. On the other hand, social, esteem and growth needs are abstract and more difficult to recognize. He suggests that each lower-order need must be at least partially fulfilled before the next higher-level need becomes dominant in terms of an individual's motivation.

In practice, assuming that concrete needs are reasonably well fulfilled, supply managers should attempt sequentially to provide satisfaction first for each employee's social needs, then for his or her esteem needs and finally for his or her growth needs. Progressive satisfaction of each of these types of needs tends to produce a higher and more positive level of motivation.

**Herzberg's Motivation-Hygiene Theory.** A related and somewhat more application-oriented theory of motivation was developed by Frederick Herzberg and his associates during the 1950s. Herzberg's Motivation-Hygiene theory (sometimes called the "two-factor" theory) separates motivational factors into two categories: (1) those intrinsic to the job and (2) those extrinsic to the job.

According to this theory, for most people the major causes of job satisfaction — and, thus, motivation — stem largely from the work itself in the form of intrinsic job-related rewards. These rewards include achievement, recognition, responsibility, personal growth and advancement. An individual gains these rewards (typically in a developmental sequence) by good job performance.

Extrinsic factors that lie outside the job itself are not considered motivators in a positive sense. Factors such as working conditions, pay, relations with coworkers, supervisory style and organizational policies tend to be "dissatisfiers" if they do not exist at an acceptable level. It seems that most people expect some minimum level of satisfaction with respect to these peripheral elements of the work environment. Beyond this threshold level, however, enhancement of these extrinsic factors does not turn them into "satisfiers" that produce a stronger positive motivation to any significant extent. Thus, Herzberg terms them "hygiene" factors.

**McClelland's Achievement Motivation Theory.** As discussed in the section on leadership, McClelland identified three needs that motivate human behavior: the need for (1) power, (2) affiliation and (3) achievement. From a managerial perspective, an assessment of employees along these lines may help a manager determine the types of activities in which individual employees might perform best, the work environments that might be most conducive for success and the rewards that might motivate.

**Expectancy Theory.** Another approach to understanding employee motivation more recently suggested by Victor Vroom, Lyman Porter and Edward Lawler is called the Expectancy theory.[50] According to this process theory, an individual's course of action will be guided heavily by two factors:

1. The importance or value attached to a successful outcome of the action and
2. The individual's assessment of his or her ability to achieve a successful outcome of the action.

This rather commonsense concept holds that people will select alternatives that they believe to be both attainable and highly rewarding.

**Equity Theory.** Another process theory of motivation is Equity theory. Equity theorists argue that the motivation level of employees is determined by how fairly or equitably they believe their work is judged in comparison to others' work. Each employee will make this assessment, and the outcome (positive or negative) will impact job motivation and performance. The original concept focused on pay, but other variables have been included in more recent research.

**Reinforcement Approach.** The Reinforcement approach to motivation is based on the work of B.F. Skinner on operant conditioning. The basic concept is that individuals will be motivated to continue behavior if the consequences are favorable, and they will be motivated to stop or alter behavior if the consequences are unfavorable.

**Measurement and Reward/Incentive Programs.** Incentive programs are designed to inspire appropriate behaviors by sharing the benefits of cost reduction and other financial improvements with those who help bring them about. For the supply management function, incentive programs may be designed to reward and motivate employees of the function and/or suppliers to the organization.

At a large consumer products company, for instance, the reward system has been changed to look at measures beyond profit, including total shareholder return — cash, profit and stock price, profit and loss, working capital and capital investment, forecast accuracy and working capital in terms of operating cash flow. Purchasing is rewarded for getting the best value, including price, supplier innovation, capital investment, etc. Customer service logistics is rewarded for on-time delivery, perfect order and combining enough volume to ship efficiently. Engineering is rewarded for service to business units on corporate initiatives, broad application of its ideas, development of new ideas and service. Total delivered cost is key to the product supply manager. The business unit is rewarded for delivering projects on time, within budget and for complexity reduction.[51]

Departmental performance measurement is discussed in greater detail in Chapter 11 and supplier performance measurement is more thoroughly explained in *Foundation of Supply Management* (ISM Professional Series).

## Management Styles

The views managers hold about theories of motivation, and about people in general, heavily influence the management styles they develop and employ in practice. The application of certain theories of motivation produces a related management style. Frederick Taylor is generally accorded the distinction of being the "father of scientific management." In studying the elements of work and job design at the turn of the century, Taylor observed that the output of individual workers increased as a job was made more specialized. Removal of the elements of planning and control, as well as some peripheral operational elements, permitted the individual to become more proficient at the core job activities and, thus, to become more productive. Subsequently, the concepts of functional job specialization and detailed job supervision became well accepted as a basic management technique. When carried beyond a certain point, however, functional specialization can produce repetitive, monotonous and, at times, demotivating jobs. In recent years, this traditional approach has been tempered or supplemented with a variety of human-centered (as opposed to job-centered) approaches. Among these are Deming's 14 Points for Management, McGregor's Theory X and Theory Y, Ouchi's Theory Z and the team concept.

> *Long-term commitment to new learning and new philosophy is required of any management that seeks transformation. The timid and the fainthearted, and the people that expect quick results, are doomed to disappointment.* W. EDWARDS DEMING[52]

**Deming's 14 Points for Management.** W. Edwards Deming was a consultant in statistical studies and a professor of statistics at New York University. He is best known for his work in applying statistical methods to the improvement of quality in manufacturing. His work was the basis for the Japanese quality movement in the 1950s and, finally, recognition and application in the United States in the 1980s. The Union of Japanese Scientists and Engineers, supported by Japanese industry, instituted the annual Deming Prizes, a sum of money awarded to a Japanese scholar for his or her contributions in statistical theory or its application, and a medal to a Japanese company for using statistical methods for the advancement of precision and the dependability of the product.

Deming's 14 points for management apply to all types of organizations, small ones as well as large ones, the service industry as well as manufacturing, and to a division within a company. According to the W. Edwards Deming Institute, these 14 points are:

1. Create constancy of purpose toward improvement of product and service, with the aim to become competitive, stay in business and provide jobs.

2. Adopt the new philosophy. We are in a new economic age. Western management must awaken to the challenge, must learn its responsibilities and take on leadership for change.

3. Cease dependence on inspection to achieve quality. Eliminate the need for inspection on a mass basis by building quality into the product in the first place.

4. End the practice of awarding business on the basis of price tag. Instead, minimize total cost. Move toward a single supplier for any one item, on a long-term relationship of loyalty and trust.

5. Improve constantly and forever the system of production and service, to improve quality and productivity, and thus constantly decrease costs.

6. Institute training on the job.

7. Institute leadership. The aim of supervision should be to help people, machines and gadgets to do a better job. Supervision of management is in need of overhaul, as well as supervision of production workers.

8. Drive out fear, so that everyone may work effectively for the organization.

9. Break down barriers between departments. People in research, design, sales and production must work as a team, to foresee problems of production and in use that may be encountered with the product or service.

10. Eliminate slogans, exhortations and targets for the workforce asking for zero defects and new levels of productivity. These exhortations only create adversarial relationships, for the bulk of the causes of low quality and low productivity belong to the system and thus lie beyond the power of the workforce.

    - Eliminate work standards (quotas) on the factory floor. Substitute leadership.

    - Eliminate management by objective. Eliminate management by numbers, numerical goals. Substitute leadership.

11. Remove barriers that rob the hourly worker of his or her right to pride of workmanship. The responsibility of supervisors must be changed from sheer numbers to quality.

12. Remove barriers that rob people in management and in engineering of their right to pride of workmanship. This means, inter alia, abolishment of the annual or merit rating and of management by objective.

13. Institute a vigorous program of education and self-improvement.

14. Put everybody in the company to work to accomplish the transformation. The transformation of the organization is everybody's job.[53]

**Theory X and Theory Y.** In the 1960s, Douglas McGregor developed his widely known "Theory X - Theory Y" approach to management. McGregor found that many managers employing the traditional approach treated their subordinates as though they were lazy, uncreative, undisciplined and generally not interested in doing a good job. He called these characteristics Theory X assumptions about the nature of people. In the work environment, Theory X assumptions tend to lead to an autocratic, close-supervision style of management.

In contrast to Theory X, McGregor proposed another set of assumptions — Theory Y— that he believed were more consistent with the underlying nature of most people. Theory Y assumptions assume that:

1. Work is a natural activity, just like recreation and rest.

2. Under appropriate conditions, most people tend to accept and to seek responsibility.

3. Creativity and imagination are possessed to a reasonable extent by a large number of people, but are not fully utilized in most jobs.

4. Most people naturally take pride in what they do and, consequently, want to do a good job if they think the job is worthwhile.

McGregor holds that managers who genuinely believe Theory Y assumptions will employ a participative management style, designed to involve subordinates more actively in the total planning/operating/controlling process. According to McGregor, the end result should be greater development of individuals' capabilities and greater fulfillment of individuals' personal goals for self-actualization.[54]

**Theory Z.** In the early 1980s, William Ouchi conducted an intensive study of major Japanese organizations to identify the management characteristics that contribute significantly to their success. He found one common thread running throughout the total fabric of Japanese management. Virtually all Japanese firms employ a companywide managerial philosophy built around an overriding concern for the individual employees and managers alike. The extensive use of quality circles and other techniques of participative management appears to the Western observer to represent, in part, an extension of the Theory Y concept. Ouchi calls this Japanese approach Theory Z. In addition, Theory Z successfully integrates achievement of personal goals of employees with the collective goals of the organization. Four key elements that characterize this type of management are:

1. Long-term employment,
2. Slow but steady advancement to higher-level positions,
3. Shared decision-making at all levels of the organization and
4. Intense individual loyalty to the organization.[55]

As noted previously, one's management style can assume two broad orientations: (1) an employee (or human orientation) and (2) a job (or production orientation). Few managers use a style that focuses completely on one orientation or the other. In daily operations, most managers employ a mix of the two orientations, depending on their commitments concerning the nature and motivation of their subordinates. Additionally, as the type of job and situational environment change, a perceptive manager will vary the management mix to suit the circumstances at hand. One of the management styles that attempts to meld the human orientation with the job orientation is the use of the team concept.

### Teams and Teamwork

The focus on teamwork has received such widespread attention in the past 20 years that it may be hard for some to comprehend that as early as 1945 Elton Mayo (famous for the Hawthorne studies) wrote in *The Social Problems of an Industrial Civilization* about the importance of groups.[56] He was interested in methods of understanding the behavior of groups, whether formally organized and recognized by management or self-constituted, informal organizations.

Today, many organizations use teams to accomplish organizational objectives. The supply management function is no exception. New product design teams, process improvement teams, source selection teams and system implementation teams, to name a few, may include team members or team leaders from the supply function. Some purchasing teams are comprised solely of purchasing department staff, while some may include personnel from other functions in the organization (cross-functional teams) and/or suppliers. At Shell Oil, for example, a cross-functional team reduced the total cost of ownership of PCs by more than 25 percent by (1) consolidating purchases with two major suppliers, (2) decentralizing buying decisions to the department level, (3) implementing electronic ordering and (4) establishing a dedicated PC support group.[57]

Regardless of its composition, a team is made up of a collection of people who work or function together in varying degrees to achieve a common goal. Many variations on the team concept exist, ranging from informal teams to highly structured to self-directed teams.

**Informal Work Groups.** Within every formal organization, experience demonstrates the existence of one or more informal groups. Typically, these groups are fairly small and structured informally around specific interests of their members. They may be social groups, special-interest groups or sometimes pressure groups pushing for change. Whatever the case, these informal groups are an integral part of the organization and their attitudes and actions can either assist or hinder the attainment of objectives.

A wise manager uses the potential influence of informal groups in a constructive manner. To do this, he or she must first recognize the existence of such a group and identify the informal group leader(s). Then, by practicing the concepts of open communication and group involvement in the decision-making process, the manager attempts to align the objectives of the informal group with the objectives of the department. This represents an extension of the participative management strategy employed in dealing with individuals and formal work groups within the department/organization. Specific approaches that can be used include:

1. Solicit appropriate input on decisions that affect individuals and the informal group through various individual, committee and brainstorming techniques. Use this input to arrive at genuinely group-oriented decisions whenever possible.

2. Create and develop a work climate and a reward system that encourage teamwork and cooperation.

3. Develop informal group cohesiveness that produces a positive influence on the activities of the formal work group.

The manager's goal in using this integrative approach is to promote cooperation of the various groups, formal and informal, in daily activities that contribute to attaining the department's overall objectives.

**Formal Teams.** Formal teams are made up of individuals who are designated members of a formal group. Cross-functional teams are assembled for many reasons in an organization, including product quality improvement, process improvements, sourcing, evaluating, selecting a supplier or new product development.

For instance, Kodak assembled a cross-functional sourcing process change management team to develop and implement a new centralized, formal sourcing process enterprisewide. The team had four sponsors: the manager of business unit worldwide operations at headquarters, the managers of business unit equipment development from two sites and the vice president of worldwide equipment purchasing. The project team was comprised of core and extended team members. The core team consisted of a project team leader (a worldwide commodity manager) and four team members (a worldwide commodity manager, a strategic cost manager, an engineer and a business unit supply chain manager).[58]

**Group or Team Management.** Managing a team or group of any size requires the skills and attributes described by Chris Chen earlier in this chapter. Chen's description of leaders as individuals who set direction, align people and motivate and inspire means that leaders empower others to work together to achieve the vision. Empowerment works to build people so they will develop and act, often without supervision, to jointly contribute to the organization and themselves.

Empowerment includes being empowered (creating power for oneself), giving empowerment (helping others grow toward a state of empowerment) and an empowering environment (giving power to other groups for organizational benefit). For empowerment to work, there must be a vision of where the organization needs to go and a strategy for getting it there. Managers need to delegate more and employees must have more to say in daily and future work. Implementing empowerment requires serious background work, preparation of all people involved, careful training and the development of interpersonal skills, incentives, resources and action plans.

## Management of the Supply Process

The many changes in the way business is conducted have had a huge impact on the way the supply management function is managed. Technology allows organizations to automate and streamline many of the activities that were historically considered the primary activities of purchasers. Even with the delays and problems that occur with the implementation of any new technology, the changes in the way that goods and services are bought and sold have allowed those in the supply function to move from a transaction-oriented activity to a knowledge and relationship–oriented role. The alignment of supply strategy with organizational strategy, the focus on the value chain starting with the needs and wants of the end customer and the drive to identify and focus on core competencies have all led to the realization that the supply process must be managed differently than it has been in the past.

If the supply function is to make a strategic and operational contribution to the organization, then how the function is organized, managed and evaluated matters. The objective of supply management is to capture the contribution of the supply base to the organization. Suppliers carry influence. Therefore the management of suppliers is critical to the success of the organization. Also, because of the influence of suppliers on an organization's success, they are too important to leave to just one department. As the purchasing or supply side of the organization comes into the spotlight, managers and owners of the supply process must drastically change their orientation to internal customers, suppliers and end consumers. Linking the contribution of the supply function and the suppliers to the overall mission of the organization is critical if the supply function is to truly make the greatest contribution to the organization. Working with, not against, internal customers is a necessity. Interdependence among functional areas requires the ability to cross functional boundaries and forge alliances within the organization as well as outside of it. Focusing on the results of supply management professionals and the supply management department rather than on activities is the difficult, but essential task of those leading, managing and assessing the supply function. For best results, the role of the supply function in the organization must first be understood.

Figure 1-4 illustrates the major roles of the supply manager or management team. These roles are discussed in detail in Chapters 5 through 11.

**Figure 1-4 Major Management Roles**

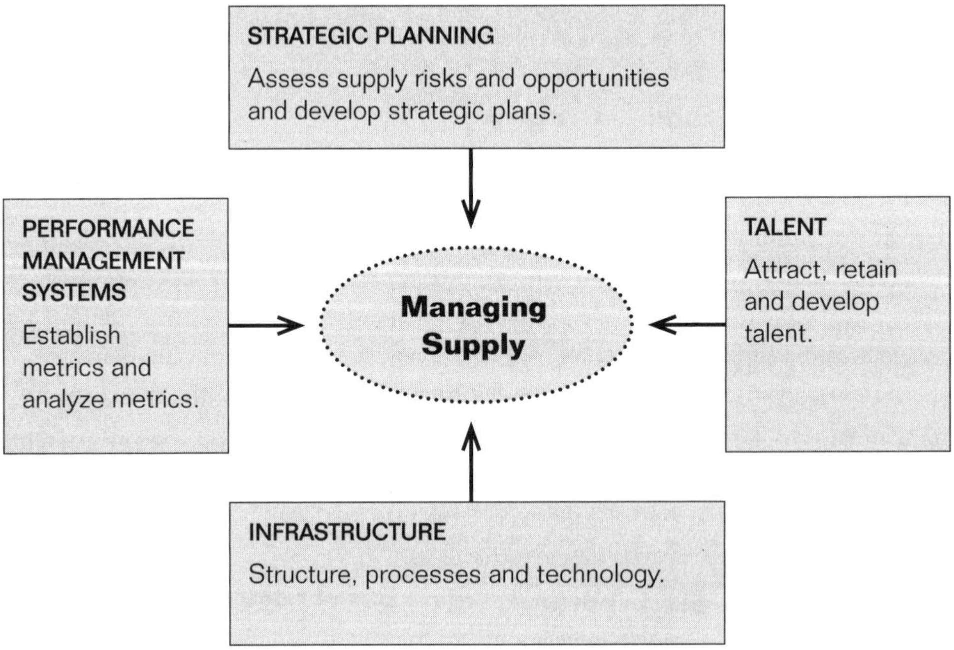

STRATEGIC PLANNING
Assess supply risks and opportunities and develop strategic plans.

PERFORMANCE MANAGEMENT SYSTEMS
Establish metrics and analyze metrics.

Managing Supply

TALENT
Attract, retain and develop talent.

INFRASTRUCTURE
Structure, processes and technology.

*Source: PRACTIX,* CAPS Research, Volume 8 (July 2005), 3.

Becoming both an effective leader and an effective manager may be the biggest challenge facing each person in an organization whether he or she is in a formal or informal leadership or management role and whether he or she manages hundreds of people or just himself or herself. Increasingly complex environments coupled with the need for rapid, dramatic change add to the pressure to deliver results quickly. These situations reinforce the importance of both the what and why and the how and when.

In an interview with *The McKinsey Quarterly,* Deere & Co. CEO Bob Lane referred to Deere's culture as being "straight down the middle." When asked if it is difficult to balance ethics and performance given the new demands on employees, he responded, "It is a challenge, but it can be done. And we have created a new set of tests to ensure that Deere will have a high-performance culture and, at the same time, retain an environment of integrity. The emphasis is squarely on 'how.' It's the only word underlined in our strategy statement. So that becomes a statement to our people — how we do our business is a very important factor. The message to our people is clear: If you get everything else done right but you don't treat people properly or you're not straightforward, you don't work here. And sometimes that hurts a lot. In fact, at our worldwide management meeting I recently announced the number of people who don't work here anymore because — even though their work was satisfactory in every other respect — how they did business was not acceptable. When I announced the number our worldwide leadership team was silent ... silent. It got people's attention."[59]

## Key Points

1. Leaders and managers do different things in organizations.

2. Leaders have three primary responsibilities: set direction, create alignment and gain commitment.

3. Managers have corresponding tasks. While the leader sets direction, the manager assesses risks and develops plans; the leader creates alignment and the manager organizes and staffs; the leader gains commitment and the manager assesses performance and establishes internal controls.

## **Appendix:** *Timeline of Major Theories of Management*

| *Dates* | *School of Thought* | *Major Contributors* | *Major Contributions* |
|---|---|---|---|
| 1850s to 1860s | Systematic Management | Daniel McCallum<br>Henry Poor | • Organization = division of labor<br>• Communication = management-reporting system<br>• Information = analysis of reports to improve operations |
| From the 1880s on | Scientific Management and Operations Research | Frederick W. Taylor<br>Henry L. Gantt<br>Frank Gilbreth<br>Lillian Moller Gilbreth<br>Harrington Emerson | • Application of scientific study<br>• Efficiency studies<br>• Wage systems and motivation<br>• Specialized management knowledge<br>• Use of mathematical models in managerial decision-making |
| 1880s through early 1900s | Administrative Theory or Universal Theory of Management | Henri Fayol | • Universality of management<br>• Principles of managerial thinking<br>• Elements of management: planning, organizing, command, coordination and control |
| 1920s and 1930s | Behavioralists Theory | Hugo Munsterberg<br>Walter Dill Scott<br>Mary Parker Follett<br>Elton Mayo | • Focused on social needs of employees and motivation<br>• Applied psychology to business<br>• Link physical and mental qualifications with ideal psychological conditions and provide optimal motivational influences<br>• Concept of working with, not under, someone |
| Early 1900s on | Organization Theory | Max Weber<br>Chester Barnard<br>Herbert Simon | • The central unit of analysis is the total organization<br>• Weber's model of bureaucracy: organization must be effective and efficient to be successful<br>• Function of management is to keep organization (decision-making structure) running<br>• Limit decision-making scope through policies, procedures, hierarchy, etc. |

| *Dates* | *School of Thought* | *Major Contributors* | *Major Contributions* |
|---|---|---|---|
| 1950s in Japan and 1980s in the United States | The Deming System of Profound Knowledge | W. Edwards Deming | • The four related parts of profound knowledge:<br>1. Appreciation for a system<br>2. Knowledge about variation<br>3. Theory of knowledge<br>4. Psychology<br>• Also included 14 Points for Management (discussed earlier). |
| 1960s and 1970s | Systems Theory | Ludwig von Bartalanffy | • Identify parallels among disciplines<br>• Integrate into one theory |
| 1970s on | Contingency Theory | Fred Luthans<br>Todd I. Stewart | • Focuses on flexibility and adaptability<br>• No universal management principles, circumstantial |
| 1980s on | Excellent Companies or Best Practices | Thomas J. Peters<br>Robert H. Waterman | • Attributes of excellent organizations:<br>1. Bias for action<br>2. Closeness to the customer<br>3. Autonomy/entrepreneurship<br>4. Productivity through people<br>5. Hands-on, value-driven<br>6. Stick to the knitting<br>7. Simple form, lean staff<br>8. Simultaneous loose and tight properties |
| 1980s and early 1990s | Management by Objectives | Peter Drucker<br>Douglas McGregor<br>Edward Schleh<br>George Ordiorne | • Integrates planning, participation, communication, managerial development, performance appraisal |
| 1980s on | Continuous Improvement (Kaizen) | Japanese management theorists such as Shigeo Shingo and Taiithi Ohno | • Collaborative, collegiate, people-based management that extends beyond the borders of the organization and aims at long-term payoffs<br>• *Kaizen* or continuous improvement: Anything and everything can be improved. If it can be, it must be; otherwise, you are creating *muda,* or waste.<br>• *Meikiki,* or "foresight with discernment," is how the Japanese describe a process that, of course, they fully understand and apply. |

(continued)

| *Dates* | *School of Thought* | *Major Contributors* | *Major Contributions* |
|---|---|---|---|
| | | | • Concept I: "Change the basis of competition continually" (as with small copiers)<br>• Concept II: "Multiple sources of competitive advantage"<br>• Concept III: "Organizing to achieve new levels of agility"<br>• Concept IV: "Sophisticated collaboration" with suppliers and customers to new heights<br>• Concept V: "Focusing on core capabilities to execute strategy successfully" |
| 1980s on | Toyota Production System | Taiichi Ohno | • Production depends on people, not just machines. |
| 1980s on | Lean Organization Theory | Shigeo Shingo<br>James P. Womack<br>Daniel T. Jones | • Precisely specify value by specific product.<br>• Identify the value stream for each product.<br>• Make value flow without interruption.<br>• Let the customer pull value from the producer.<br>• Pursue perfection. |
| 1990s on | Learning Organization | Peter M. Senge | • Systems thinking<br>• Personal mastery<br>• Mental models<br>• Building shared vision<br>• Team learning |
| 2000 on | Holistic Approach to Business | C.K. Pralahad<br>Ram Charan<br>Vijay Govindrajan<br>Dipak Jain | • Inclusive capitalism — create value and social justice.<br>• Take into account the needs of shareholders, employees, customers, society and the environment.<br>• Develop a management theory that replaces the shareholder-driven agenda with a more stakeholder-focused approach.<br>• Green is good versus greed is good. |

*Source:* Adapted from Anna Flynn and Sam Farney, *The Supply Management Leadership Process: Strategies for Organizational Effectiveness* (Tempe, AZ: National Association of Purchasing Management, 2000), 77–79.

CHAPTER

# 2

# Setting Direction

*A leader takes people where they want to go.*
*A great leader takes people where they don't*
*necessarily want to go but ought to be.*

ROSALYNN CARTER, FORMER FIRST LADY, UNITED STATES[1]

Setting direction is the primary task of a leader or leadership team. It involves clarifying the core values of the organization, identifying future opportunities and risks and devising a compelling vision, mission and strategies. According to John P. Kotter, Konosuke Matsushita Professor of Leadership at Harvard Business School, "A leader gathers a broad range of data and looks for patterns, relationships, and linkages that help explain things. He or she creates visions and strategies that describe what a business, technology, or organizational culture should become over time and articulates a feasible way to get there."[2]

The chapter is organized into three sections: (1) creating a values-based organization, (2) opportunities and risks and (3) developing vision and strategies. From a leadership perspective, how these actions unfold and what they entail depends in part on the style, role and attributes of the leader that were discussed in Chapter 1. The chapter concludes with an appendix that details the ISM Principles of Social Responsibility.

### CHAPTER OBJECTIVES

- Describe how the leader creates a values-based organization.
- Explain how opportunities and risks might be identified and assessed by the leader or leadership team.
- Discuss how a vision is developed.
- Explore how strategies are developed to support the attainment of the vision.

## Creating a Values-Based Organization

*If you lead the people with correctness, who will dare not to be correct?*

CONFUCIUS

The supply management leader and the leadership team develop the core values of the supply organization in alignment with those of the organization and instill those values in the supply management organization through words and actions. The supply leader is the primary driver of both alignment and adherence to established core values throughout strategy execution. To understand this role, it is important to briefly discuss values and ethics (covered in greater detail in *Foundation of Supply* (ISM Professional Series)). In this book, coverage focuses on the establishment of core values to guide the decisions and behavior of supply management employees, other internal stakeholders and suppliers.

### What Are Values?

The English word *value* comes from the French verb *valoir,* meaning "to be worth." Our values describe how we intend to operate, on a day-to-day basis, as we pursue our vision. Some organizations develop a set of core values with and for stakeholders to define behavior within the group and behavior with external stakeholders such as customers, suppliers and the community. The vision statement tells where the organization wants to go, and the value statement describes the means (how) the organization will use to get there. Globalization increases the pressure on each person to fully understand and live the core values of the organization.

Ethical principles are the rules of conduct that derive from ethical values. For example, honesty is a value that governs behavior in the form of principles such as tell the truth, do not deceive, be candid, do not cheat. In this way, values give rise to principles in the form of specific dos and don'ts. Figure 2-1 illustrates the relationship between values and behavior.

**Ethics and Action.** Ethics is about putting principles into action. Consistency between what we say we value and what our actions say we value is a matter of integrity. According to the Josephson Institute of Ethics, "It is also about self-restraint. Not doing what you have the *power* to do. An act isn't proper simply because it is permissible or you can get away with it. Not doing what you have the *right* to do. There is a big difference between what you have the right to do and what is right to do. Not doing what you *want* to do. In the well-worn turn of phrase, an ethical person often chooses to do more than the law requires and less than the law allows."[3]

Figure 2-1 The Relationship of Values and Behavior

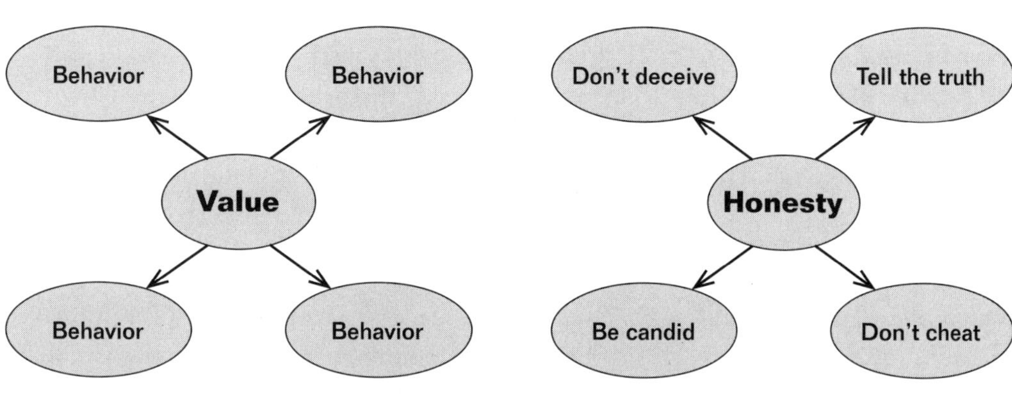


While the concern with ethical behavior in business is not new, the global business environment presents significant and unprecedented ethical challenges that are increasingly gaining attention. According to Maxine A. Dalton, group director of the Center for Creative Leadership's Leading in the Context of Difference practice area, businesses can take three steps to help ensure that their organizations' expatriates behave not only appropriately but also ethically: (1) develop a clearly articulated set of core values as the basis for global policies and decision-making, (2) train employees to ask questions that will help them make business decisions that are both culturally sensitive and flexible within the context of those core values and (3) balance the need for policy with the need for flexibility or imagination.[4] The challenge for any person operating in another culture is twofold: how to avoid moral imperialism, demanding that international organizations and colleagues act just like us, and against cultural relativism, conforming to whatever behavior is the local norm. This challenge exists for each of us whether we are Japanese sourcing in Vietnam, German sourcing in China or North American sourcing in Mexico.

## What Can a Leader Do?

> *The best thing you can give as a leader is a* ***reason*** *to trust. People want to trust. They're hungry for it. But they're selective. They'll only give it to a motivator, a communicator, a* ***teacher****, a real person. Someone who in* ***good*** *times and bad always does the right thing.*
>
> JEFFREY R. IMMELT, CEO OF GE, DARTMOUTH, 2004[5]

Armed with a better understanding of values and ethics, the question remains, how do leaders develop core values for an organization and embed them in the actions of each and every stakeholder, especially in a large global organization? Leaders can take several actions to focus everyone's attention on how results are obtained, to support the practice of ethical decision-making and to guide the behavior of others. These actions are: exhibiting ethical behavior, creating a strong ethical culture, establishing a code of conduct, including ethical issues in employment decisions, formally including ethics in performance evaluations and engaging in meaningful ethics training.

**Exhibiting Ethical Behavior.** Research findings suggest that the higher the achieved level of moral reasoning development, the more likely the person is to make an ethical decision. Leaders can support the development of moral reasoning through training and example. Transparency in the decision-making process demonstrates the thinking process used to resolve an ethical dilemma.

**Creating a Strong Ethical Culture.** Leaders make a critical contribution to ethics by creating a strong organizational culture that sets the tone at the top and establishes expectations about the use of values in guiding behavior and business outcomes.

**Establishing a Code of Conduct for the Supply Organization.** Most supply organizations have written codes of conduct for supply management personnel as well as suppliers. *Foundation of Supply Management* (ISM Professional Series) discusses this issue in greater detail. ISM's Code of Conduct can be accessed at www.ism.ws. Ethical concerns extend beyond the walls of the organization and greater focus is now on ethical supply chains.

**Including Ethical Issues in Performance Evaluations and Employment Decisions.** Leaders should openly include and weigh ethics when deciding whom to hire, fire, retain or promote. They should express this thinking in terms of behaviors so that it is evident how organizational values are translated into actions. Recall the Deere & Co. example from the end of Chapter 1 in which the CEO announced the number of people who no longer work at Deere because of how they obtained results.

**Engaging in Meaningful Ethics Training.** Leaders should avoid once-a-year mandatory reviews and individual sign-offs on the code of conduct if this is the only time employees hear the word *ethics.* Leaders should find ways to engage in frequent discussions about the ethics of supply situations and use real experiences as learning opportunities. They should support the development of moral reasoning through training.

Core values are the guiding principles behind the actions of everyone in the supply organization. Supply management leaders are well positioned to play an organizationwide leadership role in the policy and practices related to an organization's core values as well as the corresponding core values of the supply management group. For example, Deere & Co. focuses on its longevity when it states, "The company is guided today, as it has been for more than 165 years, by core values that were exhibited by its founder and have been long adopted by our employees: integrity, quality, commitment and innovation."[6] Figure 2-2 lists the core values of the procurement group of the Lenovo Group, Beijing, China.

**Figure 2-2 Lenovo's Core Values**

| Procurement embodies those core values of customer service, innovative and entrepreneurial spirit, accuracy and truth-seeking, trustworthiness and integrity that the company and all its divisions hold to the highest esteem. | |
|---|---|
| **Customer service** | Vigorously seek a full understanding of the capabilities, wants and needs of the entire supply chain: Lenovo's customers, our internal clients, our suppliers and our suppliers' suppliers. Actively articulate both Lenovo's and our suppliers' viewpoints, and facilitate communication at all levels and functions. |
| **Innovative and entrepreneurial spirit** | Continually seek to improve and never be satisfied with anything less than a competitive advantage in technology, price, quality delivery, responsiveness, speed and efficiency. |
| **Accuracy and truth-seeking** | Firmly believe in and insist on true cross-functional participation to ensure our business decisions are based on carefully understood facts. |
| **Trustworthiness and integrity** | Ensure both Lenovo and suppliers keep the letter and spirit of all agreements. Build long-term relationships with suppliers based on trust, honesty and candor. Never compromise Lenovo's overall best interests in the pursuit of local or divisional interests. Expect teamwork, integrity, respect and excellence from each other. |

*Source:* www.lenovo.com.

As Figure 2-3 illustrates, Whirlpool Corp. focuses on the importance of its values and how it does business as the key to its success internationally.

**Figure 2-3 Whirlpool Corporation's Core Values**

Our employees live by the values-based strategy that has made Whirlpool the international leader that we are today. Our values represent who we are to our customers, our investors and to each other. And the way they represent the company demonstrates how we do business: the right way.

| | |
|---|---|
| **Respect** | We've built an employee culture where all beliefs, perspectives and opinions are welcomed and valued. |
| **Integrity** | The high road is the only one we take, from the people we hire to the clients we serve. As we often say, "There's no right way to do the wrong thing." |
| **Diversity** | By constantly seeking fresh approaches, new ideas and different outlooks, we build our success and secure our future. |
| **Teamwork** | From the first to the last, we take each step forward as a team. |

*Source:* www.whirlpool.corp.

The leader is on the way to success if he or she has successfully established core values and these values drive each person's decision-making process and actions. From this base, the supply management leader or leadership team is ready to assess supply opportunities and risks.

## Opportunities and Risks

A major precursor to turning a leader's vision into a shared vision is assessing the present state of affairs. For the supply management leader this means taking a high-level view of the present state of the supply management organization to determine the external risks and opportunities, internal strengths and weaknesses and the past and present vision. The leader or leadership team then thinks about the future and asks: What are the potential changes in markets and products, key stakeholders and constituencies, and the economic, social, technical and political environments? It is only through a thorough and rigorous assessment of the present and a deep exploration of future potential that a vision can be created.

One critical aspect of creating a shared vision is stakeholder analysis. This process includes identifying all the individuals and groups, internally and externally, who have a stake in the outcome and understanding each stakeholder's underlying interests to invent options that tap into these interests. By doing this early in the visioning process, the leader stands a better chance of getting buy-in and gaining commitment.

This chapter started with the idea that the supply management leader sets direction first by creating a values-based organization. Along with creating and sustaining a values-based supply management organization, the supply leader must continually assess supply risks and opportunities. The following section explores what this means from a leadership perspective. Chapter 5 presents the managerial side of this leadership task and addresses the details of assessing risks and developing business plans.

## Recognize and Assess Organization and Supply-Related Opportunities and Risks

The type and number of opportunities and risks that exist for the organization from a supply management perspective vary with the company, industry and economy as a whole and are dynamic as situations change. Some of the areas where a leader might look for opportunities and risks include growth of markets, especially in low-cost countries or in markets concerned with sustainable products, strategic partnerships, mergers and acquisitions, financial markets and government-industry partnerships.

**Growth of Markets.** Where do market growth opportunities exist for your organization's products or services? To what extent is your supply base ready and able to support these market incursions? What are the sources of supply base vulnerability? What opportunities and risks might these new markets create from a supply perspective? Also, where are growth opportunities or risks for the supply base? Does the host government and its laws and regulations favor international businesses? Are there legal or regulatory hurdles to overcome? Is there political or social unrest?

**Growth of Markets in Low-Cost Countries.** Are there growth opportunities for selling or buying in low-cost countries? Has a decision(s) been made to stay out of low-cost countries, to go into cities and countries where operating internationally is well established or to explore second-tier cities that have not suffered from overexposure?

For example, many supply management teams are either considering or already sourcing from low-cost countries such as China and India and countries in Eastern and Central Europe. The opportunities typically come from abundant low-wage labor for items that offer high savings potential, stable quality and availability. Critical questions include: How stable and mature is the environment? To what extent is there market transparency? Are appropriate laws and intellectual property rights in place? If so, are they enforced? How wide is the regional disparity in economic development, infrastructure, traffic congestion, pollution levels, education levels, wage rates, etc.?

How might these factors affect the supply decision and goals such as savings, cycle time and productivity?

**Growth of Markets Concerned With Sustainable Products and Services.** Is there an existing or emerging market for sustainable products and services? If not, is there an opportunity for the organization to be on the forefront of this trend and manage demand in this direction? Seventh Generation, for instance, is the leading brand of nontoxic household products for a clean home, a healthy family and a safer world. Organic foods retailer Whole Foods is generally credited with rapidly and dramatically expanding the market for organic products.

**Strategic Partnerships.** Is there an opportunity to form a strategic partnership with a for-profit, not-for-profit, nongovernmental organization or governmental organization to understand emerging issues, create business opportunities, capitalize on innovation or avoid negative events or outcomes? The Environmental Defense Fund, the Rainforest Action Network and the World Wildlife Fund are three examples of organizations working with multinational companies on a variety of issues, including green product design, carbon offset programs and sustainable harvesting of forest and marine products. The Rocky Mountain Institute (RMI) is working with Wal-Mart to help reduce its fossil-fuel consumption in retail stores and transportation.[7]

**Mergers and Acquisitions.** Assess supply-related opportunities from changing internal and external environments through acquisitions, mergers and/or divestitures. What is on the horizon and how well prepared is the supply management group for any eventuality? Are there opportunities that the supply leader sees and wants to bring to the attention of key decision-makers? If a merger or acquisition is under review, the supply management team can provide valuable data and insight into two critical premerger questions: (1) Is the proposed deal commercially attractive? (2) Can the organization capture the full potential value of the proposed deal? Postmerger, the supply management team looks for risks to supply continuity and opportunities to capture synergies in five primary areas: contracts, reducing redundancy and complexity, reducing liability exposure, divestiture of assets and global economic considerations.

**Financial Markets.** Financial markets increasingly recognize and reward organizations exhibiting sustainable business practices. The number of socially responsible investors and funds is growing; sustainability is a key component of socially responsible organizations. A reflection of the growth in socially responsible investing are the Dow Jones Sustainability Indexes, created in 1999 to track the financial performance of leading sustainability-driven companies worldwide. The indexes provide objective benchmarks for the financial products that are linked to economic, environmental and social criteria. Are there supply opportunities to enhance your organization's reputation and brand image? Is your company's reputation exposed because of any existing supply policies, processes, procedures, contracts or supplier relationships?

**Government-Industry Partnership Initiatives.** Government agencies have launched programs in partnership with organizations across many industries in areas related to sustainability. Western European countries are among the leaders in sustainability programs at the local, national and European Union level; EU regulations are, in fact, driving some corporate environmental policies for multinational companies. In the United States, the Environmental Protection Agency (EPA) runs numerous industry programs that can contribute to an organization's sustainability efforts, from pollution prevention and climate change to product stewardship and green product design. Supply management can play a role by scanning the external environment for opportunities such as suppliers of green products or new technology and by assessing the needs of internal stakeholders to bring them together with innovations from the supply base.

## Assessing Risks

Risk management is the process of measuring or assessing risks and then developing strategies to eliminate, reduce, mitigate or manage the risk. In general, the strategies employed include transferring the risk to another party, avoiding the risk, reducing the negative effect of the risk and accepting some or all of the consequences of a particular risk. Traditional risk management focuses on risks stemming from physical or legal causes (e.g., natural disasters or fires, accidents, death and lawsuits). Financial risk management focuses on risks that can be managed using traded financial instruments. Supply and supplier risk management focuses on risks that are either caused by a supply-chain issue or that can be managed through the execution of the appropriate supply strategy. Regardless of the type of risk management, all large organizations have risk-management teams and small groups and organizations practice informal, if not formal, risk management.

**The Matrix Approach to Risk Assessment.** The matrix approach to risk assessment and risk management offers a higher-level focus and graphic display of risk. A matrix is formed with the organization's business units on one axis and a set of high-level risks on the other axis (see Figure 2-4). The number of risks is usually between 12 and 16, although viable models may have as few as four. A team assesses each business unit for each risk, and the results are displayed in the appropriate cell on

**Figure 2-4 Example of a Risk Matrix**

| | | | | | |
|---|---|---|---|---|---|
| **Risk 5** | W | Y | G | R | G |
| **Risk 4** | R | Y | R | Y | Y |
| **Risk 3** | Y | G | Y | R | G |
| **Risk 2** | G | W | G | W | R |
| **Risk 1** | G | R | W | W | Y |
| | BU 1 | BU 2 | BU 3 | BU 4 | BU 5 |

G = Low risk Y = Moderate risk R = High risk W = Not applicable

the matrix: G for low risk, Y for moderate risk, R for high risk and W — or blank — for "not applicable."

Advantages of the matrix approach are that it is flexible and quick to implement and it provides a three-dimensional look at risk by including the cell contents. Although assumptions are not so easily explained, the impact of the graphical representation of risk is enormous.

This approach requires that the assessment team possess a great deal of business knowledge to be credible. In addition, maintenance of the matrix can be challenging, because the assessment must be performed any time a significant change is noted. Tracking possible changes in the business units that would warrant a new assessment can be difficult, depending on the strength of management information systems and reporting. As a result, the matrix does not display the dynamics of the risk profile as easily as a database does. Alternatively, each business unit may create its own matrix using the same risks, but applying them against smaller work groups within the business unit. These assessments can then be combined to create the organization's total risk matrix.

This same approach could be used to focus on supply-related risks by business unit. The types of risks that might be applicable are (1) financial risk, (2) operational risk, including end of life cycle, (3) brand/reputation risk from either ethical, social responsibility or sustainability issues or organizational culture, (4) legal and regulatory risk (risk of litigation, Sarbanes-Oxley (SOX) compliance, employment law and

**Figure 2-5 Supply Risk Profile by Business Unit**

| | | | | | |
|---|---|---|---|---|---|
| **Technical risk** | W | Y | G | R | G |
| **Environmental risk** | R | Y | R | Y | Y |
| **Legal and regulatory risks** | Y | G | Y | R | G |
| **Brand/reputation risk** | G | W | G | W | R |
| **Operational risk** | G | G | Y | R | W |
| **Financial risk** | G | R | W | W | Y |
| | BU 1 | BU 2 | BU 3 | BU 4 | BU 5 |

intellectual property issues), (5) environmental risk and (6) technical risk. This assessment can be compiled to create a supply and/or supplier risk profile as illustrated in Figure 2-5.

Each risk factor may also be subdivided into specific aspects of risk. Figure 2-6 illustrates the subdivision of the risk factor, availability, into five categories: incoming materials, sourcing process capability, volume capacity, technologically capable and supplier lead time. In this example, each subcategory is assessed as a showstopper (the process or action comes to a standstill), a high risk, medium risk, low risk or qualified risk. An item rated a showstopper is characterized by open or unresolved critical issues that are serious enough to delay a product or service introduction. A high-risk item is characterized by a key problem that may become a showstopper, such as a reduction in yield, known reliability or defects, variability that has not been qualified or a high level of uncertainty. High-risk items require an action plan for risk mitigation. A moderate-risk item is characterized by a low to moderate impact on product performance. A qualified rating means that all key issues have been resolved and, at most, only minor issues remain. A qualified rating means that all attributes are fully qualified.[8]

The third phase of direction setting is the development of a vision of supply management and a corresponding set of broadly defined strategies to achieve the vision.

**Figure 2-6 Example of Risk Assessment for Availability**

| RISK FACTOR: AVAILABILITY | SHOW-STOPPER | HIGH RISK | MODERATE RISK | LOW RISK | QUALIFIED |
|---|---|---|---|---|---|
| **Incoming materials** | No source identified | Raw material scarcity | Sole sourced with multiple production operations in close proximity | Sole sourced with multiple production operations separated by 50 miles | Multiple sources with no supply shortages |
| **Source process capability** | Unknown, new technology or supplier | Manufacturing capability only proved on pilot scale | Manufacturing or service capability demonstrated for a similar material | Data demonstrates process is in specification | Source process is stable and capable |
| **Volume capacity** | Availability requirements not supported with existing sources | Suppliers identified. Plans to support volumes not in place | Capacity plans developed by supplier and implementation in process | Capacity mostly in place. No known issues | Capacity fully in place |
| **Technologically capable** | Industry moving toward different standards | Industry movement toward different standards known with no plans to address | Industry movement toward different standards understood with plans to address | Industry adopting multiple standards | Technology chosen is standard |
| **Supplier lead time** | No quick turn capability exists at supplier | Quick turn capable for new design is greater than lead time | Supplier lead time reduction plans on track | Quick turn capability for new design lead time or meets goals | Supplier and supplier tooling meets lead-time goals |

*Source:* George Zsidisin and Lisa Ellram, "Supply Risk Assessment Analysis," *PRACTIX,* CAPS Research (June 1999), 9.

## Developing Vision and Strategies

*Perhaps the most distinguishing trait of visionary leaders is that they believe in a goal that benefits not only themselves, but others as well. It is such vision that attracts the psychic energy of other people, and makes them willing to work beyond the call of duty for the organization.*

MIHALY CSIKSZENTMIHALYI, CLAREMONT GRADUATE UNIVERSITY[9]

A vision is a picture of the future you seek to create, described in the present tense, as if it were happening now. A statement of "our vision" shows where we want to go, and what we will be like when we get there. The word comes from the Latin *videre*, which means "to see." This link to seeing is significant; the more richly detailed and visual the image is, the more compelling it will be. Because of its tangible and immediate quality, a vision gives shape and direction to the organization's future.

A clear and compelling vision also helps people set goals to take the organization closer to the vision. As the Roman philosopher Seneca "The Younger" said, "If a man does not know to what port he is steering, no wind is favourable."[10] The leader endeavors to create a sense of shared purpose and destiny. According to Tsun-Yan Hsieh and Sara Yik of McKinsey & Co., leadership is the starting point of strategy and top managers must assess the leadership gap in the short, medium and long run for the organization to realize the full potential of opportunities.[11]

A vision statement should be a broad statement that captures the overarching purpose of the organization. It describes what the organization wants to become; it is future-oriented. A concise statement that attracts attention and interests and appeals to the audience is far better than a lengthy statement. Whole Foods' motto is "Whole Foods, Whole People, Whole Planet." IKEA, the Swedish home-furnishings company, has a very simple, yet encompassing vision statement: "A better everyday life." Maho Bay Resorts, Saint John Island, U.S. Virgin Islands, which combines ecotourism with sustainable technology (solar power, composting toilets, etc.), has this vision statement: "Environmental sensitivity, human comfort, responsible consumption." Jade Mountain, Inc., Boulder, Colorado, a supplier of more than 7,000 products including solar electric, microhydro wind generators and superenergy-efficient appliances, describes its vision as "the fulfillment of appropriate technology — less is more." The Boeing Co.'s vision is "People working together as one global company for aerospace leadership. Boeing — the future of flight."

A vision statement embodies the future that has been visualized by the leader or leadership team. Whole Foods includes this statement in its philosophy: "Our Vision Statement reflects the hopes and intentions of many people. We do not believe it always accurately portrays the way things currently are at Whole Foods Market so much as the way we would like things to be. It is our dissatisfaction with the current reality, when compared with what is possible, that spurs us toward excellence and toward creating a better person, company, and world. When Whole Foods Market fails to measure up to its stated Vision, as it inevitably will at times, we should not despair. Rather let us take up the challenge together to bring our reality closer to our vision. The future we will experience tomorrow is created one step at a time today."[12]

The vision of Deere & Co. is "Growing a Business as Great as Our Products," and the vision for Deere worldwide supply management is "Aligning the Global Value Chain." At Whirlpool, the vision is "Every Home ... Everywhere. With Pride, Passion and Performance." The vision of Lenovo is "A Worldwide Leader in Technology." These short statements quickly and successfully convey where these organizations are going.

The management of many organizations also adopts a mission statement to express the organization's purpose. The following section provides various examples of mission statements.

## Mission: Why Does This Organization Exist?

*When people can see which direction the leaders are going in it becomes easier to motivate them.* LAKSHMI MITTAL, PRESIDENT OF THE BOARD OF DIRECTORS AND CEO OF ARCELOR MITTAL STEEL COMPANY[13]

*Mission* comes from the Latin word *mittere,* meaning "to throw, let go or send." Also derived from Latin, the word *purpose* (originally *proponere*) meant "to declare." Whether you call it a mission or purpose, it represents the fundamental reason for the organization's existence. What are we here to do together? For example, the Josephson Institute cited earlier in this chapter adopted the mission: "To improve the ethical quality of society by changing personal and organizational decision making and behavior."

The mission statement of an organization should flow from its vision. It should concisely answer fundamental questions such as:

- Who are we?
- Whose needs do we want to meet?
- What needs do we want to meet?
- How do we intend to meet these needs?
- What are our central values?

A supply management organization, for example, might state its mission as: "Establish supplier relationships that bring maximum value to the customers, owners and employees of the enterprise." Or "Achieve a level of supply-chain integration that allows materials, services and information to flow uninterrupted and at continuously lower total cost year after year."

The mission statement describes the important business capabilities, based on the customers' needs identified in the market research. Themes emerge from the vision statement to form the mission statements for the business. The mission statements provide the basis for measuring success and progress. At Deere, for instance, the mission is: "We aspire to distinctively serve customers — those linked to the land — through a great business, a business as great as our products."[14]

At Lenovo, the mission of procurement is to:

- Drive quality improvements from our suppliers of goods and services,
- Deliver lowest overall cost and greatest competitive advantage,
- Improve client perception of our values through increased influence and exemplary customer service and support.[15]

At Whirlpool, the mission is "Everyone … Passionately Creating Loyal Customers for Life."[16]

It is clear from these examples what the organizations are trying to achieve and how they define and measure success. A generic vision statement for a supply management organization might be: "A team and process that produces supplier contributions to the business and is seen as the world-class benchmark of performance." At Lufthansa, the vision of supply changed as a result of the multiple pressures of 9/11, the war in Iraq and the outbreak of SARS in Asia. The new vision of purchasing was as an internal critical, problem-oriented partner and externally as a "market forces optimizer." The focus of purchasing changed from demanding cost reductions from suppliers to focusing on cost reduction potential inside the organization by increasing spending discipline in daily routines to free up internal value-creation potential and by working more effectively with suppliers. A major change as a result of this vision was that purchase decisions would be derived from the economic problem and purchasers would have some freedom in their decisions. The purchase/supplier decision would not come predetermined.[17]

Figure 2-7 illustrates the current and projected approach to an acquisition and purchasing role using the example of customer data management.

At LG Electronics (LGE), the vision is to be in the global top three by 2010. This vision is supported by a growth strategy, focus on core competencies and a

Figure 2-7 Request-Oriented Versus Problem-Oriented Purchasing Pattern

**Request-oriented purchasing pattern TODAY**

**Specify need**
Database management and server system

**Determine technical specifications**
Hardware and software solution

**Identify possible solutions**
Supplier 1, supplier 2, supplier 3, etc.

**Send out Request-for-Quotes**
Specified performance, prices for server capacity, etc.

**Discuss and preselect suppliers**
Server capacity, security, service levels, etc.

**Personal final negotiation and award of contract**
Consideration of qualitative and quantitative aspects

**Request-oriented purchasing pattern FUTURE**

**Understand economic problem**

Securing and retrieval of customer data

**Deriving value drivers and decision criteria**

Costs, security, scalability, access speed, etc.

**Determine problem-oriented specification**

Efficient, safe and need-driven data management

**Expand solution space with alternatives**
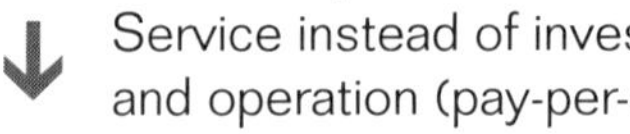
Service instead of investment and operation (pay-per-customer)

**Monetary evaluation of differences**
Bonus for service levels, scalability, etc.

**Project-specific negotiation design with clear rules**
Optimal use of solution space

*Source:* I. Bulow, U. Schott-Wullenweber and F. Hedderich, "Change Management in Purchasing: Best Practices from Germany's Number 1 Airline Deutsche Lufthansa AG," *PRACTIX,* CAPS Research 9 (July 2006).

supportive and enabling corporate culture. And, at its foundation, "Great Company, Great People." This vision is supported and enabled by LGE's global supply-chain management (GSCM) organization. LGE's GSCM system combines "design, parts supply, procurement, inventory, production, and cost management into an integrated process to enable strategic flow of information and gathering of standardized production data. The system is expected to help strengthen LGE's competitive edge with operation integration with overseas subsidiaries, to maximize operation efficiency with the introduction of advanced management system, and to save about 45 billion won per business location for the next three years."[18] LGE's global purchasing system is expected to improve the purchasing process, facilitate the implementation of global standards to help strengthen LGE's presence in e-business and to make possible real-time sharing of production cycle information.[19]

## Developing Strategies

*Vision without action is a daydream.*
*Action without vision is a nightmare.* JAPANESE PROVERB

Given the direction and vision of the future, what are the strategies that will lead the supply management organization to achieve its vision? At this point, the leader wants to develop higher-level strategies that align supply vision and strategy with corporate vision, strategy, mission and goals and objectives. This alignment might occur in specific areas such as social responsibility or technology roadmaps. For example, in its *Corporate Sustainability Report,* Procter & Gamble states the alignment this way: "Sustainable development is a simple idea — ensuring a better quality of life for everyone, now and for generations to come. P&G embraces sustainable development as a potential business opportunity, as well as a corporate responsibility. Through our activities we contribute to the economic and social well-being of a range of stakeholders. ... In summary, P&G contributes to sustainable development through both what we do and how we do it. As a result, consumers will reward us with leadership sales, profit and value creation, allowing our people, our shareholders and the communities in which we live and work to prosper."[20]

In Figure 2-8, I. Bulow, U. Schott-Wullenweber and F. Hedderich propose three implementation strategies based on the status of supply management in the organization and its developmental level.

### Aligning Supply Strategy With Organizational Strategy

A key factor in the concept and development of a strategic supply management department is that this will lead to greater alignment of supply strategy with organizational strategy. As internal alignment improves, supply management will be better able to realize its full potential as a major contributor to sustainable success. Ultimately, the true test of the vision, and the leader behind it, is results. John Kotter offers a matrix approach (see Figure 2-9) to assess if the vision will drive to sustainable success for the organization.

**Figure 2-8 Implementation Strategies Based on Supply Management's Status and Development Level**

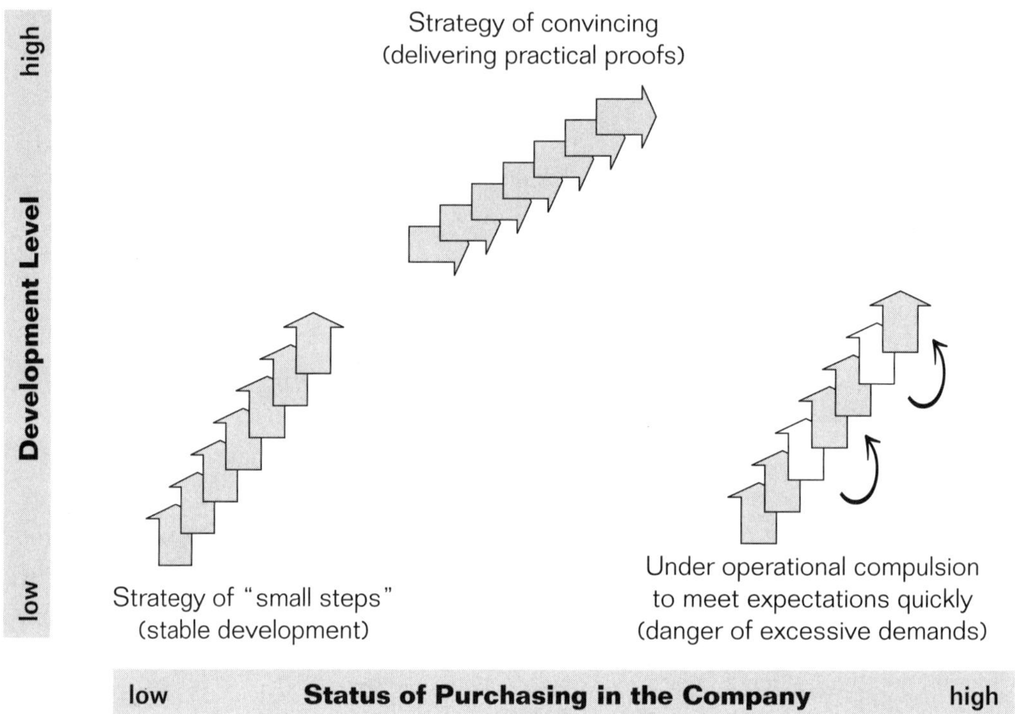


*Source:* I. Bulow, U. Schott-Wullenweber and F. Hedderick, "Change Management in Purchasing: Best Practices from Germany's Number 1 Airline Deutsche Lufthansa AG," PRACTIX, CAPS Research 9 (July 2006).

At Nissan, Carlos Ghosn found that the company had no long-term vision. The organization was in the lower left-hand quadrant of Kotter's matrix. Targets were set at the regional level (Japan, United States, Europe) and there was no coordination across regions. Suppliers were approached multiple times in a year for price reductions to offset the eroding performance of the organization. Once a strong vision was established and stakeholders bought into it, the organization was able to move to the right on the vision axis and to begin obtaining better results. Once suppliers believed that the targets were real and that Nissan purchasing employees would not keep coming back with new targets throughout the year, they could begin to turn things around.[21] Whether Nissan can sustain success through the current downturn remains to be seen.

**Figure 2-9 Vision, Results and Sustainable Success**

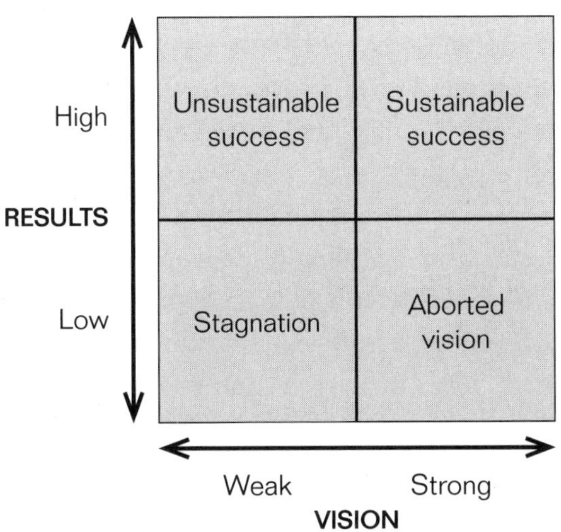


*Source:* John P. Kotter, "Winning at Change," *Leader to Leader* 10 (Fall 1998), 27–33.

How the leader of supply management aligns supply strategies, goals and objectives to effectively and efficiently contribute to overall organizational goals and objectives is the key question. To accomplish this, he or she must have access to and understand the business unit plans and objectives, ideally through involvement in their development. Then, using that knowledge, a supply management strategy is developed that best supports the organizational strategy. The alignment of supply management strategy and objectives with organizational strategy and objectives requires two-way communication during the planning process at all three levels of planning (strategic, operational and tactical). Supply management receives input from the corporate and business unit strategy process that enables the development of supply management strategy. Equally important to the success of the organization is input from the supply leaders and managers about supply opportunities and risks that may influence the development and direction of corporate and business-unit-level strategy. Strategy development is discussed in detail in Chapters 5 and 6.

Louis Chênevert, president and COO, United Technologies Corp. (UTC), recognizes the value of supply management and looks to it to contribute to the success of the company. Supply management played an important role in the development and success of the Otis Gen2 elevator, which represented about one-third of the elevators shipped by Otis in 2006. Chênevert notes, "The supply management team found suppliers with capability to reliably produce quality parts in sufficient quantity and who are committed, as we are, to continuous improvement." The effort grew market share continuously over the past several years, with orders for Gen2 elevators up by about 30 percent in 2005 over the year before. Chênevert sees supply management's use of strategic sourcing and design for manufacturing as instrumental in helping meet aggressive production goals for Pratt & Whitney's PW600 jet engine. Pratt took assembly line lead time from eight days to eight hours. "This step-change in productivity allows us to better respond to demands of the fast-growing market for very light jets, where we see potential for 25,000 or more engines. ... The supply management team deals constantly with suppliers to communicate UTC's needs and the needs of its customers," says Chênevert. "Our goal is to ensure our customers get market-leading products with perfect quality," he says. "To accomplish that, we need suppliers as dedicated to this goal as we are." Chênevert adds, "UTC's culture is one of constantly improving our performance. There are always opportunities to improve and we are pursuing those aggressively so we remain competitive and achieve the highest levels of customer satisfaction. Over the next five years, supply management will continue to seek suppliers who share our vision and commitment."[22]

As the primary owner of the supply management process, the supply leader plays a crucial role in communicating the vision and strategies of supply to internal and external stakeholders including top management, users of the process, the supplier community and the surrounding community. The supply leader's most important task may be in successfully communicating supply opportunities beyond traditional price and volume considerations and creative ways to mitigate risks. It will be through these efforts that supply management takes its place at the strategic level in the organization.

The next chapter addresses the challenges and rewards for the supply management leader who can develop meaningful internal and external business partnerships.

## Key Points

1. Direction setting is the primary task of a leader or leadership team. It involves clarifying the core values of the organization, identifying future opportunities and risks and devising a compelling vision, mission and strategies.

2. Values drive the behavior of all members of the organization and contribute to the corporate culture of the organization. They describe how we intend to operate, on a day-to-day basis, as we pursue our vision.

3. Ethical principles are the rules of conduct that derive from ethical values. These principles guide behavior.
4. A vision statement tells where the organization wants to go, and the value statement describes how the organization will get there.
5. To focus attention on how results are obtained, to support the practice of ethical decision-making and to guide the behavior of others, leaders can exhibit ethical behavior, create a strong ethical culture, establish a code of conduct, include ethical issues in employment decisions, formally include ethics in performance evaluations and engage in meaningful ethics training.
6. Supply opportunities and risks may exist in any number of areas, including growth of markets, especially in low-cost countries or in markets concerned with sustainable products, strategic partnerships, mergers and acquisitions, financial markets and government-industry partnerships.

## **Appendix:** *ISM Principles of Social Responsibility*

### *Introduction*

It is the mission of ISM to promote excellence in social responsibility through the development of principles and the sharing of tools, information and best practices that will assist in the implementation and continuous improvement of supply management organizations and professionals.

### *ISM objectives:*

1. Increase the supply management profession's awareness of social responsibility.
2. Provide tools, information and best practices for the development of a proactive social responsibility program for supply management professionals and their organizations.
3. Make available social responsibility references to supply management professionals.
4. Raise the profile of supply management through the promotion of social responsibility internally and through supplier personnel.

### *ISM will ask organizations to:*

1. Support these social responsibility principles.
2. Donate resources to support communication of the social responsibility principles and practices.
3. Share best practices and other material to assist other organizations working to improve social responsibility behavior internally and with suppliers.

### *Preamble*

ISM believes supply management is a key contributor in the development and implementation of social responsibility principles. The supply chain can be impacted both "upstream" and "downstream." The purpose of these principles is to increase supply management's awareness and to provide tools to supply management professionals for the development of a proactive supply management social responsibility program for their organization. Organizations are encouraged to promote social responsibility through participation on appropriate committees, boards and panels of governmental and nongovernmental organizations.

Creating principles applicable across social, sector, organization (public, private and nonprofit) and country boundaries is a daunting task. Additionally, federal, state and local laws and regulations, international laws and regulations, and customs and practices pertinent to social responsibility must be a relevant and integral part of the development and implementation of policies and procedures.

These principles have been written and distributed to provide "one more voice" to the importance of social responsibility in its many forms and applications. They may complement existing standards, or they may be used as a starting point from which to develop a set of standards unique to the needs of the organization.

Finally, it is recognized that individual social responsibility components or dimensions may be of greater or lesser importance depending on the context in which the organization operates.

### *Principles*

Social responsibility is defined as a framework of measurable corporate policies and procedures and resulting behavior designed to benefit the workplace and, by extension, the individual, the organization and the community in the following areas (in alphabetical order):

#### I. COMMUNITY

1. Provide support and add value to your communities and those of your supply chain.
2. Encourage members of your supply chain to add value in their communities.

#### II. DIVERSITY

1. Proactively promote purchasing from, and the development of, socially diverse suppliers.
2. Encourage diversity within your own organization.
3. Proactively promote diverse employment practices throughout the supply chain.

#### III. ENVIRONMENT

1. Encourage your own organization and others to be proactive in examining opportunities to be environmentally responsible within their supply chains either "upstream" or "downstream."
2. Encourage the environmental responsibility of your suppliers.
3. Encourage the development and diffusion of environmentally friendly practices and products throughout your organization.

### IV. ETHICS

1. Be aware of *ISM's Principles and Standards of Ethical Supply Management Conduct.*
2. Abide by your organization's code of conduct.

### V. FINANCIAL RESPONSIBILITY

1. Become knowledgeable of, and follow, applicable financial standards and requirements.
2. Apply sound financial practices and ensure transparency in financial dealings.
3. Actively promote and practice responsible financial behavior throughout the supply chain.

### VI. HUMAN RIGHTS

1. Treat people with dignity and respect.
2. Support and respect the protection of international human rights within the organization's sphere of influence.
3. Encourage your organization and its supply chains to avoid complicity in human-rights or employment-rights abuses.

### VII. SAFETY

1. Promote a safe environment for each employee in your organization and supply chain. (Each organization is responsible for defining "safe" within its organization.)
2. Support the continuous development and diffusion of safety practices throughout your organization and the supply chain.

CHAPTER

3

# Creating Alignment

> *It is not for the system to dictate the moves of people, but for people to dictate the system. A company where the system moves its people will lose its vigor and will decline. It is the company where people move the system that develops and grows.*
>
> GAISHI HIRAIWA, COUNSELOR, TOKYO ELECTRIC POWER COMPANY, INC.[1]

Creating alignment is the second stage of effective leadership. *Merriam-Webster's Dictionary* defines *alignment* as "an arrangement of groups or forces in relation to one another." When it comes to leadership, alignment is the process of arranging internal and external groups in the appropriate relationship to one another so that they are all moving in the direction set by the leader or leadership team. In this way, the leader or leadership team turns the vision into a shared vision among all key stakeholders. Communication is the key leadership task at this stage. To create a shared vision the leader must communicate in multiple ways with multiple internal and external stakeholders. During this ongoing communication process, the message must be compelling, the leader must be credible and the behaviors must be consistent.

This chapter addresses the role of the leader as the chief communicator who brings together internal and external stakeholders behind the vision. The complementary managerial concepts of organizing and staffing are addressed in Chapters 7 and 9, respectively. To attain the shared vision, the leader must then gain commitment from stakeholders to persevere throughout the change process and execute the necessary tasks. Motivating and inspiring, which are the key leadership tasks in stage three, are discussed in detail in the next chapter. This chapter is organized into four sections: (1) supply alignment and the leader's role, (2) communicating a clear understanding of vision to disparate stakeholders, (3) building credibility and (4) empowering others to own the vision.

**CHAPTER OBJECTIVES**

- Define alignment and discuss alignment in the context of supply management.
- Identify key internal and external stakeholders.
- Discuss the communication tools and techniques leaders can use to impart a clear and compelling message about the vision of supply management.
- Discuss the ways that the leader establishes and maintains credibility.
- Explore the opportunities and obstacles that might occur during the alignment process.
- Discuss the behaviors that the leader must display consistently throughout the change process to capitalize on the opportunities of alignment and eliminate or reduce the obstacles.

## Supply Alignment and the Leader's Role

In the context of supply management, alignment refers to the relationship of the supply leader to members of the supply management organization as well as the position of the supply management group relative to other major groups in the organization, such as finance, marketing and engineering; and to major groups outside the organization, such as suppliers, the community, professional associations and so on. Alignment is achieved by successfully communicating the vision of supply management to these stakeholders. Successful alignment is achieved when multiple stakeholders accept or buy in to the vision of supply management to the extent necessary to move toward attaining the vision.

The first stage of leadership — setting direction (discussed in Chapter 2) — addressed the importance of aligning the supply management vision and strategies with the organizational vision and strategies (see Figure 3-1). If this has been carried out successfully, the supply leader or leadership team will be well positioned to align internal stakeholders with the supply vision. If, however, conflicts exist between the organizational vision and strategies and those of supply management, then there will undoubtedly be problems. Likewise, if the supply vision and strategies conflict with that of individual internal stakeholders such as finance, marketing, engineering and so on, then the organization has even bigger challenges ahead. It is this lack of horizontal alignment that often creates problems between and among members of different functions and business process owners. The desire to avoid these types of conflicts affects the leaders and top managers of the various functions when they are setting direction and making plans at the organizational and functional levels.

Figure 3-1 Vertical and Horizontal Alignment of Vision and Strategies

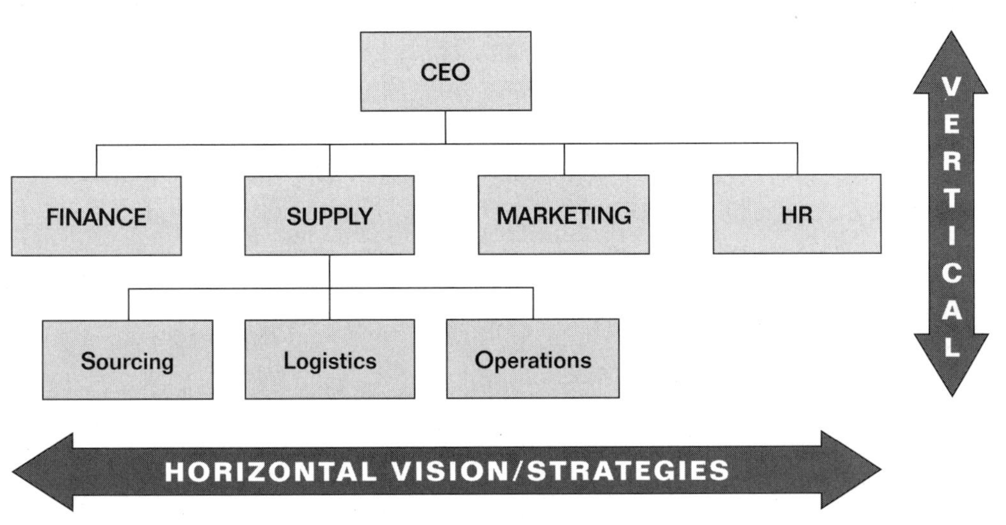


## The Importance of Alignment

The alignment role in supply management is especially critical and challenging because in many organizations the scope of supply management is expanding to include more components that are approached from a more strategic perspective. P. Fraser Johnson and Michiel R. Leenders reported that the overall trend in the aggregate was for increases in supply-chain responsibilities although there were substantial gains and losses among those organizations that participated in both their 1995 and 2003 study of roles and responsibilities. The most frequently identified responsibilities were e-procurement, supplier development, supplier cost management/value analysis, outsourcing and subcontracting, and supply-chain processes and systems.[2]

According to the Institute for Supply Management™ (ISM), supply management includes the identification, acquisition, access, positioning and management of resources and related capabilities that an organization needs or potentially needs in the attainment of its strategic objectives. This includes the following components: disposition/investment recovery, distribution, inventory control, manufacturing supervision, logistics, materials management packaging, product/service development, strategic sourcing, procurement/purchasing, quality, receiving, supply management, transportation/traffic/shipping and warehousing. This expanded scope means the supply management process involves more and different stakeholders than the historical purchasing role and often entails major changes in processes, human capital, reporting relationships and responsibilities. Reliance on strong managers may not achieve the transformation that both supply and the organization as a whole require. Consequently, strong leadership in supply management is more important than ever to successfully market the value of strategic sourcing and sourcing strategies and initiatives to management and internal customers.

In 2005, IBM Business Consulting Services conducted a survey of 45 CPOs from 14 industries and 8 European countries. These data were supplemented by a joint study with the Economist Intelligence Unit that consists of 50 CPOs and 250 other C-level executives from 64 countries. The results were distilled into five key areas for CPO success:

1. Become business partners, not just buyers. Respond proactively to broader business goals.
2. Explore new value frontiers; it is not just about price. Reorient to capability sourcing.
3. Pull suppliers inside; the best value chain wins. Champion the full contribution potential of strategic suppliers.
4. Pursue low-cost sources — a world worth exploring. Overcome cross-border challenges to tap into cost-effective sources.
5. Conduct the ultimate talent search. Equip teams with necessary skills and expertise to do the previous four items.[3]

For example, the CEO of Cable and Wireless, PLC, headquartered in London, set an aggressive vision for the organization "to lead the world in integrated communications." This vision also led to a transformation of the procurement function. Two years after the vision was set, head office procurement consisted of 25 people who handled contract administration and tactical buying while user groups handled sourcing decisions. The first expansion in role and responsibilities was the establishment of a three-year savings target of £600 million (about $1 billion) and the overall goal of making procurement accountable for adding value. A year later, a further expansion occurred when procurement's reporting line changed to the chief executive of global operations. This change positioned procurement to play a role in the development of the Cable and Wireless Global Procurement Organization. Procurement's focus changed to revenue enhancement and early supply involvement. Supply-chain responsibilities expanded to include meaningful involvement in major technology acquisitions, nontraditional purchases, new product and new business development as well as programs and bids, processes and systems, and travel. Global procurement oversaw Cable and Wireless Global in the United Kingdom and Europe, Japan and the United States.[4]

### The Leader's Role in Alignment

To successfully align people behind a vision and future direction, the leader must execute three activities: (1) Impart a clear understanding of the vision to a broad and disparate group of stakeholders; (2) build credibility with stakeholders by exhibiting consistent behaviors that support and promote the vision and strategies; and (3) empower people to take ownership of the vision and make it happen.

For example, the Supply Chain Management (SCM) division leadership at Bank of America had a vision of being recognized as world class in supply-chain management throughout the financial services industry. This vision first had to be clearly understood within the ranks of supply-chain professionals at Bank of America. Then, the SCM team worked with its leader(s) to impart an understanding of this vision throughout the organization and to external stakeholders as well. To gain credibility with stakeholders, the supply-chain professionals had to understand the business, be able to implement innovative supply-chain processes and possess the capability to flawlessly execute those processes while working as a value-adding, high-performing part of the business. A consistent display of these behaviors built credibility and further support for the vision. By working in partnership with internal customers, the supply management group empowered other bank employees to execute parts of the supply vision.[5]

## Communicating a Clear Understanding of the Vision

The first step in creating alignment is to impart a clear understanding of the vision to disparate audiences. A critical role for the supply management leader is that of chief advocate, chief communicator and chief salesperson of the transformation to the new vision and direction of supply management. The leader must answer three questions at this stage: (1) Who are the target audiences/stakeholders? (2) What are the underlying interests of each stakeholder or stakeholder group? (3) How can the leader link the supply vision and strategy to the stakeholders' interests?

### Who Are Stakeholders?

A stakeholder is someone who has a legitimate interest in the outcome of a project or decision. A stakeholder's level of interest depends on the magnitude of the potential gain or loss from the success or failure of the project. Stakeholders may be members of the organization or members of external groups affiliated with the organization in some fashion. The supply leader(s) faces the twin tasks of aligning internal stakeholders and external stakeholders with the vision.

**Internal Stakeholders.** Target audiences or stakeholder groups may be people inside the supply organization itself because without buy-in from supply professionals the leader has little chance of success at achieving the vision. Supply personnel are the people who must "flawlessly execute" the vision. Target audiences may also be inside the organization, but outside of supply management; for example, marketing, engineering, design and so on. Without alignment with these internal stakeholders, the supply leader may find it impossible to deliver on the vision. Alignment is required internally to efficiently and effectively transform the supply organization from a tactical operation to a strategic one according to the specific vision and direction set by the leader. Figure 3-2 lists some of the interests of internal stakeholder groups and examples of how the supply management team might link their goals to the stakeholders' interests.

**Figure 3-2 Internal Stakeholders and Their Interests Linked to Supply Management**

| WHO (the audience) | WHAT (is being communicated) | EXAMPLES |
|---|---|---|
| **Top leadership or management of the organization** | Supplier performance | Price and cost trends, lead times, shortages, labor strife, cartel actions, new technology, mergers affecting the supply chain. |
| | Performance to plan | Budgeted expenditures, headcount, savings plan, quality improvement, training. |
| | Supply market conditions | Present and forecast raw material availability and cost, supplier capacities, mergers and acquisitions. |
| **Employees** | Special supplier terms for employee purchases | Dell offers employee purchase discounts to customers with more than 400 employees. |
| | Terms of certain supplier agreements affecting employees | Travel, services, utilities, temporary help, printing, etc. |
| | Policies and procedures relative to supply management | Ethics policy (the organization's commitment to treat suppliers fairly and honestly; rules about accepting gifts and gratuities). |

*Source:* Anna E. Flynn and Samuel Farney, *The Supply Management Leadership Process,* Volume 4 of the *ISM Knowledge Series* (National Association for Purchasing Management, 2004), 234.

**External Stakeholders.** Lastly, target audiences may be external groups; for example, suppliers, the community, professional associations and any other group that has a vested interest in the outcomes of the organization and supply's contribution to these outcomes. Alignment is required externally to extend supply's reach and influence up and down the supply chain. Stakeholder alignment requires continuous communication about the central message embedded in the future vision. Figure 3-3 lists some of the interests of external stakeholder groups and how the supply management team might link their goals to the interests of these stakeholders.

## Building Alignment Internally

The approach taken by the leader to build alignment internally depends in large part on the drivers of change. Is the new vision the result of a crisis that threatens the survival of the organization? Or is it the result of external pressures that are negatively affecting key performance metrics, but not survival? Or is it internally driven because of a change in leadership or structure or technology? The supply leader's alignment approach will vary depending on the driver(s) and the audience.

For example, external events including 9/11, the war in Iraq and the SARS outbreak in Asia created the impetus for change at Lufthansa. Change was needed and top management was open to ideas from every segment of the business. The supply leader could make a strong case for change from a logical basis given the very real pressures caused by external events. The change in the vision of supply management at Lufthansa started with discussions between top management and supply leadership to clarify expectations. This led to a new vision, new purchasing processes and a new self-image.

The vision required three distinct activities on the part of the leader: (1) align supply management personnel behind the vision and lead them to develop the critical role of partner with internal customers; (2) lead a change in the internal perception of supply management and convince internal stakeholders of supply management's new value proposition; and (3) lead the change in interactions with, and expectations of, suppliers.[6]

External events may create a compelling situation in which it is far easier to sell people on the need for change. In fact, in the Lufthansa case, the change in supply management arose out of the purchasing organization as the leaders in that group recognized both the critical nature of the situation for the company and the opportunity for supply management to move to the "next level" in performance and contribution. In this case, alignment within supply management was extremely critical because misalignment within the group would almost certainly doom the entire change effort with top management and with internal stakeholders and the supply base.

**Figure 3-3 External Stakeholders and Their Interests Linked to Supply**

| WHO (the audience) | WHAT (is being communicated) | EXAMPLES |
|---|---|---|
| **Investors** | Cost and customer value improvements | Quality, delivery, lead time, cost improvements, specifications |
| | Key supplier relationships | Strategic alliances that may (or do) significantly impact value |
| **Community** | Supplier diversity programs | Percentage of annual spending awarded to minority-owned or women-owned businesses or small businesses |
| | Local and regional content | Percentage of end product that is composed of material made, mined or assembled locally |
| **Customers** | Product or service improvements | Quality, delivery, lead time, cost improvements |
| | Innovations in process or delivered value | Specifications — new features, advantages or benefits |
| | Faster response time | Accurate and predictable delivery dates |
| **Suppliers** | Performance feedback | Quality, delivery, lead time, cost improvements |
| | Schedule needs | Forecast, quantity versus date, annual requirements |
| | New product plans | Specifications, quantities, production dates |
| | Key expectations of suppliers | Design innovation, continuous improvement, competitiveness, speed-to-market |

*Source:* Anna E. Flynn and Samuel Farney, *The Supply Management Leadership Process,* Volume 4 of the *ISM Supply Management Knowledge Series* (National Association for Purchasing Management, 2000), 237.

At Sandvik Materials Technology, the impetus for change came, not from external pressures, but from internal pressure from organization president, Peter Gossas, to find ways to "embark on the path of broad, deep and never-ending change" to improve an already well-performing organization. According to Gossas, "When a unit is in full crisis and has, say, eight months to get its act together or face closure, the manager does not have to sell the idea of change. But you won't get automatic buy-in for a new business system in a company where many units view themselves as good — some even as very good. In that situation, the manager's message must be different from the one about survival being at stake, but it needs to be just as persuasive because a new system will not work unless everybody believes in it and is dedicated to it."[7]

At Sandvik, transformation was initiated at the top of the organization and methodically rolled out to various functions in the organization based on the assessment that manufacturing lead time was the key driver of productivity. This assessment led to a four-part transformation plan: (1) Improve material flow in manufacturing processes, (2) develop more efficient ways to market and sell products, (3) use scale to capture leverage when purchasing and (4) use these three transformations to drive more efficient product development. This fourth stage of the transformation hinged on greater alignment internally so that the links and relationships between and among people in R&D, sales, supply management, manufacturing and customers would speed up product development through parallel development of the new product, the choice of raw materials and the best way to manufacture and market.[8]

External or internal drivers may stimulate the change management initiative. The leader or leadership team must carefully assess the drivers of change and build the alignment plan accordingly.

**Create Alignment Within Supply Management.** The first place that alignment must occur is within the supply organization itself. Target audiences may include supply personnel transitioning from the old paradigm to the new as well as those being incorporated under a new and expanded supply umbrella. The level of difficulty in aligning supply personnel behind the new vision of supply management depends, in part, on the level of change or transformation that will be experienced by these people during the change process. For example, every supply management employee at Lufthansa completed a questionnaire about everyday work procedures to determine the gap between the vision and the reality of the supply management organization. Written objectives were used to help supply management personnel understand the required changes, including developing the capability to act (1) internally as a critical, problem-oriented partner and (2) externally as a "market forces optimizer" who maximizes company benefits.[9]

To be successful, the leader must clarify and communicate to supply personnel the changes in roles, responsibilities and reporting relationships, including the reasons for the changes and the expected benefits from the changes. In situations where people were involved in the visioning process, a certain level of acceptance or buy-in may have already been achieved. In other cases, there may be little or no buy-in to a vision the leader is announcing. In the latter case the leader may have a tougher job during the alignment process because stakeholders were not part of the thought process and may need to walk through the leader's thinking to accept it. The buy-in process varies depending on the circumstances and the organizational structure, culture and current state. Unlike Lufthansa, at United Technologies Corp. (UTC), the supply management process change was top-down. The CEO brought in Kent Brittan, named him vice president of supply management and made him responsible for pulling together the spending of UTC's diverse businesses and set a cost reduction goal of $750 million in four years. Brittan's challenge was rooted in the highly decentralized nature of UTC. Each UTC business — Carrier, Hamilton Sundstrand, Otis, Pratt & Whitney, Sikorsky, UTC Fire & Security and UTC Power — operates autonomously and has its own supply management operation. Brittan had to align the disparate supply groups around the new vision of supply management without changing the basic decentralized structure and culture of the organization. By focusing on common areas with clear benefits from collaborating, Brittan was able to deliver results beyond savings.[10]

Alignment within supply management at UTC was facilitated by a council composed of vice presidents of supply management at each business who meet 11 times a year to share best practices and make decisions about supply management policy and procedure. The supply group was also able to develop corporate contracts with common terms and conditions to minimize the risk of doing business in a highly regulated environment and make it easier for suppliers to do business with UTC. Supply managers at businesses within UTC with little common spend categories, and therefore little opportunity to leverage spend, communicate frequently and share supply initiatives with each other.[11]

**Create Alignment Internally, But Outside of Supply Management.** The supply leader must also develop alignment with internal stakeholders outside of the supply organization to generate buy-in and commitment to the leader's vision of supply management. To build the necessary level of connectivity between and among internal groups, the supply leader must determine who the key internal stakeholders are, what their interests are in the specific situation and how to help them meet their interests while also affecting the desired change in supply roles, processes and systems.

When it comes to these internal stakeholders, the starting point is often an assessment of the perception of supply and its role in the organization. How much credibility does the supply organization currently have in the organization? What are the sources of this credibility? Perhaps supply management has credibility when it comes to driving the lowest prices from suppliers, but no credibility when it comes to input in the design stage, assessing and delivering lowest total cost of ownership or balancing the needs of disparate stakeholders and arriving at the "best value" combination of quality, delivery, service and total cost. One result of the assessment needs to be a determination of the level of credibility relative to the vision and the changes that will be required to achieve the vision. The leader may also begin to put together a plan to build credibility where it is lacking.

This assessment might be accomplished through regular or special communication in the course of developing or maintaining "thick, informal internal networks" or it may be in a more formal manner such as with surveys of internal users of supply processes or interviews with key stakeholders. A level of trust must be developed between the parties if there is any hope of getting accurate feedback. Developing surveys that do not introduce bias and that respondents believe will be carefully considered is also important.

In some organizations, the change management process is highly structured. At Eastman Kodak, for example, the sourcing process change management team had four sponsors: the manager of business unit worldwide operations at headquarters, the managers of business unit equipment development from two sites and the vice president of worldwide equipment purchasing. The stakeholders in the process change were identified as the manager of business unit operations at Site 2, the supply chain manager for the business unit at Site 2 and the worldwide commodity manager of worldwide equipment purchasing. The project team was comprised of core and extended team members. The core team consisted of a project leader (a worldwide commodity manager) and four team members (a worldwide commodity manager, a strategic cost manager, an engineer and a business-unit supply-chain manager).[12]

**Creating Alignment With External Stakeholders.** The supply leader must also align external stakeholders behind the supply vision to the extent necessary to execute it. The supply leader represents the supply organization in meetings with corporations, government agencies, professional associations and other organizations and, of course, with suppliers.

Suppliers represent perhaps the most important external stakeholder group in the supply process. A change in the vision of supply typically entails changes in sources and the location of sources. A new vision may mean new and different demands on suppliers and very real differences in how business is executed. For example, UTC's new vision of supply management led to a transformation in the expectations of suppliers and supply managers. For instance, four purchasing professionals in UTC's aerospace businesses are dedicated to developing suppliers in the emerging markets of China, India, Eastern Europe, Turkey and Brazil. In other areas of UTC's aerospace business, the focus is on involving suppliers in design for manufacturing initiatives such as the development of its PW600 engine for very light jets to meet anticipated customer demand. On the commercial business side, Lean tools have been used to create a new supply chain to develop technology for Otis' Gen2 elevator.[13] These types of initiatives require consistent behaviors that are very different from those used by buyers and suppliers focused on prices and operating out of adversarial relationships.

External pressures from global competition and external opportunities from a global talent pool and a global supply base may also influence the change management process. For example, IBM's vision is of a "globally integrated company" and its strategy is to draw more efficiently on its global capabilities and capitalize on emerging market opportunities. To advance this vision, IBM chose Shenzhen, China, for its global procurement headquarters. IBM already has more than 1,850 procurement and logistics professionals in the region, many of them at its China Procurement Center in Shenzhen, which has been in operation for more than a decade. The center is one of IBM's largest procurement organizations outside the United States. The company also has strong and collaborative relationships with nearly 3,000 suppliers across Asia, accounting for about 30 percent of the $40 billion IBM spends annually on procurement. Although IBM has been purchasing in Asia for more than 50 years, changes in global demand for services require the development of relationships with new partners and suppliers as well as working with existing ones to help them build skills, processes and management practices to compete globally in the services market.[14]

It is just as important to clarify the expectations of external stakeholders as it is to clarify those of internal stakeholders. Supplier representatives have been through every supply management fad that has come along so it may take some time and effort to convince them that this transformation is for real. For example, a commodity manager might refer.to an online auction as an online negotiation and stress the importance of buyer-supplier relationships. However, if the supplier perceives a negotiation as involving give-and-take and the online auction as a one-way exchange mostly or solely benefiting the buyer, then the commodity manager may have little or no credibility with the supplier. The perception may not be changed until or unless the commodity manager understands the perspective of the supplier and adjusts his or her words and actions accordingly.

Scott Singer, director of global general procurement at UTC, for instance, talks about the importance of (buyer and seller) understanding and agreeing on each other's expectations for the relationship. He found that this usually leads to a discussion about mutual gains or *coprosperity,* a term used at UTC in meetings with suppliers.[15]

Understanding the interests of the other party is critical to the alignment process. For example, supply management may consider how long it takes to get innovative new products to market a key performance indicator of a successful supplier relationship. Suppliers may focus on expected revenue growth and the potential for increased business from buyers. Once both parties have a clear understanding of the key performance indicators for their respective stakeholders, this paves the way for creating options for mutual gain. Exhibiting understanding of the other parties' interests is a solid first step toward credibility. Other tools and techniques for building credibility are discussed in the following section.

## Building Credibility

> *Experto credite. (Trust one who has proved it.)* VIRGIL, 2,000 YEARS AGO

According to *Merriam-Webster's Dictionary, credibility* is "1: the quality or power of inspiring belief, and 2: capacity for belief." This is an interesting definition because it reflects action on the part of the messenger and the receiver of the message. The messenger must possess or develop the power to inspire belief, and the listener must have the capacity for belief. Even if the message is understood, how does the leader get people to believe it? The ability to build credibility requires the supply leader (messenger) to inspire belief through his or her character, words and actions. The leader must also seek to understand if he or she has credibility in the eyes of stakeholders and why or why not. A truthful message alone will not inspire belief. Building credibility with stakeholders is a critical element of successful alignment and change management.

For example, the supply management vision of an organization in the transportation sector (referred to as Fleet) was to have a "lean, focused, world-class supply base providing a competitive advantage that could be readily accessed by its end users." Part of this vision involved "purposely choosing suppliers."[16] Jeffrey A. Ogden and Matthew W. McCarter report that under the old vision of purchasing, the organization collaborated very little with suppliers and relationships were marked by short-term, price-oriented contracts, multiple suppliers and frequent supplier switching, especially if difficulties were encountered. This resulted in highly variable pricing across suppliers and locations.

Under the new vision of supply management, suppliers were gradually brought into alignment as the size of the supply base was reduced and the remaining suppliers focused on improvements in price and delivery. The benefits envisioned under the new supply direction went way beyond price improvements to lower total cost of ownership. To achieve this, Fleet and its suppliers had to collaborate through long-term, integrative partnerships and strategic alliances. Once Fleet was successful at building a supplier relationship according to this new model, other suppliers became interested in working toward a similar deal. Actual performance in accordance with supply's new vision established credibility with other suppliers as well as the partner-supplier. This example illustrates the importance of backing up words with actions. Because of past experiences with Fleet, suppliers were understandably cautious in believing that things would truly be different.[17]

## Components of Credibility

Credibility is built through a number of actions and behaviors, including demonstrated performance, consistency, commitment, existing relationships, the reputation of the messenger, the message itself, the ethics, integrity and trustworthy behaviors of the messenger and the perceived concern of the messenger for the listener's interests. Figure 3-4 captures the components of credibility.

**Ethics, Integrity, Trustworthiness and Reputation.** Ethics, integrity and trustworthiness are at the heart of credibility. If the leader is perceived by stakeholders as unethical, lacking in personal integrity or untrustworthy, it may be very difficult to bring these stakeholders into alignment with the vision and direction of supply management. While it is possible to proceed in the absence of trust, it may take skills and abilities that are underdeveloped in many people to do this successfully.

Figure 3-4 Components of Credibility

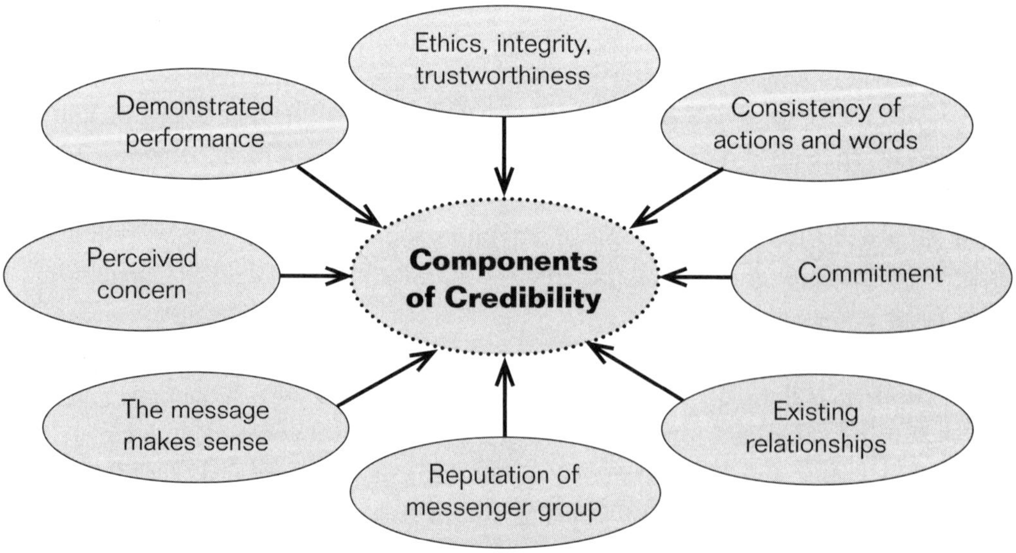

According to Deere CEO Bob Lane, "Trustworthiness is a vital part of Deere's heritage. For customers, that means if we say we'll make it right during the warranty period we'll make it right, even if it costs us a lot of money. For employees, it means people know where they stand. It's the same for suppliers too. One supplier told me, 'You know, I wouldn't call Deere supplier-friendly, but I would call Deere supplier-fair.' And I was pleased to hear it. As an organization, Deere aspires to be a transparent company: no smoke, no mirrors, no tricks. We're straight down the middle."[18]

**Demonstrated Performance and Reputation.** As the Deere example illustrates, an established reputation for fairness paves the way for change. People will tend to think, "They were fair to me in the past, I believe they will be fair to me in the future, even if some things change." Without the reputation firmly in place, stakeholders may be wary of process changes and cautious in adopting new procedures until there is evidence to support the claims of supply management.

The messenger, in this case the supply management leader or leadership team, and the supply management organization will be more believable if, individually and collectively, they have a performance track record to back up the current vision. A reputation for getting the job done may lead people to believe that the leader or team can get the current job done as well.

Often, this is not the case. If the supply organization is undergoing transformational change from a tactical to a strategic organization, building credibility with stakeholders may be the first and foremost challenge if supply management's past performance has not measured up in the eyes of stakeholders. For example, if supply and suppliers are perceived as unreliable, if the organization lacks a rigorous sourcing process or the existing process is perceived as bureaucratic, and if there is any question at all about the individual and collective trustworthiness of supply personnel, then the supply leader should expect to have to stimulate a transformational change in the perceptions of supply management.

Fleet, the company in the transportation sector, earned greater respect among people working in organizations in its supply base as a result of the behavior of its supply personnel in a partnership with one supplier. Consistent behaviors involving shared resources, open communication, shared risks and rewards and joint accountability in the partnership relationship have made other suppliers eager to develop a similar relationship. Consistency is a major driver of credibility. If the supply management team talks about the value it can add, and the actions of supply personnel consistently support this claim, then credibility will be established. If results are below projections, then a serious review of why and how to do better next time may shore up or rebuild supply's credibility.

**A Clear and Consistent Message.** Stakeholders are more likely to believe the message if it is presented in a straightforward, logical manner supported by objective data, evidence and thorough analysis. Basically, the message needs to make sense. For example, in an interview with *The McKinsey Quarterly* about the organization's transformational change, Deere CEO Bob Lane was asked about the role communications played in getting the necessary buy-in among Deere's various stakeholders. Lane said, "I think the key was that everybody — employees, dealers, suppliers — heard exactly the same message: We have to perform better for shareholders, and we're going to organize this company to have a great, sustainable business that delivers better shareholder returns. The economic profits have to increase. A clear and consistent message helped show our conviction. So even though the details were evolving, the direction was clear."[19]

**Commitment.** The supply leadership team must remain committed to the changes and demonstrate this commitment in words and actions through good times and bad. Carlos Ghosn, CEO of Nissan, put his own job on the line to demonstrate his commitment to Nissan's change strategy. CEO Bob Lane expressed his and the organization's commitment to the new business model even though the details were not all finalized. He said, "When SVA was introduced, in December of 2000, we didn't have all of the specifics developed. In fact, during one of our management meetings early in the journey, I held up a great big meat bone in front of the group and told them that while our strategic direction and performance imperative was clear, we would put more meat on the program's bones over time. This was also true of the changes around compensation. The details came after we were already sharing with everybody how the business was going to be organized around SVA." The message was clear and consistent even though the details were still evolving.[20]

The supply leader, and the entire supply management team, must build credibility and gain the trust of stakeholders. Toward this end, the supply leader or leadership team might conduct gap analysis to answer three questions: (1) What is each stakeholder group's current perception of the supply management group? (2) What is the desired perception? (3) What actions will it take to close the gap between the stakeholders' current perception of supply management and where they need to be to embrace the vision and new direction of supply management?

### What Are the Current and Desired Perceptions of Supply Management?

A primary influencer when aligning stakeholders behind the vision of supply management is the existing role and perception of supply management in the organization. A new vision typically entails a major change in the role of supply management in organizational strategies and requires a change in the perception of supply internally and externally for the vision to be realized.

At Lufthansa, the "takeoff" point for change was determined by conducting two gap analyses. First, the leadership team discussed with top management the supply management's potential functions, operating range and role in the organization. In this way the team made sure that the vision and strategies developed for supply management were aligned with top management's expectations. Second, supply management employees completed a questionnaire about everyday work procedures to determine the status quo and compare it to the requirements based on the new vision. The information gathered from these two activities fed the development of the change management plan.[21] Figure 3-5 illustrates the checklist for the analysis of the takeoff point for change management at Lufthansa's supply management organization. It illustrates the process used to ensure vertical alignment with the company and horizontal alignment with employees in other functional areas.

## How Leaders Communicate Vision

The leader must clearly and consistently communicate the vision. Jack Welch, former CEO of General Electric, said, "Without question, communicating the vision has been, and is continuing to be, by far the toughest job we face."[22] In a global organization

**Figure 3-5 Checklist for Supply Change Management Takeoff Point**

| CHECKLIST ANALYSIS OF TAKEOFF POINT (SELECTION) | |
|---|---|
| **Company** | |
| • Top management philosophy<br>• Economic situation/pressure to act | • Change readiness and tradition<br>• Status of purchasing in the company |
| **Purchasing Organization** | |
| • Development level (methods, etc.)<br>• Existing eTool landscape (experience with e-auctions, etc.) | • Change management experience in purchasing<br>• Tendency of outsourcing |
| **Employees** | |
| • Qualification profiles (capabilities)<br>• Mind-set (willingness) | • Personal traits<br>• Fear of change |

*Source:* Ingo Bulow, Ulrich Schott-Wullenweber and Fabian Hedderich, "Change Management in Purchasing: Best Practices from Germany's No. 1 Airline Deutsche Lufthansa AG," *PRACTIX* CAPS Research, Volume 9 (2006), 4.

this difficulty is compounded by numerous differences such as culture, norms, time zones and language. For example, when asked by *The McKinsey Quarterly,* "What do you consider the biggest difficulty that you've faced in your job to date?" Nissan CEO Carlos Ghosn replied, "The biggest difficulty for me by far is not mastering Japanese. You are facing a very important period of change, so obviously communication is extremely important — communication at all levels of the company, from executive committees to the workforce. I can manage [to make myself understood] in low-level Japanese, ordering a meal in a restaurant or going to a store to buy something. But I cannot sustain a business discussion in Japanese. And whatever the quality of the interpreter you have, you will never know the subtleties that people would like to communicate to you. And you'll never know how you are being translated."[23]

## Developing a Communications Plan

The supply leader needs a communication plan that fits the organizational culture and the targeted audience's preferred way of receiving and participating in communication. Carlos Ghosn spoke about the challenges of devising communication strategies in a global organization. He noted that communication strategies with the Japanese focused on the listeners gaining understanding of the concept. On the other extreme, communication strategies with Latin American or Anglo-Saxon audiences were all about execution. Ghosn said that because of the differences, delays on the front end should be anticipated in Japan until everyone understands the concept and delays in Latin American and Anglo-Saxon countries should be anticipated during execution as people start to realize they have different perceptions of the concept. As has been stated before, understanding disparate audiences is a leadership imperative and a key driver in the successful development and execution of a communications plan.[24]

Once broad approaches have been established, the leadership team can devise specific communication strategies to facilitate the alignment process. These strategies might entail verbal and/or written elements depending on the preferences of the listeners. They may be delivered face to face or in a Web-based meeting, through a video, via an iPod, in chat rooms or whatever communication media works with the intended audiences. To ensure true alignment, the leadership team must focus on developing trustworthy feedback mechanisms such as 360-degree surveys. They might also have their presentation skills assessed to determine the impact of presentation style on what listeners hear and how they react to what they hear. The last thing a leader wants to do is ruin an acceptable message with poor presentation.

**Communication Techniques.** Verbal communication obviously plays a huge role in building alignment. The supply leader or leadership team can use a number of verbal communication techniques to bring stakeholders into alignment with the vision of supply management. These range from communicating one-on-one to interacting in small groups of like-minded people to hosting large town hall–type meetings. Figure 3-6 lists different techniques and the purpose of using each one.

**Figure 3-6 Possible Components of a Verbal Communications Plan**

| TECHNIQUE | PURPOSE |
|---|---|
| One-on-one. Top leader meets one-on-one, face to face with key people internally and externally. | Sell the vision to each person by demonstrating an understanding of each person's interests and by making the connection between the vision and the stakeholder's interests. |
| Flow down. Top-level leader meets with direct reports who then meet with their direct reports. | Formulate direction and strategies for each group aligned with the overall vision and flow it down the chain of command. |
| Town-hall meetings. Top-level leader holds quarterly town hall–type meetings with large groups of stakeholders segmented by interests, reporting lines, roles, responsibilities, etc. | Recognize achievements that have been made since the last meeting. Launch next-step actions. |
| "State of the department" meetings held by managers with their direct reports. | Talk about improvements and next steps. Ensure continued alignment with and commitment to overall organizational strategy. |
| Weekly meetings with direct reports. | Keep momentum, stay on track, maintain focus. |
| Monthly meetings with different employees from each department or group within supply management. | Give multiple people a chance to voice issues and concerns and give ideas and input. |
| Monthly town hall–type meeting with organizational stakeholders who work in other functional areas. | Open forum to discuss any issues related to supply management. |
| Topical forums held by supply managers for nonsupply personnel. | Focused discussions (two-way communication, not formal presentations) on specific topics relevant to a select group of stakeholders. |
| Hold events to recognize and reward top performers. | Opportunity for top leaders to recognize and reward performance and to reinforce their commitment to the change process. |

Written communication also plays a role in building alignment. This communication might be delivered in hard copy, via e-mail and/or posted on the supply intranet. Understanding the preferred forms of communication of groups within the organization would drive the delivery decision. The author worked with a large multinational that was undergoing transformative change in its global supply-chain management organization. The change management team focused considerable resources on developing new processes, policies and procedures and acquiring technology to support the new organization. However, the team faced massive resistance from supply-chain employees around the world in large part because of how they communicated the change. All information was posted on the newly designed intranet and supply-chain employees were expected to check this site frequently and do whatever was posted. Even when the message was good, it was often badly received and adoption was slow.

Common forms of written communication used to facilitate change are listed in Figure 3-7.

**Figure 3-7 Potential Components of a Written Communications Plan**

| TECHNIQUE | PURPOSE |
|---|---|
| Monthly newsletter | Recognize and reward achievements; share information about next-stage activities; provide a means for those in the trenches to write about their experiences and demonstrate their ownership of the vision. |
| Dialogue option | Allow employees to anonymously submit questions about any aspect of the vision and change management process. |
| Charts | Capture data on key metrics and track over time. Post in high-traffic areas with lots of visibility so everyone can see the results. |
| Symbols, pictures, short phrases, simple metaphors | Short, catchy messages that grab people's attention and stay in their minds. |

Never underestimate the power of symbols, metaphors, analogies and simple phrases. For example, Deere CEO Bob Lane held up a big meat bone as he talked about putting more meat on the bone as the details of the strategy were finalized. It is easy to picture the meat bone and the image may help people remember the message.[25]

## Leadership Styles

According to the Center for Creative Leadership, versatility is a key element of leadership. Versatility relates to a leader's ability to use different ideas, tools, techniques and systems for executing leadership tasks. This is especially important for a leader trying to align stakeholders. Not all people will respond to the same leadership behavior so the leader must be versatile in his or her communication style.

Leadership styles come into play in this stage. Recall the six leadership styles presented in Chapter 1. Each style is favored by a particular type of leader and used in specific types of situations with rather predictable results. Figure 3-8 lists who tends to use each style, the behaviors of the style, when it is likely to be used and the likely outcome.

**Figure 3-8 Leadership Styles and Behaviors**

| LEADERSHIP STYLE | FAVORED BY | BEHAVIORS | APPROPRIATE APPLICATION | OUTCOMES |
|---|---|---|---|---|
| **Directive** | Achievers under stress | Command-and-control; at times coercive; tell people what to do, when to do it, how to do it and what will happen if they do not | Crises; managing poor performers | Stifles creativity and initiative |
| **Visionary** | People with a high personalized power drive under low stress and people with a high socialized power drive under high stress | Authoritative; gains employee support by clearly expressing their challenges and responsibilities in the context of the organization's overall direction and strategy | Environments of rapid change and high complexity where a new direction is required | Clear goals, energized team and increased employee commitment |

(continued)

| LEADERSHIP STYLE | FAVORED BY | BEHAVIORS | APPROPRIATE APPLICATION | OUTCOMES |
|---|---|---|---|---|
| **Affiliative** | Leaders who need to be liked and want to maintain close, friendly relationships | Emphasizes the employee and his or her emotional needs over the job; tends to avoid conflict | Dealing with employees with personal crises or in high-stress situations such as layoffs | Ineffective unless coupled with visionary, coaching or participative styles |
| **Participative** | Leaders with high-affiliation needs in high-stress situations | Engage people in the decision-making process; collaborative and democratic | Team of highly competent individuals and the leader has limited knowledge or lacks formal power and authority such as highly matrixed organizations | Builds trust and consensus |
| **Pacesetting** | High achievers in low-stress situations; leaders with high standards who make sure those standards are met even if they have to do the work themselves | Leads by example and personal heroics | Short-term crisis situations; high stakes; teams with highly competent and motivated people | Effective in the short term; demoralizing over the long term |
| **Coaching** | Leaders with a high socialized-power motive in low-stress situations | Leader engages in long-term professional development and mentoring of employees | Stable environments | Develop broad and deep knowledge base throughout the organization |

*Source:* Adapted from Daniel Goleman, Richard E. Boyatzis, and Annie McKee, *Primal Leadership: Learning to Lead With Emotional Intelligence* (Boston, MA: Harvard Business School Press, 2004).

## Empowering People

*Empowerment* is a widely used term in business and other settings. To empower, according to *Merriam-Webster's Dictionary,* means to enable or to promote the self-actualization or influence of someone. As people embrace or buy in to the vision, the leadership team must empower people to take initiative and accept joint ownership and accountability for the successful implementation of the vision. Many leaders are challenged in the goal of an empowered workplace by entrenched mind-sets, policies, procedures and other aspects of organizational culture that inhibit rather than enable empowerment. Leaders must focus on removing organizational barriers and replacing them with useful tools to aid employees in taking action associated with ownership of the vision.

Sometimes the leader is a barrier to empowerment. Talking about empowerment while micromanaging every aspect of employees' daily worklives is likely to lead to frustration on everyone's part. Review the leadership styles in Figure 3-6 and think about the effect of each style on an individual's motivation and ability to be empowered. Visionary leaders may be capable of letting others take ownership of execution, but may fail to put into place the necessary tools for successful execution. Leaders with directive or pacesetting styles may not be able to let go of control to the extent required for multiple people to take ownership. While the visionary leader may not provide enough direction, these types of leaders may establish boundaries of behavior that are too narrow and constricting for the organization to fully benefit from the talents within its ranks. Affiliative leaders may be overly interested in being liked and therefore unable to allow conflict to emerge or, if it does emerge, lack the skills to manage it constructively.

Empowerment may also be hindered by the very people the leader wishes to empower. If the organization has a long history of bureaucratic processes and procedures, it also likely has a long history of employing people who are most comfortable working in a bureaucratic environment. This is not to say that transformative change is impossible, but the leadership team (if it is capable of transformative change itself) would have to recognize the level of effort required. Coaching and facilitative leadership skills would be needed to develop the existing human capital, attract new and different talent and transition to other places those who are unable or unwilling to change.

Figure 3-9 lists leader behaviors that are typically used to foster empowerment.

At Sandvik Materials Technology, for example, each unit has full responsibility to find its own way to improve productivity and full accountability for financial results. Central management has full responsibility for the SMT Business System and for providing the toolbox and support that units may need to develop their operations. SMT offers the services of some 50 internal change leaders and technical experts, called navigators, to the business units in support of unit initiatives.[26]

**Figure 3-9 Behaviors That Empower**

| BEHAVIORS | EXAMPLES |
|---|---|
| Delegate | Tasks and responsibilities that will help develop others<br>Decision-making authority |
| Encourage people | To take initiative<br>To improve their skills<br>To expand their interests and involvement<br>Actively seek ideas and promote ideas |
| Establish | Clearly defined goals and metrics<br>Debrief and review sessions to discuss thought processes and link to and reinforce vision, mission and strategy<br>Tool sets that support the new behaviors<br>Guidelines and parameters for behaviors to limit fallout during the learning process |
| Coach | Before changes to reduce stress and anxiety about change<br>During the change process to facilitate the transition to new behaviors<br>After changes are implemented to make changes permanent |
| Reinforce, recognize and reward | Engage in informal recognition such as compliments<br>Engage in formal recognition<br>Provide incentives and rewards |
| Share | Successes with a focus on best practices that can be replicated<br>Failures with a focus on recovery and improvement |
| Build trust | Be consistent in words and actions<br>Be committed to empowerment especially when things go wrong<br>Create a safe environment for trial and error |
| Provide support | Formally through training, policies, procedures and work tools<br>Formally by removing organizational barriers<br>Informally through actions and words |

If disparate stakeholder groups are aligned around a common vision, there is less likelihood of conflict; and if it does occur, there is greater likelihood of a resolution. Leaders empower people when they provide them with the tools they need to consistently execute the new behaviors. At Lufthansa, supply management identified four action items to close the gap between the vision and reality. These were (1) knowledge transfer, (2) learning by experience, (3) practical proofs and (4) support tools for the daily work.[27] Knowledge transfer refers to supply management personnel learning and adopting the relevant concepts of problem-oriented supply management. Learning by experience was an internal case-based simulation designed to allow supply management personnel to experience their new roles as problem-oriented critical partners and competition maximizers. Practical proofs are visible and tangible examples of the outcomes of supply management's new role derived from pilot projects. Daily support tools include e-tools that guide supply management through the new process and pattern and a workflow management tool that guides the process while still allowing room for an entrepreneurial approach by the individual.

In the alignment process, the leader begins to build commitment if the message he or she delivers energizes the listener. Sandvik's Gossas refers to this energy when he says, "So the first challenge for us was to ensure that every employee understands that this business system is not an action plan; it's a religion that is about what should characterize a really good company, and there are no alternatives to this religion. We have put a lot of effort into making everybody understand this."[28]

Building alignment is a key step in transforming the supply management organization. The leader must take action to turn alignment into commitment. This leads to Chapter 4 and stage three of the leadership process — gaining commitment.

## Key Points

1. To align internal and external stakeholders, the supply management leader must impart a clear understanding of the vision.

2. The communication tools and techniques used to convey the vision depend on the drivers of change, the source of the change and the recipients of the message.

3. The leader must either already have credibility with the stakeholders or make a concerted effort to build credibility for the alignment effort to be successful.

4. The leader and the entire supply management team must exhibit consistent behaviors with stakeholders to solidify acceptance and buy-in of the vision and move stakeholders to a level of commitment necessary for success.

CHAPTER

# 4

# Gaining Commitment: Motivating and Inspiring People

> *Once you have a staff of prepared, intelligent, and energetic people, the next step is to motivate them to be creative.* AKIO MORITA, COFOUNDER OF SONY CORP.[1]

To turn a shared vision into reality, the supply leader must gain commitment from internal and external stakeholders. This is the third and final stage in the leadership process. In this stage, the leader's primary role is motivating and inspiring people to take ownership of the vision and plan, persevere throughout the change process and execute the tasks necessary to implement the vision. This chapter focuses on energizing stakeholders to successfully execute the plans and strategies required to achieve the vision of supply management. The complementary managerial tasks of measuring department performance and establishing controls and ensuring compliance are covered in Chapters 11 and 12, respectively.

As discussed in Chapter 1, *management* relates to the execution of routine activities and *leadership* relates to nonroutine activities, especially change. Generating commitment to a new way of thinking about things and doing things necessarily involves change. The leader must do everything in his or her power to create the right atmosphere for change. According to a *McKinsey* global survey of executives, "Executives further improve their chances for success if they significantly raise employee expectations, actively change people's behavior, and engage the attention of individuals at all levels of the organization, from top management to the front line."[2]

If successful, the alignment process will engage individuals at all levels of the organization. To gain commitment, the leader must focus on raising the expectations of employees and take actions that will permanently change behaviors. To this end, leaders perform three tasks: (1) motivate and inspire people, (2) build strong internal partnerships and (3) create a culture of leadership. This chapter is organized around these three leadership tasks.

### CHAPTER OBJECTIVES

- Discuss motivational techniques leaders use to energize stakeholders and generate commitment to the vision of supply management.
- Define informal internal partnerships and explain why they are so important in the leader's work of gaining commitment.
- Discuss techniques leaders use to build strong informal networks.
- Explain the concept of a culture of leadership.
- Discuss the supply leader's role in creating a culture of leadership within supply management.

## Motivating and Inspiring

*A leader leads by example, not by force.* SUN TZU, AUTHOR OF THE ART OF WAR

According to *Merriam-Webster's Dictionary, to motivate* means "to stimulate the active interest in a study through appeal to associated interests or by special devices." *To inspire* means to "to influence, move, or guide, to exert an animating, enlivening, or exalting influence on, or to spur on: impel or motivate." The leader motivates people by stimulating their active interest in the vision of supply management and influencing them to take action.

### Motivational Techniques

*Fall down seven times, get up eight.* JAPANESE PROVERB

In numerous ways a leader can motivate and inspire people to generate the necessary level of commitment to see people through tough situations and ensure the achievement of the vision (see Figure 4-1). Leaders motivate by appealing to other interests the stakeholders have that are related to supply. For example, the leader may appeal to the design group by linking the new supply vision to faster time to market for new products or services through longer-term relationships with fewer suppliers, leaner supply chains and better access to global distribution information. The leader may appeal to the marketing department by linking its objective of wider customer acceptance to early supply and supplier involvement in design.

**Figure 4-1 Motivational Techniques**

Link the supply vision and strategies to the organizational and stakeholders' vision, strategies, goals and objectives.

Stress the audiences' values.

Feed the person's need to feel important.

Involve the person or people in decision-making and feed their need for control.

Enhance the person's sense of belonging.

Enhance the audience's self-esteem.

Increase the person's sense of ownership.Listen to the concerns people have about the changes.

Model the behaviors you want people to adopt.

The leader also uses "special devices" to satisfy basic human needs. These "devices" typically stress the audience's values and feed their need to feel important; involve the audience in decision-making and contribute to their sense of control; enhance the individual's self-esteem and sense of professionalism; and recognize and reward accomplishments to feed into the individual's sense of accomplishment and belonging.

Commitment is about taking ownership of change. The leader looks for ways to incite or impel people to feel a sense of ownership and, as a result, to permanently change their behaviors. For example, Peter Gossas, president of Sandvik Materials Technology, wanted to drive change by appealing to employees' pride in improving their professionalism and achieving results. This motivation would drive the development of competence within the organization, and lead to managers and workers in each unit creating and taking ownership of their change programs.[3] According to the Center for Creative Leadership, team members are motivated to take ownership if they have opportunities to learn and develop; work on projects that build skills and experience without greatly exceeding their ability; make suggestions and give input and ideas; and have their concerns taken seriously by the leader.[4]

Acting as a role model is one motivational technique the leader may use to generate commitment. By modeling desired behaviors such as openness to criticism and active listening, the leader demonstrates the power of these behaviors and encourages others to adopt them. The leader might also identify role models within the organization. This might be individuals or teams who have achieved outstanding results by adopting the desired behaviors and committing to the vision. Sandvik's Gossas identified showcase units, manufacturing and sales units that achieved early results greater than they had expected. People from the showcase units visit others in the organization who fear the current change process will just be another fad that passes in a short time. Gossas also uses people from already high-performing units to motivate those people to greater performance levels and to influence the new business system.[5]

Another method is to assess where the supply organization is now compared to where the vision takes it and create action items based on the assessment. This approach might work quite well with achievement-oriented employees who are motivated by a challenge. The supply management leadership at Lufthansa, for example, identified the need to create new purchasing processes, new working procedures and a new self-image to turn the vision into a reality. Four action areas were identified to close the gap between the current state of supply management and the desired state: (1) knowledge transfer, (2) learning by experience, (3) practical proofs and (4) support tools for daily work.[6]

"Learning by experience" and "practical proofs" were especially useful in building commitment. Through a simulated environment with Lufthansa salespeople acting as suppliers, supply management employees were able to practice the new problem-oriented behaviors required by the new vision. In the process, salespeople were able to see and believe what supply management could contribute. These initiatives helped to change the mind-set of the entire organization and supply management's peers began to communicate the value-add potential of supply management to others in the organization. Generating "practical proofs" of supply management potential was accomplished through carefully selecting and executing pilot projects by handpicked members of the supply management group. By "practicing" the new behaviors in real settings, and capturing and communicating the results, supply management was able to build interest and momentum in its new vision.[7]

Clearly, the leader must be versatile in terms of having the ability to switch from coaching to mentoring to acting as a role model to providing feedback. Not all leaders will be equally strong in each role. Therefore, the leader may want to ensure that the leadership team includes individuals with different strengths and multiple strengths.[8]

## Influence and Influencing Techniques

*Influence* is defined by *Merriam-Webster's Dictionary* as "the act, process, or power of producing an effect without apparent exertion of tangible force or direct exercise of command and often without deliberate effort or intent." Influence techniques may be positive (build strong relationships, understand stakeholders' interests, create options, motivate) or negative (manipulate, harass or trick people to get what you want). One's span of influence is not limited by one's position in the chain of command or by formal authority. According to John Kotter, "[T]he better performers tend to mobilize more people to get more things done, and do so using a wider range of influence tactics."[9]

According to the Center for Creative Leadership, a leader may chose from three influence tactics. These are tactics that (1) depend on logic, (2) appeal to the emotions and (3) support a cooperative effort.[10]

**Logic.** Logical appeals are targeted to the listener's rational and intellectual positions. Salespeople often employ this tactic when they plan a sales strategy around the features, advantages and benefits of the sale item. When they speak with a potential customer, they typically focus on the benefits from that customer's perspective.

Ravi Kant, managing director at Tata Motors, for instance, focused on selling new ideas to people rather than giving orders. In an interview with Gautam Kumra from *The McKinsey Quarterly,* Kant said, "The most effective way to sustain change is to make those involved internalize it rather than just getting someone to come and talk about it." The leadership team exposed people to the outside world so they would see what was happening and they kept reasoning with people so they would come to their own conclusions about the changed context of the business. Customers were brought in to talk about problems and make product improvement suggestions. Competitors' products were taken apart so that Tata employees could compare them to Tata products to understand why customers chose a competitor's product over a Tata product. These logical appeals were used to sell new ideas internally.[11]

**Emotion.** Emotional tactics appeal to some affecting motivator such as the need to feel like one belongs, is providing a service or contributing an idea that supports his or her well-being. At Sandvik Materials, the senior management team became "ambassadors for change." They had to present a compelling case for change when neither outside forces nor company metrics created a compelling reason to change. Operational excellence became the focus of the organizational vision and supply management process owners and leaders were expected to change along with other areas of the organization. Peter Gossas, the president of Sandvik, made an emotional appeal based on people's pride in their professionalism and a desire to achieve better results. He said, "We [the top management team] have spent an amazing number of hours traveling and meeting people in the organization, just to be ambassadors, really. I think we have met some 5,000 employees so far, and we have penciled in more meetings this autumn."[12]

**Cooperation.** Cooperation relies on building a connection between stakeholder groups and the leader. "We are all in this together" is the basic message that depends on all parties believing there is a connection and that people are jointly accountable for mutual goals. For example, the external pressures of SARS and 9/11 brought together everyone at Lufthansa to find new ways to do business to offset the negative effects of these devastating external events.

Figure 4-2 lists these three types of influencing techniques and provides ideas for making each appeal successfully.

**Figure 4-2 Influencing Techniques**

| TYPE OF APPEAL | TECHNIQUES |
|---|---|
| **Logic** | Use facts, objective data and evidence to support your claim.<br>Present the idea clearly, logically and objectively.<br>Engage in a thorough explanation of the thought process used.<br>Compare advantages and disadvantages.<br>Focus attention on potential problems and proposed solutions.<br>Explain how the plan improves the person's job, how resources will be allocated and what the feasible benefits and opportunities are for the person. |
| **Emotional** | Focus on the listener's values and goals.<br>Link your vision and strategy to the listener's values and goals.<br>Use hypothetical statements and future-oriented scenarios.<br>Appeal to the listener's self-image and need for accomplishment. |
| **Cooperation** | Create the image of mutual goals and shared responsibility.<br>Focus on how you will help the listener make the vision happen.<br>Talk about the training, tools and other forms of support that will be available.<br>Discuss barriers and explain how you will work to remove them.<br>Reinforce your role as partners by listening carefully and thoughtfully to the person's concerns. |

Robert Cialdini, a professor of psychology at Arizona State University, founder and president of Influence at Work and author of *Influence: Science and Practice,* identified six business tools that can be used to influence people: (1) commitment and consistency, (2) reciprocation, (3) authority, (4) consensus, (5) liking and (6) scarcity.[13] These tools are explained in Figure 4-3.

These tools are used by many people in different settings. David Hannon of *Purchasing* magazine interviewed Sidney Johnson, vice president of global supply management at Delphi Corp. Several of these influencing techniques can be identified while reading the interview. For example, Johnson is recognized as an authority because of his background in operations, quality and procurement mostly in the automotive industry (Saturn and Delphi) as well as stints at General Electric and Allison Transmission. He said, "As a quality manager in operations, I knew exactly what to expect from my operations as well as our supply base. So going into a supplier's plant with the ability to identify quality systems is a big help. For example, does the supplier operate from a proactive perspective or are they more reactive to inspections, etc.? It is helpful to understand the supplier's philosophy in that regard." Johnson also talks about Delphi's supplier diversity program as "giving back to the areas in which [the company] operates" — an example of reciprocity. The organization is in a tough situation in a tough industry and its spend is more than 50 percent of sales. The organization has a commitment to wisely managing that spend and Johnson's efforts as vice president are consistent with this message.[14]

**Figure 4-3 Tools of Influence**

| INFLUENCING TOOL | DEFINITION | EXAMPLE |
|---|---|---|
| **Commitment and consistency** | Find common ground and speak the same message continuously. | Identify a commitment that has been made by the organization (for example, to contain costs) and then show how the supply management strategy is consistent with the organizational commitment. |
| **Reciprocity** | Give-and-take. | Make a concession to motivate a reciprocal concession.<br>Give time, energy and attention (legally and ethically) in return for a concession made by the listener.<br>(continued) |

| INFLUENCING TOOL | DEFINITION | EXAMPLE |
|---|---|---|
| **Authority** | Be seen as *an* authority, not *in* authority. | Ethically use authority. Supply managers need to demonstrate to suppliers and internal business partners that they are knowledgeable and credible. They must give people a reason to believe the message. Nothing sells like success. Pick pilot projects carefully, obtain measurable results and communicate them widely. Better yet, get your internal business partners to communicate your successes for you. |
| **Consensus** | Get people to realize that they are substantially in agreement. | Know the specific needs of each stakeholder and use this knowledge and understanding to link stakeholders to one another. In essence, build agreement and consensus where there was no perception of it among stakeholders. Build a consensus on some aspect of your vision, mission, plan or strategy. Use this as a takeoff point. |
| **Liking** | People tend to cooperate better with people they like. | Point out common interests.<br>Look for personal and professional similarities or goals.<br>Avoid trying too hard to gain the approval of others by using too many compliments or trying to find common ground when there is none. |
| **Scarcity** | Being one of a privileged few may influence behavior. | Technique must be used carefully. It can involve offering information selectively (always legally and ethically). Supply managers may be able to use the fact that resources are scarce as a tool to influence internal stakeholders to work with them to ensure best value decisions. |

*Source:* Adapted from Mary Siegfried, "The Power of Influence," *Inside Supply Management,* Volume 16, Number 10 (2005).

## Global Leadership Styles and Influence

Leadership styles and the effectiveness of influencing techniques vary across cultures and change with the times. Michael Jenkins, managing director of the Center for Creative Leadership-Asia campus in Singapore, notes that there is a tendency among Westerners to think about a monolithic Asian leadership style. He gives the example of the Western perception that a consensus-driven style dominates in Japan. Jenkins reports that there may very well be a behind-the-scenes leader who is orchestrating all decisions and actions. In Singapore, a strong, directive leader may set the objectives, but then people are given a lot of latitude to realize objectives. In some parts of Asia, leaders who solicit opinions are quite successful while in Spain such leaders are seen as weak. Supply managers working in global situations must take the time to understand the leadership style of the person, organization and culture in a specific situation and avoid stereotypes.[15]

In an interview with *The McKinsey Quarterly,* Carlos Ghosn, CEO of Nissan, talked about the differences he has encountered when leading change in various parts of the world. He talked about the importance of taking time to ensure that Japanese employees fully understand a concept before implementation. In contrast, Anglo-Saxons tend to jump quickly into execution. Delays then occur when it becomes evident that there is no common understanding and acceptance of the concept.[16]

Harvard Business School Professor D. Quinn Mills compares the prevalence of leadership styles in American and Asian businesses in a more general fashion. In "Asian and American Leadership Styles: How Are They Unique," he notes that while the directive style is waning in America, it is still quite common in Asia. A participative or teamwork style is common in Europe, often to meet legal requirements, and in Japan because of cultural norms.[17] An empowering style where responsibility is delegated is common in divisional structures in America and is starting to be used by some young Asian leaders. Recall the story about Lenovo in chapter 2. The story is about very successful Chinese entrepreneurs with very different leadership styles.

The rise of professional managers in developing economies and companies brings similarities in leadership styles, but cultural and national differences influence how these styles are manifested. The Center for Creative Leadership's Jenkins quotes Lin Lin Sea, an Asian business leader, who talks about an emerging internationalism among Asian business elites that combines Western charisma with Eastern pride.[18] This is evident in statements made by Eastern leaders. For example, Ravi Kant, managing director of Tata Motors, said that the organization wants to grow and produce a healthy bottom line, be seen as an innovative organization and do it "the Tata way — transparently, ethically and meeting our corporate social responsibility. We want to make India proud."[19] Likewise, in a speech at an international conference, Zhang Yue, owner and CEO of Broad Air Conditioning in Changsha, China, spoke futuristically of the world's most profitable and admired company in 2015. Although he was speaking about his own company, one that "quietly economizes on energy use around the world," he said, "It doesn't matter that people may not know the name of this company, but they should know it is a Chinese company."[20] Western charisma mixed with Eastern pride.

**Individualist or Communitarian.** In a global business environment it is also important to consider whether the individual's starting point is as an individualist or as a communitarian. An individualist values autonomy and initiative and seeks achievement through setting goals and taking action to reach them. A communitarian values group harmony and cohesion and makes decisions in consultation with other group members whose input is heavily weighted. A leader from a communitarian background seeking to generate commitment from a group of individualists may be perceived as indecisive. A leader from an individualist background may come across too strongly and autocratically for group members from a communitarian background. Recognizing these differences and respecting the preferences of parties the leader is trying to influence may increase the chances of gaining commitment.[21]

In developing economies such as that of China that have a communitarian tradition, an interesting mix of rising individualism, marked by successful entrepreneurs and a growing middle class, is emerging, while traditional collective approaches are still seen in employment, training and work practices in many successful Chinese ventures. This duality presents a challenge for a leader, especially a Western leader, who is working to turn an organization into a truly global company or trying to understand and conduct business with Chinese suppliers.

Former Singaporean Prime Minister Lee Kuan Yew and others refer to the Asian social bargain as "less individual latitude, more collective success." James Fallows wrote in *The Atlantic Monthly* about Chinese tycoon Zhang Yue who owns and runs Broad Air Conditioning that has no debt and 2005 revenues of about $300 million. The company's business is nonelectric refrigeration, which is more energy-efficient than compression coolers. Yue argues for worldwide systematic changes in energy, packaging and transportation. The company is guided by six Broad values: (1) not paying bribes, (2) paying taxes, (3) environmental protection, (4) respect for intellectual property rights, (5) no price gouging and (6) no predatory competition. The company pays good wages by Chinese factory standards and trains employees at the Broad management training center. Yue believes that if employees are comfortable and happy, this will affect their work ethic and professionalism.[22]

Hand in hand with these practices, employee training is styled after military training with employees organized into platoons that live in barracks, wear military-style uniforms and undergo a 10-day intensive boot camp. After training ends, they live on the factory grounds in company-provided housing, eat company-provided food and wear company-provided uniforms. The day starts with physical training at 6 a.m. While such regimentation may seem alien to most Westerners, it is a blend of traditions that has helped make Broad Air Conditioning a successful company in markets all around the world.[23]

## Building Strong Internal Partnerships

*The key to successful leadership today is influence, not authority.*

KENNETH BLANCHARD, MANAGEMENT WRITER AND LECTURER[24]

Motivational tools alone will not lead people to commit to change and to adopt new ways of doing things. The supply leader and his or her leadership team must also develop strong internal business partnerships throughout the organization. Management author John Kotter refers to these relationships as "thick informal networks."[25] As supply management leaders seek to transform the group, processes and functions, it becomes even more critical for them to develop a network of thick informal relationships and strong internal and external partnerships vertically and horizontally.

### Vertical Relationships

Vertical relationships are those that involve people up and down the chain of command (see Figure 4-4). For example, the vice president of supply management might work to develop thick informal networks with people in positions above his or hers as well as with people in positions below the vice-president level. The relationship that a direct report builds with his or her manager is an example of "managing up." An interesting question is, can a direct report also "lead up" the chain of command and exhibit leadership behaviors in the relationship with a superior? The relationship built with subordinates is partly based on the direct report having reporting responsibilities to the supervisor/manager. How successful a manager's relationship is with direct reports depends also on the leadership skills and behaviors exhibited by the manager.

### Horizontal Relationships

Horizontal relationships (see Figure 4-4) are those that involve peers (people at a similar level) across the organization in various functions representing different business processes. For example, the vice president of supply management would work to

**Figure 4-4 Vertical and Horizontal Relationships**

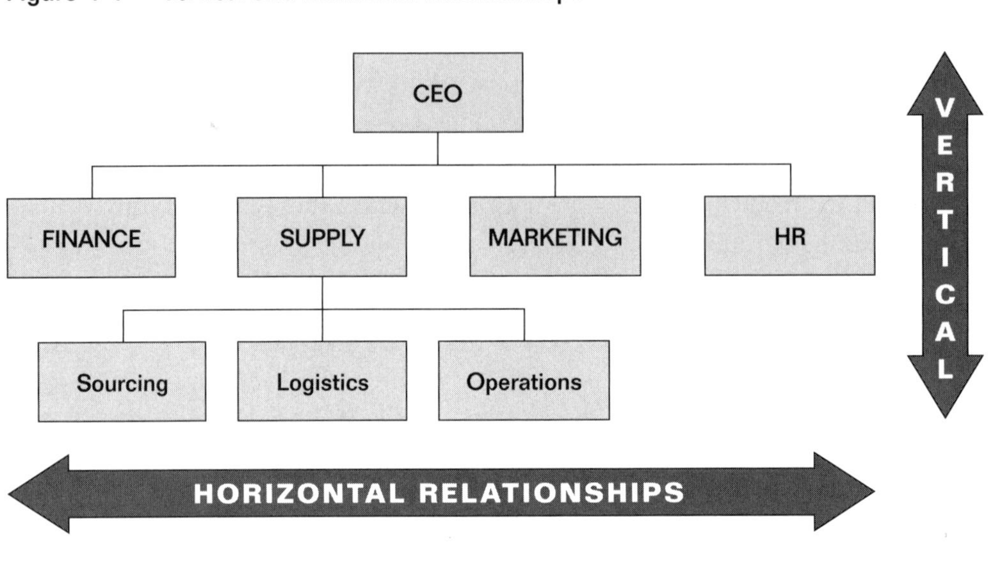


develop thick informal networks with the other vice presidents in the organization, managers with managers and so on. Strong vertical and horizontal relationships lay the foundation for effective change management.

The interrelatedness of members of an organization is called *connectivity.*[26] The supply leader must recognize the degree of connectivity present at the start of the change management process and work to strengthen connectivity with the appropriate stakeholders in ways that make collaboration possible. The leader's versatility enables him or her to enhance positive connectivity and reduce or eliminate the negative impact of connectivity that is harmful to change.

The ability to perceive the patterns of connectivity within the organization is a key leadership skill according to the Center for Creative Leadership.[27] Sandvik's Gossas is a good example of a leader who developed a deep awareness of the existing connections between and among internal groups. He then used the top management team to build stronger connections to further facilitate the organizational transformation. According to Gossas, "It is extremely important for an organization to take full ownership and develop its own model. The more people who are involved in this development, the more it will become a Sandvik Materials Technology (SMT) model, and that's what it has to be, because we have our own history, our own product range. So creating a new business system at SMT requires getting the buy-in from managers of some 80 production and sales units and over 8,000 employees. That's the big challenge."[28]

## Building Coalitions

A coalition is a temporary alliance of distinct parties, persons or states for joint action. One of the main advantages of strong one-on-one internal business partnerships is the possibility of building coalitions. Because the changes in supply management affect many stakeholders in different ways, the supply leader must consciously build coalitions to stave off resistance, increase support and drive momentum. The leader can use his or her knowledge about the interests, options and alternatives of each party to identify common interests, create a sense of interdependence and overcome resistance to change. In today's heavily team-oriented business environment, the leader is often maneuvering among multiple teams with competing goals and objectives as well as multiple individuals within these teams who may also have competing goals and objectives. The leader needs strong negotiating skills and creative thinking abilities to reap the rewards of coalition building. Geographical dispersion and lack of active sponsors or advocates may hinder the leader's ability to build effective coalitions.

For example, Bristol-Myers Squibb's supply management vision is "Procurement excellence." The Procurement Excellence Program has three phases. Phase one, Category Focus, is an ongoing effort to engage in strategic sourcing and category management. Phase two, Supplier Focus, addresses supplier relationship management. Phase three, Process and Behavioral Focus, includes value chain restructuring and consumption and specification management.[29]

A formal supply-led team at Bristol-Myers Squibb developed a consumption specification management (CSM) program to reduce demand for certain goods and services used by members of the company. The CSM project team structure included an executive committee/program office, the vice president of global sourcing and supply, the CSM program lead, the CSM management, business unit/functional advisory group part-time), an executive champion (part-time) and a category leader for each of the designated categories.

To be successful, the CSM program required both broad and deep support. Broad support meant that individuals across the organization accepted and actively participated in the program. Deep support meant that senior executives through every level in the organization played an active role in the development and execution of the program.

Executive support and data accessibility were two critical pieces of business case development on the managerial side. Communication was an important part of executive support on the leadership side. For example, the CFO issued communications around the launch of new policies. Corporate affairs also communicated the initiatives more broadly around the company.

At the business-unit level, the CSM program was a new approach. No formal mechanisms were in place to motivate commitment to the CSM program. Challenging a user's defined need and asking for changes to the specification was perceived as threatening by some users. Focus groups were held with some internal customers, such as key meeting planners and teams of scientists, to build buy-in. Typically, users already knew ways to obtain savings, and the focus groups provided a platform for getting ideas out of people's heads and into implementation. The focus groups worked to tap into people's need to belong, to achieve and to accomplish something.

The team also solicited ideas from employees and created an Idea Bank to gather ideas and create the overall climate for change. Along with these initiatives was a budgeting process change — a managerial action. By making it harder to get money, employees looked for places to standardize. Greater pricing transparency facilitated the process. For example, if scientists knew that certain laboratory items were *x* percent lower than others, they would comply. If a user has budgetary responsibility and is motivated to think about standardization and consumption patterns, then there is a great opportunity for change. This requires changing employees' "use it or lose it" budget mentality. Departments are now coming to supply management for ideas to drive out costs, especially during the budget preparation process.

The team experienced a lot of resistance from employees if ideas had been tried (and failed) before, if they believed an idea was inappropriate in a particular area or if they simply thought it would not work. Some of this resistance was overcome by giving the business-unit owner/stakeholder credit for the savings, thus appealing to people's need for a sense of accomplishment. Savings were reported up through the CFO who was very supportive of the initiative and who also knew that the CSM team was driving the process.[30]

## Lead or Participate in Teams

A team brings together interdependent people with varying knowledge, skills and expertise, often from different functional areas, to work on a common task or project. Supposedly, teams provide superior results compared to individual efforts as a result of the range of skills, knowledge and capabilities of team members. Teams also promote cross-functional cooperation, collaboration and communication and may facilitate consensus building in the organization.

Some organizations use personality profiles to foster understanding of personal differences between and among team members and to develop team contracts or charters that seek to accommodate personality differences by developing understanding and acceptance along with work rules that guide behavior and lessen the impact of differences. For example, in a supply chain organization in a major oil company, permanent supply chain teams were formed around key commodities. Team members completed the Myers-Briggs assessment and then each team spent time with an outside facilitator who explained the outcomes and worked with the teams to develop better working relationships.

In effective teams, team members have clear roles and responsibilities, share a vision and sense of purpose and are collectively accountable for reaching the team's goal. Teams often have to collaborate with people or groups outside the team who may have competing or conflicting goals and processes. The team leader and the supply leader-manager must build relationships within and outside the team, negotiate and resolve conflicts and communicate to build acceptance of team decisions.

Teams are used throughout many organizations for many purposes, including improvements in quality, cost or delivery, product development, process engineering and technology management. They can be project-oriented or ongoing. Project teams are brought together for a limited time to achieve a specific goal or outcome, such as completion of a capital project or an e-commerce initiative. Ongoing teams continue indefinitely, such as a commodity sourcing team that manages the process and the supplier relationship. The Center for Creative Leadership advises using a team when the task is complex, multidimensional, demands innovation, requires different skills, expertise, diverse thoughts and opinions, and there are significant barriers and problems that may be overcome by building better relationships that may lead to faster acceptance or buy-in from internal (multiple functions, top management) and external stakeholders (customers, suppliers).[31]

Many corporate organizational structures are leaner, flatter, more adaptive and flexible than in the past. Rigid functional structures have been replaced by a greater dependence on cross-functional teams that overlay the functional organization to push decisions lower in the organizational hierarchy. Senior management often tries to combine the flexibility of decentralized supply management and the buying power and information sharing of centralized supply through the use of teams. Cross-functional teams consist of personnel from multiple functions focused on a supply-related task. Generally, high-performing cross-functional teams will achieve better results on the task, with greater benefit to the organization as a whole, at lower costs, in less time, with greater stakeholder buy-in. Effective cross-functional teams save time by allowing a simultaneous, rather than a sequential approach. For example, if key stakeholder groups are involved in the development of a new process from concept through design, development and rollout, the process may be better to start with, more widely accepted and adopted quickly.

Various types of supply management teams may be used, including cross-functional teams, teams with suppliers or customers or both, supplier councils that include key suppliers, purchasing councils, commodity management teams, and buying consortiums.

**Role of Supply Management in Teams.** Supply professionals are increasingly called on to lead or participate in cross-functional and cross-organizational teams, including project management, process improvement and international teams. Supply personnel may play a number of roles in a team including (1) providing support, service or information, (2) project management, (3) leadership or (4) facilitation. Often supply personnel are on teams to provide support, service or information to the other team members. In these cases, supply personnel play an advisory role and may not have much say in the actual team decisions. The ability to influence without authority is an important skill in these situations. Other times, supply personnel play the role of the project manager and need skills in process, people and time management, along with a strong ability to see both the big picture of the total project and keep track of the many project details. At still other times, a supply professional is the team leader and must develop the skills to manage people, processes and time while taking primary responsibility for the outcome of the team effort. Another role is that of facilitator. A facilitator primarily manages the communication process of the team with the goal of fleshing out the thoughts and ideas of the participants rather than selling them on any one result. It is important to be clear about the role being played and to develop the appropriate knowledge, skills and expertise to fulfill the role requirements.

**Phases of Team Building.** Group dynamics play a critical role in team success. While group dynamics are driven by the interactions of the members of each team, certain dynamics may be observed in teams in general. Bruce Tuckman identified four phases of team formation (see Figure 4-5): forming, storming, norming and performing. In stage one, forming, team members get acquainted with each other and learn three important things about each other: (1) what each person brings to the team, (2) what each person wants from the process and (3) how team members will interact with one another. In stage two, storming, team members put forth their ideas, argue and test to see whose ideas will dominate. In stage three, norming, team members have developed some trust in one another and are able to focus on the substance of the project, reaching agreement on task responsibility, workload and the decision-making process. In stage four, performing, the team functions effectively and decisions are reached.[32] The supply leader-manager plays a critical role in understanding these stages, recognizing which stage his or her teams are in, and coaching and mentoring team members to move through the phases and achieve the goals of the team.

Figure 4-5 Phases of Team Building

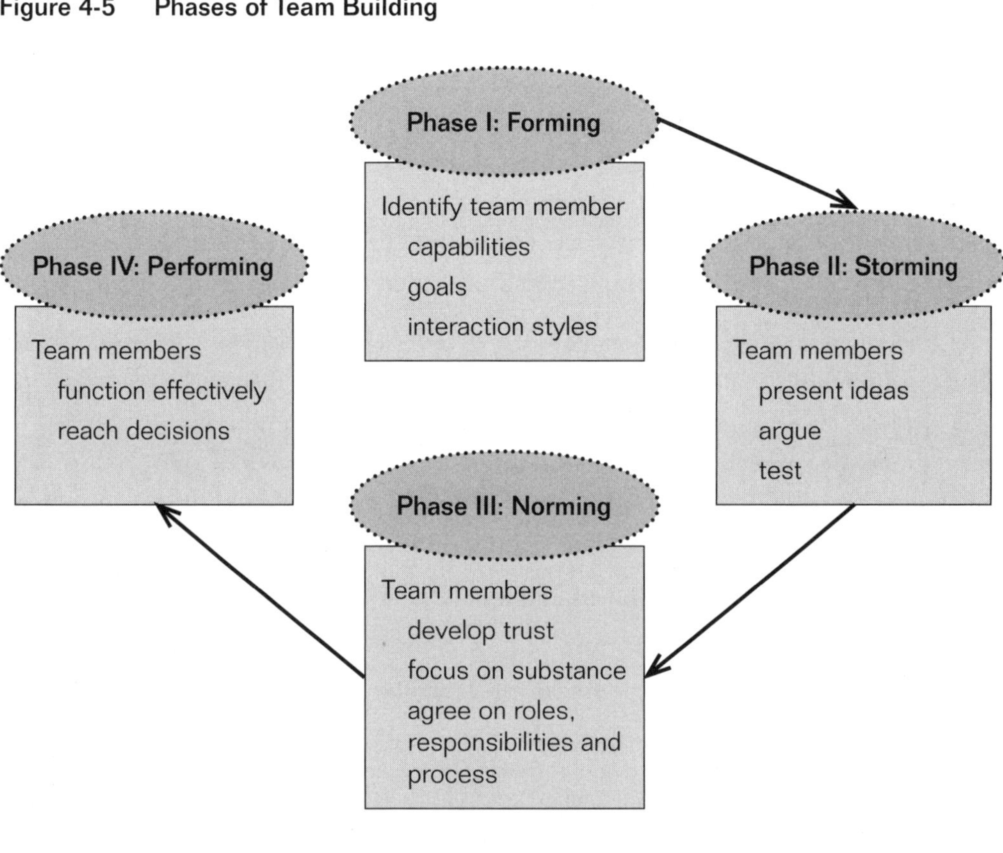


**Advantages and Disadvantages of Teams.** There are a number of advantages and disadvantages to using teams. In many ways whether something is an advantage or a disadvantage depends on the composition, structure and management of the team. Advantages and disadvantages may relate to the ability or inability to create synergy, reach a consensus, manage time to complete the task or project efficiently and effectively, introduce and manage change effectively, avoid groupthink and resolve conflicts. The supply leader-manager must be quick to recognize obstacles and find ways to turn them into opportunities.

SYNERGY. *Merriam-Webster's Dictionary* defines *synergy* as "cooperative action of discrete agencies (as drugs or muscles) such that the total effect is greater than the sum of the two or more effects taken independently — opposed to *antagonism*." In the business world, the "discrete agencies" may be individuals, groups or organizations that come together to achieve results greater than those that could be achieved independently. The possibility of synergy is a primary reason for forming teams and the inability to achieve synergy is the root of many team failures.

**CONSENSUS BUILDING.** A consensus is when a group reaches a general agreement. Teams may facilitate consensus building because key stakeholders come together at the beginning of a decision-making process and work through all the issues jointly to reach a decision. The deal may be more widely accepted and adopted because of the level of buy-in secured during the team process. On the other hand, team discord may make it impossible to reach a consensus and ultimately derail the team process.

**GROUPTHINK.** *Groupthink* is a term used to describe a decision-making process in which group members do not critically evaluate each other's ideas and proposals. The result is a poor decision reached through a faulty consensus-building process. Irving Janis did extensive research on groupthink in several critical events in U.S. history, namely Pearl Harbor, Vietnam and the Bay of Pigs Invasion. He and other researchers have found certain conditions that foster groupthink, including:

- High stress from external threats and low hope for a better solution than the one offered by the leader(s)
- Group homogeneity of backgrounds and ideology
- The persuasive strength or directive style of the group's leader
- Insulation from outside ideas, perspectives and alternate opinions

An organization faced with external threats such as global competition, rapidly rising commodity prices or increasing regulation mixed with a homogenous leadership team and inadequate research may easily fall prey to groupthink.

The leader and all team members must be sensitive to signs of groupthink and be ready to recommend alternate processes such as subgroups working independently of one another or bringing in outside experts. The leader must balance the desire for consensus against the dangers of groupthink and provide guidance and direction throughout the process.

**TIME CONSIDERATIONS.** The cycle time for a project may be less than the nonteam approach, but more of the work may be concentrated at the beginning of the process. Effective new product or service development processes can improve an organization's competitive position. Cross-functional teams can shorten development cycle times, improve quality and reduce development costs by operating concurrently rather than sequentially. Rather than each functional area performing its task and passing the project off to the next functional area, the key functional groups, usually design, engineering, manufacturing, quality assurance, supply management and marketing, work on the new-product development simultaneously. Because a large percentage of a product's cost is purchased materials, early supplier involvement is often needed. When surveyed, many supply managers report greater involvement in new product/service design and development.

Harley-Davidson, the motorcycle manufacturer, successfully uses cross-functional teams for sourcing and product development. Teams are formed for a platform or line of Harley-Davidson motorcycles and are responsible for the life cycle of their line. Each platform team consists of a program manager who is generally from the design community, as well as a lead from manufacturing, supply management and marketing. The platform team analyzes information from many sources and decides on the general design and style of the bike. Then the project is turned over to the company's engineering center of expertise, which is also a cross-functional team consisting of supply, engineers, suppliers and others who work together to integrate all design components in a cost-effective, high-quality manner. Once the design is complete, the platform team is responsible for getting the end product into the hands of customers, accumulating and analyzing field reports, surveys of owner satisfaction levels and marketing information.[33] If supply is also included in teams with end customers, there is a better opportunity to deliver the greatest value in the shortest cycle time.

**OWNERSHIP ISSUES.** Ownership of an idea, process, project or decision may be spread among the team members in such a way that buy-in across functions is achieved in less time. However, there is always the risk that no one in a team will take ownership and the lack of shared ownership and accountability causes the team process to flounder. There is less of a chance of this happening if team goals, roles and responsibility, authority and measurement and rewards are clearly defined up front. Creating shared goals and rewards among team members encourages ownership.

**MANAGING OR INTRODUCING CHANGE.** Teams may be used either to introduce change or to manage the change process. If the team is successful at creating synergy, building consensus, avoiding groupthink and taking ownership of the change process, then the team may be a successful change agent.

**Managing Multicultural Teams.** Team members, team leaders and managers face special challenges when team members come from different countries, cultures and backgrounds. From their research on multicultural teams, Jeanne Brett, Kristin Behfar and Mary C. Kern identified four categories that can create barriers to team success and four strategies for dealing with these challenges: (1) direct versus indirect communication styles, (2) trouble with accents and fluency, (3) differing attitudes toward hierarchy and authority and (4) conflicting norms for decision-making.[34]

**DIRECT VERSUS INDIRECT COMMUNICATION STYLES.** People from Western cultures tend to communicate directly and explicitly. In many other cultures, however, meaning is embedded in the way the message is presented and the listener must know about the context of the message and the presenter. Direct confrontation and moving things up the chain of command may violate norms of behavior and lead to the direct communicator being isolated socially and even physically from the team. For example, in a culture where direct communication is the norm, a team member may be expected to identify a problem and explain the implications of the problem directly to the team and to the boss. In a culture where communication is more indirect, it may be more appropriate to ask the team "what if" questions to allow them to discuss the scenario and uncover the problem on their own.

**TROUBLE WITH ACCENTS AND FLUENCY.** English may be the language of global business, but fluency, accents, translations, interpretations and usage create challenges for multicultural teams. Some native English speakers are impatient with non–native speakers and may allow the lack of fluency to influence their perceptions of the non–native speaker's competence or status. This behavior may mean that the team does not get the full benefit of the expertise in the team.

**DIFFERING ATTITUDES TOWARD HIERARCHY AND AUTHORITY.** People from hierarchical cultures may defer to higher-status team members even if the team itself has a flat structure. This behavior may damage the person's stature and credibility in the eyes of people from more egalitarian cultures. Those from more egalitarian cultures may communicate directly with people higher up the chain of command because this is commonly accepted in their culture, but their peers from a hierarchical culture would consider this disrespectful behavior.

**CONFLICTING NORMS FOR DECISION-MAKING.** In some cultures, decisions are made slowly after much analysis, while in others, for example in the United States, they are made quickly after little analysis.

The four strategies for dealing with these challenges are (1) adaptation, (2) structural intervention, (3) managerial intervention and (4) exit. Adaptation occurs when team members recognize and adjust to each other's cultural differences or learn to work around them. When they are unable to adapt, people may be reassigned or the team reorganized (structural intervention) or the manager may intervene and make decisions for the team. An exit strategy is when one or more team members voluntarily leave the team or leave at the request of management. This strategy is used as a last resort typically when permanent teams cannot function because of cultural challenges.[35]

## Conflict and Conflict Resolution

Teams, partnerships and coalitions may be challenging to build and even more challenging to maintain. It is not only common but also inevitable, then, that leaders come into conflict. This conflict may be with recalcitrant "followers" who are not yet committed to change. Or it may be with other leaders in the organization who have a competing vision to that of the supply leader. Because leaders lead in the interest of the group they represent, they will eventually encounter other leaders who are defending the interests of *their* group within the organization. These competing visions indicate that the organization as a whole has not committed to one clear vision or direction, perhaps because of a lack of direction from the very top of the organization or because of misalignment between and among business process owners and leaders. At this point, the organization needs a leader, or leaders, with the ability to avoid taking sides and work collaboratively to cross boundaries and bring visions into alignment.[36]

The benefits of thick informal networks may be less conflict generation in the first place and speedier resolution of conflict if and when it does occur. In situations where the driver for change comes from within the supply organization itself, rather than an edict from top management or from an external event that challenges the organization's survival, internal partnerships may facilitate the change process. A stakeholder may be more willing to at least listen to new ideas if the messenger is someone who is trusted and credible.

Conflict can be a powerful constructive force or a powerful destructive force in a team, partnership or coalition. If managed properly, disagreements, debate and different perspectives may be a source of creative thinking by pushing people out of their mental comfort zones. Ineffective conflict resolution may prevent the team from accomplishing its goal. Avoidance of conflict and a tendency to quickly reach consensus without debate may result in groupthink and a poor decision. Groupthink can be equally destructive because it prevents the group from capitalizing on the expertise of the team members. The challenge for team leaders is to minimize destructive conflict while encouraging constructive disagreement and open debate.

**Conflict Resolution Skills.** The ability to resolve conflicts is a valuable leader skill and important in gaining commitment. Conflict resolution is a model for resolving conflict that starts with the assumption that the parties involved in the conflict are stuck and need to get unstuck. It is a nonjudgmental model for neither side is assumed to be inherently wrong, bad or evil. Supply management professionals need to develop a conflict-resolution strategy for dealing with issues that arise out of process, policy or procedure changes, and internal or external performance appraisals or audits.

Nondefensive problem-solving is a process that focuses on finding and eliminating the root cause of a problem rather than trying to place blame on a person. An organizational culture that fosters blaming behaviors creates fear in employees. W. Edwards Deming noted that a major obstacle to process improvement is fear by the employee. Fear can be a debilitating emotion and one that often arises from the common practice of determining "who did it" when a mistake occurs.[37]

Deming also noted that even when human error is the apparent source of a problem, most often something in the system or process led to the person's making the error. He said, "Put a good person in a bad system and the bad system wins, every time."[38] Therefore, it is necessary to seek the root cause behind the error and develop and execute a plan of action to eliminate it. The plan would, of course, focus on improving the process or system. This approach is called *mistake-proofing* or *poka yoke* (pronounced POH-Ka YOH-Kay), a Japanese quality-control method developed by Shigeo Shingo, an industrial engineer at Toyota. It refers to the design of materials and assembly methods to prevent mistakes. For example, parts might be designed in such a way that it is impossible to assemble them in an incorrect configuration. Color-coding plugs and outlets helps ensure proper hookup. Or making each plug and outlet a different size or shape from each other prevents incorrect hookup.

Fostering a defensive problem-solving mentality and mistake-proofing during the design stage as part of organizational culture may help avoid the creation of some conflict and speed up the resolution of conflicts when they do occur.

Other tools and techniques available to resolve conflict include rational problem-solving methods such as the Kepner-Tregoe rational process analysis, Six Sigma processes and project management. These are discussed in detail in *Effective Supply Management Performance* (ISM Professional Series).

## Creating a Culture of Commitment

> *You do not lead by hitting people over the head —*
> *that's assault, not leadership.* DWIGHT D. EISENHOWER

The change management process requires multiple leaders throughout the organization and the hierarchy. Therefore, leaders must motivate other people to provide leadership within their sphere of influence. This is especially challenging if people perceive leadership as the equivalent of a formal position in the organization. For example, the author spent eight weeks with a company that was instituting a supply-chain management initiative. When supply-chain team members were interviewed about the change process, they typically stated that they could not move forward with the changes required by new supply processes because top management had not provided enough of the right kind of support. This perception persisted across the supply-chain organization despite the fact that top management had taken the initiative to launch a formal supply-chain management program, budgeted absolutely and relatively large sums of money to the initiative over multiple years, committed customized training resources, dedicated IT support and facilities, and despite the fact that top management had regularly communicated a consistent verbal message about the supply-chain initiative. When asked what else top management was supposed to do, most people responded: mandate the change.

A weakness in the change management process was that top management considered the leadership tasks of creating alignment and gaining commitment as the responsibility of the supply-chain management teams. Team members perceived their roles as largely managerial — plan, budget, organize, staff and control. When compliance was not forthcoming in all the operating areas, supply-chain team members were ill-equipped to cope with the lack of commitment. Individuals had the skills, qualification, education and experience to manage routine processes and procedures, but lacked the leadership capability to energize people to commit to change.

Senior executives who were interviewed stated that mandates did not work in the company's organizational culture and they expected the supply-chain team to sell the vision and concept to stakeholders and influence them to support the supply-chain initiative.

The lack of buy-in was also influenced by managerial factors such as a lack of joint goals and joint accountability across business units and functions. The presence of competing and conflicting goals raised the requirement for strong leadership, but the organization had not developed leadership skills in multiple employees and not enough leaders were ready, willing and able to fill the void.

This story is told to illustrate that organizations need more than one leader. They need many leaders at many levels, all of whom are aligned around a common vision. As these leaders develop a vision for their particular area, such as supply management, finance, marketing or engineering, the internal partnerships or thick informal networks they build enable them to align individual functional visions around the common organization wide vision. By developing the leadership capability of the organization, current leaders are also laying the foundation for the availability of leaders in the future in both formal and informal roles.

For example, Kent Brittan, former vice president of supply management at United Technologies Corp. (UTC), had no purchasing experience, but he hired people from both inside and outside the company both with and without supply management experience. All the recruits had one thing in common — leadership qualities. He provided training programs and gave the new hires freedom to take risks. Today, the corporate staff, based at UTC's Leadership Center in Farmington, Connecticut, consists of 54 purchasing professionals, of which more than 80 percent have advanced degrees. They have corporate responsibility for managing the indirect spend, quality, supplier diversity and other activities.[39]

## Eight Steps to Transform Your Organization

The previous sections of this chapter have focused on tools, techniques and actions that can be used to motivate and inspire people to adopt a vision and, more important, change their behaviors to make that vision a reality. As anyone who has ever tried to change a behavior knows, making a permanent change is very difficult. The leader must be aware of the human tendency to backslide and take actions to institutionalize the changes without creating a new, rigid, suboptimal bureaucracy. John P. Kotter of the Harvard Business School suggests eight steps for a leader to take to transform an organization (see Figure 4-6).

## Maintaining Momentum

While initiating change in an organization is typically difficult, maintaining the momentum over a long period of time is often even more difficult. According to Peter Gossas at Sandvik, "What is really encouraging is that we have reached a stage, in three years, where it looks like we have a better acceptance of, and more interest in, this way of working than I had thought possible. Actually, the bottleneck is not really a lack of interest but that our change leaders and experts — the navigators — have difficulty keeping pace with requests for help from the units. We are now introducing complementary ways to transfer knowledge between units. Management rotation is one way, and we're very excited about it."[40]

**Figure 4-6 Eight Steps to Organizational Transformation**

| STEP | ACTIVITIES |
|---|---|
| **Establish a sense of urgency** | Examine market and competitive realities.<br>Identify and discuss crises, potential crises or major opportunities. |
| **Form a powerful guiding coalition** | Assemble a group with enough power to lead the change effort.<br>Encourage the group to work as a team. |
| **Create a vision** | Create a vision to help direct the change effort.<br>Develop strategies for achieving that vision. |
| **Communicate the vision** | Use every vehicle possible to communicate the new vision and strategies.<br>Teach new behaviors by the example of the guiding coalition. |
| **Empower others to act on the vision** | Get rid of obstacles to change.<br>Change systems or structures that seriously undermine the vision.<br>Encourage risk-taking and nontraditional ideas, activities and actions. |
| **Plan for and create short-term wins** | Plan for visible performance improvements.<br>Create those improvements.<br>Recognize and reward employees involved in the improvements. |
| **Consolidate improvements and produce still more change** | Use increased credibility to change systems, structures and policies that do not fit the vision.<br>Hire, promote and develop employees who can implement the vision.<br>Reinvigorate the process with new projects, themes and change agents. |
| **Institutionalize new approaches** | Articulate the connections between the new behaviors and organizational success.<br>Develop the means to ensure leadership development and succession. |

*Source:* John P. Kotter, "Winning at Change," *Leader to Leader,* Volume 10 (Fall 1998), 27–33.

## Key Points

1. Leaders use various motivational techniques such as appealing to people's sense of belonging, need for accomplishment and sense of control to energize stakeholders and generate commitment to the vision of supply management.

2. Informal internal partnerships or "thick informal networks" are critical to successful change management.

3. Leaders build thick informal partnerships by using motivational techniques and knowledge of stakeholders' interests to build coalitions that provide enough benefit to each stakeholder group to maintain commitment.

4. A culture of leadership is created when multiple leaders exist in an organization and they are actively using their leadership skills while also developing these skills in others.

CHAPTER

# 5

# Assessing, Mitigating and Managing Supply-Based Risks

*Killing the project minimizes risks but also eliminates reward.*

JAMES MCCRODDY, FORMER CHIEF TECHNICAL OFFICER OF IBM[1]

Every organization faces a multitude of risks that must be identified, assessed, prioritized and managed either by avoiding the risk, mitigating the impact of the risk, accepting some or all of the risk or transferring the risk to another entity. The direction-setting role of leaders is complemented by the risk-assessment/risk-profiling and business-planning roles of managers. Risk is the possibility of loss or injury. Risk exposure is the probability of a loss or injury occurring and the likely impact. High-risk events are those with greater probability of occurring and higher expected impact or loss.

Supply management professionals contribute to the organizational risk profile through their assessment of supply-related risks. During the planning process they are then better equipped to develop business plans that, if executed effectively, will maximize opportunities at acceptable levels of risk. The supply leader-manager is responsible for instituting processes and procedures to identify supply-based risks from all potential sources, assess the risk exposure and work internally to determine the acceptable level of risk given the expectations from a project or event, and develop and execute the selected risk-management strategies. Therefore, the analysis of risks and risk exposure and the development of plans to manage risks are critical activities of supply management professionals.

Chapter 2 addressed the supply leader's role in setting direction for the supply organization. The managerial counterparts to direction setting are risk assessment (discussed in this chapter), planning (discussed in the following chapter) and budgeting (addressed in *Foundation of Supply Management* (ISM Professional Series)). This chapter is divided into two sections: (1) the risk-management process including risk assessment and profiling and (2) supply's role in assessing risks related to two key business decisions: insourcing/outsourcing and mergers, acquisitions and divestitures.

### CHAPTER OBJECTIVES

- Outline the steps in the risk-management process and discuss each one.
- Discuss the supply management professional's role in assessing risks related to the decision to insource/make or outsource/buy a good or service.
- Discuss the supply management professional's role in assessing risks in proposed mergers, acquisitions and divestitures.

## The Risk Management Process

The steps in risk management are: (1) identify the sources of risks, (2) estimate the probability of occurrence, (3) estimate the likely impact, (4) develop a risk profile, (5) develop risk-management strategies, (6) allocate resources, (7) execute strategy and (8) review results. Figure 5-1 illustrates the risk management process. Each step is discussed in the following sections.

### Step 1: Identify the Sources of Risks

The first step in risk management is to identify the sources of risk for each project. For example, the management of a German company in the telecommunications industry defined its risk as "the danger that events or decisions will obstruct the company's achievement of its objectives." This definition of risk was incorporated into the planning process of each functional area.[2] A team might determine typical sources of risk for specific projects or types of projects and use this information as a starting point in planning. In *Waltzing with Bears,* Tom DeMarco and Timothy Lister identify the most common software project risks:

- *An inherent schedule flaw.* Some flaw in the schedule-setting practice will result in an agreement to work to an unreachable goal.
- *Feature creep.* Or scope creep as supply professionals would call it. Changes and additions to the requirements will push the project over budget and schedule.
- *Employee turnover.* Key staff leaving the organization during the project will push up the budget and project duration.
- *An ambiguous specification.* A breakdown in communication at the specification stage leads to an ambiguous and unsuitable contract.

Figure 5-1 The Risk Management Process

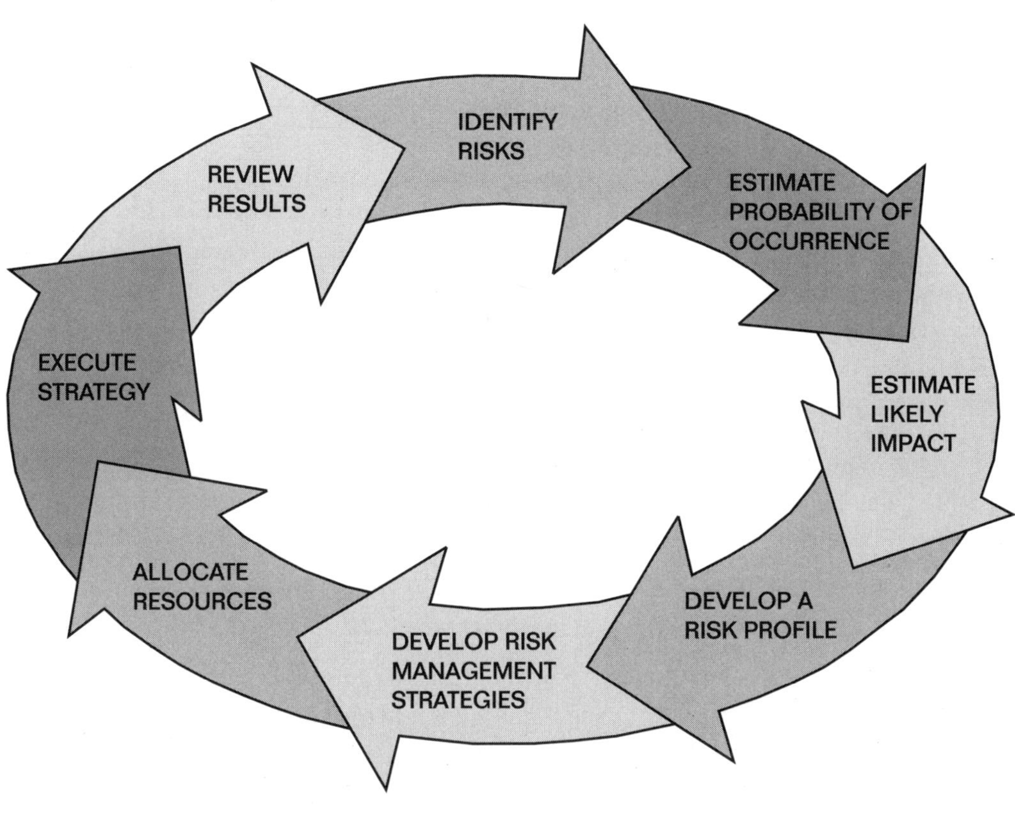


- *Poor productivity.* A failure to accurately estimate a team's performance will lead to project overrun.[3]

A software development or a sourcing team that is procuring the services of a software development company might start with this list, estimate the likelihood of each event occurring and estimate the impact. This assessment would drive the acquisition process in terms of acquisition strategy, negotiation goals, type of contract and terms and conditions.

Many sources of risks exist for every type of organization. The supply team members should continually scan the horizon to anticipate anything or anyone who creates or suggests a hazard or raises the possibility of loss or injury. A well-structured and well-staffed supply management organization should have multiple mechanisms in place, including systems, processes, policies, procedures and people, to support this internal and external environmental scan.

One approach to risk identification is to identify major categories of risk and then identify specific risks within each category. For example, a supply risk-management team might focus on identifying supply-related risks in six major categories: (1) brand or reputation risks, (2) business continuity risks, (3) financial risks, (4) operational risks, (5) legal risks and (6) technical risks. Each risk category and possible mitigation strategies are discussed in the following sections.

**Brand or Reputation Risks.** The primary risk for an organization is that its reputation or brand will be harmed by some force that either goes undetected or that is detected but not mitigated. Worse case, this risk interrupts business continuity. In a sense, all roads in an organization lead to brand and reputation. For example, the brand and reputation risks to Federal Express Corp. are outlined and discussed in its 2006 Annual Report:

- "Our businesses depend on our strong reputation and the value of the FedEx brand. The FedEx brand name symbolizes high-quality service, speed and reliability. In addition, we have a strong reputation among customers and the general public for high standards for social and environmental responsibility and corporate governance and ethics.
- We rely heavily on technology to operate our transportation and business networks, and any disruption to our technology infrastructure or the Internet could harm our operations and our reputation among customers.
- If we do not effectively operate, integrate, leverage and grow acquired businesses, our financial results and reputation may suffer."[4]

Supply leaders and managers at all levels play a role in building and maintaining the organization's reputation and brand. Their behaviors throughout the sourcing, procurement, receiving and payment processes either enhance or degrade reputation and brand. The Code of Ethics at Deere & Co. states, "Employees and directors will meet the highest standards of honesty, truthfulness and integrity in all communications, not just because it is good business, but because it is right. This applies in all our dealings, both as a Company and in our relationships with each other. We will abide by the laws that govern the states and countries where the Company operates. The Company will provide a working environment in which adherence to these high standards is clearly expected of all employees, and integrity is never compromised by pressures for immediate success."[5]

**Business Continuity Risks.** These are risks that imperil operations. The supply management team contributes to business continuity planning by anticipating supply disruptions and having emergency response plans and business recovery plans in place. In a CAPS Research white paper, George Zsidisin reported on an organization that defined business continuity planning as "having the processes, procedures, escalation paths and backup support plans in place to ensure the organization continues to operate should an interruption or crisis occur."[6]

One organization in the CAPS-sponsored event shared two series of business-continuity risks-related questions, one to ask internally (see Figure 5-2) and one to ask suppliers (see Figure 5-3).

**Financial Risks.** The supply management organization is a critical partner with the financial organization in managing financial risks and averting problems. For the supply management team, the main areas of responsibility relate to financial transactions and the organization's commitments to third parties. Supply management must

**Figure 5-2 Business-Continuity Planning Assessment Questions to Ask Internally**

Do we understand our core business vulnerabilities or potential failure points during a major, extended crisis? These would include:

- How do we redirect production and/or distribution capacity?
- What capacity is available and how quickly can we redirect?
- Do we have emergency management structures and defined roles and responsibilities in place to respond to a crisis?
- How do we procure direct and indirect materials? Manually? How are supply chain disruptions accounted for?
- Who is responsible for business continuity and crisis management at each site?
- What immediate action must we take to minimize loss and liability?
- Do you know your key support groups and their business continuity plans? Are your plans in alignment so that you would be able to continue operations?
- Do we need to prioritize customer demand? If so, which customers will be prioritized?
- What is the worst-case financial loss and legal exposure? Do you have a key contact list for individuals required to respond to the crisis?
- How long will it take to resume operations?

*Source:* George Zsidisin, "Business and Supply Chain Continuity," CAPS Research Critical Issues Report 2 (January 2007).

**Figure 5-3 Business-Continuity Planning Assessment Questions to Ask Suppliers**

What kinds of business functions are considered critical and have business-continuity plans associated with them?

What kinds of impacts are considered by your risk-mitigation and recovery-planning activities?

How does senior management support the business-continuity program? What management review and corporate governance mechanisms exist?

Does your business-continuity program ensure that all business processes and functions "critical" to your company are identified and documented?

Does the business-continuity documentation cover the components that make/support critical processes to an appropriate level of detail to ensure that single points of failure can be identified?

Does your business-continuity program ensure that business interruption risks are understood and prioritized and their impacts comprehended?

Have your business groups taken steps to reduce risks?

How frequently is the risk and impact assessment refreshed so that changes to your business are reflected in the business-continuity program?

Does your business-continuity program ensure that the plans in place are well documented and current?

Do these plans provide an effective crisis response and ensure that critical operations continue during a crisis?

Is the business-continuity plan documentation readily available to the people who need it and maintain it?

What kinds of exercises and drills are performed to ensure the completeness of the plans? Is the organization prepared to perform effectively during a crisis?

Can your senior management confidently answer "Yes" when asked if everything reasonable and prudent has been done to be able to respond to and recover from an emergency?

*Source:* George Zsidisin, "Business and Supply Chain Continuity," CAPS Research Critical Issues Report 2 (January 2007).

verify the existence, accuracy and completeness of relevant items. This is accomplished in three ways: (1) by being fully knowledgeable about and compliant with organizational financial reporting policies, (2) by being fully knowledgeable and compliant with domestic and international regulatory requirements such as the Sarbanes-Oxley (SOX) Act and (3) by working with finance to avoid getting into situations that lead to financial settlements. This responsibility means supply management professionals must link decisions and actions related to intellectual property laws, employment laws, product liability, environmental issues and end-of-life-cycle issues to the financial risks as well as the brand and reputation risks.

For example, the Code of Ethics at Deere states, "To maintain the integrity of our system of accounting and internal control, the Company's accounting and financial records must be valid, accurate and complete. All transactions should be accurately and promptly recorded in the Company's books. The Chief Executive Officer, the Chief Financial Officer and other senior financial officers of the Company shall foster practices and procedures which ensure compliance with all applicable laws and regulations, including the United States securities laws, regarding full, fair, accurate, timely and understandable disclosures of Company information, and insider trading."[7] Financial processes and controls are discussed in greater detail in Chapter 12.

**Operational Risks.** Operational risks are the risks of loss from inadequate or failed internal processes, systems and staff or from external events. Supply management plays a primary role in keeping the operation running smoothly. There are many sources of operational risks, including supply availability, intellectual property issues, data management, regulatory compliance, organizational policies, environmental issues and technology. These risks are key drivers in the development of overall supply strategy and specific category sourcing strategies.

For instance, Zsidisin reported that the German telecommunications company developed a program to explicitly measure and manage the potential financial impact of supply risks. This program was initiated to meet the legal requirements of Germany's KonTraG amendment that requires organizations to treat risk-management information similarly to financial information and to achieve greater control of inbound supply and proactively reduce the occurrence of those supply risks. The supply risk-process coordinator meets annually with each commodity and supply-line manager to initiate the process. Each commodity is evaluated for its impact on earnings before interest and taxes (EBIT) and reported quarterly to the risk manager. Thirteen risk categories are evaluated:

1. Additional costs for cancellation
2. Additional costs for transportation
3. Additional costs for material obsolescence
4. Unexpected material price increase because of allocation

5. Unexpected material price increase because of yield problems
6. Unexpected material price increase because of change of specification
7. Missing parts because of late delivery
8. Missing parts because of quality defects
9. Missing parts because of instability of supplier's country
10. Additional material costs because of single sourcing during the ramp-up phase
11. Contractual risks
12. Risk sharing on supplier investments
13. Currency risks[8]

**Legal Risks.** While the supply leader-manager may not necessarily be fully knowledgeable about the various domestic and international laws and regulations that affect the supply organization, he or she must be certain that the risks and opportunities associated with the legal and regulatory environment are considered. Legal exposure arises from a number of internal issues related to supply management processes and procedures, and from external issues related to intellectual property, the environment and various laws and regulations.

As the owner of the supply management process, one of the first orders of business is to clearly establish who does and does not have the authority to commit the organization's funds. This basic issue communicates to employees the seriousness with which senior management views spend management and fiduciary duties. It also communicates to suppliers the degree of rigor and discipline that the buying organization brings to the marketplace. Risk exposure was defined earlier as *risk exposure = the probability of a loss × the expected impact.*

In the case of agency and authority, the probability of a loss is high if an organization is not properly managing both the actual and apparent authority of employees. Likewise, the less agency and authority are controlled, the greater the impact or loss. For example, it is more difficult to track spend, improve spend visibility and manage spend when agency status is diffused. It is also easier for suppliers to gather information, possibly proprietary or damaging, when employees lacking supply management training engage in contact with suppliers. Loss may also occur in terms of paying higher prices, agreeing to unfavorable terms and conditions and compromising the buying organization's leverage in future deals. The link between process rigor and law is therefore a critical one.

The supply leader-manager must rely on his or her strong internal partnerships with chief legal counsel, peers at the executive level and influence over process integrity to ensure that the law of agency and limits to authority are calculated and understood as legal risk exposure that is endogenous in nature, meaning it is a risk that is completely within the bounds of internal actions to eliminate.

LEGAL RISKS: EMPLOYMENT. Supply management professionals may also contribute to risk assessment by recognizing legal risks related to employment in the supply management organization. In their capacity as hiring managers, they can assess the risks associated with hiring practices in the supply management organization relative to protected classes including race, color, religion, sex, national origin, disability or age. Supply professionals also bear responsibility for assessing behavior within the supply management group to prevent discrimination and harassment. This includes abiding by organizational policies and procedures and ensuring they are aligned with current laws and regulations. When dealing with contract manufacturers, the supply management professional may also need to be familiar with equivalent laws and regulations in other countries. With growing international commitments, supply professionals must be vigilant in ensuring adherence to applicable rules and regulations on an international scale.

LEGAL RISKS: INTELLECTUAL PROPERTY. Intellectual property (IP) is intangible personal property, including patents, trademarks, service marks, copyrights, technology and trade secrets. Protection of intellectual property is of growing concern to management in many industries. While IP laws exist in many organizations, these laws vary greatly. Therefore, this is a high-risk area for many organizations. Because the supply team is often heavily involved in acquiring intellectual property, the team bears a primary responsibility to recognize and eliminate or mitigate such risks. This includes educating internal stakeholders about the risks they may be exposing the organization to.

LEGAL RISKS: ENVIRONMENTAL. Environmental laws and regulations affect many industries in many countries, and they vary considerably depending on the country. The supply management team plays an important role in acquiring current information on domestic and nondomestic environmental laws and regulations and ensuring that the organization takes the necessary steps to be in compliance. Supply management professionals can assess environmental risks at three stages: (1) design stage, (2) acquisition and transformation and (3) end of life cycle.

**Technical Risks.** Depending on the nature of the business, technical risks might include infrastructure security, risks to systems, process disruptions and data-access disruptions. Risks to data include theft, alteration, destruction and loss of availability. Supply management professionals, working with IT, can assess the potential technical disruptions and the likely impact on the supply organization's ability to provide uninterrupted supply if the risk events occur.

Prioritizing risks is complicated when looking at a mix of risks where some have a high probability of occurring but a low impact and others have a low probability of occurring but a high impact. An assessment of risk exposure provides the information necessary to prioritize risks and put together an action plan that addresses risks based on exposure. It is important to have a methodical process of examining supply risk and factoring that information into the overall assessment of organizational risk.

### Step 2: Estimate the Probability of Occurrence

In mathematics, probabilities always lie between zero (an impossible event) and one (a certain event). Sometimes it is fairly easy to measure the two attributes, probability of occurrence and likely impact. Other times it is impossible to know the value of these attributes with any certitude if the necessary statistics are unavailable. In these cases, the best educated guess or a range of educated guesses is used to facilitate the process of prioritizing the actions in the risk-management plan. For example, risk managers in one organization defined the probability of occurrence as A = Very high, B = High, C = Occasional, D = Low, E = Very low, and F = Almost impossible. Calculating or estimating the likely impact or loss is the next critical step in risk assessment. This calculation may also be very difficult to quantify. The risk managers rated the likely impact if the risk event occurred as I = Catastrophic, II = Critical, III = Significant and IV = Marginal. In the software development project described at the beginning of the chapter, for instance, the loss or impact to the project might come in the form of diminished quality of the end product, increased costs, delayed completion or failure. Delayed completion or increased costs might be rated as a marginal impact; diminished quality as a significant impact; and project failure as a critical impact.

With the German telecommunications company, each of the 13 supply-risk categories is assessed by the commodity manager using an 11-step process that is based on past experience and anticipated supply trends. The assessment process results in estimates of the expected impact on earnings before interest and taxes (EBIT) and the probabilities of those events occurring. Estimates are made for commodities both before and after risk-handling measures are proposed and for the current and next fiscal years.[9]

### Step 3: Estimate the Likely Impact

Risk tolerance is the key comparison point for use as the basis of risk-management strategies. Risk tolerance, often referred to as risk appetite by enterprisewide risk-management experts, is the level of aggregate risk an organization can bear and still manage successfully over an extended period of time. Different people and groups of people — management, shareholders and so on — may have different appetites for risk. The risk tolerance of an organization is determined by its capacity for undertaking risk.

### Step 4: Develop a Risk Profile

A risk profile captures all the risk exposure and casts it in light of the organization's risk-aversion level (see Figure 5-4). Decisions about how to manage different levels

**Figure 5-4 Total Risk Profile Before Changes**

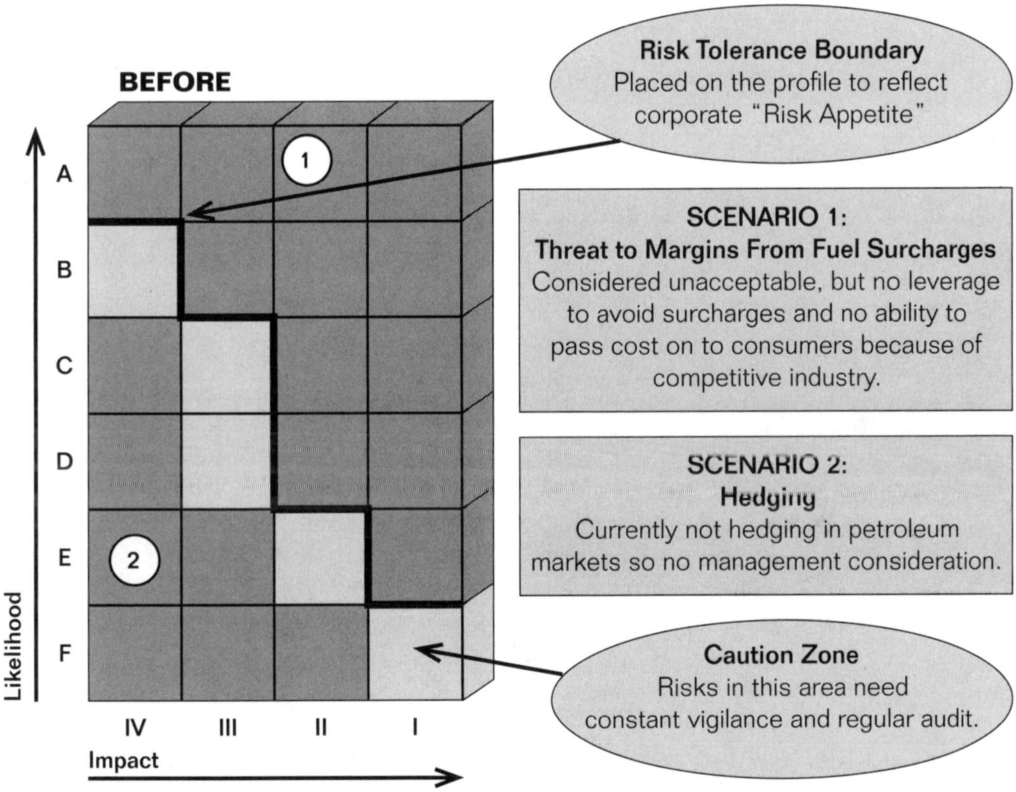

Likelihood Scale: A: Very High B: High C: Occasional D: Low E: Very Low F: Almost Impossible
Impact Scale: I: Catastrophic II: Critical III: Significant IV: Marginal

*Sources:* Adapted from "Total Risk Profiling: Process Overview," Zurich Strategic Risk; available from www.zurich.co.u/strategicrisk/services/riskmanagementprocess/Totalriskprofiling.htm and Matt A. Schlosser and George A. Zsidisin, "Hedging Fuel Surcharges," CAPS Research, *PRACTIX,* Vol. 7, May 2004, available from www.capsresearch.org/publications/pdfs-protected/practix052004.pdf.

of risks will emerge from or be based on this profile. To compile Figure 5-4, the team had to determine: (1) the organization's tolerance for risk, which is shown as the risk-tolerance boundary, (2) identify potential risks and (3) assess each risk along two dimensions, likelihood and impact.

Risk-management strategies are then developed. These include action plans and required resources to change the risk profile. The example in Figure 5-5 considers both scenarios and their relation to one another. The risk-management strategy actually moves scenario 4 into the cautionary zone to reallocate resources to move scenario 9 out of the danger zone.

**Figure 5-5 Total Risk Profile After Changes**

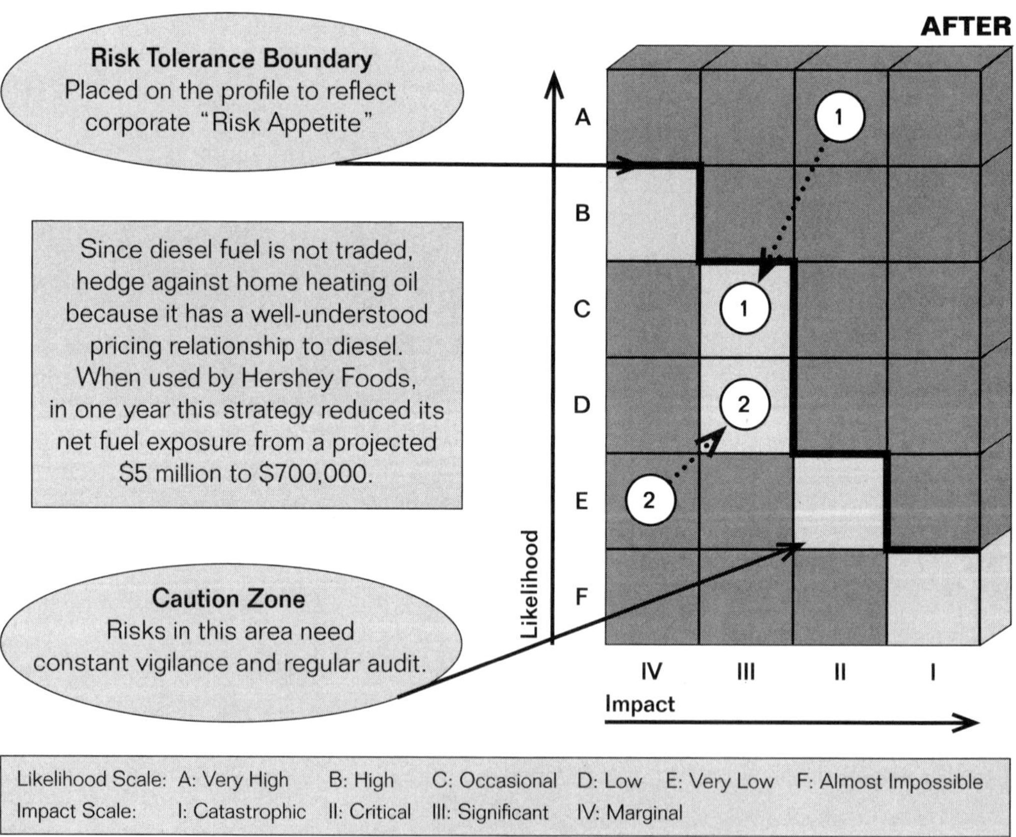


*Sources:* Adapted from "Total Risk Profiling: Process Overview," Zurich Strategic Risk; available from www.zurich.co.u/strategicrisk/services/riskmanagementprocess/Totalriskprofiling.htm and Matt A. Schlosser and George A. Zsidisin, "Hedging Fuel Surcharges," CAPS Research, *PRACTIX,* Vol. 7, May 2004, available from www.capsresearch.org/publications/pdfs-protected/practix052004.pdf.

One technique for developing a risk profile is to classify risk stakeholders. For example, contractors might be classified as prime, sub or general and the risks associated with each tier identified in accordance with existing contracts, applicable laws, regulations and organizational policy.

### Step 5: Develop Risk-Management Strategies

Once risks are identified, assessed and prioritized, risk-management strategies can be developed. Typically, supply management professionals develop strategies to reduce risks and enhance value. Opportunities cannot be fully exploited, however, without taking risks. The challenge is balancing the risks against the opportunities presented by a given situation. For example, the value of an item that is customized may be increased if that item is further refined to provide unique features valued by customers (meaning they are willing to pay for it). This action would move the item to the strategic category. It might also increase risk or leave risk unchanged. If the opportunity from the standpoint of probability of increased revenue, market share or customer satisfaction is great enough, it may make it worth taking the risks.

Managers develop business plans based on their assessment of risks and opportunities relative to the overall risk appetite (where the thick line is drawn to establish the stair step of Figure 5-4) of the organization. These strategies typically fall into one of four categories: (1) acceptance, (2) mitigation, (3) transference and (4) avoidance.

**Acceptance.** In some cases, risk is identified and accepted, and no action is taken. The team should consider contingency plans for it knows it is allowing the risk to occur.

**Mitigation.** To mitigate means "to cause something to become less harsh or hostile; to make less severe or painful; or to moderate a quality or condition in force or intensity." Risk-mitigation strategies are action plans that are designed to lessen the probability of loss or injury or to lessen the impact of the risk event. They typically focus on core drivers of loss and are designed to prevent losses or reduce the cost of losses that do occur.

**Transference.** Some or all of the risk may be transferred to another party. For example, if a request for proposal is issued along with engineering drawings and a request to build to the specification, then the buying organization has decided (consciously or not) to assume all the design risk. If, however, the request is performance-based, then the buying organization has decided (again, consciously or unconsciously) to transfer the risk of design to the supplier. If a supplier is invited into the early stages of the design process with no guarantee of the business, then the supplier is assuming a high level of risk that the ideas of the selling organization's representatives will be included in the design and someone else may receive the business. The willingness to engage in this behavior reflects the supplier's appetite for risk and the expectation for reward. Supply managers should approach projects from a risk-management perspective to ensure that the appropriate division of risk and corresponding reward is made.

**Avoidance.** Two situations may lead to a risk-avoidance strategy. With the first one, the risk profile leads the manager to conclude that the risks are too high based on the likelihood of occurrence and the expected impact. With the second one, the organization has a very low tolerance for risk and thus risk intolerance is built into the organizational culture so that individuals throughout the organization avoid taking risks. The costs associated with not taking advantage of an opportunity in an effort to avoid the expected impact of risk-taking may never be recognized or fully captured by management. Overly risk-averse decision-makers can have a very costly impact on an organization.

In a German telecommunications company, managerial activities focused on either reducing the probability of the event occurring or on reducing the impact on EBIT (earnings before interest and taxes). Typically, efforts were made to reduce the probability of occurrence. Managerial actions included more intensive relationships with suppliers, increased supplier capacity levels, the creation of improved planning processes, derivation of alternative transportation routes, development of suppliers with quality issues and adjusting forecasts to better reflect market demand.[10]

Risks are often interrelated and managers must decide where to accept more risk in one case and to reduce risks in another. The example in Figure 5-5 illustrates this action. Scenario 1, the threat to production capacity, was assessed as highly likely to occur and the impact was predicted to be critical. In scenario 2, the likelihood of occurrence of the risk to the currency hedge was assessed as very low and in the event of occurrence the impact was predicted to be marginal. Although scenario 2, the currency hedge, was considered well managed, the decision was made to take on more risks by adjusting the level of currency hedging to release resources to reduce the threat to production capacity (scenario 1). Figure 5-5 also shows that the end result is that both scenarios are now within the organization's risk-tolerance boundary. These kinds of compromises across functions, disciplines and stakeholders make risk management both critical and challenging.

Risk assessment and risk profiling are critical inputs in the planning process (discussed in Chapter 6). The organization's appetite for risk drives strategy development as well as the behaviors of those responsible for strategy execution. A strategy that is more aggressive (bears more risk) than management is comfortable with may never have the necessary resources allocated to it and a less aggressive strategy may fail to maximize available opportunities.

**Degree of Control.** To establish risk-management strategies, the risk analyst must determine the degree of control that members of the organization have over the risks. Risks may be exogenous or endogenous. Earthquakes and hurricanes are *exogenous* risks because they are not affected by our actions; we have no control over them. Building codes and architectural design are *endogenous* risks because they are affected by our actions. The probability of a risk event occurring is driven by the degree to which it is affected by our actions or endogenous risks. You may not be able to prevent a hurricane, but if you build in a hurricane-prone region, you can design and build your structure to decrease the probability that it will be demolished or severely damaged if a hurricane occurs.

For example, the risk to acquire an item in the marketplace is affected by exogenous risks (ones we cannot affect) and endogenous ones (risks we can affect by our actions). The exogenous risks might be overall supply and demand (assuming your organization is not McDonalds buying beef). The endogenous risks might relate largely to the specification that is clearly affected by the actions of people — people in the organization, people in the customer base and people in the supply base. For instance, if a requirement is external customer-driven, then this action is a key driver in the risks to acquire. If the unique specification is internally driven by a design team and supply is not represented on that team, then information about the impact of the unique design on the acquisition risk may be missing from the design team's decisions. In this case, the sourcing team leader may work internally to influence the design team without having any formal authority or membership on the team. The risk-mitigation strategy might be threefold:

1. The sourcing manager works to directly influence the design team in this specific instance.

2. The sourcing manager works with the supplier to develop a supplier relationship that ensures supply availability in the short term such as bundling this business with a more attractive piece of business and eliciting assistance from the supplier to develop ideas about how to reduce the risks by reviewing the specification.

3. The supply leader works up the chain of command to influence the perception of supply and improve its role in new product or service design.

### Step 6: Allocate Resources

Allocating resources to manage risk is also a challenge. The goal is to expend the least amount of resources possible to mitigate or lessen the impact of the risk. Assessing the impact of a risk to compare the cost of the impact to the cost of mitigation is also difficult. For example, a couple may decide to buy long-term care insurance because they assess the probability of requiring nursing home care to be quite high based on the fact that they are childless, their parents lived to an old age and required nursing home care for three years each and several debilitating and slow-moving diseases run in one or both families. The cost of care is currently high and projected to increase at an unknown rate, so they project a high impact if the risk event occurs. However, the opportunity costs of the mitigation strategy are difficult to calculate. They calculate the amount they are likely to spend on insurance over the next 30 years until the time that actuarial tables indicate they will likely require care. They then need to calculate the impact of applying those funds to other options to assess opportunity costs (the costs of a missed opportunity).

Supply management professionals and their internal partners must make these types of assessments regularly in the planning stage. The overlap between and among risk and the finite nature of resources further complicates matters. Managers need to be able to look at all the risks and how they intersect with each other to make optimal decisions about priorities and resource allocation. To aid this process, risk-management teams often develop a risk profile to compare risk exposure to the organization's appetite for risk. Determining the tolerance for risk is, of course, an equally challenging task.

### Step 7: Execute Strategy

Once risk-management strategies have been developed, they must be executed. Successful execution depends on adequate human, technical and capital resources to ensure proper support for strategy execution.

The wave of mergers among global banks and the growth of regional banks through acquisitions, for example, leave the newly created entities at high risks from redundant operations. These risks have been mitigated in many cases through an outsourcing strategy. Demand is aggregated for all combined bank divisions into one enterprisewide procurement function to gain leverage through volume discounts, synergies and scale economies. A centralized process and new policies and procedures are then imposed, often faster, by the third party than they would be by an internal group. Outsourcing, with all its inherent risks, is chosen because the risks of a drawn-out integration with limited strategic, operational and financial results is projected to have a greater negative impact on stock performance, market reputation and customer service (losing customers is one of a bank's biggest risks). By outsourcing IT, regional banks access leading-edge technology and other best practices at lower risk levels and without the intensive capital investments required.

### Step 8: Review Results

As with all plans, the assessment of results is critical to the improvement of risk-management strategy development and execution. Performance is typically measured against projected outcomes for key metrics.

Clearly, supply leaders and managers can play a valuable role in the development of an organization's risk profile. There are two strategic decisions where supply management's role may be especially critical:

1. The decision to merge with or acquire another business or to divest in a business and
2. The decision to insource/make or outsource/buy specific tasks within a function (e.g., payroll) or a whole function (e.g., human resources).

## Supply Management's Role in Assessing the Risks of Proposed Mergers, Acquisitions and Divestitures

Supply management professionals can make an important contribution to the organization's assessment of risks related to mergers, acquisitions and divestitures both pre-decision and postdecision. Supply's responsibilities extend to five primary risk areas: (1) contractual issues, (2) management of redundancy and complexity, (3) liability exposure, (4) divestiture of assets and (5) global economic considerations.

### Contractual Issues

The pertinent contractual risks in potential mergers and acquisitions/divestitures are related to: (1) assignment consent, (2) confidentiality, (3) due diligence, (4) current contractual obligations and (5) financial assessments.

**Assignment Consent.** Assignment consent refers to the transfer of a property right or title to some particular person under an agreement, usually in writing. An assignment is usually limited to the transfer of intangible rights rather than the property itself. For example, one organization buys another and the liability insurance coverage is part of the deal — the rights are assigned. An assignment may be qualified in some way, for example a partial assignment of trademark rights rather than global rights. Also, some contracts restrict the right of assignment. This might, for instance, leave the acquiring firm without liability insurance. The supply management professional may be involved in reviewing contracts to determine if there are restrictions and the extent of the associated risk level.

**Confidentiality.** Confidentiality is especially important when assessing the opportunities and risks of a merger or acquisition. Confidentiality and nondisclosure agreements are used to impose confidentiality obligations on parties receiving information on materials from disclosing parties that consider such information or material confidential. Drafting the appropriate contract requires consideration of some key issues. One important consideration is to specifically identify the information that is confidential. There may be limitations on what information is deemed confidential, such as information already known to the signing party, or information made public, through government agency order, etc. Another issue is whether the party is receiving or disclosing such information. A further issue concerns the duration for keeping the information confidential. Finally, consider whether the confidential information also qualifies as a trade secret. Also important is an explanation of the purpose for disclosure, for example, when confidential information is only revealed to another party for a specific purpose. The agreement should set forth what that purpose is.

**Due Diligence.** Due diligence is the process of analyzing information concerning the status of a target organization (for example, its intellectual property portfolio or trademarks) and assessing the risks, exposure and potential benefits associated with the proposed transaction in relation to the strategic short-term and long-term business goals of the acquiring organization. Supply management may be represented on the due-diligence team along with legal counsel and other executives and advisers. What is important in a particular deal will drive the approach to due diligence. For instance, the focus may be on intellectual property due diligence, notably trademarks and patents, trade secrets and copyright, and, in particular, software. Or due diligence may be focused on assessing any limitations to brands that are being acquired such as trademarks licensed to a third party, key agreements that are non-transferable or the seller's intention to retain some or all of the trademarks.

**Current Contractual Obligations.** Supply management professionals may also contribute to the assessment of risks by reviewing current contractual obligations of the targeted organization. They may find risks as well as opportunities that will result postmerger in terms of process, supply base, employee and technology synergies and project costs and savings opportunities that will occur during postmerger integration.

**Financial Assessments.** Auditors are typically on the lookout for undervalued or overvalued and unrecorded assets such as computer software, marketable equity securities, intangibles and inventories. The supply management professional can assist in scrutinizing obsolete inventories and assets under construction to identify liabilities such as potential penalties for noncompliance and contract obligations.

## Management of Redundancy and Complexity

Mergers and acquisitions are typically expected to bring synergies that lead to a reduction in redundancy and complexity. Premerger, supply management professionals can identify areas of redundancy and complexity and conduct a preliminary assessment of the risk associated with these areas. There may be redundancies in the supply base, contracts, supply management processes, technology staff, job descriptions and roles. For example, one of the most difficult aspects of postmerger integration for U.S.–based airlines US Airways and America West Airlines has been merging the pilots and flight attendants of the two airlines. In the process of creating a unified workforce, some employees lost seniority in the new system. This may ultimately affect customer service and customer satisfaction levels.

The risk may come from service disruptions to internal or external customers during the integration period and loss of institutional knowledge in supply management because of staffing changes. A premerger assessment will feed into the development of plans to quickly reduce these redundancies without experiencing costs that negate the expected synergies.

## Liability Exposure

A supply management professional may also contribute to the assessment of liability exposure in the event the proposed merger/acquisition is successful. The supply professional may be able to provide valuable information and insight into potential liability. For example, what is the target organization's potential exposure for liability resulting from:

- The use of its relevant assets?
- Environmental management systems, source or hazardous materials?
- Lack of compliance with laws or regulations?
- Any other supply-related areas?

## Divestiture of Assets

Supply management professionals assist in premerger assessments of the risks and opportunities associated with divesting assets in the event of the merger. Pertinent questions include:

- What relevant assets does the target organization own and what is its ability to control those assets?
- What is the asset's strategic value to the target organization's business and what is the extent of exclusivity in the marketplace that those assets provide?
- What is the target organization's potential exposure for liability resulting from the use of these assets?

## Global Economic Considerations

Supply management professionals may also provide valuable information and insights into the supply-related risks from a global economic perspective. Will the proposed merger create global market power or operational efficiencies from a supply perspective? How will the proposed merger affect the organization's global supply base and its ability to create or maintain a competitive advantage as a result of its supply base? Supply professionals might assess the risks associated with language and culture, geographical barriers and boundaries that might lead to high logistics costs, political situations that affect trade barriers, tariffs and duties, domestic laws and regulations and intellectual property rights.

A strong supply management organization can clearly be an asset in premerger risk and opportunity assessment. Supply's role in strategic and operational planning as it relates to mergers, acquisitions and divestitures is discussed in Chapter 6.

Whether to insource or outsource is the second strategic decision in which supply leaders and managers may make a valuable contribution during risk assessment and planning.

## Risks Associated With Outsourcing

One of the most fundamental strategic decisions made by management is: Should the organization make a good or service internally or should it buy the good or service (specific tasks or an entire function) from an external supplier? Insource/make or outsource/buy analysis is driven by management's perspective on ownership and control. The analysis focuses on the question of which value stream activities can be performed internally and which should be handled externally to ultimately contribute to competitive advantage. Part of this analysis involves the assessment of the risks associated with outsourcing internationally.

To assess the risks and develop appropriate risk-management strategies, it is important to define the terms and discuss the logic behind insourcing, outsourcing and offshoring. Figure 5-6 lists the definitions of the terms *make or buy, outsource, insource* and *offshore* from the *ISM Glossary of Key Supply Management Terms.* These definitions

**Figure 5-6 Definition of Terms**

| TERM | DEFINITION |
|---|---|
| Make or buy | A determination of what products or services an organization should manufacture or provide in-house, as opposed to purchasing them from outside sources. |
| Outsourcing | A version of the make-or-buy decision in which an organization elects to purchase a good or service that previously was made or performed in-house. Outsourcing may involve sourcing and using a supplier that provides the completed item or service rather than buying the components and manufacturing them in-house. |
| Insourcing | The act of bringing inside an organization a function that has been performed outside the organization (outsourced). |
| Offshore | Located or operating outside a country's boundaries. |

*Source:* A. Flynn, M.L. Harding, C.S. Lallatin, H.M. Pohlig, and S.R. Sturzl (Eds.), *ISM Glossary of Key Supply Management Terms, 4th Edition* (Institute for Supply Management, Tempe, AZ: 2006).

are used throughout this book. Some people may define these terms in slightly different ways. It is important for a practitioner to know and use these terms as they are defined by their organization. More important, the analysis and decision-making process is likely to be essentially the same even if the terms are not defined exactly as they are in the *ISM Glossary.*

**Vertical Integration.** In a vertically integrated organization, some or all of the upstream suppliers and downstream supply groups are owned and controlled by one organization. The decision to vertically integrate reflects management's perspective that risks are lessened by controlling all the input streams. In a horizontally integrated organization, subsidiaries may be formed for marketing or production purposes. For example, companies in the oil industry are highly vertically integrated. Typically, an oil company such as BP or Petronas locates crude oil deposits, drills and extracts, transports, refines and distributes fuel often to company-owned stations to sell to consumers.

Variations of vertical integration occur all over the world. In Japan, a similar business group arrangement is called a *keiretsu* (pronounced kay-ret-sue), meaning series or "related sequence," which is a set of organizations with interlocking business relationships and shareholders rather than family ties. These relationships reflect decisions about the allocation of risks and rewards among member organizations. According to the Japan Supply Management Research Group, there are six traditional horizontal keiretsu: Mitsubishi, Mitsui, Sumitomo, Fuyo, Dai-Ichi Kangyo and Sanwa, and four new vertical groups: Nippon Steel, Matsushita, Toyota and Toshiba.[11] A vertical keiretsu is an organization of buyers and suppliers. A horizontal keiretsu (financial keiretsu) is a diversified grouping with a bank or trading company at the center and includes a range of large manufacturing firms.

In South Korea, *chaebol* (pronounced jay-BOL) are large conglomerates that are owned, controlled and managed by one family group with strong ties to government. Some are one large corporation and others are loosely connected groups of separate companies. Top chaebol include Samsung, Hyundai Motor Co., LG, SK Group, Hanjin, Hyundai Heavy Industries, Lotte, Doosan, Hanhwa and Kumho. By 2003, 17 of the top 30 chaebols of 1997 were either bankrupt or in workout programs and others had spun off major subsidiaries.[12]

**Disintegrated.** The decision to outsource is a decision to disintegrate. In this case, management has decided that the risks associated with vertical integration are greater than the advantages. By disintegrating, the opportunities for competitive advantage can outweigh the risks of procuring goods, services or functions from a third party. The driver determining whether to make or buy should be based on the greater source of competitive advantage. The outsourcing decision should be based on a strengths, weaknesses, opportunities and threats (SWOT) assessment of internal strengths and weaknesses and external threats and opportunities along with a thorough cost analysis. Supply management plays a vital role by performing the due diligence required to select an external provider and ensuring successful implementation of the outsourcing business plan. Supply management's role in supplier relationship management is especially important when outsourcing. Strategic alliances with suppliers are one means of gaining the advantages of vertical integration without the costs. As owners of the supply management process, developing and managing these alliances is another way that supply contributes to the organization's competitive advantage.

Management may revisit an initial make or buy decision and reverse course depending on the strategic direction of the organization and shifts in core competencies given the dynamics of the internal and external environment. *Outsourcing* is the term used to reflect a reversal of a "make" decision so that the organization now procures something that was previously performed in-house. *Insourcing* is the decision to perform an activity internally that was previously procured from an external source.

The fundamental force behind a decision to make or buy or to bring back in-house something that had been outsourced is the concept of comparative advantage that holds that countries and organizations are best off when they focus on sectors in which they have the lowest opportunity costs of production. The challenge for the management team is determining when and where the organization has a comparative advantage. This requires the knowledge, skills and ability to assess opportunity costs to determine if a task or function should be performed internally or externally.

The same decision is made in the public sector where the term *privatization* is used to refer to the decision to transfer responsibility to perform specified activities, functions or ownership of property from the public sector to the private sector. For example, the state of California outsourced the design, development and implementation of the California Work Opportunity and Responsibility to Kids Information Network (CalWIN) to Electronic Data Systems (EDS). At full deployment, it will be the largest human-services application in the world. Privatization is a worldwide trend. According to Dr. Martin Bartenstein, federal minister, Austrian Ministry of Economic Affairs and Labor, "The outsourcing of IT services helps the Ministry concentrate on its core business and work more quickly toward meeting the government's larger reform agenda."[13]

Privatization is the opposite of nationalization, which is similar to an organization deciding to vertically integrate. For example, Hugo Chavez, president of Venezuela, announced in January of 2007 that he is planning to nationalize the country's energy sector.

**Risks of Outsourcing Onshore and Internationally.** Outsourcing tasks or functions exposes the organization to risks. These risks typically fall into the categories of capabilities, management, ethics and markets. Figure 5-7 lists the typical areas of concern within each category.

The decision to move a task, activity or function to an outside supplier naturally includes making a decision about the most desirable location for the supplier. It is fairly common for some organizations in most countries to outsource activities internationally. For example, Japanese automakers have had U.S.–based operations since the late 1970s, thus outsourcing manufacturing jobs from Japan to the United States. China and Japan outsource food production to other countries, and organizations in Japan, the United States and Europe outsource IT and back-office operations to India.

In the face of competitive pressures, financial institutions are outsourcing more business process work internationally. A 2005 business process transformation study conducted by EDS and the Economist Intelligence Unit revealed a rapid increase in financial services outsourcing. Fifty-two percent of financial services companies

**Figure 5-7 Outsourcing Risks**

| CAPABILITY RISKS | MANAGEMENT RISKS | ETHICS RISKS | MARKET RISKS |
|---|---|---|---|
| Quality | Goal alignment | Business practices | Create a competitor |
| Technology | Long-term strategies | Social responsibility | Knowledge transfer |
| Capacity | Managerial philosophies | Proprietary information | Technology transfer |
| Cycle time | Business practices | Conflicts of interest | Impact on brand |
| Financial | No succession plan | Improper reciprocity | Political backlash |
| Expertise | Control and compliance performance | Gifts and gratuities | Customer perceptions |

surveyed currently are outsourcing business processes to a local third-party provider, with 26 percent more planning to in the next three years — leaving only a fifth of the respondents not planning to incorporate outsourcing into their business strategy.[14] A 2003 Deloitte study found that one-third of the globe's major financial institutions used international outsourcing. IT processes went international first, followed by business processes. While India is the major location for business processes internationally, to reduce risks, banks also send work to secondary locations such as China, South Africa, Malaysia, Sri Lanka, Singapore and the Philippines.[15]

A critical piece of the assessment is determining why an organization might go international. Typically, the goal is to move tasks or functions to a lower-cost country (reduce cost risks). Low cost is most often driven by prevailing wage rates. The outsourcing team must either develop or acquire the ability to perform a thorough country analysis to assess the risk of doing business in a specific country compared to the opportunities.

For example, if the organization wants to expand its global footprint, then the discussion and alternatives may include outsourcing a task or function internationally. The starting point is vision and mission, not: "Should we outsource such and such a function? Should we go to China or India or Central Europe?" Outsourcing is a strategic tool, but it is not a strategy unto itself. Unfortunately, in many cases the starting point is: "Savings of *x* amount must be generated. Labor rates are cheaper in India, China and Central and Eastern Europe, so go there." Or "Everyone else in our industry is sourcing this from China, so why aren't we?"

A critical and challenging role for the supply leader may be using the "thick informal networks" (see Chapter 4) and internal partnerships he or she has developed to influence his or her peers to perform the necessary analysis and understand the long-term implications and risks, and not rush to a decision based on partial, weak or faulty information.

As discussed earlier, decision-makers should determine the country with the lowest opportunity costs. This already difficult process is complicated by the number of variables that are hard to quantify. These include the risks and related costs of differences in language, time zones, country culture and business norms, along with the uncertainties related to customs regulations, long transit times, weather, political climate and social unrest.

This chapter covered the role of supply management professionals as managers in the risk-assessment process at the organizational level and how supply and sourcing risks feed into the organizational risk profile. With a clear understanding and assessment of the risks the organization faces, the leadership and management team is ready to develop business plans to guide the behavior and performance of everyone in the organization. If supply management plans are executed properly, there is a greater probability of supply management making the maximum contribution possible to organizational goals for areas such as customer service, corporate profit and return on equity, while reducing the organization's risk exposure. Chapter 6 covers the development of business plans, including (1) the planning process, (2) supply management's role in the development of the organization's strategic plan, (3) supply's role in mergers and acquisitions, (4) the development of strategic and operational supply management plans and (5) strategies for executing the plan.

## Key Points

1. Risk is the possibility of loss or injury. Risk exposure = the probability of a loss or injury occurring × the likely impact.

2. Organizational risks must be identified, assessed and prioritized, and managed either by avoiding the risk, mitigating the impact of the risk, accepting some or all of the risk or transferring the risk to another entity.

3. Supply-related risks might be placed in five major categories: (1) brand or reputation, (2) business continuity, (3) financial, (4) operational and (5) legal risks.

4. Supply management professionals contribute to two premerger/acquisition risk-related questions: (1) What are the risks associated with the proposed deal and does the commercial attractiveness of the proposed deal outweigh these risks? (2) What are the risks associated with postmerger supply continuity and with capturing the full potential of the synergies of the two organizations and what is the probability of occurrence?

5. The supply management team can contribute to the analysis of the risks associated with outsourcing (domestically or internationally) targeted areas of expertise.

CHAPTER

# 6

# Developing Business Plans

*If birds travel without coordination,*
*they beat each other's wings.* SWAHILI/EAST AFRICA

In 1984, a man named Liu started a company named Legend Group to sell Sun Microsystems and HP computers at retail in China. In 1990, Legend began selling its own computers in China, but faced stiff competition when the market was opened to direct imports by international PC makers. As a publicly held company, Legend was ineligible for state support the way state-owned businesses were. In 1994, Liu created a separate PC division and put Yang Yuanqing in charge. By 1997, Yuanqing had turned the business into the number one PC player in China. He was named CEO in 2001. The success of the organization was built on innovation — innovation in sales and distribution by expanding from a direct sales force to a vast network of retailers, and innovation in design by focusing on low-cost, super-easy-to-use PCs based on current chip technology rather than generation-old technology.

In 2001, globalization became the organization's strategic focus. Yuanqing's vision of Legend becoming "a global leader in technology" was advanced through three primary strategic initiatives: (1) boost sales and market share in China, (2) expand to other emerging markets and (3) move into the West. The tools the organization is using include design innovation to develop a new line of PCs offered through retailers in the West as in China and other emerging markets and the 2005 acquisition of IBM's PC division that brought technology, an existing manufacturing supply chain, linkage to large corporate customers and brand and reputation spillover. The organization is now known as Lenovo and *BusinessWeek* magazine has called Yuanqing "the Bill Gates of China."[1] The vision Yuanqing has for Lenovo can happen only through planning and execution.

Chapter 2 addressed the supply leader's role in setting direction for the supply organization. The managerial counterparts to direction setting are risk assessment (discussed in the previous chapter), planning (discussed in this chapter) and budgeting (addressed in *Foundation of Supply Management* (ISM Professional Series)). The planning process at the organizational level results in business plans that guide the behavior and performance of the entire complement of people in the organization. The planning process at the supply management level mirrors this process and results in business plans that, if executed properly, meet organizational goals for such areas as customer service, corporate profit and return on equity.

This chapter contains five sections: (1) the planning process, (2) supply management's role in the development of the organization's strategic plan, (3) supply's role in mergers and acquisitions, (4) the development of strategic and operational supply management plans and (5) strategies for executing the plan.

### CHAPTER OBJECTIVES

- Explain why planning is important, what types of plans are needed and what might be achieved by investing in an ongoing planning process.
- Discuss supply management's role and contribution to organizational strategic planning, including its role in mergers and acquisitions and make-or-buy decisions.
- Explore the process of developing a strategic supply management plan, including conducting insource/make or outsource/buy decisions as part of the strategic framework.
- Explore the process of developing an operating supply management plan.
- Discuss analytical tools that enable the planning process.

## The Planning Process

*Planning* is defined by the WordReference.com dictionary as "an act of formulating a program for a definite course of action or the cognitive process of thinking about what you will do in the event of something happening." Planning is forward-looking and anticipatory. It requires thinking and action. As Peter Drucker said, "Plans are only good intentions unless they immediately degenerate into hard work."[2]

### Why Plan?

The first hurdle a leader faces is establishing a clear vision of the future. Without this, the efforts of individuals and groups within the organization are disjointed and may be counterproductive. Once a vision is established as a shared vision, not the vision of a single leader, multiple stakeholders in the organization need to understand the path to get there and what course of action to take in the event of barriers or obstacles. A good analogy is a group setting out on a trip. First, they must agree on the destination.

Second, they must agree on the route to take to get to the destination. Each possible route will likely have advantages and disadvantages, stemming from the group's individual and collective internal strengths (for example, several group members know some backroads and shortcuts) and weaknesses (no one in the group has a sense of direction so if they get off the familiar roadways the trip may go awry). The advantages and disadvantages will also be influenced by external opportunities (a new highway just opened) and external threats (the group will be on the new highway at exactly the peak of rush hour). The roadmap or route that is selected represents the best possible route given the internal strengths and weaknesses and the external threats and opportunities at the time of the analysis. Considering trends in all four factors enables the group to anticipate and develop contingency plans to lessen the impact of risk — the dynamic internal and external environment in which organizations operate.

When planning for organizations, desired routes and alternates are mapped. With effective planning, the organization has a greater probability of success in reaching its destination or vision. Effective planning is based on having a structured and disciplined planning process at multiple levels in the organization. Effective execution depends on assembling the right mix of talented people (covered in Chapter 9), structuring the organization for efficiency and effectiveness and enabling execution by applying appropriate supporting technologies based on rigorous processes (covered in Chapter 8).

## Types of Business Plans

There are two primary types of plans: strategic and operational. Strategic plans answer the question: Where do we want to go? Operational plans answer the question: How do we get there?

The word *strategy* is derived from the Greek word *strategos,* which means "art of the general." Strategic planning is a critical task of senior managers whose jobs typically include responsibilities for planning and goal setting. Strategic planning is a process in which the long-range direction of an organization is determined, and the means of reaching that goal are established. This process can be applied to businesses, agencies and organizations and to virtually any situation in which people are pursuing collective achievement.

An operational plan is the result of thinking and formulating an action plan in the context of a specific strategic plan. It answers the question: How do we get where we want to go?

Management of all types of organizations — public and private, for-profit and not-for-profit, small, medium and large — develop strategic and operational business plans to set the course and determine the actions necessary to meet goals related to areas such as customer service, organizational profit and return on equity. Within each of these entities, functional managers in supply management, marketing, finance and so on also develop strategic and operational business plans.

## Supply Management's Role in the Development of the Organization's Strategic Planning

Risk assessment, discussed in the previous chapter, considered in light of opportunities, is a foundation of good planning. Without this analysis, plans may reflect wishful thinking more than executable strategies. The functional owners of the major business processes in an organization must each answer the question: How can we effectively contribute to the attainment of the organization's vision and strategy?

In the case of supply management, the focus is on strategic resource management. Supply's contribution comes from actively participating, guiding and leading the determination of how each dollar spent does, or does not, add value in some specific way such as more services delivered or more income earned or contributed.

Supply management has not always been perceived as a key player in strategy development. One of the indicators that supply management has become a more strategic player in an organization is that supply is represented on the organization's executive planning committee and that supply-risk assessments are incorporated into the overall organizational risk profile. Supply's placement within the organizational hierarchy and the reporting relationship indicate both the perception of supply by the senior leadership team and of supply's role in setting the direction of the organization.

For example, Mark E. Brown, senior vice president, global strategic sourcing, at Whirlpool, serves on the executive committee. Whirlpool has adopted a growth strategy based on building "unmatched customer loyalty" by focusing on "winning the hearts and minds of customers." Initiatives such as the Whirlpool innovation process are expected to lead to higher levels of customer loyalty and result in improved revenue growth, margin expansion and trade support for its brands. Functions are aligned with this vision and strategy. The global procurement organization leverages the volume purchasing power of worldwide operations to eliminate costs and redundancies across regions. Cross-regional teams of product development engineers collaborate on innovation initiatives for regional and global distribution. And the information technology organization provides Internet tools that cut the complexity and costs of doing business for Whirlpool and its trade partners. The company's global platform is used to transfer key innovation and processes across regions and brands.[3]

The supply management leader's involvement in the development of the organization's strategic plan serves two major purposes. First, he or she brings to the strategic planning process valuable data and insight about the supply side of the organization and how supply management can contribute to attaining objectives (see Figure 6-1).

**Figure 6-1 Supply Strategy Integrated With Organizational Strategy**

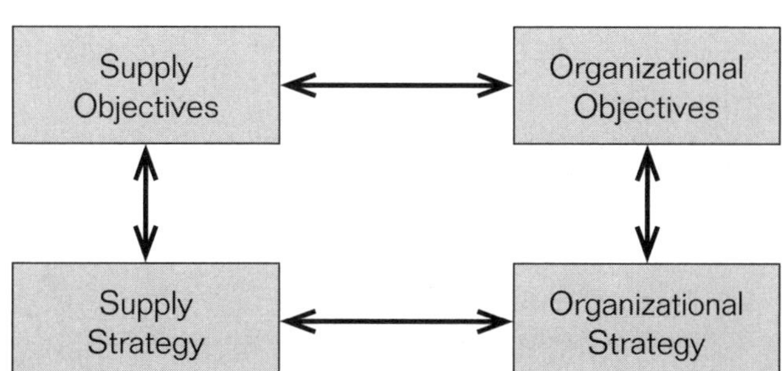


*Source:* M.R. Leenders, P.F. Johnson and A.E. Flynn, *Purchasing and Supply Management* (Burr Ridge: McGraw-Hill/Irwin, 2006), 525. Reproduced by permission of the McGraw-Hill Companies.

Secondly, the supply leader brings a thorough understanding of current and future markets and can relate this information to the current and future needs of the organization. The assessment of current and especially future markets from a risk and opportunity perspective provides much of the value of supply management's involvement in strategic planning. This is especially important for building alignment around supply's role in the organization and for generating better understanding of the supply opportunities and risks during the strategy development process (see Figure 6-2).

**Figure 6-2 Supply Strategy Links Current and Future Markets and Current and Future Needs**

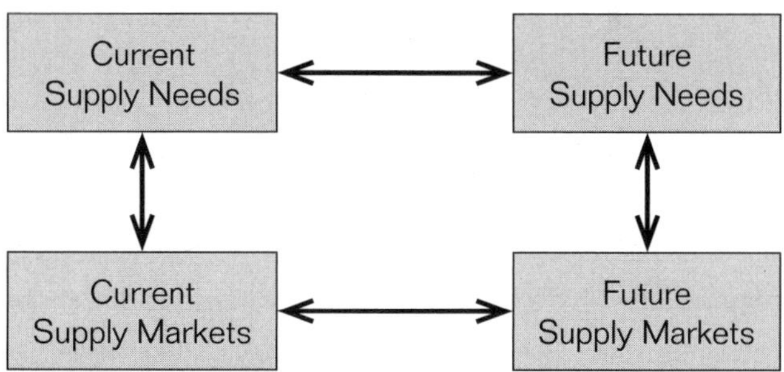


*Source:* M.R. Leenders, P.F. Johnson and A.E. Flynn, *Purchasing and Supply Management* (Burr Ridge: McGraw-Hill/Irwin, 2006), 525. Reproduced by permission of the McGraw-Hill Companies.

The involvement of the supply management leader in organizational planning ensures that the supply perspective is brought to bear on key strategic decisions and key organizational metrics.

### Strategic Tools

While a number of strategic tools are available to management, this chapter addresses two fundamental strategic decisions in which supply management can make a value-adding contribution:

1. Which areas of expertise should the organization develop and maintain as core competencies (insource) and which should it procure externally (outsource)?
2. If a growth strategy is pursued, should it be pursued organically or through mergers and acquisitions or some combination?

In both cases, the supply management team can play a vital role. As discussed in Chapter 5, in the initial strategy decision the supply management leader, as a member of the executive team, may provide valuable information about risks and opportunities from a supply management perspective. Once a strategy has been selected, the supply management team may be instrumental in the development of plans by assessing options and determining a specific course of action. Once a plan has been developed, supply managers then play a role in ensuring that full value is captured throughout strategy execution.

## Supply Management's Role in Insource/ Make-or-Outsource/Buy Decisions

One of the most fundamental strategic decisions made by management is whether or not the organization should make a good or service internally or buy the same good or service (specific tasks or an entire function) from an external supplier. Make-or-buy analysis is driven by management's perspective on ownership and control. The analysis focuses on the question of which value stream activities can be performed internally and which should be handled externally to ultimately contribute to competitive advantage.

Seven major steps are involved in this process: (1) identify an opportunity, (2) determine feasibility, (3) collect and analyze cost data, (4) assess the results of a feasibility study and make a decision, (5) develop a business plan to implement the decision, (6) audit results and (7) conduct a postaudit evaluation of the decision.

### Step 1: Identify an Opportunity

The first step in an insource/make-or-outsource/buy decision is to identify an opportunity that is driven by the organization's vision and direction. Opportunity identification is the process of developing a clearly defined outline of one or more alternatives or scenarios relative to the central business issue. Early investigation and exploration of the business idea should prevent unnecessary investment in an in-depth feasibility study. At this point the key decision is: Does the idea have market and supply-chain viability. If so, proceed with the feasibility study and include the initial market and supply-chain analysis.

The starting point should be: What business are we in, where are we going with that business and how do we get there? From this perspective, specific outsourcing decisions hinge on whether or not the item or service is strategic, and what kind of capabilities the organization has or can develop. The decision to outsource some or all of the components of a product or service should flow from the vision and mission of the organization and align components with the core competencies that give the organization a competitive advantage. Products and services may be broken into their subsystems, subsystems into their components and components into their parts to determine what is strategic and should remain in-house and what is not strategic and can be outsourced. Accurately determining this decoupling point has implications for the organization in the long term. In *Clockspeed,* Charles Fine stated that the ultimate core competency of an organization's supply-chain design is defined by choosing what capabilities to invest in and develop internally, and which to allocate for development by suppliers. In a fast clockspeed world, this means designing and redesigning the firm's chain of capabilities for a series of competitive advantages in a rapidly evolving world.[4]

In the public sector, ideas are generated about how to perform activities more efficiently and cost-effectively. Advocates of privatization argue that the private sector can perform any task more efficiently than the public sector can. Opponents believe that certain tasks and activities should be performed by the public sector because these activities have a social support focus that is in opposition to the self-serving interests of market forces. In the public sector, much like the private sector, the initial discussion is often around the applicability of privatization. This discussion is quite similar to the private sector discussion about core competencies. Political considerations are also discussion points in both private and public sector outsourcing discussions. In the public sector, these discussions might center on the public entity's role in society, and in the private sector, they might revolve around the organization's role in the community and the impact of an outsourcing decision on the local economy, especially if the decision involves outsourcing business internationally.

### Step 2: Determine Feasibility

A feasibility study is an analysis of the viability of an idea, proposed project or program. The goal is to determine the likelihood of success before a full investment of money, time and other resources in developing a course of action. The feasibility study focuses on the analysis of alternatives. After thorough analysis, the overall best alternative is identified based on pre-established decision criteria and a decision is made. A feasible idea is one that meets certain criteria such as withstanding the likely risks, long-term viability and contribution to organizational goals and objectives. A business plan is developed to execute the decision.

A feasibility study typically includes: (1) an executive summary briefly stating the major findings and recommendations, (2) a section of background information, (3) a description of the proposed project or program including advantages and disadvantages, (4) impact on key areas such as staffing, service levels and assets such as facilities, equipment and technology, (5) a comparison of the current situation to the proposed one, (6) a project schedule and (6) the final recommendation with supporting financial documentation.

The feasibility of an insource/make-or-outsource/buy decision depends on a number of influencing factors, including: (1) strategic aspects, (2) the effect on assets and (3) the degree of flexibility once the decision is implemented. Each of these factors requires careful analysis.

The strategic factors in an outsourcing decision relate to internal and external issues. Externally, these issues revolve around suppliers and the long-term implications of a buy decision such as supplier capability now and in the future, capacity now and in the future, supplier quality and technology, cycle time and cost management. Internally, there may also be concerns about the socioeconomic goals and objectives for the supply base, especially if the buying organization has a supplier diversity program.

Other strategic considerations include the impact on the organization's core competencies and related strategies, such as loss of internal skills and especially labor; the supply risks that result from the degree of control required and the security of the process; the impact on total cost of ownership; and the overall effect of the decision on competitive issues. Any decision that involves intellectual property requires special consideration of the long-term impact.

The second area of impact to consider is the impact the decision has on the organization's assets, including capital investments in equipment and technology or investments in human capital assets. Will a decision to outsource lead to the inadvertent creation of a competitor or transfer of proprietary knowledge? For example, this was the case when Intel outsourced chip manufacturing to Advanced Micro Devices (AMD) in the early 1990s. Now, AMD is Intel's biggest competitor. If assets are eliminated or reduced, what are the projected costs in the near term and far term and what if the decision is later reversed? These cost streams may be difficult to estimate.

The third consideration is the degree of flexibility to reverse course after the decision is made. If human capital and equipment are reduced or eliminated as part of an outsourcing decision, the cost and speed at which they could be reacquired may be prohibitive.

## Step 3: Collect and Analyze Cost Data

Several analytical methods and processes are useful in make-or-buy analysis, including break-even analysis, cost estimation processes and incremental cost analysis.

**Break-Even Analysis.** Break-even analysis is the process of determining the point at which revenues equal costs. It may include the expected profit or loss at different production volumes (see *ISM Glossary of Key Supply Management Terms*).

**Cost-Estimation Processes.** Estimating the cost of making versus buying or insourcing versus outsourcing is one of the most critical and most difficult tasks in the decision-making process. The first challenge is identifying all the relevant cost components and the second is estimating the associated costs. When considering outsourcing a service, the cost estimation may involve interviewing managers and line staff in addition to reviewing job descriptions to be sure that the RFP fully captures the activities and service levels performed in-house. How activities are structured, what staff and material resources go into delivering a service, how professional time is consumed during a workday, economies of scale because of equipment, setup time, coordination and supervision requirements, and learning curves may all be factors in a cost estimation process. This method compares a baseline cost (for example, the cost of performing a function internally) with the total costs if the function were performed externally. This requires a thorough understanding of the underlying events or drivers that cause major costs to be incurred. Consideration must be given to the fixed costs that will remain in the organization as well as to the incremental costs of supervising the outsourced provider.

**Incremental Cost Method.** Incremental cost-analysis methods measure the economic consequence of decision alternatives by focusing on the *relevant* costs. The overall question is: How will the total costs for the organization change if we decide to do Y rather than continue to do X? For example, the executive committee of an organization has decided on a growth strategy. The question is, "How do we achieve the targets?" Three alternatives are available: (1) continue to manufacture goods domestically and export to new international markets (status quo/baseline metric);

(2) manufacture goods in local markets (countries or regions) and sell them in those markets, (3) concentrate manufacturing in a country or countries with a comparative advantage in this type of manufacturing. The analyst identifies the set of relevant costs that are associated with this decision. This process recognizes that typically it is not possible to identify a single definitive cost per unit or total cost of the good or service.

**Total Cost of Ownership (TCO).** Total cost of ownership is defined by ISM as "the combination of the purchase or acquisition price of a good or service and additional costs incurred before or after product or service delivery." Costs are often grouped into pretransaction, transaction and post-transaction costs, or into acquisition price and in-house costs. To use cost of ownership analysis as a cost reduction tool, it is necessary to identify and analyze the cost drivers to look for any avoidable costs. TCO analysis is discussed in detail in *Foundation of Supply Management* (ISM Professional Series).

### Step 4: Assess the Results of a Feasibility Study and Make a Decision

The team must analyze the data and recommend a course of action. There is a danger at this stage that the decision had already been made (e.g., we will outsource our call centers to India) and the data are forced to support the preconclusion. Or the pressure is intense to take action and often to achieve quick cost savings so the data collection and analysis phase is weak.

### Step 5: Develop a Business Plan to Implement the Decision

Once a decision has been made, the team develops a business plan to drive the execution. This is a detailed action plan complete with task assignments, deliverables and due dates and performance metrics.

### Step 6: Audit Results

The results should be measured and compared to projections in case adjustments need to be made. Clearly, financial auditing is in order. Equally important may be a relationship audit of the third party to whom tasks or functions have been outsourced and the relationship with manager(s) internally. If the decision was made to keep tasks or a function in-house or to bring tasks or a function back in-house, then a relationship audit might be performed to assess the quality of the relationships that employees performing the tasks and/or functions have with internal and external stakeholders against the projections if outsourcing had been chosen.

### Step 7: Conduct a Postaudit Evaluation of the Decision

There are two primary benefits to conducting a postaudit of the decision. One, it may provide valuable insight into the next phase of management of a third-party provider or lead to a reversal of the original decision. Two, it is a feedback loop into the next outsourcing decision and knowledge gained during the current process may lead to a better and/or faster decision in the future.

## Supply Management's Role in Mergers and Acquisitions

Mergers, acquisitions and divestitures are also strategic tools that enable an organization to achieve its vision and mission. For example, if an organization has a vision to be a global leader in technology, it may decide that organic growth over time will not generate the growth necessary to achieve the organization's goals. The executive committee may decide to pursue a growth strategy through mergers and acquisitions or concentrate on technology by divesting in nontechnology-related businesses. Many organizations pursue growth through acquisitions. China's Legend Group did this when it acquired IBM's PC division.[5]

Supply management professionals can make a contribution to the organization's decisions and plans related to mergers, acquisitions and divestitures during both premerger analysis and postmerger integration. The supply-related risks associated with mergers and acquisitions were discussed in detail in Chapter 5. Supply professionals can provide the results of their risk analysis as inputs into the premerger planning process. Supply management expertise can be applied to two strategy-related questions: (1) Is the proposed deal commercially attractive? (2) Can the organization capture the full potential value of the proposed deal?

Postmerger, supply management's primary role is to ensure continuity of supply and capture synergies from the merger or acquisition. Supply management's responsibilities postmerger extend to five primary areas: (1) contractual issues, (2) management of redundancy and complexity, (3) liability exposure, (4) divestiture of assets and (5) global economic considerations. According to Booz Allen Hamilton, inadequacies in postmerger integration are the leading cause of failed mergers. Because procurement delivers the bulk of near-term savings in merger integration efforts, chief executives rely on procurement to deliver value from a deal.[6]

Booz Allen Hamilton recommends the following to ensure superior execution:

- Premerger planning between the CEO and the procurement chief,
- Anticipating changes and their influence on procurement, especially in the merged organization's vertical integration, product line and organizational structure and

- Developing capabilities that will enable procurement to quickly capture the required savings.

A phased work plan is recommended. This focuses first on critical operational issues, then on capturing synergies and then on achieving the ultimate value of the merger. Savings come from three sources: (1) price harmonization, (2) economies of scale and (3) adoption of sourcing best practices. "The first provides the 'low-hanging fruit,' while the second represents the value that was generally expected from the merger. The third, however, is often the greatest source of opportunity. The best way to achieve savings is to use a well-structured sourcing methodology that pursues the opportunities in waves, starting with the easiest first. If procurement is managed well, companies will capture much of the merger's potential."[7] When PC giants Compaq and HP merged in 2001, one of the immediate areas of focus was how to capture best prices and best practices of the old supply organizations into the new organization.

Clearly, there are strong linkages between supply management and organizational strategy, strategic decisions and strategic tools. Supply leaders and managers will be better positioned for success if they align functional strategy with organizational strategy. The following section addresses the development of strategic and operational plans at the supply management level and strategic plans at the sourcing level.

## The Development of Strategic and Operational Supply Management Plans

The strategic planning process may also be performed at the function level, resulting in a strategic supply management plan, a strategic marketing plan and so on. These plans should be aligned with the organizationwide strategic plan and should be congruent with one another.

### Elements of a Strategic Supply Management Plan

A strategic supply management plan typically includes:

- The shared vision of supply management (future-oriented),
- The mission of the supply management organization: what supply does, why and for whom,
- The core values of supply management that will guide its activities and
- Goals, strategies or specific courses of action to accomplish the goals and metrics for determining the degree of success.

The development of a supply management vision, mission and core values was discussed in Chapter 2. This section addresses the development of goals and strategies to attain those goals, and offers preliminary suggestions for metrics. Metrics for department performance are discussed in detail in Chapter 11 and metrics for supplier performance are discussed in *Foundation of Supply Management* (ISM Professional Series). The supply management vision statement describes what the supply organization wants to become; it is future-oriented. The mission statement(s) describes the important business capabilities of supply management based on the customers' needs identified in the market research. The core values are the guiding principles behind the actions of everyone in the supply organization.

The supply management leadership team must then focus on developing business plans that will meet customer service, corporate profit and return on equity goals. Toward this end, supply managers must understand the organization's product price structure and how supply makes a contribution to profit.

Given the current price structure, how and where does supply contribute to that pricing strategy and where are there opportunities to avoid, reduce or remove costs? Supply professionals must identify precisely what effect their actions have on various costs in the supply chain to maximize the supply-driven contribution to profit. This knowledge is fundamental to the goal-setting phase of a strategic supply management plan.

## Goals

Goals should be SMART:

*S*pecific
*M*easurable
*A*ttainable
*R*esults-oriented and
*T*ime-bound.

A visioning initiative needs not just a broad vision, but specific, realizable goals. Goals represent what people commit themselves to do, often within a few months. The word *goal* may have come from the Old English *goelan,* which means to hinder, and goals often address barriers and obstacles. Organizationwide planning typically includes a pricing strategy, as well as targets for profit and return on equity. Planning for supply management should include goals aligned with these targets, and metrics should be in place to determine the extent of supply's contribution.

At Whirlpool, strategy and goals are aligned globally. The company's vision is "Every Home … Everywhere. With Pride, Passion and Performance." Its strategy is to expand its manufacturing and marketing presence around the world through a series of acquisitions to become the world's largest major home appliance manufacturer serving customers everywhere. The company Web site states, "Whirlpool continually leverages its significant global resources, brands and business processes to offer innovative solutions that are responsive to the unique lifestyles and needs of customers in every region around the world." Goals at the functional level are aligned with the vision and strategy. Global procurement goals are related to leveraging the volume purchasing power of worldwide operations to eliminate costs and redundancies across regions. Product development engineers' goals are related to collaborating on innovation initiatives for regional and global distribution. And information technology goals are related to providing Internet tools that cut the complexity and costs of doing business for Whirlpool and its trade partners and to using the global platform to transfer key innovation and processes across regions and brands.[8]

## Market Analysis

Market analysis is the process of examining the external environment in conjunction with the internal one to develop strategies and business plans. Market analysis is a critical element in supply management especially in light of supply management's broadening scope of influence and responsibility. A number of tools and techniques are available to analyze markets. This section addresses SWOT analysis, supplier marketing strategies, and risk and benefit analysis.

**SWOT Analysis.** SWOT is an acronym for strengths, weaknesses, opportunities and threats. SWOT analysis is a strategic planning tool that starts with the desired end state or objective. *Strengths* are internal attributes of the organization that may be helpful to achieve the desired objective. *Weaknesses* are internal attributes that may be harmful. *Opportunities* and *threats* are external conditions that are either helpful or harmful. Figure 6-3 illustrates the types of areas to consider in SWOT analysis.

Following the identification of all the strengths, weaknesses, opportunities and threats, it must be decided if the stated objective is attainable. If the objective seems attainable in light of the analysis, then the strengths, weaknesses, opportunities and threats are used to develop possible strategies that maximize strengths, mitigate weaknesses, exploit opportunities and defend against threats. It is important to compare strengths to weaknesses and opportunities to threats to avoid assuming that a weak strength will overcome a strong weakness or that a weak opportunity will overcome a strong threat. The expected results of strategies should be expressed as a range of alternative assumptions. Remember that SWOTs are descriptions of conditions and possible strategies define actions.

**Figure 6-3 SWOT Analysis**

| | HELPFUL | HARMFUL |
|---|---|---|
| **Internal attribute** | Strengths<br>Resources: financial, intellectual, location<br>Customer service<br>Efficiency<br>Competitive advantages<br>Infrastructure<br>Quality<br>Human capital<br>Price/cost<br>Delivery<br>Service | Weaknesses<br>Resources: financial, intellectual, location<br>Customer service<br>Efficiency<br>Competitive advantages<br>Infrastructure<br>Quality<br>Human capital<br>Price/cost<br>Delivery<br>Service |
| **External attribute** | Opportunities<br>Governmental such as legislation<br>Market forces<br>Global<br>Technology<br>Emerging supply chain practices | Threats<br>Governmental such as legislation<br>Market forces<br>Global<br>Technology<br>Emerging supply chain practices |

## Strategies

A strategy is how the work will get done and by whom. Strategies or action plans are developed and prioritized for each goal. For each strategy, the specific action plans or tasks required to implement are defined. A strategy could be designing a new supplier relationship management program or streamlining the supply management process. For example, the strategy at Deere & Co. is: "We aspire to distinctively serve customers — those linked to the land — through a great business, a business as great as our products. To achieve this aspiration, our strategy is:

- Exceptional operating performance,
- Disciplined shareholder value add (SVA) growth and
- Aligned high-performance teamwork.

"Execution of this strategy creates the distinctive John Deere Experience that ultimately propels a great business and, for all with a stake in our success, delivers … Performance That Endures."[9]

At Whirlpool, "Whirlpool's global platform provides our operations with resources and capabilities no other manufacturer can match. Whirlpool's global procurement, product development and information technology organizations help our operations reduce costs, improve efficiencies and introduce a continuous stream of relevant innovation to consumers."[10]

## Prioritized Implementation Schedule

Goals and corresponding strategies are prioritized. A schedule, including start dates, milestone dates and anticipated completion dates for each strategy, must be documented. Resource allocations, adjustments and requirements can be developed from this schedule.

Figure 6-4 provides an overview of the supply management plan for the University of British Columbia.

## Develop a Supply Management Operating Plan

An operating plan is based on market conditions, business needs and available resources. At the organizational level, it starts with the sales forecast and flows down to a production (services or goods) plan and master schedule, with accompanying budgets for materials and services, labor, capital equipment and MRO or supplies. The operating plan provides a more detailed picture of the resource allocation decisions that have been made in support of the organization's strategic plan.

A corresponding operating plan is developed at the business unit and function levels. The supply management operating plan includes all the component areas under the supply management organization.

**Elements of an Operating Plan.** A supply management operating plan typically includes forecasts, budgets, a staffing plan and metrics.

FORECASTS. The organizational forecast of the scope and magnitude of key operating activities is used as the starting point to forecast supply management activities. Forecasting is discussed in *Effective Supply Management Performance* (ISM Professional Series).

**Figure 6-4 Supply Management Business Plan Overview, University of British Columbia**

**TREK 2000 — Mission Statement**

The University of British Columbia, aspiring to be Canada's best university, will provide students with an outstanding and distinctive education, and conduct leading research to serve the people of British Columbia, Canada and the world.

**Supply Management**

University community success through supply management leadership and services.

| | |
|---|---|
| **Best in class** | Leading-edge technology and service delivery.<br>Offer UBC community optimal customs clearance services.<br>Create effective travel management applications for UBC clients.<br>Develop key performance indicators (KPI) to benchmark functional effectiveness.<br>Introduce new supply chain processes to UBC's best advantage. |
| **Customer focus** | Achieve improved customer fulfillment.<br>Implement Web-based technology to enhance customer service.<br>Track and manage performance to approved and published standards.<br>Focus on and respond to customer needs by implementing a formal mechanism for customer feedback.<br>Track and manage supplier On-Time Delivery for all campus customers. |
| **Best value** | Maintain passion to acquire lowest overall cost of ownership.<br>Use IS technology more effectively to reduce time and costs.<br>Support sustainable development.<br>Improve functional productivity by improving negotiation skills and adoption of standard operating procedures.<br>Negotiate key strategic value agreements. |

(continued)

| | |
|---|---|
| **Best value** (continued) | Build upon and supplement customer procurement capabilities.<br>Enable system integration efforts to reduce resource costs.<br>Remove $20M from UBC capital and operating costs.<br>Use aggressive managed risk to single source large contracts for University benefit. |
| **Partnership** | Fully develop internal and external value-added relationships.<br>Encourage exchange of values and commitments with suppliers.<br>Implement guiding principles for developing partnerships.<br>Leverage contracts and supplier agreements to contribute to UBC-supported business ventures.<br>Demonstrate UBC leadership to support cost- and risk-reduction initiatives in the Canadian public sector.<br>Implement internal functional partnerships within the UBC community. |
| **Risk reduction** | Reduce all possible exposure associated with University procurement activities.<br>Strengthen and test delegated procurement authority to reduce risk.<br>Ensure University customs activity compliance to CCRA.<br>Administer an Equipment Asset Management system for the University.<br>Proactively develop and promote procurement risk management practices. |
| **People** | • World-class workforce.<br>• Improve staff fluency and depth on all systems by leveraging internal and external partnerships.<br>• Invest in professional skills for all staff.<br>• Ensure appropriate resource base to sustain infrastructure and research needs.<br>• Staff development and coaching will be provided through the use of objective performance reviews.<br>• Promote and orient staff towards all unique personal development opportunities afforded by the University.<br>• Produce a work environment that is conducive to teamwork.<br>• Recognize superior performing staff. |

*Source:* Adapted from www.supplymanagement.ubc.ca/SM_BPlan_Web.pdf, January 16, 2007.

**BUDGETS.** The supply management operating plan includes budgets for the function. These budgets define the needed resources, such as personnel, equipment, furnishings and training, and estimate their dollar value. Once funding is approved, the supply management team uses the budgets to carry out the mission of supply management, and monitor and evaluate the resources consumed in the process. *Foundation of Supply Management* (ISM Professional Series) addresses budgets and the budgeting process in detail.

**STAFFING.** The staffing plan is another critical piece of the supply management operating plan. It outlines the talent requirements of the supply management function, including existing talent and succession plans, as well as identifying staffing needs to fulfill the vision and mission of supply. The proposed operating budget should reflect and align with the staffing plan. Chapter 9 addresses staffing issues in more detail.

**METRICS.** The operating plan should include the key performance indicators (KPIs). Metrics for the supply management department are discussed in Chapter 11 and metrics for suppliers are addressed in *Foundation of Supply Management* (ISM Professional Series).

## Strategies for Executing the Plan

Planning is a waste of time if the people in the organization are unable to execute plans efficiently and effectively. It is beneficial to develop a communication plan, a rollout plan and a phased timeline to enhance the probability of superior execution.

### Communication Plan

A communication plan describes the different methods that will be used to communicate the strategic and operating supply management plans to everyone in the organization. This might involve holding town meetings face-to-face or electronically where the senior leadership team lays out the strategy, issuing newsletters, and fielding questions and concerns in an established format. The communication plan should use the types of communication tools that are preferred by employees so that the communication method itself does not hinder the delivery and receipt of the message.

At Deere & Co., CEO Bob Lane credits giving a clear and consistent message to everybody — employees, dealers, suppliers — so that even though the details of the plan were still evolving, the direction was clear.

### Rollout Plan

The rollout plan includes items such as a deployment schedule, required resources, personnel and training requirements and a budget. Flawless execution depends, in part, on a carefully developed rollout plan that takes into consideration the risks and risk exposure.

## Phased Timeline

The sequencing of the rollout is also a critical success factor. Bob Lane reflected on the company's operational and cultural transformation: "Looking back, this desire to both grow and improve operational performance at the same time created an enormous amount of skepticism early on. And if I had it all to do over again I would be clearer and crisper at the front end about the priorities. The lesson for me was that sequencing is very important in terms of establishing the right expectations with employees and investors, and when you don't get it right it causes a lot of skepticism — legitimate skepticism."[11]

This chapter covered supply management's contribution to the planning process at the organizational level and how supply management and sourcing strategies are developed to align with organizational strategy. Business plans guide the behavior and performance of supply management personnel and, if executed properly, ensure supply management's contribution meets organizational goals for such areas as customer service, corporate profit and return on equity, while reducing the organization's risk exposure.

## Key Points

1. Strategic plans answer the question: Where do we want to go?

2. Operational plans answer the question: How do we get there?

3. A strategic supply plan typically includes: (1) the shared vision of supply management (future-oriented), (2) the mission of the supply management organization (what supply management does, why and for whom), (3) the core values of supply management that will guide its activities, goals, strategies or specific courses of action to accomplish the goals and (4) metrics for determining the degree of success.

4. Supply managers contribute to two premerger/acquisition questions: (1) Is the proposed deal commercially attractive? (2) Can the organization capture the full potential value of the proposed deal? They contribute postmerger by ensuring continuity of supply and capturing synergies from the merger or acquisition.

5. The supply management team can contribute to strategic planning by involvement in decisions about which areas of expertise the organization should develop and maintain as core competencies and which it should procure externally.

CHAPTER

# 7

# Organizing and Building Supply Management Infrastructure

*An organization should, by definition, function organically, which means that its purposes should determine its structure, rather than the other way around, and that it should function as a community rather than a hierarchy, and offer autonomy to its members, along with tests, opportunities, and rewards, because ultimately an organization is merely the means, not the end.* WARREN BENNIS[1]

Chapter 3 addressed the leader's role in aligning people and resources around the direction he or she sets for the organization. From a managerial perspective, alignment relates to the infrastructure needed to support the people in their quest for the vision set forth by the leader or leadership team. In the case of supply management, this infrastructure consists of the structure of the supply management group, the human capital or talent that will carry out the strategies and plans and the technology that will support and enable strategy execution. This chapter focuses on the options, issues and considerations around structuring the supply management group. Chapter 8 focuses specifically on processes and technology to enhance efficiency and effectiveness, while Chapter 9 addresses the organization of the people in the supply management organization.

According to Institute for Supply Management™, the scope of the supply management process includes the identification, acquisition, access, positioning and management of resources and related capabilities that an organization needs or potentially needs in the attainment of its strategic objectives. This includes the following components: disposition/investment recovery, distribution, inventory control, logistics, manufacturing supervision, materials management, packaging, product/service development, procurement/purchasing, quality, receiving, strategic sourcing, transportation/traffic/shipping and warehousing. The structure around these processes and the systems and processes themselves should be aligned with the organization and contribute to the attainment of organizational goals and objectives. This chapter discusses various approaches to these issues and is organized in three major sections: (1) organizational and supply management structure, (2) systems and processes and (3) technology.

### CHAPTER OBJECTIVES

- Describe the different types of organizational structures: functional, divisional (based on project, product/brand, category/commodity or geography) and matrix.
- Discuss the implications of each type of organizational structure.
- Describe the approaches to organizing the supply management function: decentralized, hybrid and centralized.
- Discuss the advantages and disadvantages of centralized, hybrid and decentralized supply management organizations.

## Organizational and Supply Management Structure

*Eighty-five percent of the problems that affect quality reside in the organization's structure, not in individual performance.*

W. EDWARDS DEMING[2]

Organizational structure is the way interrelated people, processes and activities are arranged (see Figure 7-1). Organizational structure reflects decisions about who should do which tasks, who reports to whom and how decisions are made. Structure addresses the complexity, formalization and centralization between and among the interrelated people, processes and activities.

First, the degree of horizontal, vertical and spatial differentiation of organizational activities determines the complexity of the structure. The number of units across the organization represents its horizontal complexity. The depth of the organizational hierarchy is its vertical complexity. Flat structures have fewer hierarchical levels and each level has a wider span of control, meaning that more workers report to the same manager. Tall structures have many levels with narrower spans of control. The geographical dispersion of physical and human resources is the organization's spatial complexity. Second, the degree of standardization of rules, job descriptions, procedures and such represents the formalization of the structure. Third, the degree of concentration of decision-making reflects how centralized or decentralized the structure is.

Figure 7-1 Horizontal, Vertical and Spatial Aspects of Structure

| ELEMENTS OF STRUCTURE | ← | → |
|---|---|---|
| **Horizontal complexity** | | |
| Number of business units | Few | Many |
| **Vertical complexity** | | |
| Hierarchical levels | Few | Many |
| Span of countrol | Wide | Narrow |
| **Spatial complexity** | | |
| Geographical dispersion | Little | Much |
| **Formalization of rules, job descriptions and procedures** | Little standardization | Much standardization |
| **Centralization of decision-making** | Low | High |

Differentiation occurs through a division of labor and technical specialization. Integration occurs when specialists cooperate to achieve a common goal. Each organizational structure reflects trade-offs made between differentiation and specialization.

## Functional Structure

The structure of each functional area in an organization flows from the organizational structure. The overall goal for each function (supply management, marketing, finance, etc.) is an efficient and effective process. When considering the structure of supply management, three primary questions should be answered:

1. To what extent does the structure enable efficient and effective management of the organization's annual spend?
2. To what extent does the structure enable efficient and effective aggregation of spend across departments, divisions and business units?
3. To what extent does the structure enable efficient and effective service levels to end users of the purchased goods and services?

The supply management professional has primary responsibility for ensuring that these goals are achieved to the greatest extent possible given the organization-wide structure. Therefore, the leader-manager must fully comprehend the implications of organizational structure on supply management structure and processes.

## Organizational Structure Types and Implications

Organizations may be structured in many ways. This chapter addresses three basic types of structure: functional, divisional (based on project, product/brand, category/commodity or geography) and matrix. Ideally, structure should maximize communication and coordination internally and externally and optimize how products and services are delivered to customers. In a complex, global environment, it is especially challenging to reconcile top-down hierarchical management with matrix management at a project level and the need or requirement for organizationwide information flows.

**Structured by Function.** If an organization is structured by function, it is arranged around knowledge areas such as sales, marketing, engineering, supply management, etc. (see Figure 7-2). This structure fits well with an organization that has a dominant product or service. Each area develops functional expertise, but there may be little integration, poor communication and conflicting objectives between and among functions. While functional ownership enables the development of expertise and establishment of standards, cross-functional projects may suffer from lack of flexibility and speed because of the hierarchical nature of workflows and decision-making. In this type of structure, supply management may be organized as one primary function with subfunctions such as purchasing, logistics, operations, etc.

Figure 7-2 Structured by Function

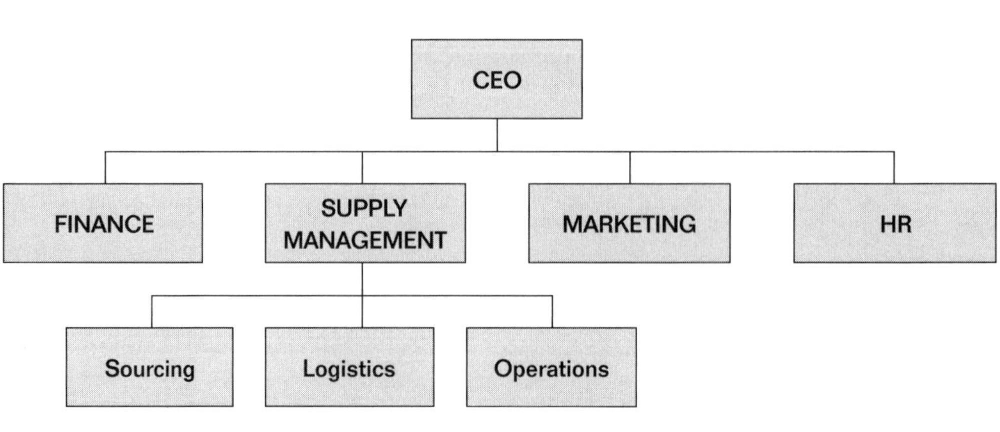

**Structured by Division.** In this organizational structure, knowledge and expertise may be grouped by product or brand, category or commodity or geography (see Figure 7-3). Product or brand management is an approach that centers organizational efforts on delivering a specific product to market or focuses on increasing the perceived value to the customer of a brand. Organizations that take a product or brand management approach may find that brand managers focus narrowly on their brand and the short-term financial objectives related to it rather than on organizationwide strategic objectives. Likewise, it may be difficult to link brand performance directly to key metrics such as shareholder equity. Different brands or products may also have conflicting objectives. For the supply management organization, the brand or product management approach may create conflicts over allocation of supply management resources, inability to consolidate spend and difficulty in standardizing inputs to aggregate spend and increase purchasing power.

Category management is an offshoot of brand management. It developed in the retail sector where retail products are grouped into categories and managed as business units. The category manager oversees products and activities across the entire category to optimize producer and retailer profits. Categories contribute to store results and contribute to brand management. In this structure, the goal is to build customer

**Figure 7-3 Product, Brand or Category Organizational Structure**

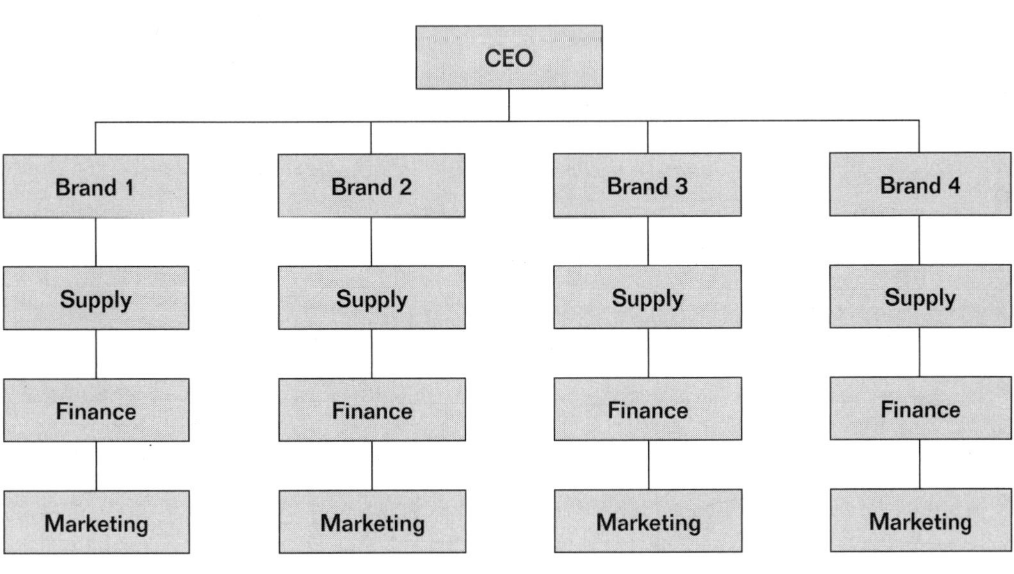

loyalty through access to better and more timely information, faster response to consumers and relationship management.

For example, the incoming CEO of German carmaker Volkswagen, AG, plans to change the corporate structure to two brands, a premium group and a volume group, replacing the existing brand structure of VW and Audi. The move is expected to better differentiate the cars within each brand in the minds of the consumers. The position of the overall development head will be reestablished on the executive board to offset the influence of the brands' chief executives.[3]

**STRUCTURED BY GEOGRAPHY.** Spatially complex organizations have wide geographical dispersion of physical and human resources. Given the difficulties created by differences in time, language, culture and business norms and practices, it may be determined that the organization is best structured around geography (see Figure 7-4). Conflicting and/or competing goals and objectives across countries or regions of activity on the sales and marketing side along with differences in location of sources increases the complexity of the business and may impede the ability to efficiently and effectively design, develop and deliver products or services to customers.

**Structured by Function and Division: A Matrix Organization.** A matrix organizational structure combines functional and divisional structures with cross-functional project teams responsible for the total project and its outcomes (see Figure 7-5). A project manager owns the project and takes responsibility for its

Figure 7-4 Structured by Geography

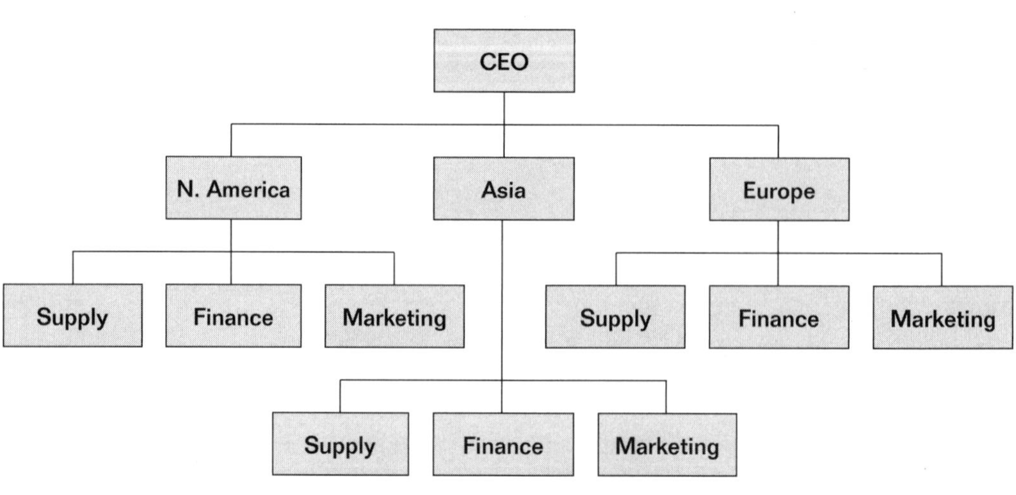

**Figure 7-5 Matrix Organizational Structure**

| | Project 1 | Project 2 | Project 3 | Project 4 | Project 5 | Project 6 |
|---|---|---|---|---|---|---|
| Supply management → | | | | | | |
| HR → | | | | | | |
| Finance → | | | | | | |
| Marketing → | | | | | | |

successful and timely completion. Matrix organizations may be complex with high communication and coordination requirements between functional and divisional levels. A matrix structure offers speed and flexibility that may not be achieved in a purely functional organization. Overhead costs, however, are typically higher than in functional organizations because sufficient expertise is necessary in various functional areas for full-time assignment to multiple and simultaneous projects. In a project-based structure, supply management personnel are assigned to project teams and serve on these teams for their duration.

Project team members report to a functional manager and to a project manager. For example, a supply management professional may be on a new product development team and report to a director of supply management and to the team project manager. There are three typical approaches to this model:

1. A project manager or administrator with limited authority oversees the project. The functional managers retain control over their resources and their aspects of the project. The project manager's role is primarily as the go-between to smooth communication flows between and among functional areas and track overall project progress.

2. A project manager oversees the project and shares power equally with the functional managers. The power-sharing aspect is the most difficult to manage and this structure tends to be complex.

3. A project manager is primarily responsible for the project and functional managers provide area expertise and resources on an as-needed basis. Competition for resources becomes a difficult issue because functional managers with finite resources are asked to provide expertise to multiple projects.

Bank of America, for example, has a matrix structure with three main lines of business: Global Corporate and Investment Banking, Global Wealth and Investment Management, and Consumer and Small Business Banking. This structure is reflected in the organization of the Supply Chain Management (SCM) group. There are two teams that handle enterprisewide sourcing: (1) technology, services and fulfillment and (2) the enterprise sourcing group. Both groups source traditional items specific to their areas and unique items specific to the line of business. Support groups within SCM also provide operational support for systems, processes, policies and procedures and a supplier development group. Housed within the lines of business are business support functions and supplier relationship management teams. SCM reports to a global SCM executive who reports to the COO within the office of the CFO.[4]

## Creating a Globally Integrated Organization

Size, geographical dispersion and cultural diversity complicate organizational structure at the enterprisewide level and at the supply management level. Management in many organizations is interested in reducing or removing the effects of organizational boundaries. These boundaries may result from differences in culture, conflicting goals or functional silos. *Barrier-free* approaches focus on removing internal boundaries to encourage teamwork and widespread sharing of information. *Virtual* and *modular* organizational forms are used to make external relations more permeable and create seamless knowledge systems across organizations. According to G. Dess, G.T. Lumpkin and A. Eisner, teams are an important part of barrier-free structures because they (1) substitute peer-based for hierarchical control, (2) often develop more creative solutions via brainstorming and other group problem-solving techniques and (3) absorb administrative tasks previously handled by specialists.[5]

For instance, Carlos Ghosn, president and CEO of Nissan, reorganized to create a more globally integrated organization. He made three major changes:

1. He reduced the number of people based at the world headquarters in Tokyo, moved part of the headquarters to the United States and Europe and made movement into and out of Tokyo more fluid based on a strong rationale for a presence there.

2. Experts were identified in a particular technology or process no matter where they are located.

3. The position of president in North America was eliminated to reduce problems with communication and information flow between headquarters and the region. The executive vice president travels every month to head the management committee of North America and Ghosn himself heads the committee every three months.[6]

Structure affects processes, procedures, systems and relationships within and between functions. Whether the organization is structured by function, division or project, supply management professionals must develop and execute strategies that maximize the advantages of the structure and minimize the disadvantages.

The organizationwide structure impacts each function (e.g., supply management, marketing, finance) within the organization. For example, if the organization tends to be highly decentralized (decision-making is spread throughout the organization), then supply management will also be highly decentralized. If the organization is highly centralized (decision-making is highly concentrated), then supply management will be highly centralized. It is the responsibility of the supply management professional to drive efficiency and effectiveness within a given structure and to use his or her influence to mold the supply management structure to achieve optimal performance. The supply management professional also uses his or her position on the senior leadership team to influence decisions about structure and to ensure that supply management processes are structured for efficiency and effectiveness.

## Centralized, Decentralized and Hybrid Supply Management Structures

As discussed earlier in this chapter, centralization is one aspect of organizational complexity and refers to the centralization of decision-making. In supply management, the degree of centralization is reflected by the percentage of organizational spend managed or controlled by supply management. Three common organizational models are:

1. *Centralized.* The authority and responsibility for most supply management–related functions are assigned to a central organization. The term refers to the locus of decision-making, not necessarily that supply management staff are all physically located in one place.

2. *Hybrid.* Authority and responsibility are shared between a central supply management organization and business units, divisions or operating plants. Hybrid structures may lean more heavily toward centralized or decentralized depending on how decision-making authority is divided. One type of hybrid supply

management structure is a center-led organization in which strategic direction is centralized and execution is decentralized. In a more decentralized hybrid structure, management may use teams and lead buyers to achieve the advantages of spend aggregation while maintaining a highly decentralized structure.

3. *Decentralized.* The authority and responsibility for supply management–related functions are dispersed throughout the organization. There is no central locus for supply management decision-making and no specialized buying expertise.

In a survey of 284 organizations, P. Fraser Johnson and Michiel R. Leenders found that the hybrid structure (centralized hybrid, hybrid, decentralized hybrid) was the most popular organizational mode, accounting for 67 percent of survey respondents. However, 66 percent of respondents "leaned" toward centralization (centralized and centralized hybrid) and 24 percent "leaned" toward decentralization (decentralized and decentralized hybrid), while only 10 percent sat in the middle of the continuum.[7] Supply management organizational structure is one of the metrics in benchmarking studies conducted by CAPS Research (www.capsresearch.org). Respondents are typically asked to identify the supply management organization as either centralized, decentralized or a hybrid. A review of the industry-specific studies reveals a mix of structures both within and across industries.

These structures actually fall along a continuum from decentralized to centralized with numerous hybrid variations, such as center-led on the more centralized end of the spectrum and teams or lead buyers on the more decentralized end (see Figure 7-6).

The supply management professional has three primary roles in terms of supply management structure:

1. Inform and influence internal partners about the advantages and disadvantages of structural types in terms of efficiently and effectively managing spend, aggregating spend and providing service to end users.

**Figure 7-6 Degree of Centralization in Supply Management**

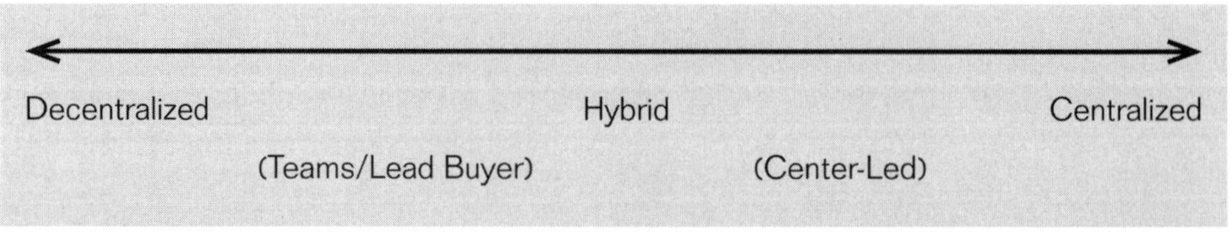

2. Develop the most efficient and effective supply management processes possible given structural constraints.

3. Enhance the ability of supply management professionals to collaborate efficiently and effectively both internally and externally by smoothing the path through structural barriers such as complicated structures, hierarchical silos and conflicting functional objectives.

To accomplish this role, the supply management professional must fully comprehend the opportunities and obstacles of various supply management structures. These are discussed in the following section in the context of degree of centralization of supply management decision-making.

**Centralized Supply Management Structure.** There are many advantages and disadvantages to a highly centralized supply management structure. Figure 7-7 summarizes the advantages and disadvantages of a centralized supply management structure.

Clearly, centralized decision-making creates an opportunity to transition supply management from a transactional to a strategic process and function by laying the foundation for spend aggregation and analysis that may lead to greater leverage in the marketplace. For example, in a Japanese organization, a parts unification committee assisted by information technology standardized commodity coding for parts. Then a centralized supply management group could more efficiently and cost-effectively order parts for multiple divisions.

The supply management professional must recognize that this transition may naturally lead to internal resistance from budget owners if they perceive a loss of decision-making control over spend decisions that affect their budgets. One of the greatest challenges may be the supply management professional's ability to create a shared vision of supply management's potential contribution and align stakeholders around this vision. A second challenge may be overcoming the difficulties in creating efficient processes when decisions are made from an organizationwide perspective rather than from a unit-level one. A third challenge may be attracting, retaining and developing the necessary talent to effectively manage resources from a centralized perspective.

**Decentralized Supply Management Structure.** Figure 7-8 summarizes the advantages and disadvantages of a decentralized supply management structure.

Clearly, decentralization offers some distinct advantages; the challenges for the supply management professional are to overcome the weaknesses, primarily designing processes, policies and procedures, overlays or temporary structures to enable the

**Figure 7-7 Potential Advantages and Disadvantages of Centralization**

| ADVANTAGES | DISADVANTAGES |
|---|---|
| Strategic focus | Lack of business unit focus |
| Greater buying specialization | Narrow specialization and job boredom<br>Cost of central unit highly visible |
| Ability to pay for talent | Corporate staff appears excessive |
| Consolidation of requirements — *leverage* | Tendency to minimize legitimate differences in requirements |
| Coordination and control of policies and procedures | Lack of recognition of unique business unit needs |
| Effective planning and research | Focus on corporate requirements, not on business unit strategic requirements<br>Most knowledge sharing one-way |
| Common suppliers | Even common suppliers behave differently in geographic and market segments |
| Proximity to major organizational decision-makers | Distance from users |
| Critical mass | Tendency to create organizational silos |
| Firm brand recognition and stature | Customer segments require adaptability to unique situations |
| Reporting line — *power* | Top management not able to spend time on suppliers |
| Cost of purchasing low | High visibility of purchasing operating costs |

*Source:* M.R. Leenders, P.F. Johnson, A.E. Flynn and H.E. Fearon, *Purchasing and Supply Management* (Burr Ridge: McGraw-Hill/Irwin, 2005), 37. Reproduced with permission of the McGraw-Hill Companies.

organization to aggregate and analyze spend and gain leverage in the marketplace when decision making authority is dispersed throughout the organization. The ability to influence decision-makers and persuade them to collaborate across organizational barriers may be the leader's greatest asset. For example, each United Technologies Corp. (UTC) business — Carrier, Hamilton Sundstrand, Otis, Pratt & Whitney, Sikorsky,

**Figure 7-8 Potential Advantages and Disadvantages of Decentralization**

| ADVANTAGES | DISADVANTAGES |
|---|---|
| Easier coordination/communication with operating department | More difficult to communicate among business units |
| Speed of response | Encourages users not to plan ahead<br>Operational versus strategic focus |
| Effective use of local sources | Too much focus on local sources — ignores better supplier opportunities<br>No critical mass in organization for visibility/effectiveness — "whole person syndrome"<br>Lacks clout |
| Business unit autonomy | Suboptimization<br>Business unit preferences not congruent with corporate preferences<br>Small differences get magnified |
| Reporting line simplicity | Reporting at low level in organization |
| Undivided authority and responsibility | Limits functional advancement opportunities |
| Suits purchasing personnel preference | Ignores larger organization considerations |
| Broad job definition | Limited expertise for requirements |
| Geographical, cultural, political, environmental, social, language, currency appropriateness | Lack of standardization |
| Hide the cost of supply management | Cost of supply management relatively high |

*Source:* M.R. Leenders, P.F. Johnson, A.E. Flynn and H.E. Fearon, *Purchasing and Supply Management* (Burr Ridge: McGraw-Hill/Irwin, 2005), 37. Reproduced with permission of the McGraw-Hill Companies.

UTC Fire & Security and UTC Power — operates autonomously and has its own supply management operation. Keeping in mind that this independence is important to the success of the organization, former vice president Kent Brittan re-energized an existing UTC supply management council and encouraged the businesses to pool their purchasing. Today, vice presidents of supply management at each business meet 11 times a year as a council under the leadership of Scott Singer, director of UTC global supply management, to make decisions on purchasing policy and procedure and share best practices.[8]

PURCHASING COUNCILS OR LEAD BUYING GROUPS. In a decentralized structure, a purchasing council or lead buying group might be created to aggregate volume and make spend decisions to maximize value. In lead buying situations, the site or group with commodity-specific expertise makes sourcing decisions for that commodity. For example, an IT commodity team might manage a structured, disciplined sourcing process in partnership with IT experts in the information technology department, and together they manage IT spend for all departments.

**Hybrid Supply Management Structure.** Many organizations attempt to capture the advantages of both centralized and decentralized structures by creating hybrid versions. One of the most common approaches is to create a small staff at the headquarters to manage common and high-impact requirements, with each individual site responsible for its own requirements for all other goods or services. In an organization with multiple business units, different divisions or business units often sell different products or services requiring a different mix of purchased items. Often the division or business unit is operated as a profit center where the division manager is given total responsibility for running the division, acts as president of an independent firm and is judged by profits made by the division. Because purchases are the largest single controllable cost of running the division and have a direct effect on its efficiency and competitive position, the profit-center manager may insist on having direct authority over purchasing. This has led firms to adopt decentralized-centralized purchasing, or a hybrid organizational structure, in which the supply management function is partially centralized at the corporate or head office and partially decentralized to the business units.

Often the corporate supply management organization works with the business unit supply management departments on those tasks that are more effectively handled on a corporate basis: (1) establishing policies, procedures, controls and systems, (2) recruiting and training personnel, (3) coordinating the purchase of common-use items in which more "clout" is needed, (4) auditing supply management performance and (5) developing corporatewide supply management strategies. Therefore, hybrid organizational structures attempt to capture the benefits of both centralized and decentralized structures by creating an organizational structure that is neither completely centralized nor decentralized (see Figure 7-9). Both the product/brand management model and the geographic model can be used in a hybrid structure. Instead of pushing

**Figure 7-9 Potential Advantages of the Hybrid Structure**

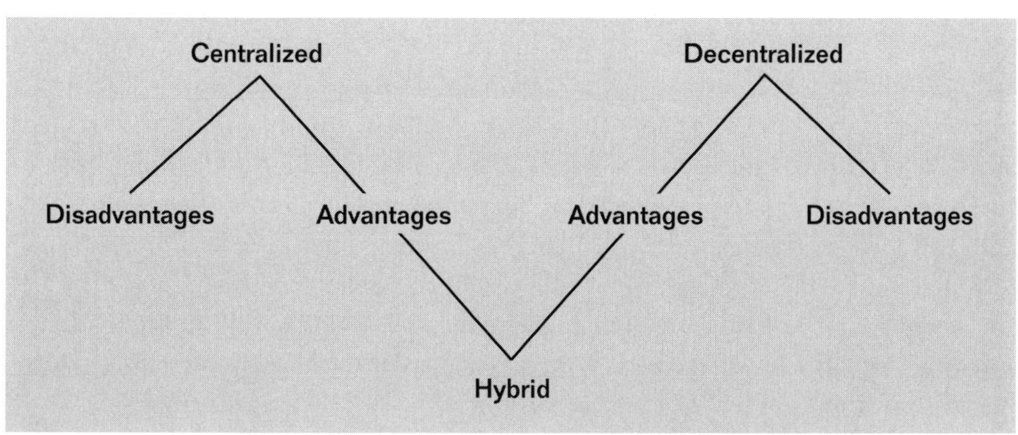


*Source:* M.R. Leenders, P.F. Johnson, A.E. Flynn and H.E. Fearon, *Purchasing and Supply Management* (Burr Ridge: McGraw-Hill/Irwin, 2005), 38. Reprinted with permission of The McGraw-Hill Companies.

all decision-making to the product/brand level or to a specific geographic location, decision-making may be shared between the corporate supply management group and the supply management professional at the product/brand or geographic level.

Organizations with a commitment to both a decentralized structure and spend aggregation find ways to leverage spend without changing the basic organizational structure. For example, Illinois Tool Works, Inc., (ITW), a $12 billion diversified manufacturing organization, with 650 decentralized business units in 45 countries, prides itself on decentralized, and relatively autonomous, management in its various divisions. Therefore, Gary Anton, vice president of strategic sourcing and IT, suggested a strategic-sourcing fleet program to senior management that would not be mandated to the divisions. Through acquisition growth, ITW's fleet had grown to 7,500 vehicles, with approximately 4,000 of these in the United States. In addition, ITW had arrangements with dozens of fleet suppliers, consisting of large and small lessors, as well as local dealerships and shops. The organization owned 20 percent to 25 percent of its fleet and leased the remainder. The problem, of course, is that savings cannot be realized until a critical mass of business units is on board in the first place. ITW estimates that it has saved about $3 million a year as a result of the centralized fleet-management program. There was not much resistance to ITW's corporate program because the costs and benefits in terms of costs, service and quality were identified and the aggressive agreements have resulted in strong benefits at the business unit level. Clearly, if it is more difficult to make the case for business unit participation or benefits are shared unequally across units, spend consolidation may be harder to sell.[9] At Rockwell Collins, the organization's two businesses — government systems and commercial systems — were brought together and their material and supply management operations were consolidated. Recently, the organization has started to organize around technologies as a way to further eliminate waste and improve processes. The material and supply management operation is a corporate shared service. Rockwell Collins has 13 manufacturing sites in the United States. Supply-chain managers at small facilities (less than $50 million) report (directly) to Kent Statler, senior vice president, operations, and on a dotted line to Roger Weiss, vice president, material and supply. Together they form a supply-chain council that meets regularly to share best practices. "We can look a supplier in the eye and say we are one company," says Weiss, who has standardized sourcing and supply-chain processes throughout his organization.[10]

## Impact of Supply Management Structure

Organizational structure affects individuals within the supply management organization and individuals in other functions and business processes as well as external players such as suppliers. It is important for the supply management professional to fully comprehend the implications of the supply management structure and anticipate the responses and reactions of those affected by the structure to ensure optimal performance. The supply management structure affects workload distribution within the organization.

**Workload Distribution.** Work must be distributed to supply management personnel no matter which structure is in place. Depending on the size and capability of the supply management group, workload is typically distributed on the basis of (1) commodity or class, (2) department, (3) special project, (4) volume, (5) rotation, (6) type of contract, (7) staff expertise or (8) supplier.[11] Each of these approaches is discussed in the following section.

COMMODITY OR CLASS. Assignments can be made to supply management professionals based on the various commodities that the organization requires. The term *commodity* means all goods and services purchased by an organization. Each supply management professional may specialize in a group of similar commodities or in a single commodity (generally in the case of large organizations), where it is a significant enough part of product cost to justify the position and where the supply management professional has a strong product orientation. There are a number of ways to categorize purchases, including monetary delineations, separating critical from standard commodities or by individual units.

*Pareto analysis* (also known as ABC analysis or the 80:20 rule) can be used to categorize purchases according to dollar value. By conducting this analysis, managers can identify the 10 percent to 20 percent of purchased goods and services on which they spend 80 percent to 90 percent of the total annual expenditures. These 'A' items, and the suppliers of these items, would be the commodities on which the greatest resources (time, people and attention) would be focused. For example, spend might be split into three major commodity groups using the ABC method with plateaus for dollar spend.

The high-value 'A' items (such as those above $5 million) might be critical mass items. These might include raw materials, such as grains, fuels, and metals. 'B' items (such as those between $1 and $5 million) might include a specific packaging item. The 'C' purchases (such as those under $1 million) could include MRO items. In each commodity grouping, supply management professionals need different levels of knowledge and skills. Commodity teams with strategic skills would handle the over $5 million items. The 'B' items require less team emphasis, and the 'C' items fall into the transactional category.

*Portfolio analysis* (presented at length in *Foundation of Supply Management* (ISM Professional Series)) is another approach that assigns risk levels to value levels to further refine the categories. Figure 7-10 is one example of this approach. This analysis recognizes the importance of marketplace risk of acquiring a category when determining resource allocation for management of a specific commodity. Portfolio analysis results in four quadrants often referred to as noncritical, leverage, bottleneck and strategic. This approach is discussed in more detail in Chapter 8 and also in *Foundation of Supply Management* (ISM Professional Series).

**DEPARTMENT.** When purchase requisitions are assigned by department orientation, this means that the supply management professional handles requests from certain departments assigned to the supply management professional. This type of supply management professonal is more oriented toward serving the department and handling all of its needs, as opposed to the commodity supply management professional whose focus is more on what is being purchased than for whom it is being purchased.

**SPECIAL PROJECT.** Requisitions may be assigned according to a special project or a new product line. The buyer may be assigned to provide the materials and services to support the needs of a certain project. This is often applied to the case of a research laboratory or construction project. For example, after a competitive source selection process, supplier partnering may be used in construction contracts. The project team, consisting of the buyer's project representatives and the contractor's representatives,

Figure 7-10 Portfolio Analysis

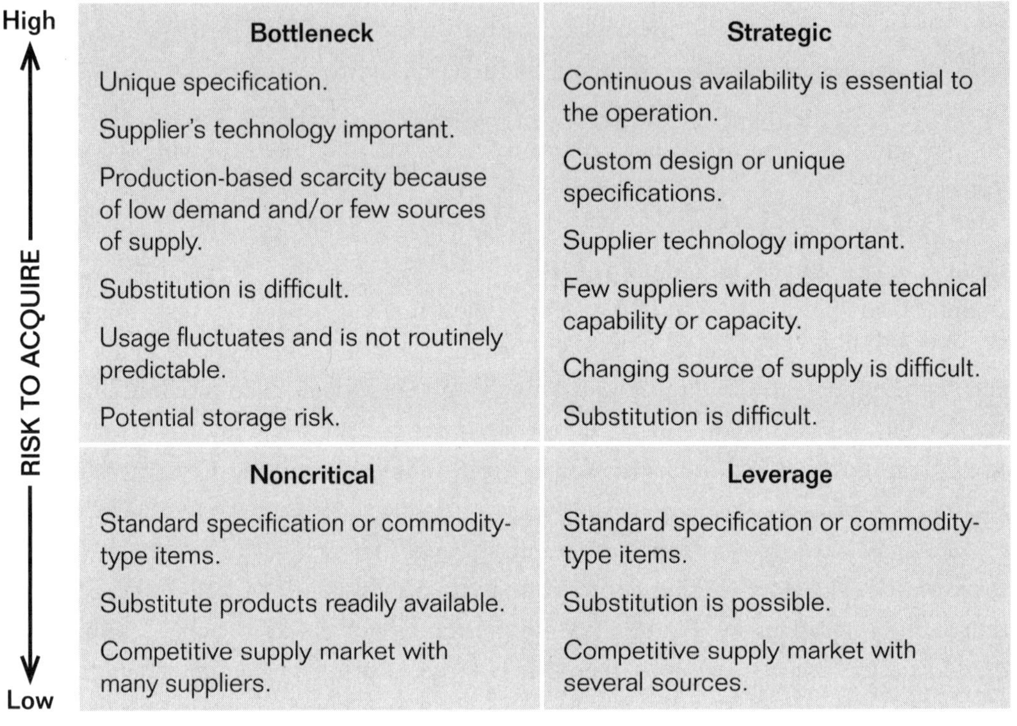


*Source:* Adapted from Peter Kraljic, "Purchasing Must Become Supply Management," *Harvard Business Review* (1983); available from www.harvard.edu.

meet to identify shared objectives and establish a decision-making process that will be applied to every issue that comes up on the job. The contracts typically contain cost-incentive provisions that encourage contractors to propose innovations to reduce costs during the contract term, and provide that they will share the benefits of the reductions. This approach typically has led to sharply reduced claims, and projects completed ahead of schedule and under budget.

**Volume.** So that the buyers in a department might have similar levels of responsibility, some departments make assignments based on dollar volume or number of requisitions handled annually. Care must be exercised in this case to ensure that the workload is reasonably distributed. Consider the difference in the nature and criticality of the tasks of an MRO buyer handling hundreds of low-value transactions versus the capital equipment buyer who spends as much on a single machine tool.

**Rotation.** Some organizations rotate supply professionals through different buying groups to develop expertise and tap as wide a range of skills as possible. The focus is less on the purchase activity itself and more on the individual's training. Rotational programs are often used to train new hires before placing them in a permanent position. This allows the new employee to understand the various jobs and functions within the supply management department, to forge relationships with coworkers and to help the employee and the manager decide where the employee's skills can best be used.

The rotational method might also be used in a very routine situation such as replenishing crib items. The supply professionals are rotated regularly to broaden their experience and to keep the work from becoming too routine.

**Type of Contract.** Assigning workloads according to the type of contract is especially useful if specific types of contracting involve a steep learning curve. One approach to delineating contracts is to apply portfolio analysis to develop a matrix of contract alternatives. For example, contracts that fall into the "Strategic" segment in Figure 7-10 represent the greatest risk, require increased resource commitments and probably entail more complex terms and conditions. Better supplier segmentation and contract selection will result in reduced cycle time of contract negotiations and more informed understanding of risk and increased optimization of the purchaser's time to achieve cost savings.

**Staff Expertise Assigned by Category.** Distributing the workload according to the skills and capabilities of the persons in the group is also used. This approach can be employed in conjunction with any number of the other methods. For instance, a manager may conduct a portfolio analysis and identify critical suppliers for each quadrant: (1) acquisition, (2) critical, (3) leverage and (4) strategic. Major categories of spend would be assigned to each quadrant based on an assessment of risk to acquire and value to the organization. For example, in a fast casual restaurant that specializes in ribs, strategic spend items might include beef ribs, signature sauces and customized seasonings. Bottleneck items might include agricultural products in short supply that season because of weather-related production problems or unavailability due to farmers transitioning to corn production for ethanol rather than for corn syrup or feed. Leverage items might include standardized restaurant supplies and food items, and noncritical items might include restaurant supplies procured on a unit rather than a corporate basis. The skills required of the supply management professional assigned to each category would be tailored to achieve the goal of each category. Figure 7-11 gives an example of possible categories, the key goal for each and the associated skill sets required of personnel.

**Supplier.** Finally, requisitions might be assigned by suppliers or groups of suppliers. This sort is according to suppliers or groups of suppliers. This is often the genesis of the supplier relationship manager concept discussed in *Foundation of Supply Management* (ISM Professional Series).

**Figure 7-11 Goals and Skill Sets by Category**

| CATEGORY | KEY GOAL | REQUIRED SKILL SET |
|---|---|---|
| Noncritical | Minimize acquisition time and cost. | Efficient, able to establish and follow simple procedures and process; can recognize and eliminate non-value-adding process steps. |
| Bottleneck | Short term: Ensure supply availability.<br><br>Long term: Eliminate. | Short term: Able to create options for mutual gain; creative thinker able to identify value for the supplier.<br><br>Long term: Strong collaboration and negotiation skills to work internally on specification or statement of work to take out unnecessary customization. |
| Leverage | Minimize acquisition time and cost and procure at lowest price/cost. | Efficient and good at price analysis, focused on total costs especially nonprice-related process costs; strong ability to identify appropriate tools to drive lowest price per unit without adverse impact on process costs. |
| Strategic | Ensure continuous availability and work with suppliers to build competitive advantage. | Strong cost analysis and cost management skills, relationship builder, good negotiator, creative thinker, strong capability to work in teams with disparate stakeholders. |

*Source:* Adapted from Peter Kraljic, "Purchasing Must Become Supply Management," *Harvard Business Review* (September/October 1983).

## Organizing Human Resources

Implicit in decisions about organizational structure are decisions that affect human resources. These decisions address three main questions:

1. What is the chain of command in the organization?
2. What authority and responsibility should be delegated and to whom?
3. What is each person's span of influence?

**Chain of Command.** The chain of command refers to the line of authority and responsibility in the hierarchy of an organization. The chain reflects the organizational structure. In a functional organization, each function reports up to a higher level of supervision within that function. All functions ultimately report up to the head of the organization. In a divisional organization, where divisions are based on geography, each function in the division reports up to the president of the division who then reports to the CEO of the organization. In a matrix organization, people report to a functional superior as well as to a project superior. The supply management professional must be aware of the chain of command and work to develop his or her abilities to operate and influence within that chain. He or she must also coach subordinates about working within the chain of command while also extending their span of influence (discussed in Chapter 4).

**Delegation of Authority and Responsibility.** Delegation is a transfer of power from a superior to a subordinate. Organizational success depends in part on the ability of managers to delegate successfully. Decisions must be made about how and to whom authority and responsibility will be delegated. This relationship requires the superior to develop and empower subordinates to make certain decisions within the scope of the superior's position. The person performing the actions and the superior share accountability for the outcome. Successful delegation depends on superiors who are willing and able to coach and develop subordinates and allow them to make decisions within established parameters and to learn from their mistakes. Employees must also be given appropriate authority to carry out the responsibilities that have been delegated. Successful delegation depends in large measure on the skills and abilities of the staff so the leader-manager must pay careful attention to hiring, retention and the ongoing development of employees. These topics are addressed in Chapter 9.

In the supply management organization, decisions must be made about what should and should not be delegated. Some of the decisions about delegation are made in conjunction with decisions about organizational and supply management structure. The decision to adopt a highly decentralized supply management structure implies that responsibility and authority will be delegated to a broad range of employees throughout the organization. In a more centralized structure, transactional activities are delegated.

The tools adopted by the supply management group also have implications for delegation. For example, the adoption of an e-procurement system carries with it the implicit decision to delegate some level of buying authority to system users. The degree of authority granted depends on the decisions made about what can be purchased through the system, which suppliers are part of the system and how those suppliers will be paid. From a policy perspective, decisions must also be made about the delegation of spending authority and the levels of approval required for specific supply management decisions.

There are three steps to successful delegation within the supply management function:

1. The objectives of supply management must be laid out along with the specific tasks that constitute execution of the objective. Then decisions can be made about the appropriate level of execution — at corporate, in the field, in the user group, etc., and the skill sets needed to execute the task.

2. Policies and procedures need to clearly articulate the plan of action for executing the tasks consistently no matter who is doing the activity. These might include desired results, guidelines, available resources, timelines and consequences.

3. The delegated tasks must be monitored for effectiveness and efficiency and adjustments made to processes, policies, procedures or people, depending on the outcome.

## Systems and Processes

Systems and processes are integral parts of the infrastructure of an organization. The supply management professional has primary responsibility for ensuring that supply management systems and processes are designed and/or redesigned to support the organization's strategy and goals, including sales goals. To ensure this alignment, the supply management professional must be knowledgeable about the link between customer requirements and supply management and ensure that supply management contributes to customer satisfaction. To this end, supply management professionals must focus on developing strong internal business relationships (see Chapter 4) based on a greater understanding of, and linkage to:

- Customer segmentation
- Product and service pricing strategy

- Sales performance to plan
- Product and technology roadmaps of key suppliers and customers
- Financial and information flows up and down the supply chain
- Critical customer service factors
- Customer and supplier collaboration processes

## Customer Segmentation

Customer segmentation is the process of grouping customers with similar characteristics to better manage customer relationships, meet existing customer needs and identifying unmet needs. Typically, segmentation focuses on identifying customer groups based on demographics and attributes such as attitude and psychological profiles. A different approach, value-based segmentation, groups customers in terms of the revenue they generate and the costs of establishing and maintaining relationships with them. According to David Ross, another approach is based on lifetime customer value (LCV). LCV calculates customer profitability by taking the total sales revenue of a customer over the lifetime of the relationship, discounted by interest and inflation. Whatever the method, the goal of segmentation is to quantitatively determine exactly how each customer segment is contributing to or detracting from the profitability of each supply-chain node and the supply network overall.[12] With the data from customer segments, managers can identify underserved segments and focus on outperforming the competition by quickly developing uniquely appealing products and services. Customer segmentation is most effective when an organization tailors offerings to segments that are the most profitable and serves them with distinct competitive advantages. This prioritization can help organizations develop marketing campaigns and pricing strategies to extract maximum value from both high-profit and low-profit customers. An organization can use customer segmentation as the principal basis for allocating resources to product development, marketing, pricing, service, sourcing, distribution and delivery programs.

Greater knowledge about customer segments coupled with equally comprehensive knowledge about strategic suppliers enables the supply management professional to enhance the abilities of the organization's supply management professionals to contribute to customer satisfaction and ultimately organizational profitability.

## Product and Service Pricing Strategy

An understanding of the organization's pricing strategy and supply management's contribution to this strategy is one of the hallmarks of a more progressive supply management organization. Too often, supply management personnel are focused on cost-cutting without necessarily connecting cost-cutting goals to overall organizational strategy. This leaves open the possibility that the supply management strategies employed will conflict with or be detrimental to the organization's ability to maintain its pricing strategy in the marketplace.

For example, an organization's products or services might be experiencing downward pressure on prices because of competition. Supply management professionals need to know what is happening and why so that they can proactively develop supply management strategies that enable the organization to remain competitive and attain projected margins. Target costing (discussed in *Foundation of Supply Management* (ISM Professional Series)) is one tool that links three critical elements: (1) pricing strategy, (2) operating profit goals and (3) cost management by designing to cost.

## Sales Performance to Plan

Knowledge of sales performance to plan is another valuable information stream that links supply management with organizational strategy. This is especially important if supply management professionals are to serve on cross-functional teams designed to determine the root cause of declining sales or slower-than-projected growth. The ability to accurately forecast and to accurately track sales performance to plan varies greatly within and across industries. For example, in the quick service restaurant business limited time offers (LTOs), such as a special salad during the summer season, are a commonly used method for testing menu items, increasing frequency of visits, bringing in new traffic and increasing revenues and margins. In many small to medium-sized chain restaurants with a large number of franchisees and no single IT platform, it is difficult to accurately forecast LTO sales and equally difficult to track actual sales and inventory in real time so that ingredients can quickly be moved to top selling locations. Food manufacturers are often asked to produce more in a shortened timeframe when sales exceed forecasts or to take back product when forecasts are too high. Implementing supply chain technology and developing appropriate relationships with supply chain members are two critical pieces of a successful program for managing sales performance to plan.

## Product and Technology Roadmaps of Key Suppliers and Customers

A roadmap is a plan that identifies the routes to a particular destination. A technology or product roadmap focuses on a single technology or product, describes the way it is expected to develop, and may include project plans to support that development. Figure 7-12 illustrates this process for the matchup of generations of technology to generations of a product. The roadmap focuses on forecasting development and

Figure 7-12 Product Planning Roadmap

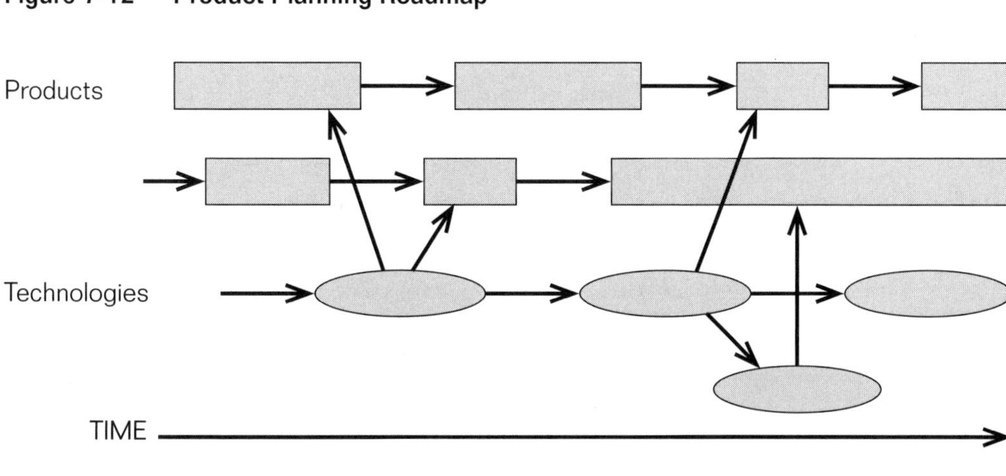


commercialization of a new technology, the organization's competitive position relative to the technology, and how the technology and the organization's competitive position will develop. The roadmap may influence resource allocation, and it may be used to form subsections of complex product maps with development time frames, milestones and ways to leverage R&D investments through coordinating research activities.

New or emerging technologies may be acquired, developed internally or developed externally with a partner. Supply management may play several roles in product and technology roadmaps, including influencing which technology will be used before new product design begins, assessing the risk of switching to new technologies, determining the impact on the supply chain, working with engineering to evaluate and determine which suppliers will be included in new product development and monitoring suppliers' investments in technologies needed in the future.

Commodity managers at Cisco Systems, Inc., in San Jose, California, work with engineers to determine which technology is the best fit for future networking products. For instance, they helped determine when Cisco's switch from synchronous DRAM to double data rate DRAMs should occur and which suppliers should be used. They also helped determine Cisco's switch from ASICs made on .13 micron technology to 90 nm process technology and are now monitoring when it makes sense to move to 65 nm technology. Commodity managers also help determine which suppliers would be included in new product development efforts and carefully monitor technology roadmaps to make sure suppliers are investing in the technologies that Cisco will need in the future. "Engaging with engineering, understanding technology roadmaps and getting lined up with the right suppliers allows us to make the right decisions to meet the requirements for our products," says John Kern, senior director for global supply commodity management. "At the same time, we can make decisions that really mitigate potential issues downstream. If you do a good job up front you have fewer quality issues, pricing related problems and delivery problems. You can focus on prevention versus chasing issues."[13]

Involving commodity management in design has resulted in a dramatic reduction in the number of suppliers, better quality and lower inventory levels and increased inventory turns. Cisco reduced its supplier base from close to 1,500 in early 2001 with 80 percent of spend with about 200 suppliers to about 650 total suppliers and 90 percent of overall spend with 93 suppliers. In addition to designing for the supply chain — for manufacturability, quality and reliability — Cisco designs for risk. Commodity management has developed a risk-rating process to help engineers avoid designing in parts that may have availability problems. The risk-rating process is an integral part of Cisco's new product introduction (NPI).[14]

At Rockwell Collins, Inc., material and supply management becomes involved early on through an online tool it developed called Impact that steers product designers to preferred or "Maximize" suppliers. Engineers who choose to use parts provided by other suppliers must get additional approvals and develop a risk-management plan. Application-engineering (AE) specialists who serve on cross-functional commodity teams are material and management supply's direct link to Rockwell Collins' product design teams. AE specialists also are deployed throughout the organization to work with engineers on products with unique requirements. And a senior operations leader serves on major new development teams (such as equipment for the Boeing 787); this individual has ties back to material and supply and works to minimize risk associated with making the move from engineering to manufacturing.[15]

### Financial and Information Flows Up and Down the Supply Chain

Supply-chain management is concerned with customers' customers' customers and suppliers' suppliers' suppliers. Financial and information flows up and down the supply chain enable better management of supply chains relative to competing supply chains. Managers and leaders of various supply management areas must partner internally with finance and information technology to ensure that financial and other information flows enable effective and efficient decision-making.

### Critical Customer Service Factors

Along with knowledge and understanding of customer segmentation, supply management professionals need to stay current on critical customer service factors. The ability of the organization to meet customer service requirements in part depends on supply management performance. Stronger links between sales and marketing and supply management may lead to better overall organizational performance.

## Customer and Supplier Collaboration Processes

Collaboration up and down the supply chain or network, from customers through tiers of suppliers, enables managers to better satisfy customer needs in a timelier manner. By aligning demand management with supply management, results can be achieved with lower levels of inventory and better asset use at a lower total cost of ownership. However, there must be greater integration of systems throughout the supplier network to capture and share this information.

Lack of systems integration internally and externally with major suppliers and major customers continues to plague most organizations. According to Noha Tohamy, a supply-chain and pricing-solutions analyst at Forrester Research, "There's no significant integration between manufacturers and their suppliers' and customers' enterprise systems."[16] Supporting her claim, more than 60 percent of organizations responding to an April 2006 Aberdeen Group survey described their current supply-chain processes as manual, spreadsheet-intensive, only partially automated and dependent on different software systems within their own organizations. According to a July 2006 IDC survey that asked organizations to describe how they collaborated with their supply-chain part-ners, the most cited method was e-mail (88 percent) followed by fax (73 percent), telephone (62 percent) and snail mail (59 percent).[17]

The time and resources required for successful integration can be daunting whether the connection is via e-mail, the Web or more complex linkages such as electronic data interchange (EDI) or RosettaNet. For example, at Agere Systems, the IT staff took nine months to set up an electronic trading connection to each major supplier or customer. Further complicating things, each connection was supported by different, inefficient processes inside the organization. Supply management staffers tracked down orders via phone, fax or e-mail, and manually keyed in EDI data into Agere's Oracle ERP system.[18]

An emerging category of integrators is third-party, hosted options that successfully blend traditional value-added network (VAN) capabilities with on-demand, hosted supply-chain software and back-office integration services. Organizations in this evolving market, such as E2open, GXS, Inovis and Sterling Commerce, offer a single point of data exchange — whether using EDI, RosettaNet or XML standards — that acts as a gateway for partner-to-partner, enterprise system integration and collaboration.

## Supply Management Technologies

The supply management process is driven by customers and it is only with a thorough knowledge and understanding of the organization's customers, product and pricing strategies and sales goals that the supply management professional can make appropriate decisions about supply technology. The technology choices come after strategy and process and should enable attainment of organizational goals and objectives. The supply management professional plays a primary role in the identification, selection and implementation of technologies that support and enhance the efficiency and effectiveness of supply management processes.

The supply management professional clearly plays a critical role in managerial decisions about the organization of supply management from its structure to its processes and technology. His or her ability to lead and manage effectively in these three areas may be one of the leader-manager's greatest contributions. Structure, processes and technology form the infrastructure of supply management and either enhance or inhibit the ability of supply management professionals to contribute to the organization's success. The next chapter addresses the strategic sourcing process and enabling technologies. Chapter 9 covers the human capital side of the equation and discusses the role of the leader-manager in attracting, retaining and developing supply management professionals.

### Key Points

1. The degree of horizontal, vertical and spatial differentiation of organizational activities determines the complexity of the structure. The structure of the supply management organization reflects decisions made at an organizational level.

2. In a centralized structure, the authority and responsibility for most supply management–related functions is assigned to a central organization.

3. In a hybrid structure, authority and responsibility is shared between a central supply management organization and business units, divisions or operating plants. Hybrid structures may lean more heavily toward centralized or decentralized depending on how decision-making authority is divided.

4. In a decentralized structure, authority and responsibility for supply management–related functions are dispersed throughout the organization.

5. The supply management structure affects workload distribution within supply management. Depending on the size and capability of the supply management group, the workload is typically distributed on the basis of (1) commodity or class,

(2) department, (3) special project, (4) volume, (5) in rotation, (6) type of contract, (7) staff expertise or (8) supplier.

6. Implicit in decisions about organizational structure are decisions that affect human resources in terms of the chain of command, how and to whom authority and responsibility is delegated and each person's span of influence.

7. The supply management professional has primary responsibility for ensuring that supply management systems and processes are designed and/or redesigned to support the organization's strategy and goals. This requires greater understanding of and linkage to: customer segmentation, product and service pricing strategy, sales performance to plan, product and technology roadmaps of key suppliers and customers, financial and information flows up and down the supply chain, critical customer service factors and customer and supplier collaboration processes.

CHAPTER

8

# Developing a Strategic Sourcing Process and Adopting Enabling Technology

*If you can't describe what you are doing as a process, you don't know what you're doing.* W. EDWARDS DEMING[1]

An organization is a collection of processes that are performed to attain the organization's goals. Managing these processes is basic to the success of the organization. However, many organizations are not organized around processes; they are organized around functions as was discussed in the previous chapter. Consequently, people are organized into functional departments such as manufacturing, supply management, sales and marketing, customer service and accounting. People in a function usually focus on performing the function rather than on managing a process. Consequently, subprocesses evolve within departments without consideration of the impact on other functional areas. The goals of the organization can easily get lost in the activities of the functions. Layers of communication and management are created to ensure desired outcomes, thus adding costs and lengthening cycle and customer response times. Inefficiency and waste become part of the system, robbing the organization of profits, productivity and competitive advantage.

Business processes must be designed to focus people's attention on what really matters: how each process and its relationship and integration with other key business processes drives toward organizational goal attainment. The objective is for the organization, or collection of business processes, to increase competitiveness by becoming more responsive in the marketplace while reducing total costs.

This chapter focuses on the strategic sourcing process and is organized in four sections: (1) an overview of the strategic sourcing process, (2) developing strategic sourcing plans, (3) leveraging spend through sourcing strategies and (4) market analysis of e-solutions.

**CHAPTER OBJECTIVES**

- Define what a process is and discuss the strategic sourcing process.
- Explain how strategic sourcing plans might be developed and executed based on a category map.
- Explore different types of leveraging strategies and when and where they are applicable.
- Discuss the role of policies and procedures in supporting a rigorous strategic sourcing process.
- Discuss the technologies that might be used to increase efficiency in various parts of the process.

## An Overview of the Strategic Sourcing Process

A process is a set of activities that has a beginning and an end; these activities occur in a specific sequence, with inputs and outputs. The process design team answers a series of questions: Where does the process start? Where does it end? What are the steps in the process and how should they be sequenced? What are the inputs and outputs? Process design teams in different organizations may arrive at different answers based on the organization's vision, mission, structure, stakeholders' interests and external forces. People may have the same starting point and ending point but consider different inputs or outputs or do things in a different sequence leading to different processes. For example, a group of parents needs to establish a process to make 100 tacos for a children's event. One person lists the inputs as hard taco shells, pork, shredded lettuce, tomato and cheese. Another lists them as soft taco shells, chorizo and cheese. One person thinks the process begins with going to the market to buy masa to make taco shells and ends with each child assembling his or her own taco. Another person thinks the process begins with going to the market to buy taco shells and ends with the parents serving assembled tacos to their children. The strategic sourcing process across organizations is a lot like making tacos. The basic ingredients are similar, but there are many variations on the theme.

Institute for Supply Management™ (ISM) defines the supply management process as the identification, acquisition, access, positioning and management of resources and related capabilities that an organization needs or potentially needs to attain its strategic objectives. This includes the following components: disposition/investment recovery, distribution, inventory control, logistics, manufacturing supervision, materials management, packaging, product/service development, procurement/purchasing, quality, receiving, strategic sourcing, transportation/traffic/shipping and warehousing. Strategic sourcing is a subprocess within the supply management process.

ISM defines strategic sourcing as "the selection and management of suppliers with a focus on achieving the long-term goals of a business." Therefore, the strategic sourcing process in any organization is a clearly defined set of steps with starting and ending points in a specific sequence focused on selecting and managing suppliers to achieve the long-term goals of the business. This section provides one approach to developing a strategic sourcing process and then gives examples from several organizations. Strategic sourcing does not apply to all purchasing situations, but is generally applied when the purchase reaches a certain organization-specific dollar threshold or presents a certain level of risk or criticality to the organization. Typically, a strategic sourcing process includes the following steps or phases:

1. Data management and analysis
2. Category strategy and development
3. Cost analysis and management
4. Select, negotiate and contract
5. Supplier development and performance management

## Step 1: Data Management and Analysis

This step includes categorizing the spend and analyzing the market.

**Categorize Spend.** To categorize spend, the sourcing team must first be able to capture spend data and analyze how much is spent on what and from whom. Spend is classified into major spend categories. This step allows for a thorough internal analysis of requirements and the role of each requirement in the organization's products and services. This is a critical first step in aligning sourcing strategy with organizational strategic goals. This helps determine the level of time and resources that supply management should invest in the strategic sourcing process for a given purchase situation.

**Analyze the Market.** Determine the market structure (monopoly, oligopoly, etc.) and the number and nature of capable suppliers globally. *Effective Supply Management Performance* (ISM Professional Series) addresses this in detail.

## Step 2: Develop a Category Strategy

Based on the internal and external scans in step 1, the sourcing team can now begin to develop a category strategy. For example, discussions might focus on the desired number and size of the suppliers, the location and proximity, and the type of relationship to be developed. This allows the team to compare where they are currently in terms of managing a specific category and where they want and need to be in the future.

**Conduct Market Intelligence.** This is a crucial element at this point. Market intelligence is the process and the result of gathering and analyzing information about the aggregate forces (including economics) at work in trade and commerce in a specific service or commodity. Using the information gathered on internal requirements and the nature of the supplier market, the sourcing team can develop a short list of potential suppliers.

## Step 3: Cost Management

Based on the organization's needs, past experience and industry data, the organization needs to develop an understanding of a reasonable expected price for the materials, goods or capital it is acquiring. This may involve some combination of the following, all of which are discussed at length in *Foundation of Supply Management* (ISM Professional Series):

- *Cost analysis.* An evaluation of actual or anticipated cost data (material, labor, overhead, general and administrative and profit). The application of experience, knowledge and judgment to data to project reasonable estimated contract costs. Estimated costs serve as the basis for buyer-seller negotiation to arrive at mutually agreeable contract prices.
- *Price analysis.* The examination of a supplier's price proposal or bid by comparison with reasonable benchmarks, without examination and evaluation of the separate elements of cost and profit making up the price.
- *Total cost of ownership.* The combination of the purchase or acquisition price of a good or service and additional costs incurred before or after product or service delivery. Costs are often grouped into pretransaction, transaction and post-transaction costs or into acquisition price and in-house costs. To use cost of ownership analysis as a cost-reduction tool, it is necessary to identify and analyze the cost drivers to look for any avoidable costs.

This will help as the organization further clarifies its specifications or statement of work. At this stage, the organization should also be ready to develop a bid package and send a RFX. The description of the requirement is a major cost driver. Therefore, the development of a clear and unambiguous description of the need is a primary focus of the sourcing team. This is also a main reason that supply management professionals must develop strong internal partnerships (see Chapter 4) to keep costs out from the earliest stages of the process. The RFX is issued to the short list of candidates (see *Foundation of Supply Management* (ISM Professional Series) for more information on the solicitation process).

### Step 4: Negotiate and Contract

This entails the evaluation and selection of supplier(s). The sourcing team analyzes responses, possibly makes site visits and narrows down the list of potential suppliers. As part of this step, the team may develop a negotiation plan (if appropriate). If negotiation is to be used, the team assesses the interests, options and walk-away alternatives of the stakeholders of both or all parties and develops a negotiation strategy. Negotiation, rather than an online or offline bidding event, which is typically used for complex items, high-dollar items and spend categories where buyer-supplier collaboration is desired, is presented in more depth in *Foundation of Supply Management* (ISM Professional Series).

This intensive step also involves putting an agreement/contract in place and managing it. A contract or purchase order is executed. The sourcing team as well as other stakeholders should see the contract as a means to an end. The real goal is performance. The team should work to ensure that the process to this point has been building commitment to perform on the parts of supply management and the supplier.

### Step 5: Supplier Development: Build and Manage the Relationship

The sourcing team should determine the appropriate buyer-supplier relationship and develop an action plan for attaining the right relationship. Monitoring and feedback loops are especially important for longer-term and more strategic relationships. If the supplier does not meet expectations initially, or as the relationship develops, and the buying organization still deems that this supplier is the best available choice, it may invest extensive assets or efforts in working with the supplier to develop its capabilities.

For example, ChevronTexaco Corp., one of the world's largest integrated petroleum companies, is active in 180 countries and employs 53,000 people worldwide. The vision of the company's Global Procurement Organization is to leverage the company's worldwide spending power: "Spending money smarter, without compromising quality and service."[2] The goal of supply management is to elevate the company's global supply management business processes to achieve a sustained worldwide competitive advantage among its peers. At ChevronTexaco, strategic sourcing consists of four distinct stages (see Figure 8-1): (1) data analysis, (2) develop strategy and set targets, (3) supplier selection and negotiation and (4) final contracting.[3]

**Figure 8-1 ChevronTexaco's Strategic Sourcing Process**

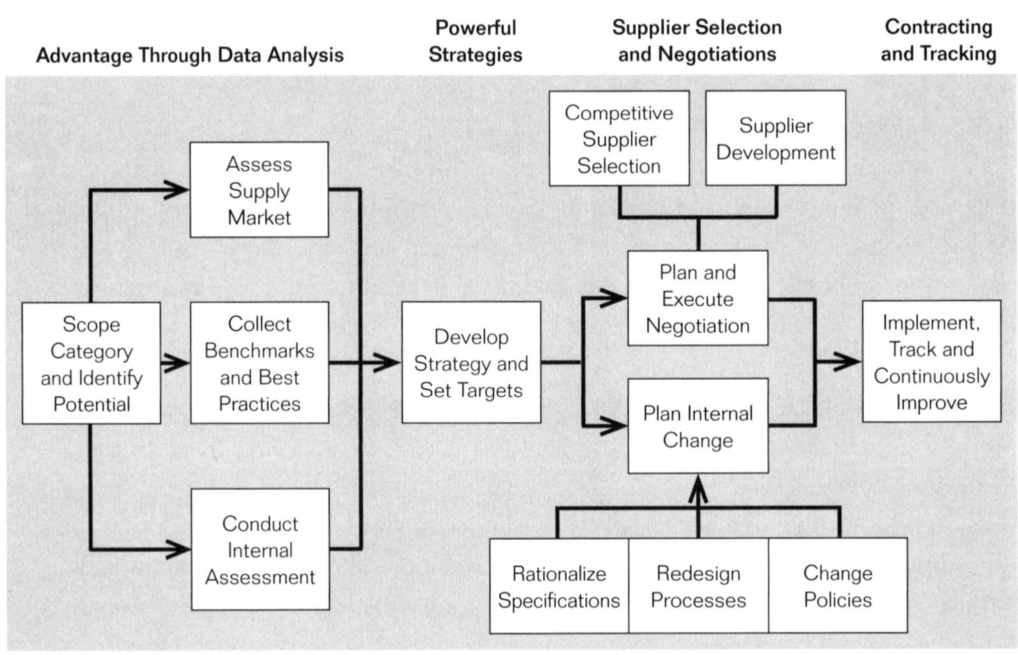


*Source:* Joseph Carter, Thomas Y. Choi and Lisa Ellram

At Bank of America, strategic sourcing is defined as:

- An organized, systematic, collaborative process for establishing and maintaining spend category relationships with suppliers.
- An ongoing process that applies joint expertise to new product and service designs, creates genuine and unique supply management advantages and revenue opportunities and spurs innovation.
- Use of a strategy to define and rule sourcing decisions.
- Consideration of the global marketplace while uniting business intelligence with market intelligence.
- Understanding the line-of-business objectives and creating strategic relationships that meet these objectives.
- Developing and institutionalizing the application of an integrated suite of sourcing tools/techniques (e.g., spend analysis, spend aggregation, demand

management, supply base rationalization, e-sourcing, supplier risk management, industry analyses).

- Creating competitive advantage.[4]

At the former Gillette Co., now Global Gillette and operating as a business unit of Procter & Gamble, the strategic sourcing process consists of seven steps: (1) develop a category profile, (2) generate the supplier portfolio, (3) develop sourcing strategy, (4) select an implementation path, (5) negotiate and select suppliers, (6) operationalize new contracts and (7) sustain the results.[5]

The basic ingredients are present in each of these examples yet they have been adapted to fit the organization.

## Developing Strategic Sourcing Plans

If supply management is to play a more strategic role in the organization, it must anticipate and guide, rather than react to, internal user requests for goods and services. This analysis and involvement in the earliest stages of strategy development and product and service design and development should align with five strategy areas: (1) operational, (2) financial, (3) marketing, (4) supply management and (5) technology. Supply management's boundary-spanning role means that supply management professionals can directly influence and impact these strategic areas.

### Operational

In any type of organization, an overriding concern is keeping operations running smoothly. The sourcing group plays a key role in the operational success of an organization. Coordination and cooperation between sourcing and operations is crucial. If sourcing is given insufficient time to obtain a needed item or service, the organization may sacrifice efficiency, competitive position or a negotiation edge. The end result of sourcing inefficiency is often higher total cost of ownership, special production runs or service delivery, or premium transportation or service provider costs and ultimately lower customer satisfaction.

### Financial

How and when an organization commits its funds depends on market trends, market and organizational forecasts and risk assessment. At the need recognition and description stages, the sourcing team should analyze the buying plan to determine its appropriateness given economic factors and overall organizational goals. Deciding to buy in advance (forward buy) because of anticipated price increases or supply shortages despite increased carrying costs may be an excellent decision if cost analyses indicate lower total cost of ownership. Forward-buying fuel was a strong factor contributing to Southwest Airline's exceptional financial performance. Southwest had strong profits when all the other U.S. airlines that did not forward buy their fuel were losing substantial sums of money.[6] Reviewing the decision to buy and carry inventory against financial and economic circumstances and cash management strategies allows supply to make the best contribution to the organization. Financial forecasts and trends provide supply management with the information necessary to make the greatest bottom-line contribution to the organization and assist in determining the appropriate exposure.

## Marketing

Sourcing plans should also fit with marketing strategies. Because sales forecasts often originate in marketing, the actual needs or purchase requirements of the organization flow down from sales forecasts. And because sales forecasts in most organizations are woefully inadequate, the sourcing group must track forecasts as accurately as possible and transmit this information to suppliers in a timely fashion so that suppliers will be able to plan and execute their fulfillment process effectively. In lieu of accurate forecasts, supply management may still contribute by sharing real-time information with suppliers and by working to develop postponement strategies and supplier-managed inventory strategies that will lessen the effects of inaccurate forecasts. Buying organizations drive up costs unnecessarily when the forecast is inaccurate and suppliers must rush to meet demand.

## Supply Management

Supply management strategies encompass all the various components of supply management. Sourcing strategies are one piece of this greater plan and must align with the plan of each of the other components. Part of the rationale for creating a supply management organization is that the structure will enable various functions and business processes to be integrated and aligned under the supply management umbrella. If this alignment does not occur, the supply management organization will find its own behavior and results undermining the business case for the supply management organization and its elevated level within the organization.

## Technology

Technology strategies at an organizationwide level are often focused on acquiring and implementing enterprisewide solutions that enable each function to work from a common database and that enhance customer interactions. As technology is used increasingly as an enabling strategy in supply management, sourcing strategies must be developed with consideration of the existing and future technological capabilities of the organization. This is especially true as an organization streamlines and automates the sourcing process and works to ensure that the supply base is appropriately electronically enabled.

## Leveraging Spend Through Sourcing Strategies

Different spend categories require different levels of resources such as money, time and the attention of people at various levels in the organization. Misallocation of resources equals waste. To avoid generating waste and ensure that spend categories are optimally managed, decisions must be made about how to segment spend. Then a sourcing strategy should be developed for each segment. There are several ways that supply management professionals segment spend, including type of spend — raw materials, packaging, services and so on; direct and indirect; and low, medium and high-dollar value through a Pareto analysis. A Pareto analysis is the process of determining the small minority of a population that accounts for the majority of a given effect. For example, in inventory management, 20 percent of the inventoried items account for 80 percent of the total dollars.

One approach that has been adapted and adopted by a wide variety of organizations is the portfolio analysis. Originally introduced by Peter Kraljic, this analysis results in a 2 × 2 matrix often referred to as the Kraljic Matrix. In this segmentation model, spend categories are assessed along two dimensions, the risk to acquire in the marketplace and the value or impact of the category on the organization.[7] Figure 8-2 describes the typical characteristics of the market and the item in each of the four quadrants. A spend and segmentation analysis may be conducted at an organization-wide level as part of an annual review of the organization's sourcing strategy. This analysis helps the supply management team identify potential risks and opportunities, and decide where it should focus attention over the coming year. Such an approach is followed by Corning Corp. and Colgate-Palmolive. Remember that data management and analysis is the first step of the strategic sourcing process, whether considering one item or the organization's entire spend portfolio.

### Developing Category Sourcing Strategies

As the second step of the strategic sourcing process, once an organization's spend has been mapped, sourcing strategies can be developed for each quadrant and refined for specific locations within a quadrant. General goals for each quadrant are listed in Figure 8-3.

**Figure 8-2 Characteristics of Quadrants**

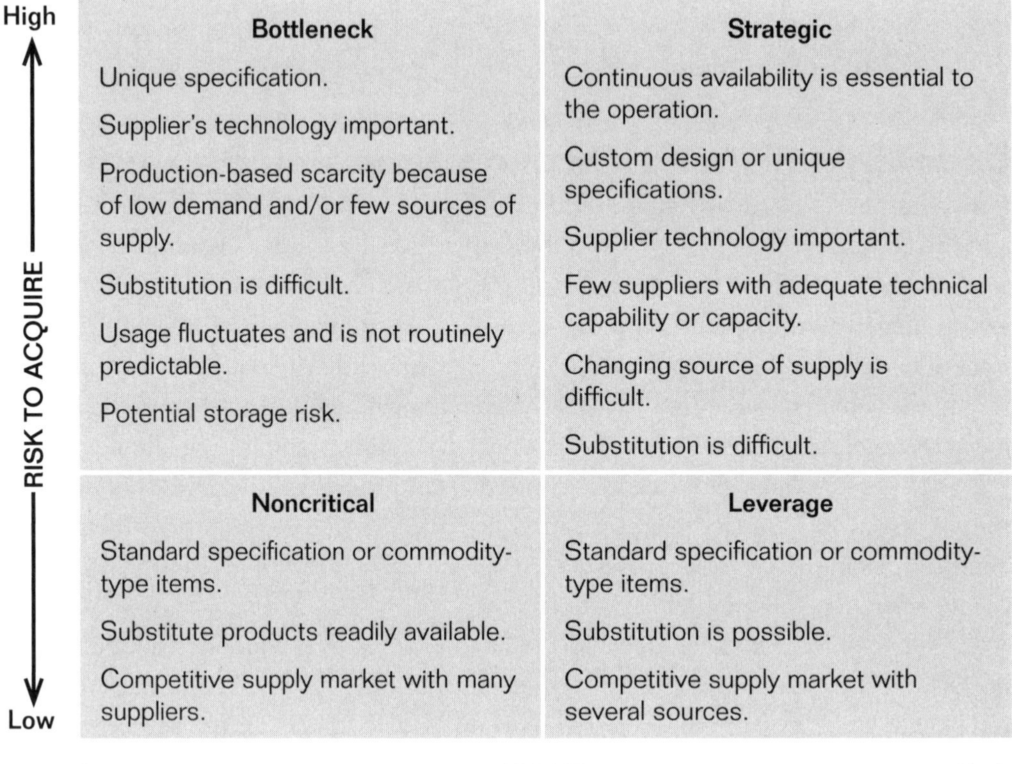


*Source:* Adapted from Peter Kraljic, "Purchasing Must Become Supply Management," *Harvard Business Review* (1983); available from www.harvardbusinessonline.hbsp.harvard.edu/b01/e/common/item_detail.jhtml?id=83509&referral=2342.

The development of a strategic sourcing process enables the organization to leverage spend through the identification, prioritization, development and execution of strategies. The implications of organizational structure on the ability to execute leveraging strategies is discussed in Chapter 7. From the supply management perspective, the opportunities that exist for an organization are driven in large part by the value of the spend category to the organization and the risks of acquiring a category in the marketplace. Supply management professionals at all levels of the supply management organization bear some responsibility for the development and/or execution of leveraging strategies.

**Figure 8-3 Basic Goals by Quadrant**

| Bottleneck | Strategic |
|---|---|
| Ensure supply availability in the short term and eliminate in the long term. | Diversify, balance or exploit.<br>To ensure continuous availability at the lowest total cost of ownership. |
| **Noncritical** | **Leverage** |
| Process efficiently.<br>Minimize acquisition cost and time. | Exploit purchasing power.<br>Focus on price or cost per unit and minimize acquisition cost and time. |

Spend segmentation enables the development of strategies that are best suited to the specific risk and value profile of the category. In general, process improvements are a primary goal when acquiring noncritical spend, spend aggregation is a useful strategy when trying to increase pricing leverage with suppliers, and capturing supplier innovation may be best suited to strategic inputs. The appropriate application of resources such as people, process, technology and money leads to greater supply management efficiency and effectiveness. Leveraging strategies may be short term, reflecting the current risk-value profile, and longer term, reflecting the targeted risk-value profile. For example, the short term strategy for a high-risk/low-value item is to ensure availability through a long-term contract, reviewing production/delivery or service provision processes to shorten lead time or bundling this item with something more attractive. Longer term, the category manager may want the supplier to work with the category team to conduct value analysis and find a lower-cost way to deliver the required function. A value analysis is a systematic and objective evaluation of the value of a good or service, focusing on an analysis of function relative to the cost of manufacturing or providing the item or service. Value analysis provides insight into the inherent worth of the final good or service, possibly altering specification and quality requirements that could reduce costs without impairing functional suitability.

Several types of analyses may be used to identify leveraging opportunities: spend, cost, risk, market and requirements. Spend analysis is one of the first steps in a structured, disciplined sourcing process. The ability to identify major spend categories and capture actual spend data is a critical first step in better managing spend.

For example, armed with these data, the category management team can make better forecasts, provide information — especially changes — in real time and present a unified front to the supply base. Spend analysis and the savings potential are discussed in greater detail in *Foundation of Supply Management* (ISM Professional Series).

Cost-analysis management is equally important in any concerted supply management process. Cost analysis moves beyond a price focus to consider the cost components relevant to a business decision. In the Kraljic Matrix, cost analysis is important in the management of noncritical and leverage spend categories where the goal is process efficiency and the cost of the acquisition process is a key driver. In the leverage quadrant, cost analysis is also important from the standpoint of achieving the lowest total cost of ownership. In bottleneck and strategic spend categories, cost analysis is focused on acquiring knowledge about cost elements and cost drivers in a good or service to develop and execute strategies to take out or reduce costs. Figure 8-4 illustrates one approach to determining if price analysis or cost analysis is the most appropriate tool, which cost tools are best suited to determining a fair price and which are best for reducing costs. The development of a strategic cost management program is discussed in *Foundation of Supply Management* (ISM Professional Series).

As discussed in Chapter 5, risk analysis is an invaluable tool in determining and assessing the possibility and probability of injury. Equally important is the development of risk-elimination and mitigation strategies. In stark contrast to this need are the results of a 2006 McKinsey survey of 3,172 executives at publicly and privately held businesses across a full range of industries worldwide about their perceptions of supply-chain risks. Nearly one-quarter said their organization does no formal risk assessment, and nearly half lack organizationwide standards to help mitigate risk. A significant number of executives said their organizations do not spend enough time or resources on mitigating risk.[8]

Market analysis is the basis of the determination of risk level in the Kraljic Matrix. This is also a critical element of the third step of the strategic sourcing process, and feeds in to supplier selection. This can be approached from two angles. One, what is the current state of the market for a specific spend category, and two, what impact does the specifying and buying community have on market dynamics? For example, the drive toward national, regional and global contracts forces consolidation in an industry and changes the dynamics between supply management and supplier. Where there may have been many small and medium-size suppliers, there are now fewer and much larger suppliers in total. Clearly, the sourcing and supplier management strategies change as the market changes. Market conditions and their impact on sourcing are discussed in *Foundation of Supply Management* and *Effective Supply Management Performance* (ISM Professional Series).

**Figure 8-4 Applying Price or Cost Analysis**

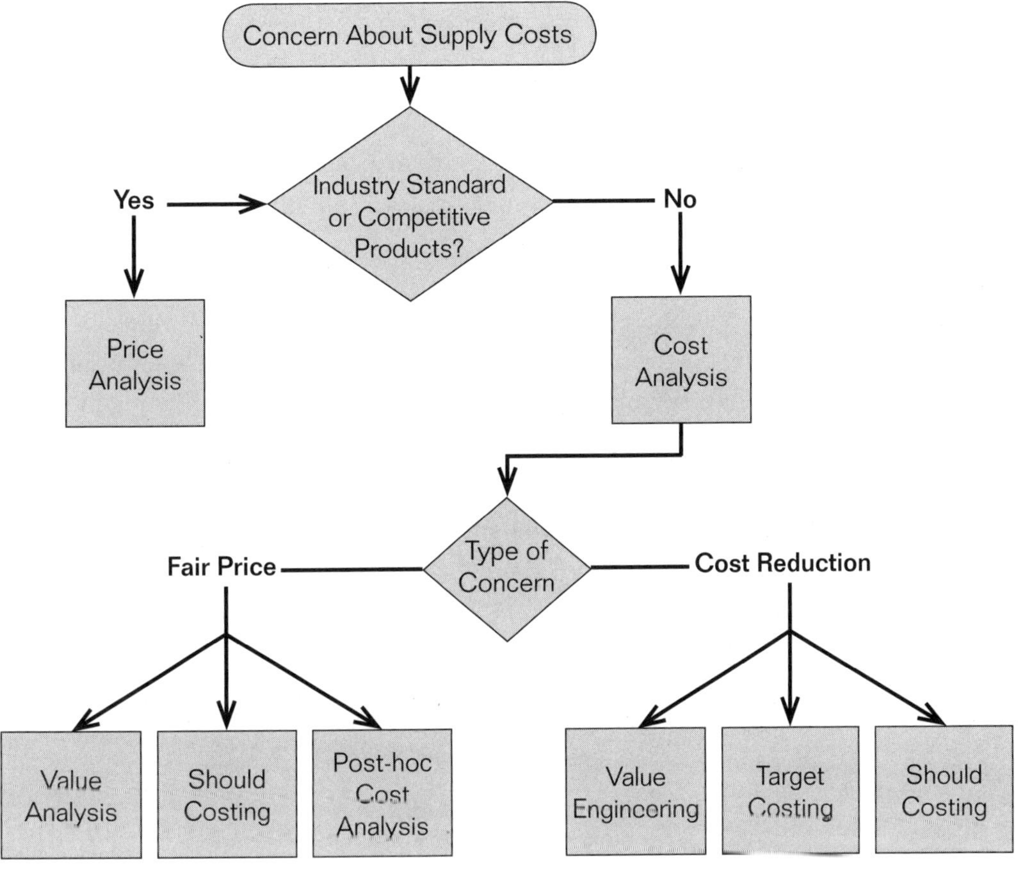


*Source:* Michael E. Smith, Lee Buddress and Alan Raedels, "The Strategic Use of Supplier Price and Cost Analysis," presented at ISM's 91st Annual International Supply Management Conference, Minneapolis, 2006.

Requirements analysis also offers leveraging opportunities. Depending on the nature of the spend category, benefits may be derived from standardization, consolidation or bundling. For example, in an organization with disparate software packages, the decision to standardize across the organization may move the category to a higher value and a lower risk. In the case of software, standardization may also increase the risk to acquire by locking into one supplier's software, but the benefits of greater data visibility and accessibility might be perceived as outweighing the risk. Then risk-mitigation strategies would be a very important part of the sourcing strategy and execution. Risk mitigation is a set of specific steps undertaken by managers to reduce the impact of factors that might lead to injury, loss, damage or failure and thus reduce the liability of the organization in its relations with various stakeholder groups, including employees and customers. These topics are discussed in detail in *Effective Supply Management Performance* (ISM Professional Series).

The sourcing analyst can also align tools and techniques (for example, price, cost and value analyses discussed in *Foundation of Supply Management* (ISM Professional Series)), knowledge and skills required of category managers, decision criteria for supplier selection and the preferred type of supplier relationship (see Figure 8-5). The end result is a comprehensive sourcing plan.

The Kraljic Matrix may also be used to make future sourcing plans by assessing the likelihood of changes in the marketplace that are expected to affect the location on the risk axis and internal changes that may affect the impact of the spend category on the organization. This analysis is critical to step 4 of the strategic sourcing process,

**Figure 8-5 Basic Strategic Tools by Quadrant**

| **Bottleneck** | **Strategic** |
|---|---|
| Value analysis<br>Cross-functional and cross-organizational teams<br>Cost driver analysis and cost management | Collaboration for innovation<br>Strategic alliances<br>Total cost of ownership<br>Cross-functional and cross-organizational teams<br>Multiple organizational levels of involvement |
| **Noncritical** | **Leverage** |
| Process efficiency<br>Standardization, bundling, consolidation to move category to the leverage quadrant | Spend aggregation<br>Price analysis<br>Total cost (acquisition price and other related costs)<br>Process efficiency<br>Ease of doing business |

*Source:* Adapted from Peter Kraljic, "Purchasing Must Become Supply Management," *Harvard Business Review* (September/October 1983).

negotiate and contract. Both supply management and the supplier attempt to negotiate to minimize their risks and build protection for contingencies into the contract.

In general, the longer-term goal is to lower risk and increase value. This is critical in both step 4 and step 5, supplier development, where the organization develops and manages the ongoing relationship with its suppliers. The analyst may identify strategies that will accomplish one or both of these goals. Risk is lowered by taking actions that make it easier to acquire an item in the marketplace, such as reducing or eliminating customization in the design specification. Clearly, this requires a cross-functional team to ensure that the uniqueness that is valued by the customer is not removed. Value may also be affected. If value has been equated to spend, the sourcing strategy may entail consolidation, bundling and standardization to move noncritical items to the leverage box. The move to commoditize everything from components to higher education shows up on the matrix as actions that will move categories to the leverage box. Then, tools that will exploit purchasing power, such as e-auctions, can be applied to the category. While this is inherently appealing to sourcing managers, it should not be entered into lightly given the possible negative impact on final customers. As Gary Hirshberg, founder of Stonyfield Farm Yogurt, said, "Quality, quality, quality: never waver from it, even when you don't see how you can afford to keep it up. When you compromise, you become a commodity and then you die."[9]

**Outsourcing Supply Management Tasks or Functions.** The outsourcing decision-making process is discussed in detail in Chapter 5. Any discussion about business processes should include the option of outsourcing tasks within the process or the entire process to a third-party provider. Business process outsourcing is growing dramatically as the number of areas targeted for consideration has expanded. For example, a major global pharmaceutical company recently identified 26 human resources–related tasks that it plans to outsource. Supply management subprocesses have been and probably will continue to be targets for outsourcing assessment. Many organizations outsource some or all inventory management, transportation and other logistics-related tasks. Some organizations have developed in-house expertise at the acquisition of production materials and outsourced the acquisition of indirect materials and services to a third party.

The decision to outsource tasks within a component or subprocess of supply management is clearly a fundamental decision in the design of organizational structure. A review of CAPS Research Benchmarking studies indicates that, to date, few participating organizations report outsourcing any supply management tasks. However, it is valid and legitimate to question whether or not an organization derives enough benefit from the development of expertise in specific supply management tasks to develop and maintain them as core competencies or if they should be outsourced.

In a study of fleet administration, M.R. Leenders, R. Kudar and A. Flynn found that specific tasks such as vehicle leasing or maintenance were successfully outsourced, and, in some cases, the entire fleet administration was outsourced. In a pharmaceutical company, the tasks of leasing, licensing and maintaining the vehicles of pharmaceutical sales representatives was outsourced to a third party while the main contact person with the individual salespeople remained an employee of the pharmaceutical company. The rationale was that the salesperson's car was a motivator and a critical tool for job performance. Because the relationship the contact person had with each salesperson enhanced that person's performance, it was decided that this relationship could not be outsourced successfully. In another case involving a municipality, the maintenance of standard cars and trucks was outsourced while the expertise required to maintain specialized and customized city vehicles was retained by the city and performed by city employees at a city-run garage.[10]

## Standardized Policies and Procedures

A strategic sourcing process gains structure and discipline through the development and consistent application of standardized policies and procedures. These are part of the foundation of a rigorous strategic sourcing process.

**Regression Analysis.** Regression analysis is one of the tools available to supply management professionals. Measures of correlation are used to describe the degree of relationship between two variables (or data series). The correlation coefficient indicates whether the relationship is positive (both increase together) or negative (one increases while the other decreases). With the use of a regression equation, the scores of one variable can be predicted based on the other variable. Correlation and regression analysis is particularly useful in forecasting. It allows forecasters to determine the relationship among variables over time. It is useful in spotting trends in usage, pricing, linking price with volumes and a variety of other factors. Any statistics textbook will provide more information on regression analysis. For example, see *Essentials of Business Statistics,* Second Edition, by Bruce L. Bowerman, Richard T. O'Connell and J. Burdeane Orris (McGraw-Hill, 2008).

**Best Practices.** A practice is only a "best practice" if it works in a given situation. In general, best practices relate to an organization having control systems and processes in place before, during and after supply management decision-making (see Chapter 12). The details of these practices are context-specific. The hallmarks of policy and procedures best practices are:

- They support the firm's vision, mission and strategies.
- They are accessible.
- People have been trained to use them.
- They are used consistently.

**Processes to Disseminate and Communicate the Policy and Procedures.** Policy and procedure changes must be communicated to stakeholders, especially those who are directly impacted either because they must execute the policies and procedures or because their work is affected by them in some way. Typical communication strategies include posting policies and procedures on the company intranet either through online manuals or online training. Communication techniques to influence and persuade people as well as gain buy-in are discussed in Chapter 4. Failure to obtain buy-in at multiple levels may result in slower process adoption that may ultimately impact sourcing-related metrics.

## Market Analysis of E-Solutions

Process first; technology last! Rigorous business processes are the critical foundation of successful technology implementation. Therefore, the supply management professional must thoroughly understand business process design and provide the resources and support needed to improve supply management–related processes and select and implement appropriate technology. He or she must also monitor the impact of supply management processes on other business processes to ensure efficiency and effectiveness.

Appropriate technology coupled with rigorous supply management processes sets the stage for a value-adding supply management organization. The supply management professional, in conjunction with internal IT and supply management specialists, must develop an overall technology strategy for supply management, determine the return on investment from IT solutions and incorporate specific technology strategies at the category level. By understanding the opportunities (data accessibility, transparency, speed, shorter cycle times, operating efficiencies, greater internal compliance, etc.) and the obstacles (user, supplier and technology limitations), the supply management professional can manage the decision-making processes surrounding technology applications. Ultimately, the leader-manager must ensure that the operating efficiencies gained from workflow improvements free up people for strategic rather than transactional activities. He or she must also ensure that the appropriate human capital is available in supply management to use the readily available data to make better decisions. Technology may lead to greater efficiency and, when coupled with human brainpower, it may also lead to greater effectiveness.

## E-Sourcing Tools

A number of e-sourcing tools are available, including purchase order systems, electronic requisitioning systems (eRFX), electronic data interchange (EDI) and e-procurement systems. The supply management professional must determine which tools are appropriate for the organization, given the capabilities of the people, the status of supply management processes and the spend categories in the organization and the likely development of these. Key questions to ask include:

1. Which spend categories are appropriate for electronic tools?
2. What are the current and projected technical capabilities of supply management personnel?
3. Are rigorous processes in place for most supply management–related activities?

Spend categories may be assessed using portfolio analysis (the previously discussed Kraljic Matrix) in which major spend categories are assessed along dimensions such as value to the organization and risk to acquire in the marketplace. Electronic tools are readily available to routinize and systematize the acquisition of lower value-adding and lower risk-to-acquire items (standard, commodity-type items), often referred to as noncritical or routine and leverage items. Electronic tools that enable collaboration at earlier and earlier stages of the process, such as design collaboration, are more appropriate for higher value-adding and riskier items, often referred to as bottleneck and strategic items.

The supply management professional must link decisions about technology applications to the framework used to categorize and manage spend. This requires strong internal partnerships with other business process owners to ensure alignment with other processes and technology and to allow the supply management professional to effectively manage change.

According to Malcolm Wheatley, the supply management professional may take one of three approaches to e-solutions: (1) use e-procurement for internal process efficiencies, (2) use it end-to-end for all spend to get price reductions on commodity-type items and process efficiencies or (3) pick individual tools for specific purposes. Wheatley gives a company example of each approach: Webasto Roof Systems, Inc., Reliant Pharmaceuticals, Inc., and Ametek, Inc.[11]

**Internal Process Efficiencies.** Webasto Roof Systems, a $300 million subsidiary of Germany-based automobile roof and thermo systems manufacturer Webasto AG, is using e-procurement strategies to make its internal process more efficient, while keeping sourcing decisions and price negotiations offline. CIO Mike Thibideau credits e-procurement with reducing inventories by 15 percent, generating $1.5 million of cash flow and reducing annual inventory carrying costs by $180,000. With all this, the system is still only 30 percent implemented. Webasto's 150 direct material suppliers download all the information they need to ship the parts and materials for Webasto's sunroofs and convertible tops. "Because all they need is a Web browser, it is less intrusive than EDI, and less expensive," says Thibideau. Suppliers log on to compare Webasto's production schedule to the inventory Webasto is holding and to the preset minimum and maximum levels and decide when and how much to ship.[12]

**End-to-End for All Spend.** Some organizations, such as Reliant Pharmaceutical, deploy e-procurement for all items where compressibility (i.e., spend aggregation leads to price reductions) and substitutability (i.e., items are standard, commodity-type items) make that possible, and settling for internal efficiencies where it is not. Reliant decided in 2002 to buy everything electronically — from janitorial supplies to the products that it sells. The relatively straightforward nature of its business made this easier; the drugs it sells are manufactured by pharmaceutical giants such as Novartis AG and Eli Lilly and Co., thus eliminating direct materials as such. Even so, says Reliant CIO Ron Calderone, "One hundred percent of our purchases now go though Ariba: lodging, travel, office supplies, sales literature, the products we sell, you name it."[13]

Previously, for Reliant to process a typical purchase order required 21 "touches" — approvals, logging, classifying and the like — and took between one and three months to move through the system. It was also difficult to enforce any consistent company purchasing policy, and Reliant's back-office system provided very little procurement information with which to leverage price concessions from suppliers. In the first year of its Ariba implementation, says Calderone, 10 percent of Reliant's purchases were electronic, contributing to an ROI of 65 percent. He estimates the second year ROI will be 400 percent.[14]

At a Japanese company in the electric equipment industry, five steps were taken to transition to an automated end-to-end system. First, the existing information system was re-examined and EDI was implemented to automate supplier delivery processes (order sheets, change orders, receiving and so on). Second, the RFQ and bid process was automated. RFQs and specifications were sent via the Internet to all suppliers using a bid-support feature that displayed price, order and delivery date. Third, the Internet was used to source long-range inventory parts. Fourth, the team ensured that technology is XML-compatible and can be customized for various users. Fifth, an automated settlement feature was created to reduce the number of mistakes in the settlement process and to reduce transaction costs. The largest value came from reducing lead times.[15]

**Pick and Choose.** Ametek, an electronic instrument and motor manufacturer, sources 12 commodity groups of substitutable and compressible items (among them machine tooling, electrical supplies and computer hardware) through an Oracle Exchange e-procurement portal. The organization has access to approximately one and a half million stock-keeping units (SKUs) (inventory items) through catalogs maintained by suppliers. Supply management also uses the Internet to locate and qualify suppliers and sometimes holds electronic auctions after which transactions are released against a contract.[16]

**Reverse Auctions.** The supply management professional must consider the appropriateness of reverse auctions as a tool in the organization's supply management strategy. A CAPS Research study identified several issues that influence the success or failure of a reverse auction:

- The ability to clearly define specifications that are universally understood by the supply base, including global suppliers.
- Identifying a sufficient number of qualified competitors who are willing to participate in the auction event.
- Potential impact on incumbent suppliers and plan to offset possible negative consequences (e.g., supplier of a strategic item).
- Understanding the unique characteristics of the item's supply market structure, degree of competitiveness, key cost drivers and current open capacity (i.e., is it a buyers', suppliers' or neutral market?). This information is essential for setting an appropriately aggressive reserve price.
- Degree of experience of both supply management and suppliers in participating in an e-RA event, including familiarity with the Web-based software being used.
- Event format — what will be revealed during the e-RA for this particular group of suppliers (price, rank, weighted price or rank, etc.), rules such as closing rule (e.g., hard close, soft close, rules for soft close), participation rules (bird-watching, offline communications) and award rule (low price guaranteed the business, post-negotiations, no award guarantee).
- Need to use a formal RFX (e-based or manual) for this particular event.[17]

**Spend Analysis.** According to *Purchasing* magazine, organizations that have constructed a complete 360-degree view of spend are able to:

- Capture large proportions, in some cases 100 percent, of the total corporate spend.

- Create dynamic, frequently refreshed and often forward-looking views of spend.
- Automate data capture, cleansing and analysis processes to minimize costly, labor-intensive work.
- Deploy innovative spend analysis capacities in a context of highly strategic, process-based and metrics-based approaches to sourcing and spend management.[18]

These organizations have gone beyond simply capturing spend data from enterprise resource planning (ERP) or transactional electronic procurement systems. Instead of relying on periodic, backward-looking spend data reports, organizations with a 360-degree view of their spend are able to generate ideas for appropriate organizational and policy structures; identify and close spend loopholes; classify, cleanse and aggregate spend data in real time and integrate it with other data sets such as supplier demographics and performance, and different technology options.

At IBM, for instance, the governance structure limits how people can spend money and policies result in immediate repercussions for violating these procedures, up to and including termination. Spend data is captured at the time of commitment and at the time of cash release or payout. Spend is classified according to commodity and supplier according to a proprietary, highly granular taxonomy that maps spend to brand and business unit accounting ledgers. Additionally, spend data is associated with other market intelligence such as competitive cost and absolute lowest cost. This enables procurement to measure the competitive advantage generated by procurement decisions. IBM's spend analysis structure allows the procurement organization to:

- Forecast what the company will spend over the coming year and how the spend will break down by business unit.
- Provide an outlook on what is likely to happen with commodity market pricing.
- Report how sourcing councils will deliver savings to specific IBM brands or business units.
- Plan with brand managers or business units how they will deploy expected savings (either "take down" or invest elsewhere) in their P&Ls.
- Close the loop by measuring performance to plans.[19]

## Contract Management

Automated contract management systems are network-based software platforms that make contract terms accessible to every person within an organization who needs access as well as customers and suppliers if desired. According to Mary Barth, CPA, the Atholl McBean Professor of Accounting at the Stanford Graduate School of Business, the contract management function has two underlying goals: (1) ensure visibility of promises an organization is making and the obligations it is taking on and (2) allow top management to see that what is being promised is acceptable. The fundamental purpose of contract management, says industry spokesperson Neil Couture, CPCM the current executive director of the National Contract Management Association (NCMA), is to fully integrate the contract management process with the rest of the organization's operations.[20]

Contract management systems provide an automated system with a central repository for all of an organization's contracts. The goal is to manage business risks, cut expenses and increase revenues by reducing pricing errors, mistaken payments, operating and processing costs and personnel. Revenue rises when organizations streamline claims-processing and improve supplier and customer relations and compliance, according to "Technology: B2B Software," a Goldman Sachs Group, Inc., report released in February of 2001.[21] "Contract-management software provides purchasing operations with the visibility and control needed to create better contracts, to ensure that suppliers meet their contractual obligations and to manage and evaluate performance against contract terms. It also helps maximize the effectiveness of other purchasing applications, accelerate cycle times from sourcing through contract and realize negotiated savings."[22]

## Key Points

1. Strategic sourcing is a process that leads to "the selection and management of suppliers with a focus on achieving the long-term goals of a business."

2. The steps in the strategic sourcing process are data management and analysis, category strategy development, cost management, negotiate and contract and supplier development.

3. Category sourcing strategies help ensure that the appropriate type and level of resources such as money, time and attention are allocated to each spend category.

CHAPTER

# 9

# Staffing the Supply Management Organization

*I believe the real difference between success and failure in a corporation can be very often traced to the question of how well the organization brings out the great energies and talents of its people.* THOMAS J. WATSON, JR., CEO OF IBM (1956–1971)[1]

The supply management leader sets direction through the creation of a vision of what supply management can be and do for the organization. He or she then aligns people around that vision and inspires and motivates them to remain committed to achieving it. Human capital, therefore, is a critical factor in achieving the leader's vision. One of the primary roles of the supply management professional is to develop talent management strategies to ensure that human capital is available when and where needed with the right knowledge and skills necessary to make the vision a reality.

Because global organizations find it harder and harder to fill critical positions, talent management strategies are even more important. Supply management professionals keen to the situation struggle to land top recruits in emerging markets and know that preparing their own staff to step seamlessly into management slots becomes a critical strategy.

The supply management professional's talent management responsibility starts with the design or redesign of roles and responsibilities within the supply management group centered on the organization's business plan and global marketing objectives.[2] The effort continues with the development of strategies for attracting, hiring and retaining supply management personnel, then continually developing and supporting supply management personnel and ensuring that the organization has a succession of qualified leader-managers. The supply management professional should be the chief knowledge officer in supply management and the chief advocate for creating and sharing supply knowledge with internal business partners and across organizational boundaries with external partners such as suppliers of strategic and critical goods and services. The supply management professional also works with his or her peer in human resources to align supply management employee practices with organizational initiatives such as employee diversity initiatives, planning career paths in supply management and ensuring compliance with employment laws and regulations. The supply management professional must also take the lead in educating employees outside of the supply management group about policies and procedures.

Chapter 3 focused on how to align people behind the vision of supply management. This chapter addresses staffing the supply management organization. It is organized around two of the supply management professional's primary managerial activities in this area: (1) design roles and assignment responsibilities and (2) developing global employment and talent management strategies.

### CHAPTER OBJECTIVES

- Develop global talent management strategies in support of a globally integrated organization.
- Describe the process of determining position requirements and writing effective job descriptions to attract highly qualified individuals.
- Discuss the skills and attributes most desirable in candidates for supply management positions given the changing role of the function.

## Designing Roles and Assigning Responsibilities

If an organization is only as good as the people who work for it, then a critical managerial task is to design roles and assign responsibilities in the form of job positions within supply management. These positions should be based on the knowledge and skills required to fulfill supply management's overall role that, according to Institute for Supply Management™ (ISM), is "the identification, acquisition, access, positioning and management of resources and related capabilities an organization needs in the attainment of its strategic objectives."[3] The supply management professional must also determine the type of person who will fit into the corporate culture of the organization. Careful consideration must be given to the short-term and long-term goals and objectives of the organization when determining individual roles and responsibilities and creating the job descriptions for each position.

The positions within the supply management group should align with organizational structure, business processes and enabling technologies to ensure that supply management professionals make an optimal contribution to the organization's success.

A 2007 joint study by *The Wall Street Journal* and the *MIT Sloan Management Review* suggests organizational success is achieved by keeping a few solutions to building the talent pool in mind: (1) make your talent plan match your business plan, (2) talent management is everyone's job, (3) global excellence needs local effectiveness, (4) support matters and (5) measure what matters.[4]

The roles played by supply management professionals, including levels of authority, actual job tasks and reporting lines and relationships, are related to the structure of the organization and to the degree of centralization of supply management. For example, the skills and knowledge required to work successfully in a functional structure may be different from the skills and knowledge needed for a divisional or a matrix structure. Functional structures tend to be more top-down and bureaucratic. People who like structure, clear chains of command and well-defined roles and responsibilities may fare best. Matrix structures tend to result in dual reporting lines and more role ambiguity and potential for competing objectives. People who prefer less well-defined roles and responsibilities, who can deal well with ambiguity and who can maneuver between two bosses may find a matrix structure to their liking.

The degree of centralization of supply management decision-making may also influence job design. In a highly decentralized structure, supply management personnel may play more of a consulting or advisory role and their most important skill and ability may be the ability to build a strong business case and influence others. Depending on the internal user group, the position may require strong analytical skills and the ability to make the case quantitatively and present it convincingly in a spreadsheet format. For other internal users, a verbal presentation or a well-written document may be preferred. In a highly centralized organization, where policy and procedures are driven from a central decision-making process, positions may require more structure and compliance.

Supply management processes and enabling technologies also influence the knowledge and skills required for supply management positions. In a highly automated environment, individuals may need more facility with various information technology tools. Or in a highly decentralized environment with multiple processes spread across divisions or geographic locations, positions may require strong process orientation and the ability to design rigorous methods. Organizations shifting more of their services internationally or locating supply management requirements closer to their international suppliers may require individuals with already developed international experience. Role and job design, individual and collective performance assessment and professional development can all be linked to and aligned with the knowledge and skills identified as critical success factors in supply management.

Job design decisions should also consider the organization and department stance on workplace issues such as flexible scheduling, compressed work schedules, telecommuting, job sharing, temporary assignments, consulting projects and part-time jobs. According to the CAPS Research study, "Supply's Organizational Roles and Responsibilities," the ratio of support staff to supply management professionals continues to drop, meaning that supply management professionals are expected to perform most position-related administrative tasks themselves.[5] Changing domestic and global workforce demographics coupled with shifting sourcing locations also affect job design decisions. The CAPS study on roles and responsibilities also reported that the number of supply management staff in U.S–based organizations located outside the United States has increased massively. As mentioned in Chapter 3, IBM announced in 2006 that it was moving its global procurement headquarters to Shenzhen, China, to reflect IBM's shift from a multinational corporation to a globally integrated enterprise. "In a multinational model, many functions of a corporation were replicated around the world — but each addressing only its local market," said Vice President and Chief Procurement Officer John Paterson, who has relocated to China. "In a globally integrated enterprise, for the first time, a company's worldwide capability can be located wherever in the world it makes the most sense, based on the imperatives of economics, expertise and open environments. IBM is a global organization. And today that is as much about making efficient and effective use of skills everywhere in the world and integrating them globally to serve clients, as it is about developing deep local relationships in markets around the world. We are becoming a globally integrated company that allows us to do both."[6]

Cultural intelligence is "the ability to adapt constantly to different people from diverse cultures and the ability to manage the interconnectedness of today's world."[7] Joo-Seng Tan states that cultural intelligence involves three things: thinking about a new culture, being motivated and feeling confident to act, and creating the actions needed for the situation. He cites IBM, Novartis AG, Nike, Inc., Lloyds TSB, Lufthansa and Barclays Bank PLC as organizations that use cultural intelligence as a source of competitive advantage.

Following its own consulting focus in this area, A.T. Kearney sums up talent management development with several keys to success. Its first suggested key to success means engaging leadership and an organization's commitment. A.T. Kearney also suggests developing a fact-based business case that creates the foundation for an ongoing talent management program. It advances frequent, open and honest communication with the organization that highlights a clear vision and objectives of the program and communicates this to all levels within the organization. Finally, any talent management strategy designed by the supply management leader must align with the existing human resources programs — recruitment, performance management, professional development, succession planning and mentoring.[8]

Clearly, numerous issues must be considered when designing roles and assigning responsibilities within a talent management strategy in supply management. These include aligning roles with organizational goals and structure, the degree of centralization, business processes, enabling technologies, workforce composition and workplace issues. Once these influencing factors are recognized and considered, the supply management professional is in a better position to determine the knowledge and skills required for success in the organization's supply management group.

## Determine Required Knowledge and Skills

The supply management professional might start the job design or redesign process by determining the knowledge and skills required for success in the supply management organization. *Knowledge* is defined by *Merriam-Webster's Dictionary* as "the fact or condition of knowing something with familiarity gained through experience or association; acquaintance with or understanding of a science, art, or technique." A *skill* is defined by *Merriam-Webster's Dictionary* as "the ability to use one's knowledge effectively and readily in execution or performance or a learned power of doing something competently." Knowledge then is knowing about something and skill is knowing how to use that knowledge to do something.

Using these definitions of knowledge and skills along with the results of the CAPS Research project, "Purchasing Education and Training II," Figure 9-1 was constructed and may be used to guide hiring, retention, promotion and professional development strategies. Certainly, the knowledge and skills in a specific organizational setting might vary from these, but this approach provides a simple tool for the supply management professional to use as a starting point for developing talent management strategies.

For global leadership, a 2007 study by the Conference Board has identified competencies and skills that apply to and enable people to work in and with other cultures.[9] The competencies and accompanying skills are:

- ***Open-minded and flexible in thought and tactics.*** The executive is able to live and work in a variety of settings, with different types of people, and is willing and able to listen to other people, approaches and ideas.
- ***Cultural interest and sensitivity.*** The executive respects other cultures, people and points of view; is neither arrogant nor judgmental; is curious about other people and how they live and work; is interested in differences; enjoys social competency; gets along well with others; and is empathetic.

**Figure 9-1 Turning Knowledge Into Skills**

| KNOWLEDGE AREAS | SKILL SETS |
|---|---|
| **Ethics** | Access ethical situations.<br>Make decisions, solve problems and resolve conflicts of an ethical nature. |
| **Markets and industries, including prices, costs, suppliers and supply chains** | Perform competitive market analysis.<br>Analyze suppliers (and make decisions, solve problems or resolve conflicts).<br>Conduct price analysis and make pricing decisions based on events such as bidding.<br>Conduct cost analysis and total cost of ownership analysis and make cost-related decisions.<br>Develop and execute supply strategies and plans.<br>Develop negotiation strategies.<br>Develop appropriate relationships internally with stakeholders and externally with suppliers and other groups. |
| **Communication techniques** | Communicate effectively, resolve conflicts, solve problems and make efficient and effective supply management decisions.<br>Execute negotiation strategies, and effectively influence, persuade and compromise.<br>Manage internal and external relationships. |

*Source:* Adapted from Larry Giunipero and Robert B. Handfield, "Purchasing Education and Training II," CAPS Research, 2004.

- *Able to deal with complexity.* The executive considers many variables in solving a problem, is comfortable with ambiguity, is patient with evolving issues, can make decisions in the face of uncertainty, can see patterns and connections and is willing to take risks.
- *Resilient, resourceful, optimistic and energetic.* The executive responds to a challenge, is not discouraged by adversity, is self-reliant and creative, sees the positive side of things, has a high level of physical and emotional energy, and is able to deal with stress.

- ***Honesty and integrity.*** The executive engenders trust and is authentic and consistent.
- ***Stable personal life.*** The executive has developed and maintains stress-resistant personal arrangements, usually family, that support (an international) commitment to work.
- ***Value-added technical or business skills.*** The executive has technical, managerial or other expertise that is sufficient to provide for his or her credibility.

For global leadership skills, the Conference Board lists establishing credibility, giving/receiving feedback, obtaining information and evaluating people as the required interpersonal skills. For global leadership, group skills such as building global teamwork, training and development, and selling and negotiating are core. Strategic planning, transferring knowledge, innovating and managing change fall into the organizational skill set a global leader needs.

These broad knowledge and skill areas can be further refined to reflect the specific duties and responsibilities of a particular position within supply management such as a position in logistics, inventory management, purchasing and so on. For example, for positions in services procurement at Bank of America, a service-based organization that relies heavily on teams, there is a strong preference for service-based supply-chain experience, strong customer service capabilities, good cross-functional team skills and leadership ability to lead teams.[10]

Many supply management leaders developing an international staff identify change management and knowledge transfer skills as very important because of the fast-paced work environment in a global setting, especially for those global organizations dealing with dramatic growth in emerging markets. One supply management professional highlights the example of working with dynamic young professionals who adapt well to changing environments and are eager to transfer their experiences to a new class of supply management professionals who are raw recruits, yet earnest to learn.

The changing nature of the supply management process, the expanding role of supply management and the demands placed on supply management professionals have altered the knowledge and skill sets required for continued success. The leader-manager of a supply management organization must be continually alert to new requirements to keep the supply management organization in a competitive position. Determining future staffing needs in supply management will derive from factors such as sales forecasts, technology applications, changes in efficiency, productivity and flexibility of labor as a result of other factors such as training or structural change, changes in employment practices such as outsourcing both domestic and international, new legislation or changes in existing regulations, policy changes that increase or decrease workload and changes to workflow.

### Assign Knowledge and Skills to Positions

While numerous job titles and positions are available in supply management, one approach to categorizing these positions is to establish a hierarchy of positions that includes levels such as vice president, directors, managers and analysts. At the vice-president level, the roles and responsibilities are driven by the organization's long-term goals and strategy. At the director level, duties and responsibilities may be segmented according to the various components of supply management. There might be a director of purchasing, a director of logistics, a director of operations and so on. While the job description for each of these would reflect the specifics of purchasing, logistics or operations, in general the director level would reflect a similar level of responsibility. At the manager level, duties and responsibilities also may be segmented according to the various components of supply management. For example, there might be multiple managers of sourcing, each with specific areas of expertise such as raw materials, packaging, services and so on. There might be managers of logistics with specific responsibility for inbound transportation — domestic, inbound — international, MRO inventory manager and so on. While the job description for each of these would reflect the specifics of the component, such as sourcing or logistics, in general the manager level would reflect a similar level of responsibility. At the analyst level, the duties and responsibilities would again be very specific to a designated area, such as buying, and focus on execution and tactical or operational activities. Positions at this level might include inventory analyst, logistics analyst, buyer, etc.

Each level in the hierarchy is based on the duties and responsibilities, the level of decision-making authority and the scope of the position in terms of supervisory or managerial oversight. These factors are reflected in the descriptions of duties and responsibilities in Figure 9-2.

Figure 9-3 describes the typical requirements for personnel at each level of responsibility.

These clearly defined roles and responsibilities set a positive course that the supply management organization's talent management strategies can adhere to. But global organizations are keen to anticipate what can be expected from future global leaders. The Conference Board's study on global leadership lists a series of additional leadership roles and responsibilities key to global leaders of the future:

- Build effective alliances with other organizations.
- Make decisions that reflect global considerations.
- Build effective partnerships across the organization.
- Consistently treat people with respect and dignity.[11]

**Figure 9-2 Duties and Responsibilities by Role**

| ROLE | DUTIES AND RESPONSIBILITIES |
|---|---|
| **Vice president** | Set strategic supply management direction, lead the development of strategies and provide managerial support for tactical execution.<br>Act as the executive sponsor of supply management initiatives that align with organizational strategy and ensure supply management's contribution as measured by key organizational metrics.<br>Build effective internal partnerships and work within these to integrate people, processes and technology across organizational boundaries.<br>Develop talent management strategies that ensure attracting, hiring, retaining and developing professional supply management personnel. |
| **Director** | In conjunction with the vice president, set strategic direction (e.g., for purchasing or logistics and so on).<br>Lead the development of (e.g., purchasing, logistics, etc.) strategies and provide managerial support for tactical execution.<br>Ensure that (purchasing, logistics, etc.) initiatives align with overall supply management strategy and with organizational strategy.<br>Develop and manage measurement systems to ensure (purchasing, logistics, etc.) contribute to key supply management metrics and feed into key organizational metrics.<br>Build effective internal partnerships horizontally (at the director level) and vertically (up the chain to the vice president and down the chain to direct reports) and work within these partnerships to integrate people, processes and technology across organizational boundaries.<br>Deploy employment strategies to the manager and lower-level employees to attract, hire, retain and develop professional supply management personnel. |
| **Manager** | Manage direct reports.<br>Efficiently and effectively manage the processes relevant to a specific area of responsibility.<br>Contribute to the development of the overall supply management strategy by providing specific area knowledge to the director (of purchasing or logistics, etc).<br>(continued) |

| ROLE | DUTIES AND RESPONSIBILITIES |
|---|---|
| **Manager** (continued) | Lead the development of area-specific strategies (for example, category strategy, raw material inventory strategy, etc.).<br>Identify appropriate tools and techniques and incorporate into management of function.<br>Provide managerial support for tactical execution.<br>Ensure that (category, inventory, etc.) strategies and initiatives align with overall supply management strategy as well as organizational strategy.<br>Measure and manage performance (of the category, inventory, etc.) and of direct reports.<br>Build effective internal partnerships and work within these partnerships to flawlessly execute strategies.<br>Attract, hire, retain and develop entry-level employees (e.g., buyers, analysts, etc.). |
| **Entry level** | Follow detailed roster of tactical activities to be executed by employee.<br>Use appropriate tools and techniques on a daily basis to make decisions.<br>Perform activities efficiently and effectively. |

The supply management professional lays the groundwork for the successful execution of plans and strategies through the development of clearly defined roles and responsibilities at each level in the supply management organization. Once these roles have been defined or redefined, usually in conjunction with human resources, the leader-manager can develop employment strategies to attract and retain highly qualified candidates to the job opportunities.

## Developing Global Employment and Talent Management Strategies

Most organizations establish employment policies that support the organization's mission and strategic plan and provide parameters for employee behavior. A broadly defined policy gives the decision-maker greater latitude than a narrowly defined policy does. For example, if an organization has a hiring policy to diversify the workforce,

**Figure 9-3 Personnel Requirements**

| ROLE | REQUIREMENTS |
|---|---|
| **Vice president** | Expert-level knowledge of processes, tools and techniques in supply management.<br>Excellent interpersonal skills.<br>Advanced degree in some area of supply management.<br>Extensive experience leading and managing a complex, diverse supply management organization.<br>May have credentials in the field. |
| **Director** | Expert-level knowledge of (purchasing, logistics, etc.) processes, tools, techniques.<br>Excellent interpersonal skills.<br>Bachelor's degree in (supply management, logistics, etc.) required and master's degree preferred.<br>Extensive experience in leading and managing a complex, diverse supply management, logistics, etc., organization.<br>Credentials in the field required. |
| **Manager** | Expert-level knowledge of (supply management, logistics, etc.) processes, tools, techniques.<br>Excellent interpersonal skills.<br>Bachelor's degree in (supply management, logistics, etc.) required and/or three to five years of experience in the specific area with supervisory or managerial responsibility.<br>Credentials in the field preferred. |
| **Entry level** | Bachelor's degree in supply management preferred.<br>Or three to five years of tactical experience in the specified area. |

then human resources managers and hiring managers will be expected to take actions that will lead to a larger pool of applicants from diverse populations and thus a larger number of new hires from diverse backgrounds. If, on the other hand, the hiring policy restricts a hiring manager to promoting from within the organization, then the hiring manager has fewer options at his or her disposal. The supply management professional's role in employment strategies may range from ensuring compliance with human resources policies to influencing these policies to developing organizational plans that serve as a blueprint for recruiting, hiring, retaining and promoting supply management personnel. One of the biggest issues the supply management professional must consider when developing employment and talent management strategies is the extent and impact of workforce diversity.

### Global Workforce Diversity

Diversity may be defined very broadly to include everyone as part of the diversity that should be valued or very narrowly according to an organization's specific need to rectify bias in employment. Workforce diversity is projected by many experts to become an increasingly important trend for the following reasons:

- More globalization of organizations, leading to a more global workforce, marketplace and economy;
- Diverse work teams becoming prevalent in organizations;
- Movement of diversity as more of a business concern than a social concern, closely linked to competitive strategies;
- Making and spending more money by diverse populations, empowering diversity;
- More involvement by senior managers in diversity issues as they realize that the diverse workforce needs to be better utilized to be competitive;
- More training professionals will face the challenge of dealing with adverse reactions backlash; and
- More integration of diversity training with other types of training.[12]

Workforce diversity, then, is a reality in most organizations either because of the presence of heterogeneous populations, migration patterns, marketing and sourcing locations, or laws and management initiatives that require managers to hire, retain and promote a wide mix of people. As the workforce composition changes throughout the world, multiethnic, multicultural and multilingual issues arise in the workplace. A global economy and shifts in economic centers with accompanying shifts in labor pools bring the question of managing a diverse workforce into focus for many managers no matter their location, nationality, race or ethnicity. For example, IBM has procurement professionals in 60 countries and 400 cities worldwide. Supply management professionals cannot afford to lose the competitive advantage that procurement provides. In the case of IBM, the organization has a strategy to locate procurement skills close to clients and suppliers around the world. This strategy affects employment and professional development strategies.[13]

Recruitment and employee selection strategies must take into account shifts in workforce composition that come from an increasingly diverse mix of potential employees in terms of race, ethnicity, gender, age, sexual orientation and geographic location. For example, rapidly aging populations in the economically developed world, including the United States, Germany, France, Italy, Canada, Japan, Australia and the United Kingdom, have huge implications for workforce composition, size and labor costs in those countries as well as spillover effects into other countries. According to the Migration Policy Group, if present trends continue, the European Union (EU) working age population will fall by approximately 40 million people between 2000 and 2050 as a result of low fertility and increased life expectancy. As Europe's population diminishes in size and becomes older, the number of people of working age declines. Moreover, many women still do not form part of the labor market, and early retirement has lowered the participation rate of older workers — at the moment, less than a quarter of people age 60 to 64 are employed.[14]

According to McKinsey & Co., there are 33 million university-educated young people in the economically developing world. This is more than twice the number in the economically developed world.[15] The rising number of college-educated people in the developing world opens up opportunities for employers and employees alike as labor pools continue to shift. Young, educated professionals may emigrate from the developing to the developed world on work visas. Most countries in the developed world have visas similar to the H1-B (distinguished alien) visa in the United States. Technological improvements will continue to loosen the constraints of geography, thus enabling more of these college-educated young people to work from their native countries for organizations based anywhere in the world. Supply management professionals face many challenges when developing strategies for hiring, retaining, managing and developing a globally diverse and geographically distributed workforce. The supply management professional must lead the supply management group in recognizing and optimizing the opportunities presented by a diverse workforce and in developing an organizational sensitivity to the challenges employees face while learning to work with one another.

An employee base of different age groups may have the advantage of a steady inflow of current thought and practice melded with institutional knowledge and experience. Age diversity often brings its own set of challenges as well. A number of situations may arise, including (1) younger workers supervising older workers, (2) more formally educated younger workers being supervised by older, less formally educated managers, (3) differences in ethics, work ethic, dress, behavior and personal and career goals. These issues may take different forms depending on the culture in which they occur. For example, in a culture where elders are revered, a younger person may be very uncomfortable in a position of authority over an elder.

A commitment to diversity is also about bringing together people with very different viewpoints and creating an organizational culture based on a positive work environment. General Mills, Inc., supports seven employee networks based at its world headquarters, including the American Indian Council; the Asian American Employee Network; Betty's Family, a network for gay, lesbian, bisexual and transgender employees and supporters; the Black Champions Network; the Hispanic Employee Network; the South Asian American Employee Network; and the Women's Leadership Forum. "Network members share insights, help in recruiting and retaining employees, and give input regarding culture-building initiatives and the broader organizational climate."[16]

According to management expert and author Anthony Mayo, "Businesses that will succeed in the 21st century will be those that embrace the diversity of their workforce, can compete in a global, competitive landscape, and can differentiate their products and services for a more discriminating customer base. The changes in the social context of business will require leaders (both men and women) who have a global perspective and who can harness talent and sustain innovation."

Mayo studied the factors that paved the inside path to success in the 20th century. He found that a shift has occurred and education is far more important today and a global perspective will be increasingly vital. Managing the level of complexity of a global organization requires a broader view — "one that is not restricted to a single gender, race, or nationality. In fact, a diverse perspective at the top may be a key to unleashing talent and fresh opportunities throughout the firm."[17]

## Attracting Diverse Talent

The process an organization uses to attract talent can take several forms depending on the employment strategies in place and, more specifically, on the level of the position(s) to be filled, the required knowledge and skills and the speed with which the position must be filled. Campus recruiting, search firms and internal and external job postings can all be used to solicit résumés from potential hires.

## Recruiting Strategies by Level of Position

Different strategies may be deployed depending on whether the job opening is an entry-level, midlevel or upper-level position.

**Entry-Level Positions.** For entry-level positions in supply management, many organizations require a bachelor's degree, often in supply management or some other area of business. Building a strong campus presence through on-campus recruiting, participation in career fairs and involvement with faculty and student professional associations can result in a steady inflow of new, educated talent in entry-level positions. Developing a summer internship program or a six-month cooperative program for continuing students can give an organization the opportunity to check out potential hires and employ hardworking, talented temporary help.

**Midlevel and Higher-Level Positions.** Midlevel and higher-level positions may be filled by newly graduating MBA candidates who also have several years of work experience or through a search firm to find a working professional interested in changing positions. Many hiring managers are finding that the demand for highly qualified supply management professionals is so high it takes months of diligent searching and very competitive packages to attract the best candidates. Supply management professionals who must employ search organizations are looking for organizations that specialize in supply management and that have track records of successfully placing high-quality supply management candidates. These organizations are also called on to help supply management leaders assess the market and attempt to take a measure of current conditions. The successful search organizations have some market research capabilities behind them.

## References, Experience and Education/Training

Reviewing the references, experience and training of job candidates is the first step in creating a short list of people for personal interviews. The résumé is usually the first step in the process. The hiring manager should have a clear understanding of the roles and responsibilities of the position and the education, training and experiences that would indicate a high likelihood of success. The hiring manager, often in conjunction with a human resources professional, will develop a list of questions to ask all job candidates.

**Questions in the Interview Process.** A recruiter may take a number of different approaches when interviewing a job candidate. These include behavioral interviewing, case study responses and discussion, team interviews and problem-solving exercises. The type of questions asked and the way in which they are posed should be driven by a clear understanding on the part of the interviewer of the true purpose of the question. The interviewer must be aware of the questions or types of questions that are inappropriate and possibly illegal to ask a job candidate. For example, interviewers should never ask about marital status or number of children or plans to have children. A guiding rule should be that the questions have relevance to the job itself. If a job requires extensive travel, then this information should be made available to the job candidate in the initial job description. An interviewer should not assume or presume that a working mother would be unable to meet the travel demands of the job. It would be inappropriate to pursue a line of questioning regarding children and child-care arrangements. However, an interviewer could ask the interviewee about his or her interest and willingness to travel and about past jobs that involved traveling. Interviewers should check with the organization's human resources professionals regarding the legality of specific questions.

The appendix at the end of the chapter includes sample questions that might be asked to assess an interviewee's skill level for specific skill areas. These are merely samples and in no way are intended to be all-inclusive.

## Employee Retention

Retaining high-performing employees requires as much thought and planning as attracting them in the first place. Authors Gary Berg, Mihaly Csikszentmihalyi and Jeanne Nakamura write that "good work is likely to happen when three conditions are met: (1) the work lives up to the best practices of the domain, (2) it responds to societal needs and (3) it is experienced as meaningful and enjoyable by those who do it."[18] Retention plans focus on fostering, measuring and maintaining these conditions and typically addresses how to:

- Compensate employees in salary and benefits,
- Assess and recognize the value generated by each employee,
- Develop a career progression pathway,
- Measure and increase the employee's job satisfaction level,
- Create a supportive work environment and
- Assist employees in balancing work and life.

**Compensation.** As the added value of supply management employees increases, so does the total compensation package. Total compensation includes benefits such as the ability to telecommute some or all of the time, flexible work hours, the ability to take time off for extended travel and educational opportunities. Employees at different ages and life stages may place more value on time than money. Organizations whose management allows flexibility in crafting the compensation package may be more attractive to some groups of job candidates.

**Value Assessment.** Assessing the value generated by each employee in a manner that is perceived as fair and equitable by employees is an ongoing challenge for human resources staff and managers throughout the organization. Recall the discussion about motivational theories from Chapter 1 and motivational tools and techniques in Chapter 4. Typically, individuals perform better, or at least try to, if they believe their efforts make a difference and that they will be valued.

**Career Progression.** In today's flatter organizations, often fewer opportunities for upward mobility and more for lateral moves or the expansion of responsibilities in an existing position exist. Selling employees on the value of lateral moves may be difficult in light of the individual's career aspirations and the value that society places on attaining higher levels of managerial responsibility. As an executive in a pharmaceutical organization said recently, "We can't hire them and we can't keep them." One of the advantages of a broad-based, strong supply management organization is that it offers diversity in jobs, duties and responsibilities. Supply management employees may be satisfied if they are able to learn and rotate through various components of supply management. Managers must also recognize that some people will use the opportunities to move to a higher-level position in another organization. By understanding what motivates a person, the manager may be able to tailor experiences and opportunities to the individual's motivational drivers.

**Job Satisfaction.** People are often motivated by what is measured and rewarded. Therefore, identifying and measuring the level of satisfaction with different aspects of a job is an important tool in improving overall job satisfaction. Often, human resources administer an annual survey that may be supplemented with anecdotal evidence as well as the perceptions and perspectives of people at various levels in the organization. Surveys might address salary, benefits, the work environment, the availability of proper tools to execute job responsibilities, educational opportunities, flexibility and so on.

**Work Environment.** The leadership and management team defines what constitutes a supportive work environment and is then responsible for fostering it through policies, processes and procedures. For example, Google offers an impressive array of benefits and conveniences to make employees' lives easier so they can focus on productivity without sacrificing their personal lives. The Google work environment appeals to self-motivated, high-energy people.[19] Broad Air Conditioning in Changsha, China, also provides amenities such as clothing, housing and plenty of good food. Unlike Google, it does so in a factory setting that is styled after a military organization complete with uniforms, on-site housing and meals and required physical activities. Young Chinese who are determined to make better lives for themselves forgo a measure of freedom and flexibility for the opportunity to improve their standard of living.[20]

**Balance of Work and Nonwork Lives.** In an environment marked by complexity and rapid change, there is perhaps nothing as challenging, individually and collectively, as the balancing act between worklife and nonworklife. Stories abound of employees who are essentially on call 24/7 because of the global reach of their activities. The culture of some organizations is such that the focus is on results and how and when employees do their work is less important than the results. Other organizational cultures embody the belief that employees require constant hand-holding and supervision and that presence on the job for long hours equates to productivity. The ability to retain high-performing individuals depends in part on the extent to which individual managers and the organizational culture overall fit with worklife requirements.

**Employee Promotion.** The management of an organization must have some means of identifying employees with promotion potential as well as a plan for grooming these individuals for greater levels of responsibility or for higher positions in the organization. In many organizations the number of layers of management has been reduced and there are consequently fewer rungs on the ladder. This means that there will be fewer slots available for employees with managerial capability. This creates a dilemma for an organization whose management wants to retain its best people. Developing lateral moves with increasing responsibilities, challenges and rewards is essential to retaining the best and the brightest. Management may also have to accept that certain individuals or categories of individuals may not be long-term employees. For example, hiring someone with an MBA degree may be desirable, but it may be realistic to expect that employee to stay for only four or five years before he or she will have peaked in the organization's hierarchy.

Developing solid promotion practices and communicating those practices to all employees can eliminate much of the confusion and anger that the promotion process can generate in an organization. For instance, an organization may require attaining a professional certification as a first step in career advancement. Linking the organization's training program and training requirements to specific jobs and job levels will make it clear to everyone what the basic body of knowledge is for different levels of authority in the organization. In some organizations, promotions always come from within the ranks of the organization, thus signifying to current employees that career advancement is a real possibility. Other organizations take the opposite approach and hire from the outside for management slots in an effort to cross-fertilize from other companies and industries. The behavior of employees will be driven by whichever approach an organization takes on a regular basis.

**Career Advancement.** The supply management professional must also consider the pathways for career advancement within supply management and in other areas of the organization. The size of the supply management organization, the span of control in the organization and the pace of employee turnover affect career advancement opportunities. Hiring managers strive to hire and develop ambitious, promotable people to build a strong and creative supply management organization. However, not all entry-level and buyer's jobs should be filled with individuals who will become readily promotable. Usually, there are not enough vacancies into which all can be promoted. And when a person's job no longer offers a challenge, he or she may become discontented and leave the organization or perform less effectively. For these reasons, it is essential that personnel be selected with care. During the hiring process, most managers attempt to match an individual's qualifications both to current and anticipated future job requirements of the department. It is much easier and less costly to address such issues before, rather than after, hiring has occurred. A good supply management person properly trained is invaluable; a poor one is a major liability.

At HP, diversity is included in the talent management process and the organization offers accelerated leadership development programs for employees in underrepresented ethnic groups, including a five-day training program delivered in partnership with the Society of Hispanic Professional Engineers. HP also sponsors numerous professional conferences, including the Simmons Leadership Conference, which about 500 HP women attended in 2005, and the Women's Information Network (WIN) Conference, which nearly 60 HP women from across the Europe, Middle East and Africa (EMEA) region attended.[21]

**Promoting From Within.** Some organizations are committed to promoting from within the ranks of existing departmental employees. The advantages and disadvantages to this policy are listed in Figure 9-4.

**Recruiting/Hiring From Outside the Department or Organization.** A wise manager promotes from within the department when it is practical. When such action tends to generate problems, however, personnel should be drawn from external sources. The advantages and disadvantages of recruiting or hiring employees from outside the department or outside the organization are described in Figure 9-5.

## Employee Termination

Consistent documentation and evaluation is the key to ethical and aboveboard termination of employees. For global organizations, supply management leaders must be familiar with various countries' employment laws. For example, Mexico and Brazil have what are considered more onerous requirements for termination and penalties for any terminations considered unjust. In Japan, an employee must be given 30 days' prior notice of a termination before his or her exit day. Regardless of a country's laws, employees should never be terminated on a "whim" or for vague, personal reasons; the organization's human resources policy steps for termination must be adhered to.

**Figure 9-4 Advantages and Disadvantages of Promoting From Within the Department**

| ADVANTAGES | DISADVANTAGES |
|---|---|
| Keeps morale high because employees know that they are not "trapped" in dead-end jobs. | One promotion may result in a chain of lower-level promotions, simultaneously moving several people one step up the organizational ladder. If chain promotions occur frequently, the organization tends to lose its stability because a large number of individuals are continuously learning new jobs. |
| Stimulates individual performance by offering an avenue of advancement. | When an organization is growing rapidly, this policy sometimes results in a promotion of people who are not ready to be promoted. The mediocre performance resulting from such action simply compounds the problem of instability. |
| Reduces total training costs because the employee already has substantial institutional knowledge. | Finally, promotion from within produces "inbreeding." If carried to extremes, it may stymie the flow of new ideas into the organization. |
| Shortens ramp-up time to new position because the individual already has established relationships in the organization. | |

These policies are designed to protect the organization against improper terminations, protect against personal vendettas and possibly turn a failing employee into a successful contributor to the organization.

Generally, employees should be terminated for consistent poor performance, insubordination, serious violations such as theft or chronic substance abuse. The employee should be given a reasonable amount of time to improve the poor performance or change behavior (except, perhaps, in the case of theft). The reasons for termination should be documented in accordance with human resources' documentation direction, and it is advisable that the employee be made aware that he or she is on probation prior to any termination action. Otherwise, the manager may leave the organization open for legal action by the employee.

**Figure 9-5 Advantages and Disadvantages of Hiring From Outside the Organization**

| ADVANTAGES | DISADVANTAGES |
|---|---|
| **Transfers From Other Departments** | |
| Familiarity with the organization's operations may help the transfer assume full job responsibilities sooner than a new employee. | May have a negative effect on morale and/or productivity within the department. |
| The transfer brings experience in a related functional area that may be useful in supply management activities and may provide a strong liaison with user departments. | If high-performing members of the department perceive this action as a comment on their promotability, this may lead them to look elsewhere for advancement. |
| | Also, the ability of an outside person to implement change, and the speed at which change can occur, may be hindered if existing employees resist the new person. |
| **Hiring From Outside the Organization** | |
| Hiring people from other organizations has considerable merit, particularly in the case of special staff and managerial jobs, because it brings new ideas into the organization. | May have a negative effect on morale and/or productivity within the department. |
| It also prevents the substitution of seniority for management ability. | If high-performing members of the department perceive this action as a comment on their promotability, this may lead them to look elsewhere for advancement. Also, the ability of an outside person to implement change, and the speed at which change can occur, may be hindered if existing employees resist the new person. |

**Adherence to Established Process.** Most organizations have well-outlined policies for the termination of employees. These may include personnel policies and procedures, union requirements and due process. Due process refers to the rights of the individual to the administering of law through courts of justice in accordance with established and sanctioned legal principles and procedures, and with safeguards for the protection of individual rights. In the case of union employees and layoffs, union contracts usually specify a laid-off worker's right to be recalled based on seniority. Most organizations have established procedures and documentation requirements for ensuring that termination of employees is handled as objectively as possible. Critical to the process, the leadership of global organizations must have available the employment laws of the various countries they operate in and methods in place to keep up-to-date on any laws that would change the current employment law of a country the organization works in.

**Outplacement.** Many organizations offer some form of outplacement especially for employees whose positions are eliminated by downsizing. Often in the United States an outside agency is hired to counsel former employees and assist them in moving on to another position. In areas of the country where similar jobs are unavailable, outplacement may focus on helping individuals identify transferable skills and find different types of positions that require those same skills.

**Exit Interviews.** Although more common in the United States, exit interviews with employees who are leaving the organization can be useful tools for feedback about the climate and culture of the organization. People leave organizations for many reasons. If employees are leaving because they perceive that there are better opportunities elsewhere, perhaps with a competitor, then an exit interview might provide useful information for the planning process at the human resources level.

## Succession Planning

Another critical aspect of talent management is ensuring that the supply management organization has qualified, experienced people at all levels ready to move into different positions as the need or opportunity arises. Management succession planning is the formal plan that management makes for replacement of key executive personnel. The supply management professional has primary responsibility for creating and managing a succession plan for the supply management organization and allocating work assignments in such a way as to provide career development and growth opportunities. This might be accomplished by developing a management replacement chart that lists the name of the current holder of a specific position and the names of one or two replacements for each of those positions. Another method is to develop a prediction of each individual's expected job in five years and at the end of his or her career.

This chapter focused on the managerial task of staffing that has taken on even greater emphasis in an age when knowledge is a key source of competitive advantage and knowledge may reside anywhere in the world. The primary staffing roles for the leader-manager discussed in this chapter are: (1) designing roles and assigning responsibilities and (2) developing global employment and talent management strategies. Chapter 10 addresses the supply management professional's role in creating, providing and sponsoring professional development opportunities.

## Key Points

1. The supply management professional must design roles and assign responsibilities in alignment with organizational goals and objectives and be flexible to prepare for the future.

2. Matching positions with knowledge and skills and supporting this structure with professional development opportunities will help to ensure effective organizational performance and ensure a qualified pool of candidates at each level in the group.

3. Recruitment and selection strategies must consider the increasingly diverse nature of the workforce domestically and globally.

## Some Sample Labor Law Sites

Mexico and Brazil:
www.mexicolaw.com/LawInfo11.htm
www.fredlaw.com/articles/international/intl_97sp_jlv.html

European Union:
www.ec.europa.eu/employment_social/labour_law/index_en htm
www.fedee.com/natlaw.html

Canada:
www.canlii.org/ca/sta/l-2/index.html

Japan:
www.japanlaw.info/law2004/JAPANBIZLAWLITE4GAIJIN_LABOR_LAW.html#EMPLOYMENT_RULES

India:
www.indianembassy.org/newsite/Doing_business_In_India/Labor_Laws.asp

## **Appendix:** *Sample Interview Questions*

### *Interpersonal Communication*

- What writing achievements are you most proud of?
- What are some of the most difficult writing assignments you have been given or taken on? Explain.
- Describe how you go about preparing for written or oral presentations.
- Do you prefer to communicate verbally or in writing? Why?
- Tell me about a situation when you had a personality conflict with a team member and what you did about it.
- Give an example of a time when you were able to successfully communicate with another person when that individual may not have personally liked you, or you them.
- Tell me about a time when you had to use your spoken communication skills to get a point across that was important to you.

### *Team Skills and Facilitation*

- Give an example of a time in which you felt you were able to motivate your co-workers or teammates.
- What did you do in your last job to contribute toward a team work environment?
- Tell me about a time when there was a conflict in your team and how the team handled it. Explain your role in the situation.
- Have you ever led a team of people who did not report to you? How did you gain their commitment? How did you motivate them?
- Have you led or been a member of a multicultural team? What challenges did the team face because of cultural differences? How did team members learn to work together to complete the project?

### *Analytical Problem-Solving*

- Describe a situation where you had to do a great deal of analysis to make a decision.
- Tell me about the courses or training programs you have taken that deal with research and data analysis.
- How do you determine when you have gathered enough data to make a decision?
- Tell me about a time when you had to be relatively quick in coming to a decision.

- Give me an example of a time when you had to use your fact-finding skills to gain information to solve a problem. Tell me how you analyzed the information to come to a decision.

### *Technical Competence*

- Describe your level of involvement in budget preparation or financial analysis.
- Tell me about your approach to cost analysis when making a purchasing decision.
- Tell me about courses or training programs you have taken that increased your technical knowledge and/or skills in any area.
- Tell me about a time when you did not understand something technical that related to your job and what you did about it.
- Describe the process you usually go through to get up to speed technically with a new supplier, commodity or process.

### *Web-Based Research and Sourcing Analysis*

- Describe your level of facility with conducting online research.
- Tell me about the information technology courses or training that you have had.
- Describe a time when you used Web-based research to analyze and solve a problem or to access and analyze data.
- How do you go about using a new software package?

### *Negotiation Aptitude*

- Give an example of a situation when you had to negotiate an agreement. Did you reach a win-win agreement?
- What are the steps you go through when you find you are in a situation of conflicting interests and you must get something done or make a decision?
- How do you know if an issue is negotiable?
- What steps do you take to persuade someone?
- What was the best idea you ever sold to your boss? Why did he or she buy into it?

### *Education and Professionalism*

- Why did you or did you not attain a professional certification in your field?
- What have you done most recently to increase your knowledge or ability in a job-related area?

- What is your plan for the next 6 to 12 months as far as your personal training and development?

### *Continual Learning*

- Are you satisfied with your current level of training and education? Why or why not?
- To what extent do you think training and professional development is driven by the organization not the individual?
- What magazines, newspapers, trade journals or online sources do you read regularly? How does this help you on the job?

CHAPTER

# 10

# Developing Supply Management Talent

*When planning for a year, plant corn.*
*When planning for a decade, plant trees.*
*When planning for life, train and educate people.*

CHINESE PROVERB

As discussed in Chapter 9, human capital is a critical factor in achieving the leader's vision. One of the primary roles of the supply management professional is to develop talent management strategies, including creating, providing and sponsoring professional development opportunities to ensure that supply management employees have the right knowledge and skills necessary to make the vision a reality, especially in complex, rapidly changing environments.

In a recent global survey of supply management executives at more than 200 organizations conducted by McKinsey & Co. and the Supply Management Institute of the European Business School, researchers found that nearly 60 percent of the difference between the financial performance of high-performing and low-performing organizations was because of three talent dimensions: (1) the capabilities of the supply management units themselves, (2) the way supply management professionals view their roles and the aspirations they associate with these roles and (3) the involvement of supply management executives in broad business planning.[1]

In high-performing organizations, capabilities included analytical expertise and general management background. Supply management executives felt that their CEOs expected more than cost cutting; the supply management executives had a clear vision of how to achieve these other goals; and they believed they contributed to an organizational culture of continuous improvement. Supply management executives were also included in the concept phase of product development, they engaged with sales and marketing for innovation, and they were involved in premerger due diligence and postmerger value capture.[2] This survey illustrates the level of expertise required of supply management executives in the most progressive organizations.

Chapter 3 focused on how to align people behind the vision of supply management. Chapter 9 addressed the supply management professional's responsibility for designing roles and developing strategies for attracting, hiring and retaining supply management personnel. This chapter continues the talent management discussion by focusing on the leader-manager's role in continuously developing supply management personnel and ensuring that the organization has a succession of qualified leader-managers.

### CHAPTER OBJECTIVES

- Identify the types of professional development opportunities available to supply management personnel.
- Develop a means of assessing the effectiveness of the professional development program.

## Professional Development Opportunities

> *The illiterate of the 21st century will not be those who cannot read and write, but those who cannot learn, unlearn, and relearn.* ALVIN TOFFLER[3]

The supply management professional must transform the supply management group into a learning organization. Peter Senge, author of *The Fifth Discipline: The Art and Practice of the Learning Organization,* defined a learning organization as one "where people continually expand their capacity to create the results they truly desire, where new and expansive patterns of thinking are nurtured, where collective aspiration is set free, and where people are continually learning how to learn together."[4] According to Arie de Geus, former head of planning for Royal Dutch/Shell, a pioneer of organizational learning and author of *The Living Company,* "The ability to learn faster than your competitors may be the only sustainable competitive advantage."[5]

Individual commitment to continual learning reflects a perspective that is not focused merely on acquiring skills on an as-needed basis; rather, it reflects a desire and drive on the part of the individual for continuous personal improvement. Chapter 1 addressed theories of motivation such as Maslow's Hierarchy of Needs and different management styles that may contribute to the development of employees with a commitment to continual learning. Identifying, hiring and retaining individuals who are committed to continual learning is critical for organizational success in a rapidly changing business world. Identifying these individuals can, however, be a difficult process.

If a manager expects to use employees effectively over the long term, he or she must assume the responsibility for assisting and guiding them in the continued development of their capabilities. For example, part of the rationale for relocating IBM's global procurement headquarters to Shenzhen, China, and for John Paterson, vice president and chief procurement officer, to relocate is the development of future leaders. "Once this shift occurs, it requires a focused and thoughtful approach to simultaneously transfer knowledge and build the management capabilities to lead the work. Mr. Paterson is in Asia to do just that; to expand and strengthen IBM's internal procurement skills in the region; develop leaders and prepare them to take on global roles."[6]

In a 2006 global survey of business executives, *The McKinsey Quarterly* found that two out of three respondents say that "They face increasing risks to their ability to supply their customers with goods and services cost-effectively. … topping the list is the availability of well-trained labor."[7] While labor, regulation and suppliers ranked as the top three risks, the availability, cost and quality of labor was the most cited concern in every region except Latin America, where regulation was the top concern.

Many organizations face challenges in planning and executing the professional development of a global workforce. Formal management education, and the development of a managerial class, is fairly new in many emerging markets. The number of domestic management schools are growing in many regions of the world and so are joint ventures with Western business schools. Educators face a challenge similar to that of managers: Western-style management education cannot always be overlaid on a non-Western culture. The globalization of management education is critical for people and their organizations if they want to be truly global.

Determination of an individual's specific development needs is a product of observation and periodic counseling by the manager with the individual employee. These needs should be determined jointly, and plans for subsequent training experiences should also be planned jointly for the ensuing 6- to 12-month period.

Developing global leaders is so important that many organizations seek to accelerate leadership development for leaders that have global potential. The 2007 study by the Conference Board suggests supply management leaders must provide an international training framework, offer early assessment and experience, implement career stage development, devise accelerated career tracks, modify an organization's current succession planning strategy, implement rotational assignments in growth areas and provide access to internationally experienced coaches, mentors and role models to help speed up global leadership development.[8] Young potential leaders must be sent on international assignments very early in their careers, and these talented prospects must be given special projects, task forces, temporary assignments and committees that are international in scope. Additionally, international management education and training opportunities are maximized.[9]

Organizations can take a number of different approaches to determine training and development needs. The basic process should include some comparison of job requirements to the skills needed to achieve desired performance levels in each position.

### Skills Assessment

One process that might be used to assess skills and determine training needs involves three phases. Phase one is the development of a mission statement for supply management and a clear description of the underlying assumptions about the supply management function and exactly what is required to perform the job. Phase two entails the development of a list of the supply management skills required and the competencies needed to function at various levels in the supply management organization. Profiles of specific positions can then be developed for use in attracting candidates and selecting employees, assessing performance and developing career paths and professional development opportunities. Phase three involves the ongoing comparison of desired competency levels with actual performance on an individual basis. This evaluation process feeds directly into the professional development goals and programs for supply management professionals. In a dynamic environment, the required skills, desired competency level, or actual performance may change because of internal or external forces.

### Job Analysis/Diagnostic Evaluation

Some organizations develop a diagnostic tool to target specific training and development needs for their supply management personnel. The diagnostic program typically begins with a job analysis that identifies the important tasks of the supply management department in question. Next, each participant is given a diagnostic test that measures his or her comprehension of the basic tasks surveyed in the job analysis. Then participants are compared to norms to determine their strengths and weaknesses in the various supply management tasks. Lastly, the results of the job analysis and the diagnostic are combined to create a customized training program, targeted to the areas that are important to the organization but still to be mastered by individual staff members. In this way, the training programs are designed to maximize the performance of the personnel in the most efficient way possible.

During a traditional diagnostic process and while engaging some of the typical methods of assessment to measure comprehension and skill sets, some global leaders watch for learning agility and use it as a selection criterion for global talent.[10] Learning agility — the enthusiasm and ability to learn what is to be learned and the application of that learning to other situations — is one of a small number of cultural traits associated with leaders in a business context. While most executives admit that no instrument can be used to accurately detect learning agility, they insist on its importance for the potential global candidate.

## Gap Analysis

Gap analysis refers to the process of measuring the difference (and distance) between the actual skill level of an employee and the desired skill level for the employee's job position combined with the importance rating of the skill to determine training priorities. Figure 10-1 shows a sample gap analysis process.

This profile can be used by an employee and his or her supervisor in conjunction with performance appraisal or coach and counseling sessions. The profile allows the individual to first conduct a self-assessment of current skill levels and then, with his or her supervisor, establish an action plan providing opportunities, both in training and on-the-job experiences, to enhance personal skills consistent with his or her current position. The profiles also can serve as discussion tools for supervisors to explain how skill requirements differ for other job assignments.

The Conference Board's 2007 study on developing global leadership uses a list with three sections — interpersonal, group and organizational — to explain global leadership skill set requirements. Relationship building underpins the list, while leadership sits at the top. Then the following 12 skill sets are required that move from the bottom of the list up:

1. Establishing credibility
2. Giving/receiving feedback
3. Obtaining information
4. Evaluating people
5. Building global teamwork
6. Training and development
7. Selling
8. Negotiating
9. Strategic planning
10. Transferring knowledge
11. Innovating
12. Managing change.[11]

**Figure 10-1 Gap Analysis Example**

**1. Identify Relevant Skill Areas**

MANAGERIAL SKILLS

- Planning and strategic development
- Project management
- Supply base management and development
- Contract development and administration
- Time management

INTERPERSONAL SKILLS

- Effective cross-cultural communications
- Negotiating within and across cultures
- Global business ethics
- Professional development
- Leadership skills/team building
- Problem-solving skills

ANALYTICAL SKILLS

- Accounting/microeconomics/financial aspects
- Business math/statistics
- Material management
- Cost and price analysis

COMMERCIAL SKILLS

- Macroeconomics
- Domestic and international business law
- Risk management
- Industrial processes
- Transportation basics
- Quality
- Global supply management
- Supply management methods and practices
- Social responsibility
- Supplier certification

**2. Establish Degree of Importance (Weight) of Skill to Job and Measure Current Competency (typically based on responses from multiple people)**

Managers assess the degree of importance of each skill to each position on a scale of 1 to 5 where 1 = least important and 5 = most important.

x = average response for recommended competency to perform the job.

Managers assess each employee's actual performance.

o = average response for perceived skill level of today's supply management staff.

**3. Measure Gap Between Importance and Skill Level to Prioritize Improvement Efforts**

Difference between o (perceived skill level) and x (recommended competency), multiplied by the average weight assigned to skill.

## Determining Training and Development Needs

> *Managers should focus on people's strengths instead of their weaknesses. Rather than dwell on the areas where a worker is weak, find out what he does well, determine the context in which he is able to exercise his positive capabilities — and let him do it. Make his shortcomings irrelevant. The function of an organization is to make human strength productive — and this is accomplished by building on people's assets, not by bemoaning their limitations.* PETER DRUCKER[12]

After the initial orientation and job training, the supply management professional must be concerned with the continuing professional development of supply management personnel. The framework developed around necessary knowledge and skills earlier in this chapter can be applied when identifying, developing or acquiring professional development opportunities. Different approaches are taken in different regions of the world. In China, for example, business enterprises run schools and schools operate businesses on a substantial scale. In Germany and other European countries, employers take major responsibility for the education and training of young people. In the United States, there has historically been a clearer separation between schools and businesses, although there are changes as businesses work with colleges to design and offer organization-specific or organization-tailored MBA programs and executive education or corporate learning.

In their research report, "Key Skill Sets for the Supply Manager of the Future" completed in 2004, Giunipero and Handfield used the input from 55 supply management executives in large organizations with global operations to identify the top training requirements now and in the future (see Figure 10-2). Clearly the acquisition and application of these skills becomes more complex in a global organization where there are multiple cultures, business norms, languages, communication styles, and decision-making processes.

## Team Building: Leadership, Decision-Making, Influencing, Compromising

Teams are a way of life in many organizations. Learning to serve as a team leader, team member or team facilitator, therefore, is critical to the success of most people. Management must decide how teams will be used, who will serve on teams and how they will be structured. Especially in an international setting, individuals should be willing and able to listen to other people, approaches and ideas. They must respect other cultures and not be judgmental or arrogant. If team members are to work in a self-directed team,

**Figure 10-2 Top Training Requirements Referenced by Focus Group Participants**

| TOP TRAINING REQUIREMENTS | |
|---|---|
| **Team building** | Leadership, decision-making, influencing and compromising |
| **Strategic planning skills** | Project scoping, goal-setting and execution |
| **Communication skills** | Presentation, public speaking, listening and writing |
| **Technical skills** | Web-enabled research and sourcing analysis |
| **Broader financial skills** | Cost accounting and making the business case |
| **Relationship management skills** | Ethics, facilitation, conflict resolution and creative problem-solving |
| **Legal issues** | Contract writing and risk mitigation in a global environment |

*Source:* Larry Giunipero and Robert Handfield, "Key Skill Sets for the Supply Manager of the Future," CAPS Research, 2004

then they must receive appropriate training from the organization before embarking on a self-led project. In some organizations, personality profiles are used to assist team members in appreciating and understanding differences and to enhance team productivity. For example, the Myers-Briggs Type Indicator (MBTI) identifies each person as one of 16 personality types. This information is then used to learn to work better with others and to better manage one's own work. The DISC profile uses a four dimensional model that includes dominance, influence, steadiness and conscientiousness.

Each of us has leadership opportunities within our sphere of influence. The supply management professional must also take responsibility for supporting the development of each subordinate's leadership potential. The supply management professional can mentor, coach and train or provide training for people to fully develop their leadership potential. A person's span of influence is probably a better indicator of his or her leadership ability than his or her formal span of control. Internationally, a person should be open-minded, flexible and culturally sensitive. Likewise, a person's ability to effect transformational change in the organization depends on his or her ability to create a shared vision and motivate and inspire others to remain committed to that vision through good times and bad. Developing one's own ability to cooperate, collaborate and build consensus and fostering those abilities in others are key components of leadership development and especially critical to succession planning.

Employers responding to the *Job Outlook 2007* survey of the National Association of Colleges and Employers (NACE) said that the job candidate who has held leadership positions has the edge over those who have no such record.[13] Likewise, in a recent *Wall Street Journal* article, corporate recruiters stated that the most valued leadership characteristics are being honest and trustworthy, accomplishing what one sets out to do, working well with others in a team setting and motivating and inspiring others. In general, recruiters believe men and women demonstrate leadership characteristics equally. But some said women are more inclined to care about others, are open to opposing viewpoints, work effectively in teams and demonstrate honesty and trustworthiness. As for men, recruiters believe they are more likely to motivate and inspire others and are more "consistent, focused and *able to stay the course during difficult times.*"[14] This type of understanding of leadership strengths and differences might be useful when designing leadership development programs as well as recognizing the complexity of skills needed for international teams and leadership.

Being an effective decision-maker is also a critical leadership skill. Decision-making includes a number of skills, including information gathering, analysis, selecting an option from a number of choices and implementing or overseeing implementation. Decisions are rarely made in an atmosphere of complete information or complete certainty. Being decisive means being able to recognize when enough information is available and enough analysis has been conducted to make a decision. The ability to act on the decision rounds out the process. It may be difficult to find individuals who can conduct the analysis, make the decision and implement or oversee the implementation of the decision.

Analytical problem-solving refers to an individual's ability to apply basic problem-solving steps to analyze any type of problem, reach a decision and act on that decision. The basic steps in problem-solving are to identify the problem, determine its importance and urgency, analyze the problem quantitatively and qualitatively, generate alternatives, compare alternatives to a set of decision criteria, make a decision and develop and carry out an action and implementation plan. Being analytical refers to the ability to identify and gather relevant information; to synthesize, compare and interpret such data in light of the problem; and to recognize relationships, issues, obstacles and opportunities in the process of generating alternative courses of action. A problem-solver is one who can take this analysis (whether self-generated or provided by someone else) and select an appropriate course of action.

The ability to influence and persuade people and to compromise effectively becomes more important in organizations where empowerment, shared control and individual and team commitment is the prevailing management philosophy rather than a top-down, command-and-control philosophy. In the supply management arena, managing relationships with key internal stakeholders and suppliers is largely a continuing process of influencing, persuading and resolving conflicts.

## Strategic Planning Skills: Project-Scoping, Goal-Setting and Execution

A second area of importance is strategic planning skills, especially the ability to scope out a project, set goals and execute.

**Project-Scoping.** According to the Project Management Institute, project scope management is the process of ascertaining that the project includes all the work required, and only the work required, to complete the project successfully. The project scope management processes include:

- *Scope planning.* Documents how the project will be defined, verified and controlled and how the work breakdown structure will be created and defined.
- *Scope definition.* A detailed project scope statement that serves as the basis for future project decisions.
- *Create work breakdown structure (WBS).* Subdivide major project deliverables and project work into smaller, more manageable components.
- *Scope verification.* Fformalizing acceptance of the completed project deliverables.
- *Scope control.* Controlling changes to the project scope.[15]

**Goal-Setting.** The ability to set goals is also part of the strategic planning skill set. Goals lead to performance if they motivate individuals by focusing attention, directing actions, increasing commitment and encouraging planning. Therefore, effective goal setting is a skill needed by everyone in the organization. In the hiring and development processes, the leader-manager should try to assess the individual's goal-setting ability.

While there are many goal-setting techniques, one that is frequently cited for its effectiveness is the SMART system attributed to Kenneth Blanchard and Spencer Johnson.[16] SMART is an acronym for

*S*pecific
*M*easurable
*A*ttainable
*R*ealistic
*T*ime-bound/trackable

The leader-manager should try to assess an individual's ability to set goals prior to hiring and continue to develop this skill in his or her direct reports.

**Execution.** The ability to execute plans efficiently and effectively and attain goals is as important as the ability to develop goals and plans. The supply management professional must also ensure that people who can execute or oversee the execution of plan are hired, trained and promoted. The right people can only execute flawlessly if the organization also has enabling, instead of disabling, structures, technologies and processes in place and the leader-manager must work to ensure these enablers exist.

### Communication Skills: Presentation, Public Speaking, Listening and Writing

Interpersonal communication often appears at the tops of lists of desired attributes of employees in general and supply management professionals in particular. According to the NACE *Job Outlook 2007,* "Year after year, the number one skill employers say they want to see in job candidates is good communication skills: the ability to write and speak clearly. Unfortunately — in spite of requesting this skill year after year — many employers also report that college graduates lack good grammar and writing skills."[17] The interest in the interpersonal communication skills of job candidates is not new. This emphasis on interpersonal communication represents a shift from transaction-oriented communication to communication that optimizes the whole relationship with others (both suppliers and customers).

Emotional intelligence is as important as IQ for success in today's workplace. "Most innovations today involve large teams of people," says former Lockheed Martin CEO Norman Augustine. "We have to emphasize communication skills, the ability to work in teams and with people from different cultures."[18]

Many people are fearful of public speaking and even highly educated people can have weak writing skills. The leader-manager must work with people to recognize where they can contribute the most to the supply management organization and how the team can compensate for individual weaknesses to create a strong and diverse communication capability.

### Broader Financial Skills: Cost Accounting and Making the Business Case

Supply management personnel are increasingly expected to possess and use broader financial skills such as cost accounting and be able to build a strong business case for a recommendation. A professional development program for supply management personnel might include seminars, courses and on-the-job training in acquiring and applying cost-accounting knowledge to conduct cost analysis and better manage costs.

### Technical Skills: Web-Enabled Sourcing Analysis and Market Intelligence

For the supply management professional, technical knowledge and skills refers to the ability to maximize the effectiveness of e-sourcing and enterprise resource planning (ERP) tools and analyze the information gathered in the sourcing process. The supply management professional must be able to acquire and analyze relevant data online and within existing organizational information technology systems and adapt quickly and easily to emerging technologies. Familiarity with different types of hardware, software and systems has become a basic requirement of employment in organizations as well as their use to proactively assess sourcing opportunities, identify alternatives and evaluate markets and supplier proposals. Supply-chain management is largely driven by the ability to manage information flows within and among organizations and information technology is a key tool in the growth of effective supply-chain management.

While many organizations will seek individuals who already know how to use the exact system employed by the organization, in the long run it is far more important for individuals to be able to quickly become proficient with any hardware, software or system. The computer is merely the tool; the real talent for a supply management professional lies in being able to identify relevant information in a format that will facilitate decision-making.

### Relationship Management Skills: Ethics, Facilitation, Conflict Resolution and Creative Problem-Solving

Chapter 2 addressed the importance of creating a value-based, ethical organization as the basic foundation of the supply management organization. Chapters 3 and 4 addressed the tools and techniques that can be used to build and maintain internal and external partnerships.

According to Roger M. Schwarz, author of *The Skilled Facilitator,* group facilitation is a process in which an outside person intervenes to help the group improve the way it handles and solves problems and makes decisions to increase the group's effectiveness. The outside facilitator must be acceptable to all members of the group and must be substantively neutral, with no decision-making authority. Schwarz goes on to say that a member of a team can adopt the skills of a facilitator to act as a facilitative leader who focuses attention on group processes used to solve problems and make decisions.[19] Developing facilitative leaders who possess the skills of a facilitator and creating the core principles and values necessary for open, free communication are challenges for team-based organizations.

**Conflict Resolution.** Conflict is inevitable in many situations. Individuals deal with conflict in a number of ways, including fleeing, fighting, smoothing, capitulating and resisting. Cross-functional and cross-organizational teams with competing or, worse, conflicting objectives will undoubtedly experience conflict. Efforts must be made to train people to manage conflict in a constructive manner. Research suggests that team results are better if there is some conflict and team members work through it rather than if the team smoothes over the conflict to keep the peace.

**Creative Problem-Solving.** Problem-solving is defined as a higher-order cognitive process that requires the modulation and control of more routine or fundamental skills that occur when a person does not know how to proceed from a given state to a desired goal state.[20] Difficult problems have typical characteristics, including lack of clarity of the situation, multiple goals, complexity, dynamism and unpredictability.

Creativity is a mental process that generates new ideas or concepts or new associations between and among existing ones. "One thing we know about creativity is that it typically occurs when people who have mastered two or more quite different fields use the framework in one to think afresh about the other," said Marc Tucker, head of the U.S.–based National Center on Education and the Economy.[21] Two common characteristics of creative output are that it is both novel and useful. According to George Kneller, "Creativity, it has been said, consists largely of rearranging what we know in order to find out what we do not know. Hence to think creatively, we must be able to look afresh at what we normally take for granted."[22]

Teresa Amabile argued that to enhance creativity in business, three components were needed: (1) expertise (technical, procedural and intellectual knowledge), (2) creative thinking skills (how flexibly and imaginatively people approach problems) and (3) motivation (especially intrinsic motivation).[23] While management of most organizations states that creativity and the ability to "think outside the box" is desired in employees, large, rule-bound, hierarchical organizations may not foster an environment that is conducive to creative thinking and creative problem-solving. Supply management professionals are challenged to create a workplace environment that is conducive to creative thinking. More recent research by Amabile suggests that "Managers should try to avoid or reduce the 'obstacles to creativity' (time pressure and organizational impediments like political problems, harsh criticism of new ideas and emphasis on the status quo) and enhance the 'stimulants to creativity' (freedom, positive challenge in the work); sufficient resources (work-group supports, putting together diversely skilled teams that communicate well, are mutually committed to the work and constructively discuss ideas); supervisory encouragement (team leaders who communicate effectively with the group, value individual contributions, protect the group within the organization, set clear goals while allowing freedom in meeting the goals and serve as good work models); and organizational encouragement (like conversations about ideas across the organization, and a top management focus on rewarding and recognizing good creative work)."[24]

**Legal Issues, Contract Writing and Risk Mitigation in a Global Environment.** Supply management personnel must also have knowledge about the legal environment, including relevant laws and regulations, the ability to write sound contracts or recognize the need for legal advice and to mitigate risks.

## Designing and Planning Training Programs

*I hear and I forget. I see and I remember. I do and I understand.*

CONFUCIUS, 551–479 BC

Once training needs have been determined, it must be decided how to provide the training that will achieve the desired results. A number of approaches can be taken to design training programs.

Globally, because the demand for talent outstrips supply in certain parts of the world, designing and planning training programs must take this into account. Supply management leaders must ask themselves what types of training can be implemented quickly and effectively.

**Competency-Based Training.** Competency-based training is driven by the idea that training should result in trainees knowing how to do something specific. For managers and developers of training, the key issues are: (1) What are the specific skills trainees should acquire? (2) How should these skills be taught? and (3) How will results be measured? This approach is very practical and rooted in employee behaviors. Learning objectives are then written specifically around something that trainees will be able to do and something that is measurable. For example, the statement "Seminar participant will understand total cost of analysis" does not give any indication of how this understanding will be assessed. On the other hand, the statement "Seminar participants will be able to identify critical cost components, estimate value and discuss missing relevant cost data" gives a clearer picture of what the training will entail and what is expected of trainees after the session. The documentation of expected competencies and the resources available to train personnel in the skills needed to achieve them are the responsibility of every supply management department.

For example, one global financial services firm was forced to use competency-based training as a result of its various acquisitions of other firms over the past several years. The supply management division of the organization had to fast-track train some of its newly acquired supply management professionals from the acquired firms in certain areas of supply management such as total cost management and asset management. They were able to measure the success of the training the professionals received by testing their competency levels as they performed in the new areas and then would make adjustments where needed.

## Types of Training

Several types of training may be offered to supply management employees, starting with orientation training for new hires and continuing with on-the-job training, rotational programs and mentoring. These activities might be supplemented by on-site or off-site seminars or classes and online courses to support the existing and changing requirements of a position. Training might also include professional certification, formal degrees and professional association involvement.

**Functional Orientation.** Orientation to the supply management function, including supply management processes, policies, procedures and technology, is typically the first form of training that most employees undergo. This is typically conducted during new-hire orientation and on-the-job training in a new position.

**Initial Job Training or Orientation.** Employee orientation involves the introduction of the new person to the job and the organization. The primary goals are often to explain the organization's history, products, services and operations; clarify job expectations; and relieve feelings of insecurity in a new environment. New or untrained personnel may be overwhelmed with job requirements and organizational systems. These orientations often include formal instruction, and the use of personnel manuals, employee handbooks, policy and procedures manuals and tours. These manuals, often maintained online for ease of access and revision, make supervision easier, define standard practices, ensure consistency of results and aid in training. Usually, human resources departments run orientation programs in person or on the intranet with the new employee's supervisor playing a major role.

**On-the-Job or Learning by Doing.** The most basic method of training is to give general guidelines about what needs to be done and let the employees teach themselves. Of course, this method cannot be employed in all instances and should be used with caution. Learning by doing is probably most effective when the employee is already well trained or experienced in the work he or she has been hired to perform.

This may be the only available method if no peer, supervisor or training facilities are available as knowledge resources.

**Sponsor/Mentor Program.** Another commonly used practice is to assign a sponsor, mentor or buddy to the newly hired person. The sponsor is typically an experienced employee doing similar work. The sponsor acts as an informal trainer during the entire period the new person is learning the job. A sponsor should be chosen for his or her experience and, more important, his or her teaching ability. The sponsor may require training to perform this role effectively. For example, at General Mills, Inc., the organization provides a mentoring program in which minority employees are paired with senior-level managers and executives to improve communication and understanding at all levels of the organization.[25]

This approach can be quite effective if the sponsor is a good teacher. The probable disadvantage, however, is that it restricts the new person's initial training to a single job. Some time may elapse before he or she fully realizes the many implications of the activities of the job and how they relate to departments outside supply management. Also, the time devoted to such training activities may significantly reduce the sponsor's productive output.

A joint *Wall Street Journal* and *MIT Sloan Management Review* study suggests coaching and mentoring but advocates frequent interaction for global candidates so they can share concerns and best practices, and offer executive-education opportunities that will supplement the candidates skills and perspectives.[26]

**Functional Rotation.** To minimize its shortcomings, many organizations modify the sponsor or mentor system by adding a functional rotation program. Before a new employee is assigned to a specific job, he or she is considered a trainee for a period varying from several weeks to several months. Much of this initial training is frequently spent in various functional areas such as purchasing, operations, inventory, marketing, materials management, strategic planning and finance. The basic idea is to expose the individual to a number of functional activities both within and outside the supply management area. This will facilitate understanding the needs of various stakeholders in the organization and the relationship of supply management to other operating functions. Specific assignments vary depending on the person's background and on his or her first permanent job assignment. The program's objective, however, is to develop a general understanding of key processes in the organization. On completion of rotational training, the new employee is assigned to a specific job where he or she may receive further job training from a mentor or supervisor.

Functional rotations on an international scope can take on slightly different characteristics such as maintaining three-year rotation plans for key leader successors to top leadership positions to guide their development. On the other hand, some organizations use international rotational assignments sparingly, believing that the logistics of making them work can be complex and costly.[27]

**On-Site or Off-Site Classroom Training.** Training may also consist of a series of short-duration classroom courses dealing with theoretical principles underlying supply management's role and related tools and standard practices. These programs can be designed to provide substantive training and practice along with the opportunity to build rapport with other supply management personnel and, in some situations, with people from related departments. These courses may be offered on-site or off-site and taught by internal trainers, managers or executives or by outside professors or practitioners.

Globally, classroom-structured education and training has become a way to discover new talent, especially in places where demand outstrips supply.[28] Because recruiting and retaining local business leaders in developing countries around the world has its challenges, supply management leaders are meeting with international leaders and educators at various global business schools to establish ongoing relationships. Supply management leaders even give lectures, talk to students about the supply management profession and about leadership. By getting into schools early and working together, global students become potential hires. They can also become familiar with the supply management leaders established in their specific global regions.

**Professional Certification.** Institute for Supply Management™ (ISM) has been offering a certification program for supply management professionals for more than 30 years. The Certified Professional in Supply Management (CPSM) designation originated in 2008. Prior to this certification, ISM offered the Certified Purchasing Manager (C.P.M.) certification, consisting of a four-module exam (along with other requirements). Attaining a certification level requires commitment and dedication to professional development. Other professional associations offer certifications for supply management or related fields.

For the individual, certification may lead to peer recognition, better job opportunities, enhanced value to the employer and faster professional advancement. For the employer, it provides evidence that the supply management professional has met standards deemed important by the profession and has the tools to do a good job. Certification as one criterion for promotion may help the employer establish sound requirements for knowledge acquisition and application in place of loose, haphazard or arbitrary promotion practices.

**Formal Education and Advanced Degrees.** Many employers require or prefer supply management employees to have a formal education and possibly an advanced degree in supply management. Now many colleges and universities offer face-to-face, online or blended programs at the associate's, bachelor's, master's and doctoral levels in supply management and related areas. The supply management professional may define the criteria for targeting schools or assist in the assessment of degree programs to best match the needs of the supply management group with the school's program.

More and more supply management leaders are working with international business schools in developing countries to develop or help in the development of supply management coursework. For educational programs already in existence, supply management leaders try to work with the educational institution to enhance the coursework by contributing real-life case studies or becoming available to lecture.

**Professional Association Involvement.** Another means of improving oneself professionally is through active involvement in a professional association such as a local affiliate of ISM. This may take the form of active membership or leadership.

Professional association involvement is offering an ever-increasing value network domestically and globally as members use every opportunity to seek out talent. Organizations are losing leaders at a much faster pace than they are producing them. More than 30 million managers and leaders will be retiring within the next several years as the baby boomers retire.[29] Supply management leaders who make full use of their affiliation with professional associations can tap into resources relating to recruiting, retaining and training development. Professional associations can also become the recruiting ground for future supply management leaders.

# Assessing the Effectiveness of the Professional Development Program

## Training, Cost Efficiency and Measurement of Outcomes

The outcomes of training should be measured in behavioral and operational terms to determine the effectiveness of the training effort (including how trainees actually behave back on their jobs) and the relevance of their behavior to the organization's objectives. In this way, the utility or value of the training can be assessed. Questions usually addressed when evaluating training programs are:

1. Was there a change in knowledge, skills and/or abilities related to supply management effectiveness in the various participants?

2. Were these changes because of the training?

3. Are the new skills positively related to the organization's goals?

4. Will similar changes occur for new participants in the training program?

5. Was the training cost-effective? Was it worth the expense to the organization? Could the same effect have been achieved with another less expensive training mode?

To determine the answers to these questions, techniques of educational research — tests, questionnaires, interviews and experimental design — need to be employed by trained researchers. The evaluators can answer the previous questions using objective, quantitative and qualitative research methods, and provide data for making decisions on whether to continue, discontinue or modify a training program. Only in this way can an objective, informed assessment of a training mode be made.

This chapter focused on the managerial task of staffing that has taken on even greater emphasis in an age when knowledge is a key source of competitive advantage. The primary roles for the leader-manager are: (1) design roles and assign responsibilities, (2) develop global employment and talent management strategies, (3) create, provide and sponsor professional development opportunities. Chapter 11 covers the measurement of supply management department performance.

## Key Points

1. Many believe that a learning organization will provide a significant competitive advantage through continual knowledge creation and sharing.

2. The supply management professional must design roles and assign responsibilities in alignment with organizational goals and objectives and be flexible to prepare for the future.

3. Matching positions with knowledge and skills and supporting this structure with professional development opportunities will help to ensure effective organizational performance and ensure a qualified pool of candidates at each level in the group.

4. Recruitment and selection strategies must consider the increasingly diverse nature of the workforce domestically and globally.

5. Three elements to achieve the best training results are: (1) job analysis, (2) diagnostic testing and (3) gap analysis.

CHAPTER

# 11

# Measuring the Supply Management Department Performance

*In the business world, the rearview mirror is always clearer than the windshield.* WARREN BUFFETT[1]

**A** department-level performance measurement and management system must be developed and implemented to ensure that supply management is maximizing its contribution to the organization. The figure in the "How to Use This Book" section of this book identified human resource management, development and measurement as a supporting structure in supply management strategy and philosophy. Chapter 6 addressed the development of strategic and operational plans for supply management. These plans should include the goals and objectives of the department. These goals and objectives should then drive the behavior of the department staff. Individual performance should be linked to the achievement of overall department goals that, in turn, should contribute to the achievement of organizational goals and objectives. The supplier community has been described as the "extended enterprise." In this context, the performance of the suppliers under the leadership of the supply management team is a critical element of the enterprise's overall results. Supplier performance measurement and management is covered in *Foundation of Supply Management,* (ISM Professional Series).

To be effective, the performance evaluation and reward system must be aligned with the goals and objectives of the organization. For example, if a major organizational initiative is continuous quality improvement, but the individual is evaluated and rewarded primarily for price reductions, then the individual may be more concerned with price reductions than quality improvements. Unless credit is given for reducing the cost of quality, the means used to achieve the necessary price reduction may work against the ability of the supply management function to contribute to the overall organizational goal of quality improvement. If top management wants supply management to support the achievement of the organization's goals and achieve its mission, then behavior that leads to attaining organizational goals must be recognized and rewarded. Developing a flexible performance evaluation system that can be adjusted to accommodate changes in strategic plans is a difficult task for the supply management team and their peers in human resources management.

Chapter 4 addressed the *leadership* task of gaining commitment to the new supply management vision and strategies. This chapter addresses the complementary *management* task of measuring and managing supply management department performance. This chapter focuses on four key questions relating to performance measurement systems and performance management:

1. *Why* should we measure?
2. *What* should we measure?
3. *How* should we measure?
4. *What* can supply management professionals do with the results?

### CHAPTER OBJECTIVES

- Explain the importance of aligning departmental performance metrics with organizational objectives.
- Discuss the reasons and methods for evaluating performance at the department level.
- Identify the key steps in performing a department-level evaluation.

## Aligning Department Performance Metrics With Organizational Objectives

There are many reasons why management might measure the supply management department performance:

- To determine the departmental effectiveness in meeting organizational needs,
- To determine the effectiveness of department management,
- To measure improvement/deterioration,
- To provide incentives for improvement,

- To determine the resources needed for improvement and
- To determine if value is added to the process.

## Effectiveness in Meeting Organizational Needs

The overriding purpose of measuring departmental performance is to determine and ensure that the department is effectively meeting the needs of the organization. This purpose drives the development of the key performance indicators (KPIs) for the department. To be effective, these KPIs must be rooted in the objectives of the department, function and process of supply management, and the objectives of supply management must be aligned with organizationwide objectives.

Likewise, each function, department and process within the organization must have objectives that are also aligned with the organizationwide objectives. This vertical alignment helps keep everyone in the organization conscious of, and contributing to, the success of the organization in achieving its vision and mission. There must also be horizontal alignment between and among departments, functions and processes to eliminate or at least minimize productivity-sapping conflict within the organization caused by conflicting and competing objectives.

**Congruence With Organizational Objectives.** To determine departmental or functional effectiveness in meeting organizational needs, the mission of the total organization and the specific objectives of the supply management organization must be understood. Chapter 6 discussed the importance of aligning functional or departmental strategy with organizational strategy. Once the organizational mission is understood, this information can be related to the ability of those in the supply management function to perform tasks that, when combined, ultimately contribute to organizational goals.

The specific objectives of a supply management function may be described as obtaining maximum value, prescribed quality and continuity of supply in keeping with the organizational objectives of continuous improvement and quality. Benchmarks then can be established to measure the impact of the departmental efforts. Much emphasis is placed on cost/benefit analysis. Supply management contributes to organizational goals in many ways, including cost, quality, technology and speed. This makes the supply management function's "added value" and, in the private sector, contribution to profit possible to document. Other ways that supply management professionals can contribute to organizational goals, such as through the quality of supplier relationships, may be harder to measure. These "softer" measures may actually contribute more to organizational success, but because of the difficulty in documenting and measuring them, they may be left out of the appraisal system.

For example, the scorecard of Roger Weiss, the vice president of material and supply at Rockwell Collins, Inc., aligns with the operations and corporate scorecards. Team performance of each is measured on three key metrics: (1) material availability, (2) asset management and (3) total cost of ownership. These objectives are outlined in the organization's annual strategic and financial plan and flow directly from Clayton M. Jones, chairman, president and CEO of Rockwell Collins. According to Jones, "It is one of the things that can keep me awake at night — ensuring that we have a source of supply at the right cost to be competitive and to meet the commitments of our customers."[2] Figure 11-1 shows the metrics for each of the three objectives for material and supply management.

**Figure 11-1 Key Performance Indicators at Rockwell Collins**

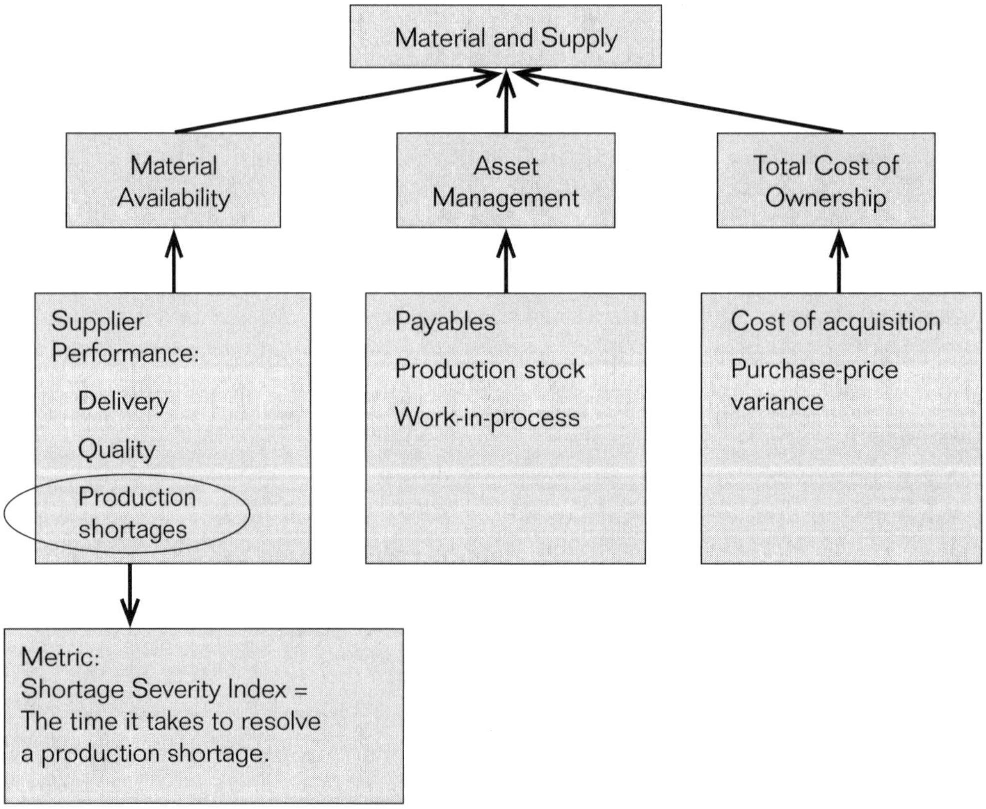

Material and Supply

Material Availability

Asset Management

Total Cost of Ownership

Supplier Performance:
Delivery
Quality
Production shortages

Payables
Production stock
Work-in-process

Cost of acquisition
Purchase-price variance

Metric:
Shortage Severity Index = The time it takes to resolve a production shortage.

*Source:* Adapted from Susan Avery, "2005 Medal of Excellence Winner: Lean, But not Mean, Rockwell Collins Excels," *Purchasing* (September 1, 2005), available from www.purchasing.com/article/CA6250270.html.

Each individual within material and supply management, operations and corporate also has a scorecard that aligns with the three key metrics. Alignment of goals and objectives across functions essentially creates shared goals and helps to build commitment to goal attainment. Commitment is further solidified if individuals also have shared accountability reflected in the organization's performance measurement and reward system. Activities are often executed in a cross-functional team, making it easier for people from different backgrounds working in different functions to learn to work together through conflicts that arise to attain shared goals and reap the benefits of shared accountability. All these alignment activities are managerial tasks that are complementary to the leadership tasks (discussed in Chapter 4) of appealing to people's basic human needs to motivate and inspire them to commit to the vision and strategies.

For example, cross-functional commodity teams at Rockwell Collins are accountable for supplier performance. Teams include representatives from application engineering, design engineering, supply quality assurance and procurement. These teams develop sourcing strategy and contribute continuous improvement ideas through the organization's life-cycle value-stream management activities.[3]

**Congruence With Supplier and Customer Objectives.** Just as the objectives of supply management should be aligned with organizational objectives, they must also be aligned with the supplier and internal and external customer objectives. The supply management organization must be structured to facilitate the flow of information between end customers and supply management and internal stakeholders. This may be accomplished through cross-functional sourcing teams or by the efforts of individual supply management professionals working with internal partners within the "thick informal networks" discussed in Chapter 4.

For example, Rockwell Collins formed a Supplier Alliance Advisory Council (SAAC) as a forum for information sharing and education. This council is composed of representatives from top suppliers who serve three-year terms and meet three times a year. SAAC members helped Weiss and his team create a supplier scorecard that measures quality, delivery, technology, responsiveness and integrity. The scorecard is used to track performance at all 13 manufacturing sites. Suppliers receive monthly performance updates via e-mail and have Internet access to the scorecards.[4]

**Organizational Expectations of Supply Management.** To achieve vertical and horizontal alignment of objectives, and consequently of metrics, there must be a clear understanding of the organizational expectations of supply management. As the Rockwell Collins example indicates, it is this set of expectations that drives goal and objective setting, the establishment of key performance indicators and the assessment of performance.

### Determine Effectiveness of Department Management

Measurement can help top management determine if the supply management department is being well managed. Overall department performance is essentially the collective performance of each individual in the department. The management team in supply management influences and affects the behavior of each individual in the chain of command. Measuring and monitoring the performance of the management team helps to ensure that the right direction, tools and techniques are provided to those responsible for executing strategies and plans.

### Measure Improvement or Deterioration

Measurement can provide evidence of improvement or provide early warning signals of deterioration of performance. This allows managers and individual employees in supply management to either use the success of improvement as leverage in internal negotiations or to take corrective action if performance is slipping in some area.

### Provide Incentives for Improvement

Leadership techniques for motivating and inspiring people were discussed in Chapter 4. From a managerial perspective, measurement systems and metrics provide a clear opportunity to develop and execute an incentive program linked to the attainment of improvement goals and as a means of motivating people to continue to improve performance on key metrics. Incentive programs are often difficult to develop because it is fairly easy to drive behavior in the wrong direction. According to a 2005 CAPS Research and McKinsey & Co. study, metrics must be tied to performance-based compensation and promotion opportunities such as individual or team incentive compensation, variable salary increases and/or promotions tied to the achievement of critical supply management metrics.[5] Because measurement is a key motivator of individual behavior, care must be exercised to assure that measurements encourage the desired behaviors. For example, if only purchase price variance (the difference between actual prices paid and a preset standard or estimate) is measured, price may become the only target for improvement, possibly at the expense of other key performance elements such as quality, delivery and lead time. Figure 11-2 from the 2007 *ISM Salary Survey* shows incentives based on bonuses and stock options.[6]

### Determine Resources Needed for Improvement

Measurement can also provide the data needed to make a business case for the allocation or reallocation of resources to achieve needed improvements. Changes in a variety of factors such as sales, product or service mix, manufacturing capacity or service delivery capacity and raw material or services prices may require a reallocation of

**Figure 11-2 2007 ISM Salary Survey**

| BONUS | | |
|---|---|---|
| **By Job Title** | **Percentage of Respondents** | **Percentage of Gross Salary** |
| Chief, Purchasing/Supply Management/Sourcing | 69.2% | 27.1% |
| Vice President, Purchasing/Supply Management/Sourcing | 86.0% | 21.6% |
| Director, Purchasing/Supply Management/Sourcing | 74.8% | 16.8% |
| Manager, Purchasing/Supply Management/Sourcing | 65.3% | 11.9% |
| Purchasing Agent, Buyer, Senior Buyer, Planner, Purchaser | 50.9% | 11.3% |
| Consultant | 65.0% | 22.4% |
| Other | 67.3% | 9.0% |
| **Criteria for Bonus** | | |
| Company results | 57.5% | |
| Department/team results | 14.5% | |
| Individual results | 24.0% | |
| Other | 4% | |
| **STOCK OPTIONS** | | |
| **By Job Title** | **Percentage of Respondents** | |
| Chief, Purchasing/Supply Management/Sourcing | 30.8% | |
| Vice President, Purchasing/Supply Management/Sourcing | 42/2% | |
| Director, Purchasing/Supply Management/Sourcing | 28.6% | |
| Manager, Purchasing/Supply Management/Sourcing | 15.3% | |
| Purchasing Agent, Buyer, Senior Buyer, Planner, Purchaser | 8.8% | |
| Consultant | 15.0% | |
| Other | 10.2% | |

*Source: ISM Salary Survey*, 2007.

resources. Measurements must be relevant and flexible to help predict these changing needs and to suggest an appropriate response.

### Determine If Value Is Added

Many activities have been performed for many years simply because they have not been re-examined since they were initiated. Today, most areas of the organization are subject to analysis to reduce, realign or eliminate items that no longer add value. This, of course, requires some level of agreement about what truly adds value to the organization. The process of bringing objectives and metrics into vertical and horizontal alignment and creating shared goals, metrics and accountability will help to define value for everyone in the organization.

## What to Measure: Linking Metrics to Goals

*The result of long-term relationships is better and better quality, and lower and lower costs.* W. EDWARDS DEMING[7]

What to measure is a critical question in all organizations. People tend to do those things that are measured and rewarded and ignore those that are not. For example, *The McKinsey Quarterly* reported on a cable organization that was trying to reduce the resolution times of its help desk and service calls. After call-duration goals were set, resolution times shrank, but total service costs rose. To meet their goals, help-desk representatives shortened the amount of time they spent on calls and quickly referred cases to field-service representatives. The field-service representatives improved their metrics for speed and resolution with these referrals. But, again, costs rose because field-service calls are far more expensive than help-desk calls. Finally, management combined call centers and field services into a single cost tree and monitored the percentage of calls passed to the help desk and the time spent on each type of call. Call-center representatives were encouraged to spend more time trying to resolve difficult calls before passing them along to field services. Although this increased the average call, it also reduced total costs. The change in metrics encouraged both help-desk and field-service representatives to take into account both call duration and costs. Management was able to see how better (or worse) performance in one area might affect another.[8]

Measurement systems are designed to assess the degree to which various aspects of the organization (including processes, functions, people, structure and technology) are contributing to the success of the organization. Therefore, metrics should be selected because they provide a link to organizational strategy and the key performance indicators connected to that strategy. Robert Kaplan and David Norton, the creators of the balanced scorecard approach, advocate using the scorecard to create a strategy-focused organization. This approach captures the activities of leaders (create a vision, build alignment and generate commitment) and those of managers (plan, organize, budget, staff, measure and ensure compliance).

The factors that the supply management professional may want to rate include the skills and knowledge of personnel, the appropriateness of the organizational structure, the scope and accountability of each job and the departmental plans, policies, procedures and so forth. These factors influence the potential level of a department's performance and, thus, are useful indicators of capability. In the Rockwell Collins example and in Figure 11-1, the key metrics were material availability, asset management and total cost of ownership. These aligned directly with the organizational strategic plans, including financial plans, and were driven by a focus on satisfying final customers.

A CAPS Research focus study identified nine categories of strategic measures: (1) price/cost, (2) revenue, (3) inventory, (4) availability, (5) technology, innovation and new product introduction, (6) workforce, (7) supplier performance, (8) operational and (9) customer satisfaction.[9]

Clearly, the categories must fit the organization, its vision and mission and the established roles and responsibilities of supply management. For example, the strategic performance measures for a food manufacturer in the CAPS study focused on financial, customer satisfaction, operational excellence and innovation (see Figure 11-3).

Efforts to create a strategic supply management department include focusing on more higher-value-adding activities and designing metrics to capture this value. Relying on historical metrics such as old price versus new price or actual versus budget may not drive behavior in the right direction or communicate to stakeholders exactly what supply management contributes to organizational success. Many supply management professionals are focusing on metrics with more strategic impact such as:

- Speed to market
- Asset/resource utilization
- Revenue growth and cost reduction
- Process improvement such as cross-enterprise collaboration or improved execution that resulted in revenue growth
- Improved level of service
- Revenue growth and risk mitigation
- Increased ability to win work
- Increased profitability
- Improve supply-chain efficiency and effectiveness

**Figure 11-3 Performance Metrics for a Food Manufacturer**

| FINANCIAL | CUSTOMER SATISFACTION |
|---|---|
| **Cost Reduction/Cost Effectiveness**<br>Actual cost per case by product platform<br>Actual market price versus prices via futures and options contracts<br>**Cash Flow**<br>Average accounts payable (AP) days<br>**Inventory Levels**<br>Number of days supply in inventory | **External Customer**<br>Quality<br>Percent and/or number of defects in shipment<br>Number of defect-free shipments<br>Complaint-free materials received<br>**Internal Customer**<br>Internal customer service<br>Compliance with measured specs<br>Percent Minority and Women Business Enterprises (MWBE) spend |
| **Operational Excellence**<br>Acquisition cycle time<br>Collaboration to adopt lean into suppliers<br>Management of strategic supplier relationships<br>Leverage of technology<br>Raw materials logistics improvement | **Innovation**<br>New product introduction<br>Met product launch milestone<br>Effectiveness of launch<br>Percent market share won from competition<br>Percent volume from new SKUs<br>Product line expansion<br>Met milestone<br>Individual development programs and review |

*Source:* Phillip L. Carter, Robert M. Monczka and Trish Mosconi, "Strategic Performance Measures for Purchasing and Supply," CAPS Research (2005), 31.

## Measure Outsourced Supply Management Functions

In organizations that have outsourced specific supply management tasks or functions, the department performance measurement system might include an assessment of these providers. The metrics discussed in this section also could be used, depending on the circumstances. Also, this review is, in essence, an assessment of the outsourcing decision.

As such, the important question from a department perspective is: Has anything changed in the internal or external environment to lead management to believe that the organization needs this type of in-house expertise?

## How to Measure: Steps in Department-Level Evaluation

How to measure can be answered at two levels. First, in the broadest sense: How can a performance measurement system be put in place that will deliver significant benefits to the organization? Second, in the strictest sense: How should the performance measurement system be structured? The first question was addressed in a recent CAPS Research study, "Strategic Performance Measurement for Purchasing and Supply." The authors identified eight items that were present in 15 large organizations with outstanding performance measurement systems:

1. Vertical alignment with organization goals and horizontal alignment with strategic business units (SBUs) and other functional units
2. Comprehensiveness
3. Dynamic and aggressive
4. Transparency: Communication throughout the organization by both the CPO and executive leadership
5. Closely tied to performance-based incentives
6. Backed up with the appropriate level of organizational resources
7. Backed with appropriate systems
8. Strong leadership[10]

The second question — how to structure such a system — is answered by devising a systematic process for a department-level evaluation. There are five basic steps to a department-level evaluation system. These are listed in Figure 11-4 and discussed in the following section.

### Step 1: Identify Department Objectives

When a manager develops a system to evaluate the performance of any department, the logical starting point is an analysis of the objectives of the department. As discussed in Chapter 6, departmental objectives should flow from, and be aligned with, the objectives of the organization. Once departmental objectives have been defined,

Figure 11-4 Steps in Departmental Evaluation

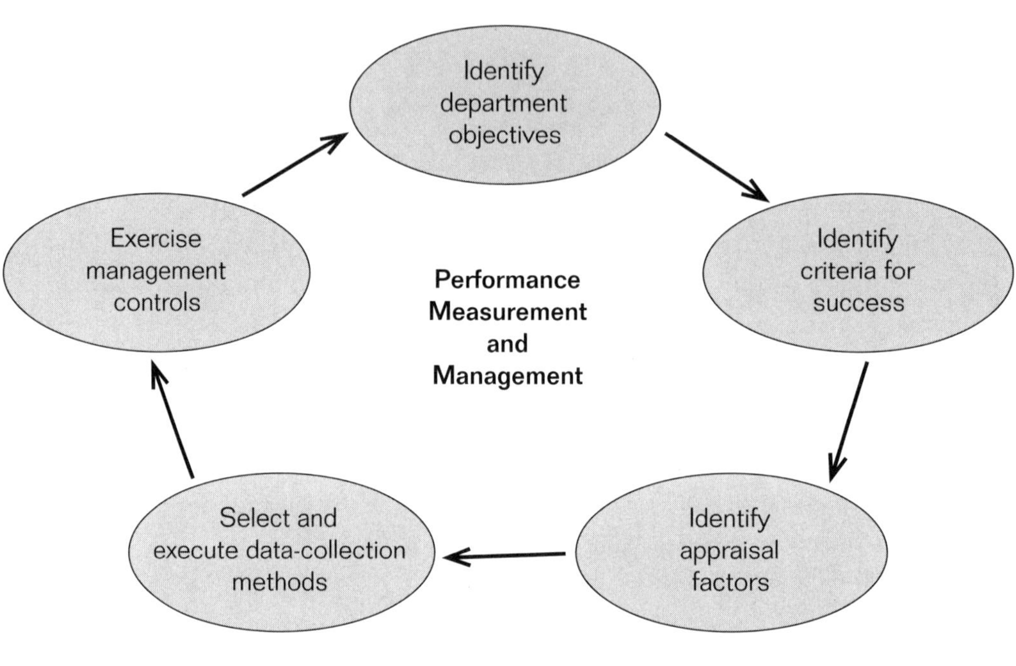


the organization structure and the responsibilities assigned to each work group should be examined to determine the impact each operating activity has on the attainment of each departmental objective. This procedure normally discloses the critical activities in the operation where evaluation and subsequent control are most important.

Often, managers find that the "easier to quantify" metrics lead to an overemphasis on objectives such as price and an underemphasis on more strategic activities such as contributing to developing and maintaining end customers through effective buyer-supplier relationships.

### Step 2: Identify Criteria for Success

The criteria for success must be established for each task that is to be measured. Performance evaluations are meaningless unless the individuals managing and working in the department know up front what constitutes success and how the degree of success or failure is to be determined. At Deere & Co. for example, CEO Bob Lane chose one key metric, shareholder value added (SVA), to guide Deere's transformation. SVA is essentially the difference between operating profit and pretax cost of capital. To get employees to align their behavior with the new goals, the senior management team first had to establish how high the metric for performance would be. The organization also adopted an online performance management system that was implemented across the 18,000 salaried employees. Each person had to develop goals explicitly aligned with the organization's goals. Next the team developed specific targets for operating assets and operating returns at different places in the business cycle. According to Lane, "This performance line was considered to be a very high bar, but it gave everybody in the organization clear goals to work on — anywhere in the world, and in any market condition."[11]

## Step 3: Identify Appraisal Factors

Areas of appraisal may be related to tactical (day-to-day) operations, strategic (commodity or category management) or integration with product or market creation (strategic and technical). At Siemens AG, the director of vehicle operations for Siemens Shared Services convinced 23 independent operating organizations to buy fleet services jointly. He developed a Vehicle Management System (VMS) program to manage the $60 million spend and partnered with a third-party vehicle supplier and leasing organization. Together they created a *Performance Index Review,* a quarterly report, focusing on three objectives or categories identified by the operating organizations: low-cost transportation (50 percent), driver productivity and satisfaction (35 percent) and administrative support (15 percent).[12]

While many factors can be considered when evaluating a supply management department's performance, typical appraisals consider one or more of the following elements.

**Contributions to Profitability/Success of Core Activity.** Contribution to profitability is a primary concern in a business. Government agencies and institutions are concerned with total value and maximization of resource use. How the supply management function's contribution to these results will be measured is a more difficult question. Customer satisfaction, cost, quality and speed are all key areas of attention for the purpose of tracking supply management's contribution to the organization's goals.

**Customer Satisfaction.** Feedback from user departments or internal customers as well as external or end customers can be a good source of data on the functioning of a supply management department and how well it is serving its customers. Feedback can be obtained informally or through structured questionnaires and surveys. The decision about what information to collect and how to collect it depends on the costs associated with data collection compared to the benefit of having the knowledge. If there is no concrete plan in place for using the information to increase efficiency and/or effectiveness, then it may not be worth the data collection and analysis costs and the ill will the activity may generate among customers.

Feedback mechanisms such as internal 360-degree surveys may be used to assess the supply management department's performance along dimensions such as responsiveness, cooperation and collaboration. While these items are more difficult to measure than something that is more easily defined and counted, these types of items may provide a better indication of the success of supply management's role in the organization.

Linking the supply management department's performance to final customer satisfaction is also difficult in many organizations. This is more realistic if management has established shared goals, shared metrics and shared accountability. Without these factors, a starting place is ongoing cross-functional discussions about customer-related metrics such as lost sales. Another starting place might be supply management's performance in areas such as delivering the appropriate quality of uninterrupted supply at minimal inventory levels.

**Timeliness of Actions.** One of a supply management department's primary responsibilities is to support operations or the satisfactory completion of the organization's tasks. Three measurements that indicate how efficiently this responsibility is fulfilled for a production or retail operation are:

1. Percentage of overdue orders,
2. Percentage of stockouts caused by late deliveries, and
3. Number of production stoppages or lost sales and/or customers caused by late deliveries.

Depending on the need and purpose of evaluation, these data can be categorized by material classification, supplier or buyer.

In a government or service industry, the focus will be on cycle time or supplier lead time. For example, if the maintenance of a police or emergency vehicle is not completed on schedule, the consequences can be very serious. If operating room supplies are not delivered as promised, then the required supplies may not be available to meet scheduled surgical needs.

Obviously, a number of different performance factors can be measured to provide a basis for appraising supply management efficiency. These factors differ in importance among different organizations depending on the nature of the business and the materials or services purchased. Each organization selects those measures most useful and cost-effective to its own specific situation.

**Material/Service Costs.** Five techniques provide a cross-check on the reasonableness of prices paid for materials (see Figure 11-5). All these measurements can be classified and subclassified in various ways to pinpoint the cause of the problems they reveal.

**Figure 11-5 Five Techniques to Assess Material/Service Costs**

| TECHNIQUE | DESCRIPTION |
|---|---|
| Compare actual prices to standard or target prices. | Establish standard or target prices for major materials or services. Chart prices actually paid against the target figures to display any significant differences. Or compare to a materials budget, utilizing standard price data or to a rate sheet that has been established for service providers. |
| Develop average price paid indices for each major class of material or service. | Develop average "price paid" indices for major classes of materials or services. The trends of such price indices are valuable guides in assessing the effectiveness of performance. If developed on a comparable basis, these indices can also be charted against various national commodity price indices published by the Bureau of Labor Statistics, the Department of Commerce and others. This comparison reveals cases in which an organization's costs are rising at a greater rate than market prices during an inflationary period. |
| Track cost savings and identify cost-saving activities. | Periodic cost savings figures can be individually charted for savings arising from such activities as negotiation, value analysis, design and material changes, suppliers' suggestions, change of supplier, packaging improvements and transportation cost-reduction projects. |
| Track results of forward buying and assess forecasting effectiveness. | If an organization engages in forward-buying activities, gains and losses from it can be periodically reported to determine forecasting effectiveness. |
| Track purchase orders that lack firm prices. | A report of the percentage of purchase orders that are issued without firm prices provides another basis for evaluating and controlling costs. |

*Source:* Anna Flynn and Sam Farney, Chapter 8, "Performance Tracking and Improvement," in *The Supply Management Leadership Process* (ISM Knowledge Series), Volume 4 (2000), 208–9.

**Material/Service Quality.** Once material or service specifications have been established, the most direct measure of quality performance is the number of delivered materials or services that are rejected or found unacceptable by the inspection and using departments. The number of such items is usually compared with the total number received and the defect rate expressed as a percent defective. Because even a small percentage can be a significant and unacceptable rate of defects, many organizations track defects in parts per million (ppm). To understand the significance, 1 percent defective is equal to 10,000 ppm. Many manufacturers have found that customers demand defect rates of 100 ppm or less. To check on the improvement of quality specifications, the supply management professional can also review the value analysis reports dealing with design or service changes and material substitutions. While the same concepts apply to service purchases, there are clearly some distinct differences primarily driven by the degree of intangibility of the service and the resulting difficulty in measuring service performance against the scope of work. Efforts must be made to develop clear, unambiguous descriptions of services to be performed and effective measurement systems to compare actual services received to the original scope of work. Often, this measurement process is based on surveys of service recipients and may be highly subjective or biased. It is the responsibility of the supply manager to root out subjectivity in service performance assessments as much as possible.

**Supplier Reliability.** Five measurements can be used to indicate the reliability of major suppliers (see Figure 11-6).

**Supplier Development.** Suppliers impact a significant part of the cost. Their failure to perform must be considered in the search for maximum value. *Foundation of Supply Management* (ISM Professional Series) addresses supplier performance evaluation in detail. The more reliable the supplier, the less costly it is to deal with the supplier's organization. It is difficult to measure the costs an organization incurs from poor supplier performance, but some of the many sources of such costs are expediting, inspection and sorting, rework, returning defective goods, missed customer promises and warranty claims. Many sourcing teams have begun to work very closely with key suppliers to improve both supplier and customer processes to attack these sources of unnecessary cost. If supplier relationship management processes are improved, the result may be less time spent correcting problems or time spent to better measurable results. Closer collaboration with suppliers might be measured by productivity levels, quality improvements, shorter cycle times, better service or knowledge-sharing across organizations.

**Figure 11-6 Supplier Reliability Metrics**

| METRIC | DESCRIPTION |
|---|---|
| On-Time Performance | Percentage of late deliveries or late completion of services and percentage, or ppm, of rejected items, further analyzed and classified by supplier, buyer, etc. |
| Correctness of Materials or Services | Percentage of orders on which incorrect materials were shipped or unacceptable services were provided |
| Quantity Accuracy | Percentage of orders on which incorrect quantities of materials were shipped or incorrect number of service calls was performed |
| Partial Shipments/ Performance/Back Orders | Percentage of orders on which split shipments were made or it was necessary to accept partial completion of the service on the due date |
| Transportation | Quality and reliability of transportation service offered by various carriers |

*Source:* Anna Flynn and Sam Farney, Chapter 8, "Performance Tracking and Improvement," in *The Supply Management Leadership Process* (ISM Knowledge Series), Volume 4 (2000), 210.

**Order Quantity and Inventory Effectiveness.** The failure to buy the right quantity (i.e., the quantity that keeps the operation functioning yet minimizes the amount tied up in inventory investment) jeopardizes the cost structure or misuses resources that may be better used elsewhere. Four measurements useful in evaluating how well funds are invested are described in Figure 11-7.

**Creativity and Value Creation.** Value creation is becoming an important factor in the success of firms. Value creation includes insightful initiatives undertaken to enhance the worth, relevance or importance of a product, service or system. The degree to which creativity and value can be obtained from suppliers is something that supply management professionals can facilitate.

Deciding what to measure is the first step in developing a performance appraisal system. The next step is choosing appropriate methods of performance data collection.

**Figure 11-7 Assessment of Investments in Inventory**

| METRIC | DESCRIPTION |
|---|---|
| Compare Inventory Carrying Costs and Material Acquisition Costs | A chart showing target and actual inventory levels in the aggregate and by major classifications along with a chart showing inventory turnover rates for the same material classifications. When analyzed together, these charts point out imbalances between inventory carrying costs and material acquisition costs. |
| Inventory Turnover Effectiveness | A report of "dead stock" materials carried in stores, resulting from overbuying or less-than-planned use. Inventory may be measured in "days-on-hand" to indicate the effective rate of turnover. |
| Buying Effectiveness | The number of stockouts and production stoppages, or customer orders not filled, attributed to underbuying. |
| Inventory Savings | A list of supplier stocking arrangements that have been negotiated, along with an estimate of resulting inventory savings. |

*Source:* Anna Flynn and Sam Farney, Chapter 8, "Performance Tracking and Improvement," in *The Supply Management Leadership Process* (ISM Knowledge Series), Volume 4 (2000), 211.

## Step 4: Select and Execute Data-Collection Methods

A number of data-collection methods may be used in a performance measurement and management system. This chapter addresses the following methods: internal audits, self-governance or self-assessment methods; customer and supplier feedback; process benchmarking; and best practices studies. Figure 11-8 lists the pros and cons of each method; the following section expands upon self-governance and process benchmarking.

**Internal Audits/Self-Governance/Self-Assessment.** An internal audit is a comprehensive, systematic, independent and periodic examination of an organization's supply management environment, objectives, strategies and activities. It is used to identify strengths and weaknesses and to develop a plan of action to improve performance. Regular and unbiased feedback is needed and an audit is one way to gather this information.

Often, audits are conducted by outside consultants to ensure the necessary objectivity and independence of judgment. Audits are, however, also conducted internally.

**Figure 11-8 Pros and Cons of Data-Collection Methods**

| METHOD | PROS | CONS |
|---|---|---|
| Internal Audits<br>Self-Governance<br>Self-Assessment | Familiarity with processes, systems, people | Auditor may be too close to be critical<br>Process may be highly politicized |
| Customer and Supplier Feedback | May get end-to-end supply chain perspective<br>Input may identify new opportunities to exploit or risks to mitigate | Lack of trust may preclude honest assessment<br>Resource constraints make it difficult to collect and analyze data |
| Process Benchmarking | Makes everyone aware of industry leaders<br>Draws attention to cross-industry practices | May lead to overemphasis on copying what others are doing<br>May set target too low |
| Best Practices | May identify a practice that will lead to competitive advantage | What is a best practice in one organization may not translate well in another organization |

At Sandvik Materials Technology, for example, the leaders of product areas meet at monthly performance reviews to describe the operational progress each of their units has made or not made as measured against selected key performance indicators (KPIs), such as delivery reliability, lead time and quality. Unit managers are also asked to audit their own performance quarterly and to compare the current status to where they need to be to become excellence-driven units. According to Peter Gossas, president of Sandvik, "This hammers home the point that to achieve the required results, they must develop their ways of working. The monthly performance reviews and quarterly self-audits are just as important as the financial results."[13]

**Process Benchmarking.** Process benchmarking refers to a performance comparison of business processes against an internal or external standard of recognized leaders. Most often the comparison is made against a similar process in another organization considered to be "best" in a particular area. In other words, process benchmarking provides an answer to the question: How are we doing compared to other leading-edge organizations? The answer to this question should lead an organization toward the development of best practices for its own internal operations.

At Siemens AG, each measurement category has best-in-class benchmarks based on information from the client database of the third-party fleet vehicle supplier and leasing organization, Wheels, Inc. "There are 40 metrics in total, but we only track 20 or 25 at a time, because we feel 40 is overkill," explains Jim McCarthy, director, vehicle management services, Siemens Shared Services LLC. For example, the best time to purchase vehicles is in the fall, so the VMS (Vehicle Management System) team created a metric that calls for replacing 60 percent of the organization's vehicles in the fall. "We monitor this carefully, because the resale value of vehicles is adversely affected if we don't reach this target," he notes. The index also provides data to identify operational enhancements and recommendations for implementation of cost savings. The composite score in fiscal year 2004 was 91.4 percent.[14]

Before initiating process benchmarking, several questions need to be answered, including:

- Are we willing to make a major change? Change may be difficult to foster if there is no agreement that the current situation is not acceptable.
- Is the expected improvement worth the expenditure?
- Are the results important to us?
- Does the process impact a critical success factor?
- Have all investigations related to this process been completed? Have all other alternatives been explored?
- Have we begun measuring the current process?
- Do we know the major cost components and service factors of our process?
- Are we willing to wait for a benchmarking study to be completed before implementing any changes?
- Are we willing to reveal information about our own processes to outside organizations?

Process benchmarking may actually involve the division of the functions of an organization into several modules analyzed as independent processes. Such a study may find, for example, that one organization has the best order processing, another has the best inventory control and so on.

## Step 5: Exercise Management Control in Response to Results

Evaluation should be an ongoing process, a catalyst for improvement in the supply management function and processes and a means of validating performance to management's expectations. Once the results of a performance appraisal are obtained, management must be sincere in its efforts to reward exceptional performance, find the root cause of problems and focus resources on correcting these problems. Otherwise, the entire performance appraisal process will serve no useful purpose. Measuring performance is only half the battle. Deciding what to do with the results of the measurement and how to do it is the other half.

At Siemens AG, the VMS team has been able to maintain a 1 percent out-of-stock rate on vehicles, meaning that only 1 percent of vehicles must be purchased from dealers rather than directly from manufacturers, compared to the national fleet industry average of 12 percent. In the past five years, the VMS team has been able to bring more than $30 million in savings to Siemens AG's operating organizations with 75 percent of the savings tied to leveraging spend across operating units and 25 percent tied to departmental expertise. The initiative has been so successful that Siemens AG is beginning to leverage the approach globally.[15]

Management can take a number of actions in response to departmental performance data, including taking corrective action, encouraging employee accountability, determining compensation, making promotion decisions, promoting personal and career development, fostering employee engagement and morale building, justifying disciplinary action, recognizing employees and motivating performance improvement.

**Taking Corrective Action.** The corrective action required will vary depending on the magnitude and root cause of the problem. In general, the process will include establishing timeframes for improvement, prioritizing the steps in the improvement plan and conducting cost/benefit analysis to determine the appropriate level of resources to allocate to the corrective action plan implementation.

ESTABLISHING TIMEFRAMES. It is necessary to establish timeframes for corrective action. This may take the form of a final due date along with milestones and timeframes leading up to full implementation of the corrective action. The manager must be clear about the purpose of the corrective action. In some cases, the first step may be to take the time to determine the root cause of the problem and then develop an action plan for dealing with the root cause. In other cases, interim measures may be taken in the short term to deal with what are really symptoms of the real problem while a plan is developed for getting at the root cause.

PRIORITIZING. Whatever the process, prioritizing the steps in the implementation plan is critical. This process should include an understanding of the resources needed for the action and their availability.

ANALYZING THE COSTS AND BENEFITS. Corrective action must be cost-effective given the expected benefits if the action is undertaken. A comparison of resources (people, time, equipment, money, etc.) and availability to the expected value (quantified in some way) should be performed. An ability to quantify the value of the benefits achieved is paramount, and in most process improvements this benefit is in the form of saving people's time. Therefore, one of the most commonly used methods of quantifying the savings is through activity-based cost analysis. Activity-based cost analysis is discussed in more detail in *Foundation of Supply Management* (ISM Professional Series). It is a cost-management method for attributing indirect costs to the activities that drive cost. This approach is in contrast to more traditional accounting methods that pool and allocate indirect costs on a formulaic basis that does not necessarily reflect the true cost structure.

**Encouraging Employee Accountability.** A good performance appraisal will identify for the employee those areas in which he or she has problems and will specify what he or she needs to do to correct them. The appraisal thus provides the employee with guidance on how to improve, and makes him or her accountable for that behavior with a definite time span for improvement. It is also important to identify and build on areas in which the employee is doing well.

**Adjusting Compensation.** No department operates at its full potential for long if its salary structure fails to reward individuals in relation to their respective performance levels. A good performance appraisal program does not guarantee an equitable salary structure. It does, however, provide data that can be used in developing a sound compensation plan or in correcting an inadequate one.

At Nissan Motor Co., Ltd., for example, the bonus system is linked strictly to the operating profit of the organization or of the subsidiary and to one or two critical objectives, growth and profits.[16]

At Deere & Co., compensation is aligned with the key metric of shareholder value added (SVA). As a result, all incentives in the short and medium term are related to economic profit; long-term compensation for Deere's top 1,000 employees is linked directly to the company's stock price. The short-term incentive applies to all salaried employees worldwide and is linked to the sales cycle. The midterm incentive applies to about 6,000 people who are treated as one worldwide team. When economic value is created, the incentive is accrued in one year, but the bonus is at risk because it is paid out over four years and the loss of economic value during that period drains the bonus. This incentive is designed to promote shared goals and accountability and is based on sustained performance. Deere has also worked with union members who have contributed to the progress and shared in the benefits of improved productivity.[17]

**Making Promotion Decisions.** How do managers know which people in their departments are likely to become candidates for the top positions? They determine this by analyzing each aspect of an individual's performance record. These analyses must be made using detailed and accurate written data. A well-designed appraisal program provides the required data.

In an interview about the transformation at Nissan, CEO Carlos Ghosn said, "You can't start with performance-based management at the base; you start at the top and cascade. First, we established a team that we call the nomination advisory committee over which I preside. No promotion in top management — in Japan or outside Japan — is approved without a review of the [candidate's] specific contribution to the performance of the organization. If, at the nomination advisory committee, somebody comes and says, 'This is a great guy, we had a great time with him,' I'll say, 'What is his specific contribution to growth, profits or cost reduction?' I can tell you that we've eliminated a lot of people from promotions. For us, the main question about high potential is not only how brilliant the guy is, but what are the breakthroughs or the specific contributions that he has concretely achieved in the last two to three years."[18]

**Guiding Personal and Career Development.** The most important benefit that can result from a good employee-evaluation program is the information needed to stimulate and direct each individual employee's professional development. A manager's prime responsibility is to develop capable and effective personnel. The data provided by appraisals can be analyzed to determine each employee's strengths and weaknesses. This determination facilitates the development of a realistic professional improvement program for each individual.

**Fostering Greater Employee Engagement and Morale.** Every supply management professional must develop a well-structured program for appraising the performance of personnel. Nothing is more disastrous to the morale of a department than haphazard or inconsistent evaluations of individual employee performance.

**Taking Disciplinary Action.** A well-designed employee performance appraisal is a necessary guide for disciplinary actions that are focused and fair and that provide direction for employee improvement.

**Recognizing High-Performing Employees.** Employees want to know that diligence and attainment of performance goals will be recognized and rewarded. When departments reward their most effective workers, heavy workloads are viewed as an opportunity to win recognition, earn respect and be included in the most interesting and high-profile projects. Most supply management employees are motivated when their managers make them feel good about quality work through acknowledgment of superb efforts. Programs that allow supply management professionals to be recognized and rewarded for their performance benefit the entire organization.

**Motivating Performance Improvements.** One of the key purposes of staff appraisal is to motivate employees to improve their performance. Well-designed systems will provide each employee with the feedback and guidelines necessary to achieve higher levels of performance in the next measurement period. Employees should have the sense that continuous improvement applies to their efforts as well as the efforts of suppliers.

At Sandvik Materials Technology, directional arrows for how each unit has developed compared with where it was before, and based on selected KPIs, are published on the organization's intranet. This process provides a visual reminder of current unit performance and provides a high level of transparency about the development of the different units. The organization tries to have a very open climate in the organization, and the published arrows have started an open and constructive discussion in the different units. The performance data has also changed the daily performance discussions between shift leader and workers to include not only new production issues but also a review of action taken on action points agreed to the previous day.[19]

This chapter focused on the managerial task of measuring and managing department performance. It is complemented by the leadership tasks of motivating and inspiring people to commitment to achieving the vision of supply management. Managers must make a strong case for the importance of having departmental objectives that are linked to organizationwide objectives. Then they must determine what and how to measure to ensure that metrics drive appropriate behaviors at the individual level and that performance data are accurate and useful. Lastly, they must use the performance data to guide decisions about supply management processes, people, technology and structure.

Recall the example in Chapter 1 of Ken Newton's role as chief procurement officer at Texas Instruments, Inc. Newton described his view of success as, "We'll know when we have achieved our vision when, first, worldwide procurement and logistics (WPL) is widely recognized by TI executives and the TI organizations it serves as a core competency and a key contributor to TI's success. Second, when WPL is an employer of choice within TI and an essential career path experience. Top tiers want to work here! Finally, when WPL is recognized as world class by TI's competitors and the procurement and logistics professions. Top students and professionals want to work here."[20]

## Key Points

1. Performance tracking is important to recognize and reward behaviors that lead to attaining organizational goals. A vital source of information about behaviors is feedback from internal and external customers of the supply management processes.

2. The supply management organization needs to be structured in such a way as to facilitate the flow of information between end customers and supply management personnel.

3. Measurement is needed to track trends in performance that will provide evidence of improvement or provide early warning of deteriorating performance. Data capture should be unbiased, at regular intervals and should be made as much a part of the normal functioning of the unit as possible. Information gathering should be built into the process wherever possible.

4. Management's response to information gathered from measurements is as critical as the measurement itself. The information must be used in guiding decisions and actions with respect to organization structure, individual development and staffing needs.

5. Feedback must be as unbiased as possible. One method of assuring this is to gather information from several perspectives as is done in the case of 360-degree personnel evaluations.

6. The supply management function is in a position to contribute substantially to the results desired by the organization, whether it is profitability for a business or effective resource use for a not-for-profit organization.

CHAPTER

# 12

# Establishing Internal Controls and Ensuring Compliance

*This isn't just a legal compliance issue for us. We consider the privacy issue to be an opportunity to reinforce brand image.* THOMAS WARGA, SENIOR VICE PRESIDENT, GENERAL AUDITOR AND CHIEF PRIVACY OFFICER, NEW YORK LIFE INSURANCE COMPANY[1]

The final, but by no means least valuable, managerial role is to establish internal controls and ensure compliance. These activities are critical managerial tasks that support organizational success and, in some cases, ensure survival. Today's business climate of ethical lapses and accounting scandals coupled with public outcry and government regulation have brought control and compliance issues to the forefront in many organizational settings. However, as the opening quote indicates, treating these situations strictly as control and compliance issues may be too narrow a perspective. Leaders and managers may also create an opportunity to enhance the organization's reputation and brand image by the way they manage the risks associated with operational, financial, legal and regulatory control and compliance. As discussed earlier, risk management is one of the overarching concerns of supply management strategy and philosophy.

The managerial control and compliance role corresponds to the leadership task of gaining commitment. The leader uses influence and develops partnerships to generate commitment to achieving a vision. The manager uses control mechanisms to compare actual behavior with planned behavior, determine the root cause of discrepancies and implement corrective action when there is a discrepancy. Instrumental to managers executing their control responsibilities is the organization's capability to identify risks, assess the level of risks and develop risk-mitigation and management strategies. These tools and techniques are discussed in Chapter 5.

The supply management professional has overall responsibility, both individually and in his or her ability to delegate responsibility, for establishing supply management controls before the fact, during the fact and after the fact and for ensuring compliance with the established controls. In one sense, this means there are three chances to get it right, but at each stage the costs of risk mitigation and compliance increase, sometimes exponentially.

The Committee of Sponsoring Organizations (COSO), formed in 1985, is a voluntary private sector organization dedicated to improving the quality of financial reporting through business ethics, effective internal controls and corporate governance. The sponsoring organizations include the American Accounting Association, the American Institute of Certified Public Accountants, Financial Executives International, the Institute of Internal Auditors and the Institute of Management Accountants. The COSO Internal Control Integrated Framework is the U.S. standard on internal controls. According to COSO, "Internal control may be broadly defined as a process, affected by an entity's board of directors, management and other personnel, designed to provide reasonable assurance regarding the achievement of objectives in the following categories:

- Effectiveness and efficiency of operations
- Reliability of financial reporting
- Compliance with applicable laws and regulations."[2]

Similar issues are being addressed by the International Accounting Standards Board (IASB). The IASB is an independent, privately-funded accounting standard-setter with board members from nine countries. The organization is "committed to developing, in the public interest, a single set of high quality, understandable and enforceable global accounting standards that require transparent and comparable information in general purpose financial statements. In addition, the IASB co-operates with national accounting standard-setters to achieve convergence in accounting standards around the world."[3]

This chapter starts with a general discussion about establishing an effective internal control system and the nature of management controls before, during and after the fact. The remainder of the chapter covers these three categories: (1) operational effectiveness and efficiency, (2) financial reporting and (3) legal and regulatory compliance.

## CHAPTER OBJECTIVES

- Discuss the purpose of management controls, different types of controls and when each is used.

- Discuss supply management's role in establishing internal controls and ensuring compliance in the areas of:
  - Reliability of financial reporting,
  - Operational effectiveness and efficiency and
  - Compliance with laws and regulations.

## Establishing an Internal Control System

The supply management leadership team must establish and maintain an effective and efficient internal control system that aligns with organizationwide risk management and internal controls. The success of this initiative depends in part on: (1) strong internal partnerships, especially with legal counsel, internal auditors, the chief financial officer, the chief information officer and the chief executive officer; (2) rigorous processes supported by appropriate policies, procedures, desk routines and documentation; and (3) fully engaged supply management professionals committed to achieving the organization's goals in an ethical and honest fashion. COSO outlined five essential components of an effective internal control system:

1. The *control environment* establishes the foundation for the internal control system by providing fundamental discipline and structure.
2. *Risk assessment* involves the identification and analysis by management — not the internal auditor — of relevant risks to achieving predetermined objectives.
3. *Control activities,* or the policies, procedures and practices that ensure management objectives are achieved and risk-mitigation strategies are carried out.
4. *Information and communication* support all other control components by communicating control responsibilities to employees and by providing information in a form and timeframe that allows people to carry out their duties.
5. *Monitoring* covers the external oversight of internal controls by management or other parties outside the process or the application of independent methodologies, such as customized procedures or standard checklists, by employees within a process.[4]

Clearly, control mechanisms are more than afterthoughts. They may be in place at three points in time: (1) before the fact, (2) during the fact and (3) after the fact (see Figure 12-1).

**Figure 12-1 Types of Controls**

| TYPE OF CONTROL | EXAMPLE |
| --- | --- |
| Before-the-fact controls | Budgets<br>Plans<br>Forecasts<br>Policy and procedures manuals |
| During-the-fact controls | Structured processes<br>Adherence to policy and procedures<br>Specifications<br>Industry standards |
| After-the-fact controls | Reports<br>Reviews<br>Audits |

## Before-the-Fact Controls

Before-the-fact controls establish a benchmark against which actual performance can be measured. Before-the-fact controls include budgets, plans (strategic, operational and disaster recovery), forecasts and policy and procedure manuals.

**Budgets.** One of the more obvious ways to establish management control is through the organization's budgets. Funds are allocated to projects based on prioritization, which is based, in part, on the assessment of risk exposure and expected rewards. *Foundation of Supply Management* (ISM Professional Series) provides a detailed description of the different types of budgets used by organizations and the role each of these plays in management control.

**Plans.** Business plans incorporate the budget process with the assessment of other areas such as organizational mission, market penetration, market share, competitive analysis, staffing and other managerial concerns that affect the strength of the organization. The strategic and operational planning process is discussed in detail in Chapter 6.

**Business Continuity (Disaster Recovery or Contingency) Planning.** Business continuity planning is one type of contingency plan that has received much attention by many supply management professionals. These "what-if" plans focus on courses of action to take in the event of earthquakes, hurricanes, major fires, international government issues and so forth. From a supply management perspective, a disaster plan may include backup suppliers in the event the usual supplier is incapacitated in some way.

For example, a manufacturer of gardening tools and accessories had a supply management strategy that relied heavily on single sourcing. When the organization's single-source provider of gardening gloves was wiped out by the tsunami in 2005, the organization had no contingency plan. This led the supply management leadership team to review all single-source decisions from the perspective of risks as well as opportunities and focus more attention on developing contingency plans.

**Forecasts.** Forecasts generally relate to the demand for finished goods or services, but also relate to the concern for internal capacity and external availability of materials and services. *Effective Supply Management Performance* (ISM Professional Series) describes different ways of forecasting demand both internally and externally.

**Policies.** The management of an organization or department typically establishes policies to cover normal operating conditions. These policies then guide the behavior of employees and standardize the response to typical events. In this way, employees can routinize their behavior for most activities and develop customized ways of dealing with ad hoc situations. Policies help to ensure that everyone in the organization is moving in the same direction on a daily basis. Supply management personnel must be sensitive to overall organizational policy as well as departmental policy. This includes policy not always found in the department manual, but in the overall organization policy, or policy from functional areas such as safety, operations, quality assurance and human resources.

**Procedures Manual.** A procedures manual outlines in detail the specific actions to be taken to accomplish a given task. It establishes guidelines for achieving an organization's objectives and contains an organization's major procedures for easy reference by users.

## During-the-Fact Controls

During-the-fact controls are put in place to monitor and measure the task while it is occurring or before it is finalized so that adjustments can be made as early as possible to stay within the designated parameters. During-the-fact controls may be in place to monitor any process such as requisitioning and procurement, sourcing, contract writing and administration, inventory management, environmental management, material transfers, quality and so on. These controls are especially important for compliance with the Sarbanes-Oxley (SOX) Act in the United States, which is discussed later in this chapter.

**Structured and Disciplined Supply Management Processes, Policies and Procedures.** A structured and disciplined supply management process with supporting policies and procedures is perhaps the best during-the-fact internal control system. The ISM Professional Series is essentially about establishing and maintaining such a system.

Process reviews can be used to ensure that these during-the-fact controls are efficient and effective. For example, a leading document solutions organization used the services of Protiviti, Inc., a wholly owned subsidiary of Robert Half International, Inc., a provider of independent internal audit and business and technology risk-consulting services, to review its supply-chain procurement processes for MRO and manual PO processing. The goal was to improve the organization's ability to monitor noninventory purchases and reduce total MRO purchasing. The review identified critical control gaps, major process deficiencies and opportunities for improvements in data processing, management reporting and policy and procedure definition, documentation and training.[5]

In another case, Protiviti consultants reviewed the internal audit function of an international wireless telecommunications organization. This led to a review of three years of accounts payable disbursements to identify duplicate and erroneous payments and missed credits. Recoverable costs of $3 million were identified and several key supplier contracts were reviewed for contract payment compliance issues.[6]

INDUSTRY STANDARDS. Industry standards, such as ISO 9000 for quality management and ISO 14,000 for environmental management, are also ways that control can be exerted.

MILITARY SPECIFICATIONS. Military specifications are one type of standard that relates to quality and may be used commercially.

**Information Technology.** During the execution of various business processes, information technology is used to capture data and monitor progress. Partnering with IT to ensure the collection, accessibility and transparency of data is a foundation of a rigorous internal control system.

For instance, the supply management team at a large consumer products organization struggled with how to turn external information and knowledge into strategic innovation. A new CEO had focused everyone in the organization on the vision of "Choose and Use" to reflect the goal of having consumers choose and use the organization's products consistently. The supply management team's corresponding initiative, "Better Buying," focused on collecting data on all spend, aligning all stakeholders and asking suppliers what worked. The supply management master plan included sound business strategies enabled by technical strategies and architecture: (1) leverage scale, technology and knowledge, (2) supplier connectivity and capability and (3) sourcing optimization. The technology strategies were (1) identify game-changing capabilities that enable strategy, (2) select best-in-breed and (3) plug-and-play. The purchaser's dashboard (see Figure 12-2) was designed to enable better decision-making through data integrity and visibility. It consists of a roll-up of information from various electronic tools to enable externalization and sourcing optimization. All tools and levels are work process–driven and depend on rigorous processes.[7]

## After-the-Fact Controls

After-the-fact controls are reviews that measure what actually happened so actual performance can be compared with planned benchmarks. This type of gap analysis can provide information that will lead to improvements in processes, products and/or services. The supply management organization should also perform internal audits

**Figure 12-2 Data Roll-Up on Purchaser's Dashboard**

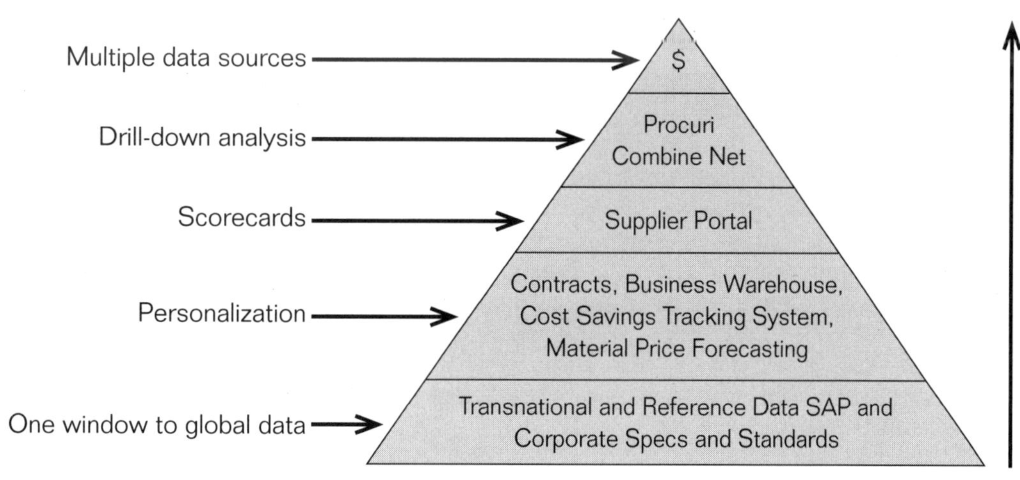


*Source:* Anna E. Flynn, "Developing and Implementing E-Sourcing Strategy," CAPS Research Critical Issues Report (September 2004), 14.

to measure compliance with contract terms and conditions and relevant laws and regulations.

**Periodic Reports.** The periodic report is another means of review that can be used to compare actual performance with the plan. The timeframe for periodic reviews should be established during the planning stage, and the quantitative information should be summarized at intervals that will facilitate the review process.

**Procedures Reviews.** Procedure reviews are initiated to ascertain if those charged with following established procedures are indeed doing so.

**Audits.** Audits are performed to (1) prevent problems, (2) gauge system and process efficiency and effectiveness and/or (3) meet a regulatory requirement. There are three basic types of audits: internal, external and self-inspection. An internal audit is performed by a person or a team of people from inside the organization who have no vested interest in the outcome of the audit. An external audit is performed by an outside party. It is critical to have policies and procedures in place, but there must be an auditing mechanism for determining if there are process shortcomings within these policies and procedures. If the policies and procedures are sound, an audit may reveal whether or not personnel are adhering to them. Audits are conducted to see if the work performed mirrors the original intent. Generally, a sample of transactions is taken by the auditor and compared to established benchmarks. The auditor usually reports his or her findings and leaves the development of conclusions to management.

The following steps outline the auditing process and provide an example of an audit of a newly acquired operating unit or field office:

1. Determine the scope of the audit.
2. Determine how the results will be used.
3. Determine the standard.
4. Determine what type of audit is appropriate.
5. Establish the format of the audit.
6. Prepare and distribute the final audit report.
7. Establish a corrective action plan.

Auditors at Boeing developed an evaluation form based on the COSO operating categories and the COSO internal control integrated framework (see Figure 12-3).

**Figure 12-3 The Boeing Control Evaluation Form**

| **Report Title** | | | |
|---|---|---|---|
| **Project No.** **Report No.** | **Report Date** | | |
| **Project Leader** | **Chief auditor** | | |
| RATINGS | COSO OPERATING CATEGORIES | | |
| S = Satisfactory<br>U = Unsatisfactory<br>I-S = Incidental Satisfactory<br>I-U = Incidental Unsatisfatory | Effectiveness and Efficiency of Operations | Reliability of Financial Reporting | Compliance With Laws & Regulations |
| Control Environment | | | |
| Risk Assessment | | | |
| Control Activities | | | |
| Information & Communication | | | |
| Monitoring | | | |
| Overall | | | |
| **Rationale for Unsatisfactory Rating:** | | | |

*Source:* Dennis Applegate and Ted Wills, "Struggling to Incorporate the COSO Recommendations Into Your Audit Process? Here's One Audit Shop's Winning Strategy," *Internal Auditor* (December 1999).

The control mechanisms discussed so far can be applied to many organizational settings. The three primary objectives of an internal control system are to ensure (1) efficient and effective operations, (2) accurate financial reporting and (3) compliance with laws and regulations. Supply management plays a role in each of these three areas.

# Internal Operations Controls

As discussed in Chapter 5, operational risk is the risk of loss from inadequate or failed internal processes, systems and staff or from external events. Internal operating controls are put in place to ensure efficient and effective use of resources. Effectiveness means that the operation being evaluated achieved the specific pre-established management objectives. Efficiency means that this was accomplished with an optimum level of resource inputs to productive outputs. An operations audit should determine whether the organization can be reasonably assured that no material inefficiencies or ineffectiveness exist in the audited organization or process. Internal operations controls and audits provide information about compliance with laws and regulations as well as compliance with internal policies and procedures.

For the supply management organization, operations controls are valuable for assessing the efficiency and effectiveness of processes, policies and procedures and measuring and ensuring internal compliance. Areas of concern include requisitioning, sourcing, procuring, contract writing and administration, hazardous and regulated materials management and end-of-life-cycle materials management.

## Internal Environmental Controls

Environmental laws and regulations affect many industries in many countries, and they vary considerably depending on the country. In the United States, environmental compliance regulations are primarily set forth by the Environmental Protection Agency (EPA), the Council on Environmental Quality (CEQ), the Chemical Safety and Hazard Investigation Board and the ISO 14001 environmental system standard. The environmental laws and regulations of other countries and regions may impact nondomestic or nonregional organizations just as U.S. laws and regulations affect non-U.S. organizations doing business in the United States. The supply management team plays an important role in acquiring current information on domestic and nondomestic environmental laws and regulations and ensuring that the organization takes the necessary steps to be in compliance. The supply management leadership team in each organization must develop a means of assessing environmental risks, putting appropriate internal controls in place, determining compliance levels and making necessary adjustments to improve performance.

**Life-Cycle Assessments.** Efforts are under way in some settings to conduct a life-cycle assessment to measure the environmental impacts of products over their entire life cycle from cradle to grave and they are shifting even more to cradle to cradle. The goal is to use life-cycle approaches to develop product systems with lower environmental impacts. In Germany, the government is drastically limiting what can go into the landfills.

Baxter, for example, produces and sells a wide range of products that help save, extend and improve the quality of people's lives worldwide. At each stage of the product life cycle, Baxter encounters social and environmental issues, from clinical trials and materials selection in research and development (R&D) to energy efficiency and waste minimization in manufacturing to advertising and promotion and access to healthcare during product use and, finally, to responsible product disposal. Baxter has policies and programs to address these important issues. Quality and safety are two issues that cut across the entire product life cycle. Baxter has programs to ensure the highest standards in these areas.[8]

**Corporate Social Responsibility and Ethics.** In addition to legal and regulatory reasons for environmental controls, some also make a case for environmental management on the basis of corporate social responsibility and ethics. Institute for Supply Management™ (ISM) defines social responsibility as "a framework of measurable corporate policies and procedures and resulting behavior designed to benefit the workplace and, by extension, the individual, the organization and the community in the following areas (in alphabetical order): community, diversity, environment, ethics, financial responsibility, human rights and safety." The ISM statement on the environment says:

1. Encourage your own organization and others to be proactive in examining opportunities to be environmentally responsible within their supply chains either 'upstream' or 'downstream.'
2. Encourage the environmental responsibility of your suppliers.
3. Encourage the development and diffusion of environmentally friendly practices and products throughout your organization.

Strategic approaches to environmental risk management range from a strict interpretation based on compliance with laws and regulations to a much broader view that focuses on looking for opportunities to enhance the brand, reputation or image of the organization through a more assertive commitment to environmental stewardship. Management teams in affected industries must develop an environmental risk profile and risk management strategy (see Chapter 5). The risk of loss stems from contractual, insurance and legal issues. Supply management professionals are in an excellent position to mitigate or eliminate risks from environmental violations occurring in the use, handling and disposal of hazardous materials. To maximize their contribution, the supply management team must have strong internal partnerships with design and environmental engineers and legal counsel. They must be recognized as key contributors starting with the earliest phases of the design process and continuing through disposal or reclamation. External customer requirements often drive design decisions. In this case, a cross-organizational initiative involving customers, designers and supply management professionals may be needed to eliminate or mitigate environmental risks.

**Supply Management's Role.** Supply management can potentially contribute to environmental management in three major ways: reduce or eliminate hazardous materials and nonhazardous materials that must be disposed of at the end of their useful life; manage the process from cradle to grave and document quantities, use, storage and handling and use the information as a resource for planning and improvements.[9]

First, supply management may contribute to reducing or eliminating the use of hazardous materials by focusing on the design and sourcing stage. If supply management can find a nonhazardous substitute that does not require costly processing and tracking, then several cost categories are reduced. These might include lower process costs (no or less tracking), lower capital expenditures (avoid investment in costly capital equipment) and lower legal exposure and avoidance of legal processes and potentially huge settlements. The design stage offers the greatest opportunity to reduce or avoid costs.

Supply management professionals can also be instrumental in programs designed to reduce consumption of materials and reduce the amount of waste that goes into landfills through the development of corporate collection and recycling programs. These programs may be internally or externally focused. There are many collection programs for computers, PDAs and cell phones. Usable materials are reclaimed and recycled, thus reducing landfill waste and organizational cost. Also, new businesses are created to collect, recycle and reuse these materials.

In the 1990s, Hong Kong native Zhang Yin started a Los Angeles–based venture, America Chung Nam, to collect waste paper from the United States and Europe, ship it to China and recycle it into corrugated cardboard for boxes. Many of these boxes are returned to the United States, filled with toys, electronics and furniture. The boxes are then collected, procured by America Chung Nam and begin the cycle again. The organization is one of the world's biggest paper-trading organizations, with ties to recycling yards in New York, Chicago and California. It was named the top American exporter to China by volume for the fifth consecutive year in 2005, the most recent ranking, according to PIERS Global Intelligence, which tracks import and export data. Yin's organization, Nine Dragons Paper, is China's biggest papermaker.[10] Because China's paper industry is fueled by coal, the organization faces environmental risks depending on the government's steps toward cleaning up the air. Until then, the Chinese papermaker has an advantage over paper organizations operating in countries with more stringent environmental standards and therefore a higher cost structure.

Second, supply management professionals may be able to better manage and track hazardous materials from "cradle to grave" or even "cradle to cradle" to lessen or eliminate the organization's liability should environmental problems occur downstream, especially in the disposal phase of the product life cycle. For instance, in 80 percent to 90 percent of the cases concerning the U.S. Comprehensive Environmental Response Compensation and Liability Act (CERCLA) and the Resource Conservation and Recovery Act (RCRA), a bankrupt hauler or bankrupt landfill operator caused the release of the pollutant. The EPA turns to the waste generator who is responsible for the waste from "cradle to grave." Because responsibility flows back upstream, the sourcing manager must be especially diligent in evaluating and selecting waste-handling organizations. Evaluations might include criminal checks, court checks and site visits preaward. Postaward actions might include annual site visits and a requirement for certificates of destruction.[11]

Third, supply management records may be a prime source of information for determining the organization's compliance with environmental regulations and for providing insight into environmental risks and liabilities. Valuable data include information about quantity, usage, storage, hazard and disposal. The information may also be used to identify and evaluate options for improving production methods.

**Conducting Environmental Audits.** An audit may be performed on internal environmental processes, policies and procedures and on the supply chain. From a supply-chain perspective, an environmental audit requires assessing both upstream and downstream activities. If customer-driven requirements are creating or increasing environmental risk, then efforts must be made to influence customers to see the benefits of design change, use of less hazardous substitutes and other initiatives that will mitigate the risk. As with most of the strategies discussed in this book, strong internal partnerships, and often external ones as well, are required for supply management to optimize its contribution.

ISM has developed a supply management audit instrument as part of its principles of social responsibility. It includes general questions applicable across all categories:

1. Does your organization comply with all applicable laws and regulations covering the ISM social responsibility principles?

2. Does your organization have written policies in place that cover the ISM principles?

3. Are goals in place for each principle? What are they? How are improvements incorporated?

See Figure 12-4 for ISM's specific environmental audit questions.

**Figure 12-4 ISM's Environmental Audit Questions**

1. Is your organization environmentally responsible? What specific programs and procedures are in place?
2. Does your organization recycle? What percent of disposable waste is recycled? What does your organization do to reduce the volume of waste created that must then be recycled?
3. How does your organization comply with laws and regulations in the handling of hazardous waste?
4. How does your organization report its results?
5. How does your organization continue to learn what it needs to know about environmental and waste issues?
6. Does your organization collect copies of environmental plans? Are the plans of suppliers assessed and approved by your supply management organization?
7. Does your organization work with engineering in the design of products for disassembly, reuse and recycling?

*Source:* www.ism.ws/SR/content.cfm?ItemNumber=4755&navItemNumber=17088.

**Reporting Requirements and Certification.** The supply management team must also stay abreast of industry-specific and government-reporting requirements and any certifications that are required or advisable for the buying organization and its domestic and international suppliers. To meet these requirements the correct data must be collected, analyzed and prepared in the appropriate format and submitted in a timely manner. These steps should be built into supply management processes and systems to facilitate enterprisewide collection and reporting. The steps to acquiring the appropriate certification are:

1. Determine which laws and regulations and corresponding certifications apply to your business.
2. Develop an environmental management system (EMS) that meets the appropriate regulations.
3. Conduct an internal audit of the environmental management system.

4. Have an accredited external audit performed.

5. If the audit is successful, receive certification by the accredited external auditing body.

6. Maintain certification.

**Life-Cycle Controls.** The supply management team may also be involved in assessing what, if any, risks exist if product components are available in the marketplace over the product's life cycle. The design stage offers the greatest opportunity to add value in terms of providing customers with the functionality they seek at the lowest total cost with the least harmful environmental impact. At Baxter International, Inc., the new product development process consists of five phases: concept, feasibility, development, launch and postlaunch support. A product sustainability review (PSR) is included in the design of all new medical devices. This review is a thorough assessment of the environmental, health and safety and social impacts of a product, its materials and processes throughout its life cycle. A preliminary PSR in the concept stage identifies high-level sustainability issues, and a complete assessment in the feasibility stage identifies sustainability impacts across the life cycle. The information gathered during the review helps establish product requirements, influence design and confirm product feasibility. The PSR is designed to benefit Baxter, its customers and the environment in the following ways:

- *Compliance.* Assesses current and future regulatory concerns to ensure market access;
- *Customers.* Optimizes environmental attributes of products and facilitates response to environmentally preferable purchasing guidelines in customer requests for proposal;
- *Operational improvement.* Identifies cost-cutting opportunities, for example through decreased energy use or packaging reduction; and
- *Environment.* When possible, minimizes adverse life-cycle environmental impacts and risks.[12]

**Life-Cycle Costing.** Life-cycle costing is the process of calculating the cost of a product over its life cycle, from cradle to grave, to maximize life-cycle profits. It is a cost-analysis tool that incorporates the purchase price of a piece of equipment and all operating and related costs over the life of the item. It is a valuable tool that may be applied to environmental life-cycle assessments. The life-cycle cost components might include costs for planning, research and development, production, operation, energy costs, maintenance, cost of replacement, disposal or salvage. This cost analysis depends on values calculated from other reliability analyses such as failure rate, cost of spares, repair times and component costs.

**Life-Cycle Analysis.** Life-cycle analysis is part of the ISO 14000 environmental management standards. It refers to the process of including all tangible and intangible costs from conception (cradle) to disposal (grave). In the energy industry, for example, a life-cycle analysis of energy production starts with the initial project conception to the final step of returning the land to its original or next-use state. Tangible costs might include a range of cost components from facility construction to fuel source development and postextraction land remediation to waste disposal. Intangible costs might include estimates of the impact because of the release of carbon into the environment or costs caused by unusually long licensing processes or political resistance for new or innovative methods of energy production as well as the cost of plant decommissioning or funding needed, for example, to reclaim strip-mined areas. The goal is to calculate true lifetime costs and profitability of energy production.

**End of Life Cycle.** All too often, the costs associated with a product at the end of its life have not been fully considered in the earlier stages, such as design, or some change has occurred in laws and regulations, public perceptions or organizational risk tolerance. Part of an organization's risk profile includes projected issues related to end-of-product-life issues. Some organizations respond to laws and regulations and others are more proactive in taking voluntary action. For example, Fisher & Paykel Appliances, Ltd., has a whiteware take-back scheme in North Island, New Zealand. It offers dealerships and service centers an alternative to disposing of appliances in landfills. Fisher & Paykel can reuse or recycle 75 percent of appliances by weight. With sales of recyclable materials and internal savings from the reuse of packaging materials, the take-back center is making a profit.[13]

Two European Union (EU) directives, Waste Electrical and Electronic Equipment (WEEE) and the Restriction of the Use of Certain Hazardous Substances in Electrical and Electronic Equipment (RoHS) have far-reaching effects on electrical and electronic equipment manufacturers and distributors. The key objectives of the WEEE directive are the avoidance and reduction of waste from electrical and electronic equipment (EEE) and the recovery, recycling and reuse of EEE products. Compliance processes and procedures vary across the EU because the government of each EU country decides how to execute these directives.[14]

China is also developing its version of the EU's Restriction of the Use of Certain Hazardous Substances directive, which took effect March 1, 2007. China's RoHS, officially known as the Administration on the Control of Pollution Caused by

Electronic Information Industry, is expected to be implemented through the development of nine standards. Those standards will cover issues involving product design, development, manufacturing and the sale of products.[15]

According to Baxter's 2005 Sustainability Report, "The responsible disposal of electronic healthcare products is an emerging issue of concern worldwide. For example, the European Union's (EU) Waste Electrical and Electronic Equipment (WEEE) Directive impacts a range of products that Baxter sells in Europe, including dialysis machines, automated blood-component collection systems, intravenous infusion pumps and other electronic hardware. The WEEE Directive, effective August 13, 2005, requires organizations to arrange for the take-back of electronic products at end-of-life to enable the recovery and recycling of product components."[16]

Prior to WEEE regulations, Baxter embraced the principles behind the WEEE directive by repairing and refurbishing medical equipment, when appropriate, to extend its useful life. However, Baxter is also working to ensure full compliance with WEEE as the regulations take effect in individual EU countries and appropriate registration bodies and compliance schemes are established.

Environmental regulations in Europe often influence those in other nations, and several other countries, such as China, Korea, Taiwan and some U.S. states, are implementing or considering legislation similar to WEEE. Baxter anticipates that its EU-based programs and experience in this area will help it comply with regulations worldwide.[17]

Supply management may be involved in deciding to what extent, if any, these and other laws, regulations and directives apply, determining the rules for compliance and developing and executing an action plan to ensure compliance. Supply management is in an excellent position to manage end-of-life-cycle programs because of strong relationships with suppliers, mechanisms in place to gather market intelligence and processes in place to collaborate with suppliers.

## Internal Records Management

Records management is an organizationwide concern, especially with the increasing use of enterprisewide information technology, the importance of information in regulatory compliance and the role information plays in strategic and operational decision-making. Clearly, records and information management is a critical piece of organizational infrastructure that supports and enables far more than control and compliance. Some of these areas were discussed in Chapter 7. This section focuses on control and compliance aspects of records management, data management, information flow and the interface between and among various systems, such as materials management and financial systems, which reinforce the importance of the supply management team building strong internal partnerships with finance and IT.

Supply management professionals facilitate communication with internal partners and external suppliers, often within complex networks. To fully extract the competitive advantage available from strategic supply management, decision-makers need easy access to reliable data and information and the ability to manage documents and records in a consistent manner. How the supply management group manages information may distinguish the highly effective supply management organization from a less effective one. Effective records management allows for smoother communication processes, provides internal control of transactions, funds and schedules and provides a record of activities. These records are needed to research information, prove that actions did or did not occur, provide audit trails and meet legal conditions and requirements. Standardized documentation allows for consistency, which helps ensure that all pertinent information is included, improves efficiency and makes it easier for users to access information.

The supply management team must develop, implement and maintain a database and/or physical filing system of relevant information. The goal should be to create a credible records and information management strategy that meets regulatory requirements, provides clean, transparent and accessible data for decision-makers and incorporates the changing value of data over its life cycle to better control the cost of data and records management.

**Regulatory Requirements.** In many organizations, management has supported the effort to develop an enterprisewide document management system to facilitate compliance with internal, external and regulatory requirements. These include compliance with country-level regulatory agencies, such as the Securities and Exchange Commission in the United States, and with regulatory directives of self-regulatory organizations; state, province and regional directives; and international laws.

Certain records are required by law or regulation. For example, the Sarbanes-Oxley Act (discussed in Chapter 5 and later in this chapter) focuses on internal controls and is a key driver in records management systems at publicly traded organizations in the United States. The U.S. Uniform Commercial Code (UCC) influences records management because physical or electronic documentation of certain types of information is required. For example, a contract for the sale of goods valued at $500 or more must be in writing to be legally enforceable. Even if there is no legal requirement, good judgment may lead decision-makers to document actions as part of a risk-mitigation strategy to prevent the need for legal action or assist in the successful resolution if legal action is required.

The U.S. Privacy Act places restrictions on access to some types of information. It is important to understand this when designing documents and systems. In governmental purchasing, most (if not all) purchasing documents are a matter of public record and are subject to public view. Legal advice is often necessary when dealing with Privacy Act/public information implications of document design and management.

Organizational policies are also developed to define internal rules, regulations and guidelines for records and database management. These policies align with management's interpretation of applicable legal and regulatory requirements, support internal strategies and goals and reflect organizational risk profiles and risk appetite.

**Domestic and International Issues.** Organizations that operate outside the borders of their own countries and trading blocs face similarities and differences in records management requirements. Common external forces include:

- Increasing litigation, legislation and government oversight.
- Demand for business process transparency.
- International sourcing and transparency.
- Privacy and data security concerns.

Differences may exist in requirements around the world. Even if regulations and laws are not that different, cultural or local approaches to record-keeping and information management still may present challenges for the supply management leadership team that is trying to standardize data classification, collection and reporting.

**Records Management.** Records management is the systematic control of records or documentation from creation or receipt through processing, distribution, maintenance and retrieval to ultimate disposition. Records policies typically address the following items:

1. Define what information constitutes a record.
2. Establish a records classification system.
3. Establish standard operating procedures and tag new and existing records accordingly.
4. Develop a storage plan to house physical and digital records for the short term and the long term.
5. Establish a policy for internal and external access to classes of records.

6. Establish a retention policy to archive records and determine when and how records will be destroyed based on internal and external needs and requirements.
7. Establish audit metrics.

The International Organization for Standardization has established ISO 15489:2001, which includes the following activities in records management: setting policies and standards; assigning responsibilities and authorities; establishing and promulgating procedures and guidelines; providing a range of services relating to the management and use of records; designing, implementing and administering specialized systems for managing records; and integrating records management into business systems and processes.[18]

**Data/Records Management System Requirements and Capabilities.** A records management system is a computer program (or set of programs) used to track and store records. Records management systems commonly provide specialized security and auditing functionalities tailored to the needs of records managers. Establishing system requirements and capabilities is complicated by the volume and complexity of data that must be managed. A strong partnership with IT is necessary to determine which IT systems will best serve the strategic and operational needs of supply management.

ISO 17799 provides a framework for creating an information security program, including policies and procedures, assigning roles and responsibilities, documenting operational procedures, preparing for incident and business continuity management and complying with legal requirements and audit controls.[19]

**Data Classification.** Data classification is the process of assigning a level of sensitivity to data as it is being created, amended, enhanced, stored or transmitted. The classification of data determines the extent to which the data needs to be controlled or secured based on the risk of loss if the data were lost, stolen or revealed. Organizational policies are developed to protect the confidentiality, integrity and availability of data generated, accessed, modified, transmitted, stored or used by the organization.

The supply management organization generates and/or maintains various types of information, including specifications, supplier data, supplier performance data, products/services, contracts, spend, tariffs, routing guides and technical assistance agreements. These data sets must be categorized and coded in a standard way if decision-makers are to access and use the data. For example, data may be classified as public, official use only and confidential. The supply management team may decide that requests for proposals with attached specifications, the supplier ethical code of conduct and information on doing business with the organization and goods and services that the organization routinely purchases are tagged as public. Supplier information including performance data may be tagged as official use only with individual suppliers granted access to their data, but no one else's. Contracts, spend data and supply management strategy documents may be tagged as confidential with access limited to specific people.

One of the biggest challenges for many supply management teams is having access to clean, current spend data. In a benchmarking study of its customers, solutions provider Emptoris, Inc., found that its customers find value in classifying data along multiple dimensions, including basic supplier, category, time, supplier diversity status, preferred supplier status, supplier performance and scorecard information, budgetary information, on/off contract, contract performance and ISO certification. More than 60 percent of Emptoris' customers look at spend data across 12 dimensions and more than 30 percent look across 15 dimensions. Customers are also classifying spend at deeper levels of granularity. More than 70 percent classify three to six levels deep in the commodity taxonomy.[20]

Data-classification schemas for commodity coding are developed by individual organizations, industries and national and international organizations. One data-classification system that is widely used in organizations around the world is the United Nations Standard Products and Services Code (UNSPSC). This open, global electronic commerce standard provides a logical framework for classifying goods and services and allows commodities and products to be properly and uniquely classified. The hierarchical structure of the UNSPSC allows drilling down and rolling up, which is integral for tactical and strategic spend analysis. It is a global standard and is freely available to the public with no copyright protection issues. Many organizations develop their own customer taxonomies because of the perceived added value. Solutions provider Emptoris reported that more than 60 percent of its recently surveyed organizations reported using a custom taxonomy.[21] Figure 12-5 lists and describes some cross-industry commodity coding schemas commonly used in the international arena.

The chief supply management professional can lay the foundation for strong internal controls on records and information in three ways: (1) consider the risks associated with information and records when developing strategies, policies and processes; (2) incorporate short-term and long-term technology needs into talent planning and role redesign; (3) build a strong alliance with the chief information officer. Operational leaders and managers will have to deal with the daily challenges of building and maintaining the IT infrastructure necessary to support supply management strategies.

**Figure 12-5 Common Cross-Industry Commodity Coding Schemas**

| CODING SYSTEM | | DESCRIPTION |
|---|---|---|
| **CPV** | Common Procurement Vocabulary | Used in the European Union in public procurement transactions to group together the products of similar producers. A unique number system, nonhierarchical, does not allow for aggregation for financial reporting. Will continue to be required for OJEC Notices. |
| **EAN** | Euopean Article Number | Most widely used. Used in conjunction with the Uniform Code Council to form the EAN/UCC product codes. EAN-129 provides an application identifier that identifies products by barcode. A unique number system, nonhierarchical, subsequently will not allow aggregation for financial reporting. |
| **ISIC** | International Standard Industry Classification | Nonhierarchichal (does not provide MI potential). Geared towards central economic statistical gathering of industry information. There is a UK version just called SIC, which is tailored to the UK market and UK suppliers. |
| **NAICS** | North American Industrial Classification | Shallow hierarchichal (does not provide product-based MI potential), classification at supplier level, code not applied to the product itself. Widely used adopted standard in the U.S. Supplier-related application. |
| **NSV** | National Supply Vocabulary | A centralised commodity coding service specifically for the public sector, initially it was focused on providing a coding structure to the NHS but since then has expanded to other uses. Not widely used/ semiproprietary, three-level hierarchical structure, mixture of product classification, product identification and, in some instances, supplier-specific product identification. |
| **UNSPSC** | United Nations Standard Product and Services Code | Hierarchichal, product classification, provides opportunity for complex MI reporting. Widely used at present, although there are many different versions. Most consistently referred to code among E-Commerce systems providers, on the buy and supply sides. |

*Source:* "A Guide to eProcurement for the Public Sector, Appendix B: Standards and Security, Commodity Classification Coding," Autumn 2002, available from www.forumpa.it/archivio/0/500/520/529/eprocguide9.pdf.

## Internal Financial Controls

Financial controls relate to the financial reporting process that is designed to ensure that financial statements prepared for external reporting comply with generally accepted accounting principles (GAAP) in the United States or IFRS (International Financial Reporting Standards) globally. These controls generally include policies and procedures that enable an organization to properly initiate, record, process and report financial data consistent with the assertions embodied in either the annual or interim financial statements.

The supply management team has a duty and responsibility to verify the existence, accuracy and completeness of relevant financial transactions and commitments to third parties. This is accomplished in two ways: (1) supply management must ensure that these transactions and commitments are made in accordance with organizational financial reporting policies; (2) supply management must adhere to the requirements of laws, such as Sarbanes-Oxley; to applicable regulations from regulatory bodies, such as the Federal Energy Regulatory Commission (FERC); and to any applicable international regulations. A strong internal partnership between supply management and finance with accurate and timely communication provides the basis for fulfilling supply management's role in financial reporting.

### The U.S. Sarbanes-Oxley (SOX) Act of 2002

The Sarbanes-Oxley Act was the U.S. government's response to a series of large corporate financial scandals involving major corporations. It focuses on corporate governance and financial disclosure. Effective in 2006, *all* publicly traded corporations are required to submit an annual report of the effectiveness of their internal accounting controls to the SEC. Provisions of the Sarbanes-Oxley Act detail criminal and civil penalties for noncompliance, certification of internal auditing and increased financial disclosure. It affects public U.S. organizations and non-U.S. organizations with a U.S. presence.

Each organization must report on a quarterly basis:

- Design of controls over relevant financial statement assertions
- Information about how significant transactions are initiated, recorded, processed and reported
- Sufficient information to identify where material misstatements because of error or fraud could occur
- Controls designed to prevent or detect fraud, including who performs them and the related segregation of duties

- Controls over period-end financial-reporting processes
- Controls over safeguarding of assets
- Results of management testing and evaluation[22]

Sections 401(a), 404 and 409 of Sarbanes-Oxley have the most relevance for supply management.

**Section 401(a): Off-Balance-Sheet Obligations.** This section requires all financial obligations to be transparent. For the supply management organization, four areas involve off-balance-sheet obligations: (1) supplier-managed inventory systems where the purchasing organization has an obligation to pay for cancellation or other penalties, (2) long-term purchase agreements that have a penalty clause, (3) lease agreements where there is a financial obligation if the purchasing organization terminates the lease and (4) letters of intent where the purchasing organization commits to a supplier to get in a long lead-time production schedule and there is a cancellation clause with financial impact. The chief financial officer needs to be informed quarterly of such agreements and the potential financial obligations.

In its 2006 Annual Report, for example, Federal Express Corp. reported other cash obligations not included in its balance sheet. These included amounts to "cover noncancelable agreements to purchase goods or services, such as aircraft, aircraft modifications, vehicles, facilities, computers, printing and other equipment and advertising and promotions contracts." Also, the amounts reflected for operating leases "represent future minimum lease payments under noncancelable operating leases."[23] Figure 12-6 is an example of the format used for capturing the data related to off-balance-sheet contractual obligations. The supply management organization may be a primary source of data for leasing information and purchase obligations.

**Section 404: Internal Controls.** The supply management team must address four areas related to internal controls: (1) inventory and inventory write-offs, (2) material transfers, (3) after-the-fact purchase orders and (4) segregation of duties. Internal inventory controls relate to financial transparency. This means that what is on the books as a financial asset can be physically located, the stated value reflects true market value and the accounting and materials management systems are in sync. Accurate information about material transfers should be transmitted from the supply management system to the financial system to reflect the current financial condition of the organization. The supply management organization must also demonstrate that established purchase policies and procedures related to requisitioning and purchasing authority are communicated internally and controls are in place to ensure internal compliance. To prevent, deter and detect fraud, SOX also focuses on segregation of

**Figure 12-6 Off-Balance-Sheet Contractual Obligations**

| CONTRACTUAL OBLIGATIONS | PAYMENTS DUE BY PERIOD | | | | |
|---|---|---|---|---|---|
| | Total | Less than 1 year | 1–3 years | 3–5 years | More than 5 years |
| Long-Term Debt | | | | | |
| Capital Lease Obligations | | | | | |
| Operating Leases | | | | | |
| Purchase Obligations | | | | | |
| Other Long-Term Liabilities Reflected on the Registrant's Balance Sheet under GAAP | | | | | |
| Total | | | | | |

*Source:* Federal Express 2006 Annual Report, p. 52, available from www.fedex.com/us/investorrelations/financialinfo/2006annualreport/online/fin_pdfs.html

duties. For supply management, it is especially important to ensure that those with the authority to purchase goods and services cannot receive and pay for goods and services.

Compliance with the internal controls requirements of SOX supports the business case for developing a structured, disciplined supply management process with complete spend visibility, controlled procurement and optimized contracts and contract compliance. For example, many food-service organizations find it difficult to get full spend visibility and contract compliance from each and every restaurant unit as well as difficulties in reconciling the back end of the process and ensuring that pricing agreements and rebates are accurate. SOX requirements can be used to drive improvements in the procure-to-pay flow path while also enabling the supply management team to drive down food costs, rationalize SKUs and suppliers, improve back-end processes and monitor unit compliance.

**Section 409: Timely Reporting of Material Events.** A material event is one that will materially impact financial reporting. Two situations may be material events on the supply management side: (1) late supplier deliveries that cause revenue forecast to be missed and (2) third-party providers (outsource partners) who cannot provide goods and services, resulting in a misstatement of revenues.

For example, a commodity manager is notified by a first-tier supplier that it is unable to meet the agreed-on delivery schedule because a second-tier supplier is unable to obtain critical inputs from a sole source. This would be reported as a material event if the supply disruption prevented customer deliveries and adversely affected revenue projections.

## Internal Legal and Regulatory Controls

Supply management processes, policies and procedures include many components that are affected by laws and regulations. For this reason, internal legal controls are especially important areas for the supply management professional. The primary responsibility is to assess and forecast legal exposure arising from supply management before, during and after the execution of an activity and from all sources, including processes, policies and procedures or noncompliance with laws relating to contracts, intellectual property, employment and the environment both domestically and internationally. For this reason, one of the supply management professional's most important internal relationships is with chief legal counsel.

Four major legal areas are addressed in this section: (1) agency law and authority, (2) regulations influencing the development of solicitations, (3) intellectual property laws and (4) employment laws.

### Agency and Authority

*Agency law* defines the legal relationship that exists between two parties by which one (the agent) is authorized to perform or transact specified business activities for the other (the principal or employer). First, an agent has a *fiduciary duty* to the principal meaning that the agent's obligation in any transaction is to conduct business in the best interests of selected stakeholders, especially those of his or her employer or principal in an agency relationship. Violations of fiduciary duty occur if, in making a deal, an agent accepts a gratuity or kickback or has some personal interest (financial or otherwise) in the supplier. Second, the principal is bound by the agent's action. The organization is legally obligated to perform under a contract signed by an agent. Third, by corollary, the agent has no personal liability under the contract, assuming the agent had actual authority and did nothing wrong.

*Authority* is the right granted to an agent to engage in legally binding transactions on behalf of a principal (the employer). Three types of authority affect the supply management organization: actual, implied and apparent authority. *Actual authority* is the specific authority that is delegated to an individual. Along with actual authority, an individual is granted incidental authority or *implied authority.* Implied authority is part of actual authority given by a principal to an agent. When the principal is less than comprehensive in describing the actual authority given, the law implies whatever is necessary to accomplish the principal's expressed intent. *Apparent authority* is the type of authority created in an agency relationship when a principal permits an individual to operate in a fashion that allows third parties to believe that the individual is an authorized agent of the principal. It represents unauthorized purchasing or bypassing of the purchasing function by other functions within an organization. For example, someone in an organization without actual authority orders goods and services that are received and payment is made. To the supplier, the person appears to have the authority to purchase based on the actions taken: receipt and payment. By making payment on an unauthorized purchase, the organization makes it look as if the actions of the buyer were authorized. Apparent authority is just as valid legally as actual authority as far as the contracting parties are concerned. The difference is for the agent: agents acting with apparent authority expose themselves to personal liability to the principal. *Ratification* is the after-the-fact approval by a principal of an otherwise unauthorized action taken by an agent. Ratification (1) creates a valid contract between the principal or employer and the supplier and (2) excuses the agent from any personal liability.

Typically, authority is delegated based on some criterion such as financial levels or budget ownership and limits are placed on this authority. For example, purchasers (agents) in the supply management department are given the authority to purchase specific goods and services with set dollar limits.

By defining authority for purchasing and contracting, top management communicates to employees the seriousness with which senior management takes spend management and fiduciary duties. It also communicates to suppliers the degree of rigor and discipline that the buying organization brings to the marketplace. Risk exposure was defined earlier as the probability of a loss multiplied by the expected impact. In the case of agency and authority, the probability of a loss is high if an organization is not properly managing both the actual and apparent authority of employees. Likewise, if agency and authority are loosely controlled, there is the potential for a greater impact or loss. For example, it is more difficult to track spend, improve spend visibility and manage spend when agency status is diffused. It is also easier for suppliers to gather information, possibly proprietary or damaging information, when employees lacking supply management training engage in contact with suppliers. Loss may also occur in terms of paying higher prices, agreeing to unfavorable terms and conditions and compromising the supply management organization's leverage in future deals.

The link between process rigor and law is therefore a critical one. The supply management professional must rely on his or her strong internal partnerships with chief legal counsel, peers at the executive level and influence over process integrity to ensure that the law of agency and limits to authority are calculated and understood as legal risk exposure that is endogenous in nature, meaning it is a risk that is completely within the bounds of internal actions to eliminate.

## Regulations Influencing the Development of Solicitations

Two major areas of law affect the development of solicitations in the private sector. These are the (1) the Uniform Commercial Code (UCC) specifically Article 2, Sales, and (2) antitrust and trade regulation laws, specifically the Sherman Antitrust Act, the Clayton Act, the Robinson-Patman Act and the Federal Trade Commission (FTC) Act. On the public purchasing side, a number of federal acts regulate federal procurement and public projects. The appendix at the end of this chapter includes a description of each piece of legislation.

**The Uniform Commercial Code Article 2, Sales.** The UCC is a statutory collection of provisions governing various aspects of commercial transactions such as Sale of Goods (Article 2), Lease of Goods (Article 2A), Letters of Credit (Article 5) and Secured Transactions (Article 9). Statutory language is recommended by the National Conference of Commissioners on Uniform State Laws (NCCUSL) to encourage uniformity among the states, but must be adopted by individual state legislatures to become effective.

The supply management leadership team must ensure that supply management personnel and all other personnel abide by contract laws and regulations. In the case of public purchasers, the regulations prescribing contracting processes are more stringent than in the private sector. In both cases, the supply management professional should put proper policies and procedures in place to drive behavior internally and support these with training and ongoing managerial support (coaching, mentoring, advising) and ensure that suppliers are made aware of the organization's stance on legal issues.

**Antitrust and Trade Regulation.** The purpose of antitrust legislation is to maintain a competitive and fair market. Many countries have such legislation. In Canada and the European Union, it is referred to as competition law. In the United States, four pieces of legislation lay the foundation for the U.S. approach: (1) the Sherman Antitrust Act, (2) the Clayton Act, (3) the Robinson-Patman Act and (4) the Federal Trade Commission (FTC) Act (see the appendix at the end of this chapter). The Sherman Act prohibits restraint of trade by any "combination" or group or contract and prohibits monopolistic activities. The Clayton Act deals with growth and distribution and prohibits "tying" arrangements. Robinson-Patman primarily deals with discriminatory pricing. The FTC Act created the Federal Trade Commission, which is partially responsible for enforcing antitrade laws. There may also be laws and regulations at the state level. It is important for the supply management professional to be aware of country-specific laws when working with multinational organizations.

Supply management professionals are in a prime position to alert management to possible violations such as price-fixing. They are also in a vulnerable position in terms of their actions, which might put their employer at risk for charges of collusion on the buying side. The supply management leadership team must partner with legal counsel to ensure the appropriate training is provided to supply management personnel. Supply management professionals are also well positioned to scan the environment for any antitrust actions in the supply management base that might adversely affect the organization. For example, when General Electric Co. attempted to acquire Honeywell International, Inc., U.S. authorities approved the merger but the EU Commission did not. If Honeywell was a key supplier to an organization, the supply management team might develop contingency plans in the event the merger occurred as well as consider any disruptions that might occur during the review period. Potential sources of risk include possible changes in processes, personnel, contracts and so on in the event the merger occurred.

**Regulation of International Commerce.** The supply management team must also develop internal controls to ensure that global sourcing and supply management activities meet the requirements of domestic laws such as the Trade Agreements Act and the Foreign Corrupt Practices Act (FCPA); international treaties such as the North American Free Trade Agreement (NAFTA), the General Agreement on Tariffs and Trade (GATT) now the World Trade Organization (WTO) and the United Nations Convention on Contracts for the International Sale of Goods (CISG). Each of these is defined in the appendix at the end of this chapter.

The primary areas of concern are (1) business practices and ethics and (2) contracts. The supply management professional should take the lead in defining internally what is and is not acceptable behavior in the international arena in light of both laws and the organization's ethical framework. Policies, procedures and training must be provided and supported by managerial action. In terms of contracts, the supply management team should work with legal counsel to ensure that the organization is complying with regulations related to international transactions.

**Regulation of Federal Procurement and Public Projects.** Supply management employees in the public sector and those doing business with federal government agencies must adhere to the various rules and regulations that govern public purchasing. The appendix at the end of this chapter defines the relevant U.S. federal laws.

Control mechanisms and audits are highly structured in the federal procurement arena. For example, the internal control matrix for the audit of purchasing controls (version 4.2, October 2006) provides a detailed matrix that includes control objectives, examples of control activities and audit procedures. Control objectives include contractor compliance, training, policies and procedures; purchase orders and subcontract clauses; management of purchasing; selecting sources, pricing and negotiation; subcontract award and administration.[24]

In this audit, two tiers of contractors are covered: the prime (or general) contractor and subcontractors. A prime contract is a contract agreement or purchase order entered into by an organization with a supplier that acts as the primary point of contact for awarding pieces of the prime contract to other suppliers (subcontractors), often smaller businesses. The prime contractor is responsible for awarding business to the subcontactors, managing the workflow and paying the subcontractors from the original prime contract. Prime contracting is used extensively in the construction industry and in government procurement.

## Intellectual Property Laws and Regulations

Intellectual property (IP) is various types of intangible personal property that has an inherent commercial value and is protected by the government in different ways. IP includes patents, trademarks, servicemarks, copyrights, technology and trade secrets. Protection of IP is of growing concern to management in many industries. While IP laws exist in many countries, they vary greatly, making this is a high-risk area for many organizations.

For example, Ethiopia recently filed with the U.S. Patent and Trademark Office to trademark the names of three of its major coffee-producing regions: Yirgacheffe, Hirrar and Sidamo. The coffee company Starbucks had already filed to trademark its Sidamo coffee. The organization suggested that Ethiopia should be filing for geographic certification, which requires products to be certified that they do, in fact, come from the specified region. This type of intellectual property protection is the standard for agricultural products. Examples of regionally certified products include Florida oranges, Roquefort cheese, Champagne and Idaho potatoes.[25]

Although Starbucks procures only about 2 percent of its beans from Ethiopia (representing about 2 percent of the annual crop) and made investments and loans of $2.4 million since 2002, the situation presented an interesting legal and ethical situation for an organization that has established an image as a socially responsible organization based in part on its fair-trade practices in the procurement of coffee beans as well as other organization practices.[26]

On February 18, 2007, Starbucks and the government of Ethiopia issued a joint press release stating that they have a shared vision of increasing the incomes of Ethiopian farmers and enhancing the sustainable production of coffee. Starbucks will not oppose Ethiopia's trademark efforts. The organization will double its purchases from East Africa, provide technical support and capacity building through a farm support center it will open in East Africa and expand microcredit facilities.[27]

Because the supply management team is often heavily involved in acquiring intellectual property, they are in an excellent position to develop and manage internal controls. While the supply management professional may not necessarily be fully knowledgeable about the various laws and regulations that affect the supply management organization, he or she must be certain that the risks and opportunities associated with the legal and regulatory environment are considered. For example, as an author I may not fully understand copyright law, but I do recognize that it presents both opportunities for me to have my work protected and it leaves me exposed to the risks associated with violating someone else's copyright. The recognition of both the upside and downside of being an author may be enough for me to take action to mitigate risks. I may mitigate the risk by hiring a copyright lawyer (cost) to look after my interests (benefit). Supply management professionals execute a risk-mitigation strategy every time they incorporate an indemnification clause in a contract.

From a strategic perspective, supply management professionals should be looking for opportunities to bring in suppliers who own intellectual property that may have value to the buying organization and also to be vigilant in recognizing potential risks associated with acquiring such property. For example, the supply management professional charged with the responsibility of purchasing drawings or models of a scientific or technical nature; artistic, audiovisual or literary works; or computer software must understand the fundamentals of the law dealing with copyright "works," "authors" and "works for hire." He or she should work with the legal department to develop the appropriate documentation for each situation.

## Employment Laws

Many countries have employment laws and they vary greatly. In the United States, certain discriminatory practices are prohibited by law. (See "Employment Law" in the appendix at the end of this chapter for specific laws.) Under Title VII of the Civil Rights Act, the Americans with Disabilities Act (ADA) and the Age Discrimination in Employment Act (ADEA), it is illegal to discriminate in any aspect of employment, including hiring and firing; compensation, assignment or classification of employees; transfer, promotion, layoff or recall; job advertisements; recruitment; testing; use of organization facilities; training and apprenticeship programs; fringe benefits; pay, retirement plans and disability leave; or other terms and conditions of employment.

Discriminatory practices under these laws also include harassment on the basis of race, color, religion, sex, national origin, disability or age; retaliation against an individual for filing a charge of discrimination, participating in an investigation or opposing discriminatory practices; employment decisions based on stereotypes or assumptions about the abilities, traits or performance of individuals of a certain sex, race, age, religion or ethnic group or individuals with disabilities; and denying employment opportunities to a person because of marriage to, or association with, an individual of a particular race, religion, national origin or an individual with a disability. Title VII also prohibits discrimination because of participation in schools or places of worship associated with a particular racial, ethnic or religious group.

The chief supply management professional sets the tone for fairness in employment in the supply management organization. Internal partnerships with human resources professionals and legal counsel will provide the framework for attracting, interviewing, selecting and hiring supply management employees. The supply management professional must also ensure that work environments, performance measurement systems and the behavior of each supply management employee is also in compliance.

The final, but by no means least valuable, managerial role is establishing internal controls and ensuring compliance. These activities have always been critical managerial tasks that support organizational success and, in some cases, ensure survival. Today's business climate of ethical lapses and accounting scandals coupled with public outcry and government regulation have brought control and compliance issues to the forefront in many organizational settings. However, as the opening quote of this chapter indicates, how managers and leaders manage the risks associated with operational, financial, legal and regulatory issues may create an opportunity to enhance the organization's reputation and brand image. By thinking of controls and compliance in this way, the leader-manager comes full circle back to the questions: What is our vision of our future? How will we get there? Sound leadership combined with strong managerial action will result in visionary strategies supported by processes, policies and procedures that enable skillful execution leading to desired results. Controls will be built in from the beginning so that compliance occurs before and during activities and after-the-fact controls are primarily for record-keeping and reporting purposes.

## Key Points

1. Management controls are designed to provide reasonable assurance regarding the achievement of objectives in the areas of (1) effectiveness and efficiency of operations, (2) reliability of financial reporting and (3) compliance with applicable laws and regulations.

2. There are three different types of controls: (1) before the fact, (2) during the fact and (3) after the fact:
   - Before-the-fact controls establish a benchmark against which actual performance can be measured. Before-the-fact controls include budgets, plans (stratgic, operational and disaster recovery), forecasts and policy and procedure manuals.
   - During-the-fact controls are put in place to monitor and measure the task while it is occurring or before it is finalized so that adjustments may be made as early as possible to stay within the designated parameters.
   - After-the-fact controls are reviews to measure what actually happened so actual performance can be compared with planned benchmarks and improvements can be made.

3. The supply management team plays a role in establishing internal controls and ensuring compliance in the areas of reliability of financial reporting, operational effectiveness and efficiency and compliance with laws and regulations.

## **Appendix:** *Laws and Regulations*

### *Regulation Influencing the Development of Solicitations*

**Uniform Commercial Code (UCC) Article 2, Sales, and Article 2A, Leasing.** Statutory collection of provisions governing various aspects of commercial transactions such as Sale of Goods (Article 2), Lease of Goods (Article 2A), Letters of Credit (Article 5) and Secured Transactions (Article 9). Statutory language is recommended by the National Conference of Commissioners on Uniform State Laws (NCCUSL) to encourage uniformity among the states but must be adopted by individual state legislatures to become effective.

### *Antitrust and Trade Regulation*

**Sherman Antitrust Act.** Federal antitrust law, passed in 1890, that makes it illegal for parties to act in combination, conspiracy or collusion with the intent of restricting competition in interstate commerce. Price-fixing, reciprocity and group boycotts fall within the parameters of this law.

**Clayton Act.** Federal antitrust law that lists specific practices that are unlawful where the effect may be to substantially lessen competition or tend to create a monopoly in interstate commerce; includes tying arrangements (where the seller requires the buyer to purchase Product B in order to acquire Product A).

**Robinson-Patman Act.** Federal antitrust law that requires a supplier engaged in interstate commerce to sell the same item to all customers at the same price (assuming the same purchase quantity). Exceptions permit a lower price: (1) for a larger purchase quantity, providing that the supplier can justify the lower price through lower costs; (2) to move obsolete or distress merchandise; or (3) to meet the lower price of a competitor in a certain geographic region.

**Federal Trade Commission (FTC) Act.** Federal law passed in 1914 to create the Federal Trade Commission and prohibit deceptive and unfair trade practices such as false advertising.

### *Regulation of Federal Procurement and Public Projects*

**Federal Acquisition Regulation (FAR).** The body of regulations used by all federal executive agencies in the acquisition of supplies and services with appropriated funds.

The FAR is a compilation of all the laws and policies governing the federal procurement process.

**False Claims Act.** Federal law that provides for the recovery of damages and remedies on proof of loss to the government, sustained through fraud in the award or performance of government contracts.

**Davis-Bacon and Related Acts.** Federal law passed in 1931 intended to give local laborers and contractors a fair opportunity to participate in federal building programs and to protect local wage standards. Some state and local governments have similar laws.

**Prompt Payment Act.** Federal law imposing certain requirements on government procurement offices to ensure that federal contractors supplying goods and services are paid on time. Many state and local governments have similar laws.

**Service Contract Act.** Federal law passed in 1965 giving the Wage and Hour Division of the Employment Standards Administration responsibility for predetermination of prevailing wage rates for federal service contracts.

**Walsh-Healey Public Contracts Act (PCA).** Federal law passed in 1936 requiring no more than 40-hour workweeks and minimum age limitations for workers and outlawing unsanitary, hazardous or dangerous working conditions. Contractors who breach these requirements have their names listed and distributed and are ineligible for federal contracting for three years. Applies to federal government purchasing and contracts for material, supplies and equipment exceeding $10,000.

**Small Business Act.** Federal law adopted in 1953 expressing government policy to aid, assist and protect the interests of small business concerns to preserve free competitive enterprise. One objective is to ensure that a reasonable portion of government purchases and contracts go to small business.

**Buy American Act.** Federal law requiring that government purchases for public use consist only of raw materials mined or produced in the United States, or manufactured items that are made in the United States from materials or items mined, produced or manufactured in the United States.

**Freedom of Information Act.** Federal law passed in 1966 requiring the federal government to disclose certain records upon request. Many state and local governments have similar laws in place.

### *Regulation of International Commerce*

**Trade Agreements Act of 1979.** Federal law enacted to facilitate approval and implementation of various trade agreements, foster growth and maintenance of an open world trading system, expand opportunities for U.S. commerce in international trade and improve the rules of international trade.

**Foreign Corrupt Practices Act (FCPA).** Adopted in 1977 and amended in 1988, the provisions prevent bribery of foreign government officials by U.S. persons and prescribe accounting and record-keeping practices.

**North American Free Trade Agreement (NAFTA).** International treaty between and among the United States, Canada and Mexico breaking down trade barriers between these countries.

**General Agreement on Tariffs and Trade (GATT).** Multilateral agreement created in 1947 to reduce barriers to world trade. Succeeded by the World Trade Organization (WTO).

**United Nations Convention on Contracts for the International Sale of Goods (CISG).** International treaty covering the sale of goods between business entities in participating countries called "contracting states." By 2006, the CISG had been ratified by 72 countries accounting for three-quarters of world trade. The CISG is similar to the UCC Article 2, but differs in some significant respects. Unless excluded by the express terms of a contract, the CISG is deemed to be incorporated into (and supplant) any otherwise applicable domestic law(s) with respect to a transaction in goods between parties from different contracting states.

### *Employment Law*

Many countries have laws regulating employment. In the United States, these laws deal with the following: wages and hours of work, safety and health standards, health benefits and retirement standards, other workplace standards, work authorization for non-U.S. citizens, federal contracts: working conditions, federal contracts: equal opportunity, and acts by specific industry, including agriculture, mining, construction and transportation. Specific laws that affect many employers include:

**Federal Equal Employment Opportunity (EEO) Laws.** The laws prohibiting job discrimination include:

**Title VII of the Civil Rights Act of 1964,** which prohibits employment discrimination based on race, color, religion, sex or national origin.

**The Equal Pay Act of 1963 (EPA),** which protects men and women who perform substantially equal work in the same establishment from sex-based wage discrimination.

**The Age Discrimination in Employment Act of 1967 (ADEA),** which protects individuals who are 40 years of age or older.

**Title I and Title V of the Americans with Disabilities Act of 1990 (ADA),** which prohibit employment discrimination against qualified individuals with disabilities in the private sector, and in state and local governments.

**Sections 501 and 505 of the Rehabilitation Act of 1973,** which prohibit discrimination against qualified individuals with disabilities who work in the federal government.

**The Civil Rights Act of 1991,** which, among other things, provides monetary damages in cases of intentional employment discrimination.

The **U.S. Equal Employment Opportunity Commission (EEOC)** enforces all these laws. The EEOC also provides oversight and coordination of all federal equal employment opportunity regulations, practices and policies.

### *Some International Employment Law Sites*

**Mexico and Brazil:**
www.mexicolaw.com/LawInfo11.htm
www.fredlaw.com/articles/international/intl_97sp_jlv.html

**European Union:**
http://ec.europa.eu/employment_social/labour_law/index_en.htm
www.fedee.com/natlaw.html

**Canada:**
www.canlii.org/ca/sta/l-2/index.html

**Japan:**
www.japanlaw.info/law2004/JAPANBIZLAWLITE4GAIJIN_LABOR_LAW.html#
EMPLOYMENT_RULES

**India:**
www.indianembassy.org/newsite/Doing_business_In_India/Labor_Laws.asp

# Endnotes

## How to Use this Book

1. Craig Hickman and Michael A. Silva, *Creating Excellence: Managing Corporate Culture, Strategy and Change in the New Age* (New York: Plume, 1986).

## Chapter 1

1. Warren G. Bennis, *On Becoming a Leader* (Upper Saddle River: Addison Wesley, 1989).
2. Marcus Buckingham and Curt Coffman, *First Break All the Rules* (New York: Simon & Schuster, 1999).
3. Bennis, *On Becoming a Leader.*
4. P. Fraser Johnson and Michiel R. Leenders, "Supply's Organizational Roles and Responsibilities," CAPS Research (2004): 15.
5. Michiel R. Leenders and P. Fraser Johnson, "Major Changes in Supply's Responsibilities," CAPS Research (2002), 101.
6. Debashis Chatterjee, *Leading Consciously: A Pilgrimage Toward Self-Mastery* (New York: Elsevier, 1998).
7. Diane Dreher, *The Tao of Personal Leadership* (New York: Collins, 1997).
8. Ibid.
9. Paul R. Bemthal, Jason Bondra and Wei Wang, "Leadership in China," *Development Dimensions International (DDI)* (2006): 10.
10. Geert Hofstede, http://feweb.uvt.nl/center/hofstede/index.htm
11. Lynn Sharp Paine and Jennifer Benqing Gui, "An Interview With Zhang Ruimin, CEO, The Haier Group," *Harvard Business Review* (December 1, 1998).
12. John H. Zenger and Joseph Folkman, *The Handbook for Leaders: 24 Lessons for Extraordinary Leadership* (New York: McGraw-Hill Professional Education, 2004).
13. James M. Kouzes and Barry Z. Posner, *The Leadership Challenge: How to Keep Getting Extraordinary Things Done in Organizations* (Hoboken: John Wiley & Sons, Inc., 2003).
14. Tsun-yan Hsieh and Sara Yik, "Leadership as the Starting Point of Strategy," *The McKinsey Quarterly* 1 (2005).
15. www.whirlpoolcorp.com/governance/managementteam/default.asp
16. Mark Gerzon, "Leaders and Leadership" in *Beyond Intractability*, Guy Burgess and Heidi Burgess, eds. (Boulder: Conflict Resolution Consortium, September, 2003), available from www.beyondintractability.org/essay/leaders/?nid=1097
17. Allan R. Gold, Masao Hirano and Yoshinori Yokoyama, "An Outsider Takes On Japan," *The McKinsey Quarterly* 1 (2001).
18. Warren Bennis, "The Secrets of Great Groups," *Leader to Leader* 3 (Winter 1997): 29–33.
19. Joseph Rost, *Leadership for the Twenty-First Century* (New York: Praeger, 1991).
20. Ibid.
21. Johnson and Leenders, "Supply's Organizational Roles and Responsibilities."
22. Gerzon, "Leaders and Leadership."
23. Peter Drucker, www.thinkexist.com/quotation/the-leaders-who-work-most-effectively-it-seems-to/347344.html

24. Peter Engardio with Jena McGregor, "Karma Capitalism," *BusinessWeek* (October 30, 2006).
25. Ibid.
26. Ibid.
27. Ibid.
28. Geert Hofstede, www.geert-hofstede.com/index.shtml
29. Tom Peters, www.leadershipthatlasts.com/quotes.html
30. John Wooden, *Wooden on Leadership* (New York: McGraw-Hill, 2005).
31. John H. Zenger and Joseph Folkman, *The Extraordinary Leader: Turning Good Managers into Great Leaders* (New York: McGraw-Hill, 2002).
32. Charles M. Farkas and Suzy Wetlaufer, "The Ways Chief Executive Officers Lead" in *Harvard Business Review on Leadership* (Cambridge: Harvard Business Review Publishing, 1998): 115–46.
33. Leenders and Johnson, "Major Changes in Supply Responsibilties."
34. Ram Charan, *Know-How: The Eight Skills That Separate People Who Perform From Those Who Don't* (New York: Crown Business, 2007).
35. Ibid.
36. Chris Chen, "Managing and Leading," *NAPM Insights* 6(4) (April 1995): 5.
37. David C. McClelland, *Human Motivation* (New York: Cambridge University Press, 1988).
38. *The Ins and Outs of Effective Leadership* (Boston: The Hay Group): 5, available from www.haygroup.com/tl/Downloads/Leadership_booklet.pdf
39. Daniel Goleman and The Hay Group, www.haygroup.com and www.danielgoleman.info
40. Warren Bennis, "The Leadership Advantage," *Leader to Leader* 12 (Spring 1999): 18-23, available on the Leader to Leader Institute Web site, www.leadertoleader.org/leaderbooks/L2L/spring99/bennis.html
41. Dave Ulrich, Jack Zenger and Norman Smallwood, *Results-Based Leadership* (Cambridge: Harvard Business School Press, 1999).
42. www.whirlpoolcorp.com/governance/managementteam/default.asp
43. Cynthia D. McCauley, *Developmental Assignments: Creating Learning Experiences Without Changing Jobs* (Center for Creative Leadership, 2006).
44. Zenger and Folkman, *The Extraordinary Leader,* 117.
45. Peter F. Drucker, *People and Performance* (Burlington: Butterworth Heinemann, 1995).
46. Lester C. Thurow, *Building Wealth: The New Rules for Individuals, Companies, and Nations in a Knowledge-Based Economy* (New York: Collins, 2000).
47. Henry Mintzberg, "The Manager's Job: Folklore and Fact" in *Harvard Business Review on Leadership* (Boston: Harvard Business School Press, 1998).
48. Chris Chen, "Managing and Leading," 5.
49. Anna E. Flynn and Samuel D. Farney, "Leading, Managing and Supervising" in *The Supply Management Leadership Process: Strategies for Organizational Effectiveness* (Tempe, AZ: National Association of Purchasing Management, Inc., 2000).
50. Victor H. Vroom, *Work and Motivation* (Hoboken: John Wiley and Sons, Inc., 1964; Melbourne, FL: Krieger Publishing, 1982).
51. Lisa M. Ellram, "Strategic Cost Management in the Supply Chain: A Purchasing and Supply Management Perspective," CAPS Research (2002): 91.
52. W. Edwards Deming, *Out of the Crisis* (MIT Press, 2000).
53. W. Edwards Deming Institute, www.deming.org/theman/teachings02.html

54. Douglas McGregor, *The Human Side of Enterprise* (McGraw-Hill, 1960; 25th Anniversary Printing, 1985).
55. William Ouchi, *Theory Z: How American Business Can Meet the Japanese Challenge* (Avon, 1982).
56. Elton Mayo, *The Social Problems of an Industrial Civilization* (Cambridge: Harvard University Publishing, 1945): viii.
57. "Total Procurement Process: An Overview," *Supply Chain Management*, Shell Services Company: 7.
58. Anna E. Flynn, "Eastman Kodak Company Worldwide Purchasing Sourcing Process," *PRACTIX,* CAPS Research 8 (July 2005): 3.
59. Rodger L. Boehm, "Leading Change: An Interview With the CEO of Deere & Company," *The McKinsey Quarterly* (December 2006).

## Chapter 2

1. Josephson Institute of Ethics, www.josephsoninstitute.org/businessethics_quotations.html
2. John P. Kotter, *John Kotter on What Leaders Really Do* (Cambridge: Harvard Business School Press, 1999).
3. "Making Ethical Decisions," Josephson Institute for Ethics, available from www.josephsoninstitute.org/MED/MED-1makingsense.htm
4. Meena S. Wilson and Maxine A. Dalton, *International Success: Selecting, Developing and Supporting Expatriate Managers* (Greensboro: Center for Creative Leadership, 1998).
5. Jeffrey Immelt, Dartmouth Commencement Speech, June 13, 2004, available from www.dartmouth.edu/~news/releases/2004/06/13a.html
6. www.deere.com
7. "Wal-Mart Announces Plans to Double Its Heavy-Duty Truck Fleet's Fuel Efficiency," available from www.rmi.org/store/p15details10.php?x=1&pagePath=00000000
8. George Zsidisin and Lisa Ellram, "Supply Risk Assessment Analysis," *PRACTIX,* CAPS Research (June 1999): 9.
9. Mihaly Csikszentmihalyi, *Leadership: Leadership, Flow and the Making of Meaning* (New York: Viking Press, 2003): 197.
10. The Classic Quotes Collection contained in The Quotations Page, www.quotationspage.com/quotes/Seneca
11. Hsieh and Yik, "Leadership as the Starting Point of Strategy," 67–73.
12. www.wholefoodsmarket.com/company/declaration.html
13. Angela Jameson, "Man of Steel Who Wants to Forge His Empire out of Limelight," *The London Times* (31 January 2005): 44.
14. John Deere Strategy, available from www.deere.com/en_US/compinfo/strategy/index.html
15. Global Procurement, available from www.pc.ibm.com/ww/lenovo/procurement/
16. "Whirlpool Vision and Strategy," available from www.whirlpoolcorp.com/about/vision_and_strategy/default.asp
17. Ingo Bulow, Ulrich Schott-Wullenweber and Fabian Hedderich, "Change Management in Purchasing: Best Practices at Germany's Number 1 Airline Deutsche Lufthansa AG," *PRACTIX,* CAPS Research 9 (July 2006).
18. "LG Electronic's Global Supply Chain Management System Goes Live," LGE press release, September 11, 2001.

19. "LG Electronics Builds Global Purchasing System," LGE press release, July 31, 2001.
20. "Designed to Grow...Sustainability," 2007 Global Sustainability Report, available from www.pg.com/company/our_commitment/pdfs/gsr07_Web.pdf
21. Gold, Hirano and Yokoyama, "An Outsider Takes On Japan."
22. Susan Avery, "Purchasing Presents Its Medal of Professional Excellence for 2006 to United Technologies Corporation," *Purchasing,* (September 7, 2006).

## Chapter 3

1. Howard Marketing Service, *Asian Words of Wisdom,* available from www.howard-marketing.com/products.php?mid=7&id=16
2. Johnson and Leenders, "Supply's Organizational Roles and Responsibilities."
3. IBM Business Consulting Services, "Taking Center Stage: The 2005 Chief Procurement Officer Survey," available from www.ibm.com/bsc
4. Leenders and Johnson, "Major Changes in Supply Chain Responsibilities."
5. Lisa Ellram and Wendy Tate, "Bank of America: Services Purchasing and Outsourcing," *PRACTIX,* CAPS Research 9 (May 2006).
6. Bulow, Schott-Wullenweber and Hederich, "Change Management in Purchasing: Best Practices From Germany's Number 1 Airline Deutsche Lufthansa AG."
7. Johan Ahlberg and Tomas Nauclér, "Leading Change: An Interview With Sandvik's Peter Gossas," *The McKinsey Quarterly* (Web exclusive) (January 2007), available from www.mckinseyquarterly.com
8. Ibid.
9. Bulow, Schott-Wullenweber and Hedderick, "Change Management in Purchasing: Best Practices From Germany's No. 1 Airline Deutsche Lufthansa AG."
10. Susan Avery, "UTC: Purchasing's Medal of Honor Winner," *Purchasing,* (September 7, 2006), available from www.purchasing.com
11. Ibid.
12. Flynn, "Eastman Kodak's Worldwide Purchasing Sourcing Process."
13. Avery, "UTC: Purchasing's Medal of Honor Winner."
14. IBM press release, available from www.ibm.com/news/us/en/2006/10/2006_10_12.html
15. Avery, "UTC: Purchasing's Medal of Honor Winner."
16. Jeffrey A. Ogden and Matthew W. McCarter, "Better Buyer-Supplier Relationships Through Supply Base Reduction and Supplier Performance Management," *PRACTIX,* CAPS Research 8 (December 2004).
17. Ibid.
18. Boehm, "Leading Change: An Interview With the CEO of Deere & Company."
19. Ibid.
20. Ibid.
21. Bulow, Schott-Wullenweber and Hedderick, "Change Management in Purchasing: Best Practices from Germany's No. 1 Airline Deutsche Lufthansa AG."
22. John P. Kotter, *Force for Change: How Leadership Differs From Management* (New York: Free Press, 1990): 51.
23. Gold, Hirano and Yoshinori, "An Outsider Takes on Japan."
24. Ibid.

25. Boehm, "Leading Change: An Interview with the CEO of Deere & Company."
26. Ahlberg and Nauclér, "Leading Change: An Interview With Sandvik's Peter Gossas."
27. Bulow, Schott-Wullenweber and Hedderick, "Change Management in Purchasing: Best Practices from Germany's No. 1 Airline Deutsche Lufthansa AG."
28. Ahlberg and Nauclér, "Leading Change: An Interview With Sandvik's Peter Gossas."

## Chapter 4

1. Akio Morita with Edwin M. Reingold and Mitsuko Shimomura, *Akio Morita and Sony: Made in Japan,* (New York: Signet, 1986), 160.
2. "Organizing for Successful Change Management: A McKinsey Global Survey" (Web exclusive) (July 2006), available from www.mckinseyquarterly.com/article_page.aspx?ar=1809&L2=18&L3=27
3. Ahlberg and Nauclér, "Leading Change: An Interview With Sandvik's Peter Gossas."
4. Kim Kanaga and Michael E. Kossler, *How to Form a Team: Five Keys to High Performance* (Greensboro: Center for Creative Leadership, 2001) available from www.ccl.org/leadership/forms/publications/publicationProductDetail.aspx?productId=1-882197-68-2&pageId=1250
5. Ahlberg and Nauclér, "Leading With Change: An Interview With Sandvik's Peter Gossas."
6. Bulow, Schott-Wullenweber and Hedderick, "Change Management in Purchasing: Best Practices from Germany's No. 1 Airline Deutsche Lufthansa AG."
7. Ibid.
8. Glenn L. Hallam, *The Adventures of Team Fantastic: A Practical Guide for Team Leaders and Members* (Greensboro: Center for Creative Leadership, 1996), available from www.ccl.org/leadership/forms/publications/publicationProductDetail.aspx?productId=1-882197-17-8&pageId=1250
9. Kotter, *Force for Change: How Leadership Differs From Management.*
10. David Baldwin and Curt Grayson, *Influence: Gaining Commitment, Getting Results,* (Greensboro: Center for Creative Leadership, 2004): 11.
11. Gautam Kumra, "Leading Change: An Interview With the Managing Director of Tata Motors," *The McKinsey Quarterly* (January 2007)
12. Ahlberg and Nauclér, "Leading Change: An Interview With Sandvik's Peter Gossas."
13. Mary Siegfried, "The Power of Influence," *Inside Supply Management* 16(10) (October 2005).
14. David Hannon, "Interview With Sidney Johnson, Vice President of Global Supply Management, Delphi Corporation," *Purchasing* (September 21, 2006).
15. Michael Jenkins, "A Question of Leadership," *Leadership in Asia* 24 (5) (November–December 2004), available from www. ccl.org
16. Gold, Hirano and Yokoyama, "An Outsider Takes On Japan."
17. Jenkins, "A Question of Leadership."
18. Ibid.
19. Gautum Kumra, "Leading Change: An Interview With the Managing Director of Tata Motors," 7.
20. James Fallows, "Mr. Zhang Builds His Dream Town," *The Atlantic Monthly* (March 2007).
21. Michelle LeBaron, "Communication Tools for Understanding Cultural Differences" in *Beyond Intractability,* Guy Burgess and Heidi Burgess, eds. (Boulder: Conflict Research Consortium, June 2003), available from www.beyondintractability.org/essay/communication_tools/
22. Fallows, "Mr. Zhang Builds His Dream Town," 85–92.

23. Ibid.
24. www.quoteworld.org/quotes/1544
25. Kotter, *Force for Change: How Leadership Differs from Management.*
26. "The New Work of Leadership: Connectivity, Creativity and Continuity," *Leading Effectively: eNewsletter* (The Center for Creative Leadership, April 2004).
27. Ahlberg and Nauclér, "Leading Change: An Interview With Sandvik's Peter Gossas."
28. Ibid.
29. Anna Flynn, "Consumption and Specification Management Bristol-Myers Squibb Company," *PRACTIX,* CAPS Research 8 (February 2005).
30. Ibid.
31. "Taking on Teams: Understanding the Fundamentals of Working in Teams," *Leading Effectively eNewsletter* (The Center for Creative Leadership, September 2003).
32. Bruce W. Tuckman, "Developmental Sequence in Small Groups," *Psychological Bulletin* 63 (1965): 384–99; and Bruce W. Tuckman and Mary Ann Jensen, "Stages of Small Group Development Revisited," *Group and Organizational Studies* 2 (1977): 419–27.
33. "How Harley-Davidson Uses Cross-Functional Teams," *Purchasing* 4 (November 1999): 144.
34. Jeanne Brett, Kristin Behfar and Mary C. Kern, "Managing Multicultural Teams," *Harvard Business Review* (November 2006): 84–91.
35. Ibid.
36. Gerzon, "What Is Leadership."
37. Deming, *Out of the Crisis.*
38. Ibid.
39. Avery, "UTC: Purchasing's Medal of Honor Winner."
40. Ahlberg and Nauclér, "Leading Change: An Interview With Sandvik's Peter Gossas."

## Chapter 5

1. Lewis M. Branscomb and Phillip E. Auerwald, *Taking Technical Risks: How Innovators, Managers and Investors Manage* (Cambridge: MIT Press, 2001): 47.
2. George Zsidisin, "Measuring Supply Risk: An Example From Europe," *PRACTIX,* CAPS Research 4 (June 2001): 2.
3. Tom DeMarco and Timothy Lister, *Waltzing With Bears: Managing Risk on Software Projects* (New York: Dorset House Publishing, 2003).
4. "Risk Factors," *Federal Express Annual Report 2006,* 59–60, available from www.fedex.com
5. Deere & Company, *Code of Ethics,* available from www.deere.com
6. George Zsidisin, "Business and Supply Chain Continuity," CAPS Research Critical Issues Report 2 (January 2007).
7. Deere & Company, www.deere.com/en_US/investinfo/corpgov/ethics.html
8. Zsidisin, "Measuring Supply Risk: An Example From Europe," 3.
9. Ibid.
10. Ibid.
11. Supply Management Research Group, Japan, "Japan's Keiretsu as a Strategic Relationship With Suppliers," CAPS Research (2005): 8.
12. Report by the Secretariat, World Trade Organization, available from www.wto.org/English/tratop_e/tpr_e/s137-1_e.doc

13. "EDS Helps Welfare and Benefits Organizations and Agencies Design and Implement New Models of Service Delivery," available from www.eds.com/industries/welfareandbenefits/
14. "Better, Faster, Cheaper? Business Process Transformation in Financial Services," *The Economist Intelligence Unit* (July 2005).
15. Beth Ellyn Rosenthal, "Deloitte Study Discovers 75 Percent of Global Financial Institutions Plan to Outsource Offshore," *BPO Outsourcing Journal* (June 2003).

## Chapter 6

1. Steve Hamm and Dexter Roberts, "China's First Global Capitalist," *BusinessWeek* (December 2006), 11.
2. www.brainyquotes.com/quotes/authors/p/peter_drucker/html
3. "Vision and Strategy: Future Growth Through Global Presence," available from www.whirlpool.com/about/vision_and_strategy/globalplatform.asp
4. Charles Fine, *Clockspeed: Winning Industry Control in the Age of Temporary Advantage* (New York: Perseus Books Group, 1998).
5. Hamm and Roberts, "China's First Global Capitalist."
6. "Managing Procurement Through a Merger: Capturing the Value of the Deal," 2006, available from www.boozallen.com/publications/article/657849
7. Ibid.
8. "Vision and Strategy."
9. John Deere Strategy, available from www.deere.com/en_US/compinfo/mission/mission_strategy.html?location=ourcompany&link=strategy
10. "Vision and Strategy."
11. Boehm, "Leading Change: An Interview With the CEO of Deere & Company."

## Chapter 7

1. Warren G. Bennis, *On Becoming a Leader* (New York: De Capo Press, 2003): 182.
2. W. Edwards Deming, The Deming Institute, www.deming.org
3. Michael Brendel, "New VW Chief to Reorganize Firm's Brands," *The Wall Street Journal* (15 November 2006), available from www.online.wsj.com/article/SB116355821732923475.html
4. Ellram and Tate, "Bank of America: Services Purchasing and Outsourcing."
5. Gregory Dess, G.T. (Tom) Lumpkin and Alan Eisner, *Strategic Management: Text and Cases* (Burr Ridge: McGraw-Hill/Irwin, 2007).
6. Gold, Hirano and Yokoyama, "An Outsider Takes On Japan."
7. Johnson and Leenders, "Supply's Organizational Roles and Responsibilities."
8. Avery, "UTC: Purchasing's Medal of Honor Winner."
9. William Atkinson, "Driving Efficiency," *Purchasing* (November 8, 2005).
10. Ibid.
11. Anna Flynn and Sam Farney, "Operating Policies, Guidelines and Procedures" in *The Supply Management Leadership Process,* Volume 4 of the ISM Knowledge Series (Tempe, AZ: NAPM, 2000): 145–70.
12. David F. Ross, "The Intimate Supply Chain," *Supply Chain Management Review* (July 1, 2006).
13. James Carbone, "Buyers Link Hands With Designers," *Purchasing* (March 16, 2006).

14. Ibid.
15. Susan Avery, "Lean, But Not Mean, Rockwell Collins Excels," *Purchasing* (September 1, 2005).
16. Thomas Wailgum, "Integration Liberation: A New Way to Integrate Your Supply Chain," *CIO* (October 15, 2006), available from www.cio.com/article/25784/Integration_Liberation_A_New_Way_to_Integrate_Your_Supply_Chain
17. Ibid.
18. Ibid.

## Chapter 8

1. www.thinkexist.com/quotation/if_you_can-t_describe_what_you_are_doing_as_a/12330.html
2. Audrey Going Brichi and Paul L. Massih, "Strategic Sourcing and Supplier Diversity — Strategies for Success," ISM's 87th International Supply Management Conference, San Francisco, 2002.
3. Ibid.
4. Richard D. Jones, "Organizing for and Capturing the Value of Strategic Sourcing," 7th Annual ISM Services Group Conference, 2006.
5. Tim Dolan and Karen Fedele, "Strategic Sourcing: Reducing Costs and Supporting Diversity Goals," ISM's 89th Annual International Supply Management Conference, Philadelphia, April 2004.
6. Joe Mahon, "Taking the Shears to Fuel Costs," *Fedgazette* (May 2006), available from www.minneapolisfed.org/pubs/fedgaz/06-05/fuel.cfm
7. Peter Kraljic, "Purchasing Must Become Supply Management," *Harvard Business Review* (September/October 1983).
8. "Understanding Supply Chain Risk: A McKinsey Global Survey," *The McKinsey Quarterly* (October 2006).
9. www.thinkexist.com/quotation/quality-quality-quality-never_waver_from_it-even/206864.html
10. Michiel Leenders, R. Kudar and Anna E. Flynn, "Fleet Management's Contribution and Outsourcing," an unpublished manuscript based on a study conducted for the National Association of Fleet Administrators, 1995.
11. Malcolm Wheatley, "How to Know If E-Procurement Is Right for You," *CIO* (June 15, 2003): 1.
12. Ibid, 2.
13. Ibid.
14. Ibid.
15. "Strategic Supply Management at Japanese Companies," Supply Management Research Group, Japan, Case Study: Company B, CAPS Research (2006): 17.
16. Wheatley, "How to Know If E-Procurement Is Right for You."
17. Stewart Beall, et.al., "The Role of Reverse Auction in Strategic Sourcing," CAPS Research (2003): 44–45.
18. Anne Millen Porter, "Super Spend Analysis," *Purchasing* (March 18, 2004), available from www.purchasing.com/article/CA403250.html?text=anne+millen+porter
19. Ibid.

20. Eric Laursen, "Cut Down on Contract Stress," *Journal of Accountancy* (January 2002), available from www.aicpa.org/pubs/jofa/jan2002/laursen.htm
21. Ibid.
22. Susan Avery, "How to Use Software to Manage Contracts," *Purchasing* (June 16, 2005), available from www.purchasing.com/article/CA607271.html

**Chapter 9**

1. Thomas J. Watson, Jr., *A Business and Its Beliefs: Ideas That Helped Build IBM.* (New York: McGraw-Hill Professional, 1963): 4.
2. Douglas A. Ready and Jay A. Conger, "How to Fill the Talent Gap," *The Wall Street Journal* (15 September 2007), available from www.online.wsj.com/public/article_print/SB118841695428712511.html
3. *ISM Glossary of Key Supply Management Terms* (Tempe, AZ: Institute for Supply Management, 2006).
4. Ready and Conger, "How to Fill the Talent Gap."
5. Johnson and Leenders, "Supply's Organizational Roles and Responsibilites," 36.
6. "IBM Shifts Global Procurement Headquarters to China" October 12, 2006 IBM press release, available from www-03.ibm.com/press/us/en/pressrelease/20422.wss
7. Joo-Seng Tan, "Cultural Intelligence and the Global Economy," *Leadership in Action* 24(5) (November/December 2004).
8. A.T. Kearney, "Impacting the Supply Management Profession: Charting and Navigating Strategies for the CPO and Your Team's Evolution" (2007).
9. The Conference Board, "Developing Global Leaders."
10. Ellram and Tate, "Bank of America: Services Purchasing and Outsourcing."
11. The Conference Board, "Developing Global Leaders."
12. Rose Mary Wentling, *Diversity Initiatives in the Workplace* (Champaign: The National Center for Research in Vocational Education NCRVE, University of Illinois), available from www.vocserve.berkeley.edu/CW82/Diversity.html
13. "IBM Shifts Global Procurement Headquarters to China."
14. Jan Niessen, "Immigration: The Role of Civil Society in Promoting Integration" (August 25, 2002), available from www.migpolgroup.com/documents/2513.html
15. Ian Davis and Elizabeth Stephenson, "Ten Trends in 2006," *The McKinsey Quarterly* (2006), available from www.mckinseyquarterly.com/Ten_trends_to_watch_in_2006_1734
16. "General Mills Corporate Social Responsibility 2006," available from www.generalmills.com/corporate/commitment/workforce.aspx
17. Sean Silverthorne, "Who Rises to Power in American Business?" *Harvard Business School Working Knowledge Newsletter* (January 8, 2007), available from www.hbswk.hbs.edu/item/5504.html
18. Gary A. Berg, Mihaly Csikszentmihalyi and Jeanne Nakamura, "Mission Possible? Enabling Good Work in Higher Education," *Change* 35 (5) (2003): 41–7.
19. "Life at Google," available from www.google.com/support/jobs/bin/static.py?page«out.html
20. Fallows, "Mr. Zhang Builds His Dream Town."
21. "HP Corporate Citizenship Report, 2005," available from www.hp.com/hpinfo/grants/us/reports/hp2005pe_ar.pdf

## Chapter 10

1. Nicholas Reinecke, Peter Spiller and Drew Ungerman, "The Talent Factor in Purchasing," *The McKinsey Quarterly* 1 (2007), available from www.mckinseyquarterly.com/The_talent_factor_in_purchasing_1927
2. Ibid.
3. www.brainyquote.com/quotes/authors/a/alvin_toffler.html
4. Peter Senge, *The Fifth Discipline: The Art and Practice of the Learning Organization* (New York: Currency, 2006).
5. Arie de Geus, *The Living Company: Habits for Survival in a Turbulent Business Environment* (Cambridge: Harvard Business School Press, 2002).
6. "IBM Shifts Global Procurement Headquarters to China."
7. "Understanding Supply Chain Risk: A McKinsey Global Survey," *The McKinsey Quarterly* (September 2006), available from www.mckinseyquarterly.com/Understanding_supply_chain_risk_A_McKinsey_Global_Survey_1847
8. The Conference Board, "Developing Global Leaders."
9. Ibid.
10. Ibid.
11. Ibid.
12. Larry Giunipero and Robert Handfield, "Key Skill Sets for the Supply Manager of the Future," CAPS Research (2004).
13. "NACE Job Outlook 2007" (December 13, 2006), available from www.naceweb.org/press/display.asp?year=&prid-248
14. "Recruiters Sound Off," *The Wall Street Journal* (20 September 2006), available from www.online.wsj.com/public/article/SB115862959400467098.html?mod=2_1245_3
15. *A Guide to the Project Management Body of Knowledge,* Third Edition (PMBOK Guide), (Newton Square, PA: Project Management Institute, 2004): 34.
16. Ken Blanchard, Chapter 8 in *Leading at a Higher Level: Blanchard on How to Be a Higher-Performing Leader* (Upper Saddle River: FT Press, 2006).
17. "NACE Job Outlook 2007," available from www.jobweb.com/joboutlook/2007/student2.htm
18. Claudia Wallis and Sonja Steptoe, "How to Bring Our Schools out of the 20th Century," *Time* (December 9, 2006), available from www.time.com/time/nation/article/0,8599,1568429,00.html
19. Roger M. Schwarz, *The Skilled Facilitator: A Comprehensive Resource for Consultants, Facilitators, Managers, Trainers and Coaches* (Chapel Hill: Roger Schwarz and Associates, 2002): 5.
20. F.C. Goldstein and H.S. Levin, "Disorders of Reasoning and Problem-Solving Ability" in *Neuropsychological Rehabilitation,* M. Meier, A. Benton and L. Diller, eds., (London: Taylor & Francis Group, 1987).
21. Thomas L. Friedman, "Learning to Keep Learning," *The New York Times* 13 December 2006.
22. Quotation found in www.quotemountain.com/famous_quote_author/george_kneller_famous_quotations/
23. Teresa M. Amabile, "How to Kill Creativity," *Harvard Business Review* 76(5) (1998).
24. Sean Silverthorne, "Time Pressure and Creativity: Why Time Is Not on Your Side," *Harvard Business School Working Knowledge Newsletter* (July 29, 2002), available from www.hbswk.hbs.edu/item/3030.html

25. "General Mills Corporate Social Responsibility Report," available from www.generalmills .com/corporate/commitment/2006_CSR.pdf
26. Ready and Conger, "How to Fill the Talent Gap."
27. The Conference Board, "Developing Global Leaders."
28. Mary Siegfried, "Filling the Leadership Void," *Inside Supply Management* (April 2007).
29. "How to Fill the Talent Gap."

## Chapter 11

1. Warren Buffet, www.thinkexist.com/quotation/in-the-business-world-the-rearview-mirror-is/357219.html
2. Susan Avery, "Lean, But Not Mean, Rockwell Collins Excels."
3. Ibid.
4. Ibid.
5. Phillip L. Carter, Robert M. Monczka and Trish Mosconi, "Strategic Performance Measures for Purchasing and Supply," CAPS Research (2005), available from www.capsresearch.org/ publication/pdfs-protected/carterp2005.pdf
6. *2007 ISM Salary Survey* (Tempe, AZ: Institute for Supply Management), available from www .ism.ws, Tools.
7. W. Edwards Deming, *Out of the Crisis,* 42.
8. Eric Harmon, Scott Hensel and Tim Lukes, "Measuring Performance in Services," *The McKinsey Quarterly* 1 (2006), available from www.mckinseyquarterly.com/Measuring_ performance_in_services_1730
9. Carter, Monczka and Mosconi, "Strategic Performance Measures for Purchasing and Supply" CAPS Research (2005): 31.
10. Ibid., 6.
11. Boehm, "Leading Change: An Interview With the CEO of Deere & Company."
12. William Atkinson, "Driving Efficiency," *Purchasing* (August 11, 2005), available from www. purchasing.com/article/CA631812.html?text=vehicle+management+system
13. Johan Ahlberg and Tomas Nauclér, "Leading Change: An Interview With Sandvik's Peter Gossas," *The McKinsey Quarterly* (January 2007), available from www.mckinseyquarterly.com/ article_page.aspx?ar=1894&L2=18&L3=27&srid=17&gp=0)
14. William Atkinson, "Driving Efficiency," *Purchasing* (August 11, 2005), available from www .purchasing.com/article/CA631812.html?text=vehicle+management+system
15. Ibid.
16. Gold, Hirano and Yokoyama, "An Outsider Takes On Japan."
17. Boehm, "Leading Change: An Interview With the CEO of Deere & Company."
18. Allan Gold, Masao Hirano and Yoshinori Yokoyama, "An Interview With Nissan's Carlos Ghosn," *The McKinsey Quarterly* 1 (2001).
19. Ahlberg and Nauclér, "Leading Change: An Interview With Sandvik's Peter Gossas."
20. Leenders and Johnson, "Major Changes in Supply's Responsibilities," 101.

## Chapter 12

1. Tom Warga, NY Life Insurance, quoted in "Get Ready for the Privacy Backlash," *Darwin Magazine* (2001).
2. COSO, The Committee of Sponsoring Organizations of the Treadway Commission, www.coso.org/publications/executive_summary_integrated_framework.htm
3. www.iasb.org/About+Us/About+IASB/About++the+IASB.htm
4. www.coso.org/audit_shop.htm
5. "Supply Chain Procurement Process Review at Document Solutions Corporation," Protiviti, available from www.protiviti.com/portal/site/pro-us/menuitem.7a3f342125b0b542d1505d86f5ffbfa0
6. "Internal Audit Transformation at International Wireless Telecommunication Corporation," Protiviti, available from www.protiviti.com/portal/site/pro-us/menuitem.9bc660ab7a0042b1d1505d86f5ffbfa0
7. Anna E. Flynn, "Developing and Implementing E-Sourcing Strategy," CAPS Research Critical Issues Report (September 2004): 14.
8. "Baxter 2005 Sustainability Report; Product Life Cycle," available from www.sustainability.baxter.com/documents/old_reports/sustainability_report_2005_eng.pdf
9. Steven M. Taber, "Understanding Liability Under Environmental Laws," *Purchasing Today* 7(7) (July 1996): 20.
10. David Barboza, "Blazing a Paper Trail in China; A Self-Made Billionaire Wrote Her Ticket on Recycled Cardboard," *The New York Times* (16 January 2007).
11. Taber, "Understanding Liability Under Environmental Laws."
12. "Baxter 2005 Sustainability Report; New Product Development," available from www.sustainability.baxter.com/documents/old_reports/sustainability_report_2005_eng.pdf
13. "Simply Sustainable, Product Life Cycle," Ministry for the Environment, available from www.mfe.govt.nz/issues/sustainable-industry/tools-services/topics.php?id=3
14. European Commission, www.ec.europa.eu/environment/waste/weee/index_en.htm
15. www.aeanet.org/GovernmentAffairs/gabl_ChinaRoHSpage0905.asp
16. www.ec.europa.eu/environment/waste/weee/index_en.htm
17. "Baxter 2005 Sustainability Report; End of Life Cycle," www.sustainability.baxter.com/product/product_end_of_life.html
18. International Standards Organization, available from www.iso.org/iso/iso_catalogue/catalogue_tc/catalogue_detail.htm?csnumber1908
19. International Standards Organization, http://www.iso-17799.com
20. Susan Avery, "Emptoris Releases Updated Spend Analysis Tool," *Purchasing* (November 15, 2006), available from www.purchasing.com/article/CA6391908.html?text=emptoris+releases+updated+spend+analysis+tool
21. Ibid.
22. The American Institute of Certified Public Accountants, www.aicpa.org/audcommctr/spotlight/SOX_Section_404.htm
23. "Federal Express 2006 Annual Report," 52, available from www.fedex.com/us/investorrelations/financialinfo/2006annualreport/online/fin_pdfs.html

24. "Internal Control Matrix for Audit of Purchasing Controls," Defense Contract Audit Agency, available from www.dcaa.mil/sap/PURC-Internal_Control_Matrix.pdf.
25. European Commission, Agriculture and Food, http://ec.europa.eu/agriculture/foodqual/quali1_en.htm
26. Stephan Faris, "Starbucks vs. Ethiopia," *Fortune* (February 26, 2007), available from www.money.cnn.com/magazines/fortune/fortune_archive/2007/03/05/8401343/index.htm
27. "The Government of the Federal Democratic Republic of Ethiopia and the Starbucks Coffee Company Joint Statement" (February 18, 2007), available from www.starbucks.com/aboutus/pressdesc.asp?idw0

# References


## Chapter 1

Fiedler, F.E., and M.M. Chemers. *Improving Leadership Effectiveness: The Leader Match Concept,* Second Edition. John Wiley and Sons, New York, NY, 1984.

Hayashi, M. "A Historical Review of Japanese Management Theories: The Search for a General Theory of Japanese Management." *Asian Business & Management,* (1), 2002, pp. 1–19, http://cfaculty.tamacc.chuo-u.ac.jp/~hmasaki/JMTen.pdf

Lewis, C.P. *Building a Shared Vision: A Leader's Guide to Aligning the Organization.* Productivity Press, Portland, OR, 1997.

Morrisey, G.L. *Morrisey on Planning: A Guide to Strategic Thinking.* Jossey-Bass, San Francisco, CA, 1996.

Rogers, J.L. "Leadership Development for the '90s: Incorporating Emergent Paradigm Perspectives." *NASPA Journal,* Summer 1992, pp. 243–51.

Rost, J.C. "Leadership Development in the New Millennium." *The Journal of Leadership Studies,* November 1993, pp. 91–110.

Thurow, L.C. *Building Wealth: The New Rules for Individuals, Companies, and Nations in a Knowledge-Based Economy.* HarperCollins, New York, NY, 1999.

## Chapter 2

Bulow, I., U. Schott-Wullenweber and F. Hedderich. "Change Management in Purchasing: Best Practices at Germany's Number 1 Airline Deutsche Lufthansa AG," *PRACTIX,* CAPS Research 9, July 2006.

Carter, C.R. "Ethical Issues in Global Buyer-Supplier Relationships." CAPS Research, Tempe, AZ, 1998.

Carter, C.R., and M.M. Jennings. "Purchasing's Contribution to the Socially Responsible Management of the Supply Chain." CAPS Research, Tempe, AZ, 2000.

Dalton, M. A. "Cultural Adaptability: It's About More Than Using the Right Fork." *Leadership in Action,* (21:6), January/February 2002, pp. 8–11.

Flynn, A., and S. Farney. Chapter 2, "The Strategic Planning Process," and Chapter 4, "Leading, Managing and Supervising." In *The Supply Management Leadership Process:*

*Strategies for Organizational Effectiveness.* National Association of Purchasing Management, Inc., Tempe, AZ, 2000.

Flynn, A., M.L. Harding, C.S. Lallatin, H.M. Pohlig and S.R. Sturzl, (Eds.). *ISM Glossary of Key Supply Management Terms,* Fourth Edition. Institute for Supply Management, Tempe, AZ, 2006.

Hedderich, F., R. Giesecke and D. Ohmsen. "Identifying and Evaluating Chinese Suppliers: China Sourcing Practices of German Manufacturing Companies." *PRACTIX,* CAPS Research 9, August 2006.

Kotter, J.P. *A Force for Change.* The Free Press, New York, NY, 1990.

Kotter, J.P. "What Leaders Really Do." *Harvard Business Review,* May–June, 1990.

Kotter, J.P. "Winning at Change," *Leader to Leader,* (10), Fall 1998, pp. 27–33.

Lewis, C.P. *Building a Shared Vision: A Leader's Guide to Aligning the Organization.* Productivity Press, Portland, OR, 1997.

Zsidisin, G. and L. Ellram. "Supply Risk Assessment Analysis." *PRACTIX,* CAPS Research, (2:4), June 1999, pp. 9–12.

**Chapter 3**

Goleman, D., R. Boyatzis and A. McKee. *Primal Leadership.* Harvard Business School Press, Boston, MA, 2004.

**Chapter 4**

Chan, C. "Is There Such a Thing as an Asian, as Opposed to a Western, Leadership Style?" *Leadership in Asia,* (24:5), November–December 2004, www.ccl.org

**Chapter 5**

Caniels, M.C.J., and C.J. Gelderman. "Power and Interdependence in Kraljic's Purchasing Portfolio Matrix." Competitive paper presented at the IPSERA 2005 Conference, Archamps, France, March 20–24, 2005.

Fine, C. *Clockspeed: Winning Industry Control in the Age of Temporary Advantage.* Perseus Books, Reading, MA, 1998.

Leenders, M.R., P.F. Johnson, A.E. Flynn and H.E. Fearon. Chapter 18. "Make or Buy, Insourcing or Outsourcing," and Chapter 20, "Strategic Supply." In *Purchasing and Supply Management,* McGraw Hill, Burr Ridge, IL, 2005.

Stokes, M. "Taking Full Advantage of Enterprisewide Risk Management." *The Treasurer,* Association of Corporate Treasurers, London, England, May 2004.

### Chapter 6

Flynn, A., M.L. Harding, C.S. Lallatin, H.M. Pohlig and S.R. Sturzl, (Eds.). *ISM Glossary of Key Supply Management Terms,* Fourth Edition. Institute for Supply Management, Tempe, AZ, 2006.

Morrisey, G. *A Guide to Long-Range Planning: Creating Your Strategic Journey.* Jossey-Bass, San Francisco, CA, 1996.

Morrisey, G. *A Guide to Tactical Planning: Producing Your Short-Term Results.* Jossey-Bass, San Francisco, CA, 1996.

### Chapter 7

Flynn, A., M.L. Harding, C.S. Lallatin, H.M. Pohlig and S.R. Sturzl, (Eds.). *ISM Glossary of Key Supply Management Terms,* Fourth Edition. Institute for Supply Management, Tempe, AZ, 2006.

Flynn, A., and S. Farney. Chapter 6, "Operating Policies, Guidelines, and Procedures," and Chapter 7, "Tools to Manage Workflow." In *The Supply Management Leadership Process: Strategies for Organizational Effectiveness.* National Association of Purchasing Management, Inc., Tempe, AZ, 2000, pp. 145–70.

Leenders, M.R., and P.F. Johnson. "Major Changes in Supply Chain Responsibilities." CAPS Research, Tempe, AZ, 2002.

### Chapter 8

Caniels, M.C.J., and C.J. Gelderman. "Power and Interdependence in Kraljic's Purchasing Portfolio Matrix." Competitive paper presented at the IPSERA 2005 Conference, Archamps, France, March 20–24, 2005.

Fine, C. *Clockspeed: Winning Industry Control in the Age of Temporary Advantage.* Perseus Books, Reading, MA, 1998.

Flynn, A., M.L. Harding, C.S. Lallatin, H.M. Pohlig and S.R. Sturzl, (Eds.). *ISM Glossary of Key Supply Management Terms,* Fourth Edition. Institute for Supply Management, Tempe, AZ, 2006.

**Chapter 9**

Aranda, E.K., and L. Aranda, with K. Conlon. *Teams: Structure, Process, Culture, and Politics.* Prentice Hall, Upper Saddle River, NJ, 1998.

Flynn, A.E., and S. Farney. Chapter 5, "Selecting, Recruiting and Retaining Personnel." In *The Supply Management Leadership Process,* Volume 4. Institute for Supply Management, Tempe, AZ, 2000.

Flynn, A., M.L. Harding, C.S. Lallatin, H.M. Pohlig and S.R. Sturzl, (Eds.). *ISM Glossary of Key Supply Management Terms,* Fourth Edition. Institute for Supply Management, Tempe, AZ, 2006.

Giunipero, L., and R.B. Handfield. "Purchasing Education Training II." CAPS Research, Tempe, AZ, 2004.

GLOBE: Global Leadership and Organizational Behavior Effectiveness Research Project Home Page, www.thunderbird.edu/wwwfiles.ms/globe/

"Impacting the Supply Management Profession: Charting and Navigating Strategies for the CPO and Your Team's Evolution" A.T. Kearney Inc., 2007.

Kramer, R.J. "Developing Global Leaders." The Conference Board Working Group Report, December 2005.

Ready, D.A., and J.A. Conger. "How to Fill the Talent Gap." Joint study by *MIT Sloan Management Review* and *The Wall Street Journal,* September 2007.

Schwarz, Roger M. *The Skilled Facilitator.* Jossey-Bass Publishers, San Francisco, CA, 1994.

Senge, Peter M. *The Fifth Discipline: The Art and Practice of the Learning Organization.* Doubleday/Currency, New York, 1990.

**Chapter 10**

Aranda, E.K., and L. Aranda, with K. Conlon. *Teams: Structure, Process, Culture, and Politics.* Prentice Hall, Upper Saddle River, NJ, 1998.

Flynn, A.E., and S. Farney. Chapter 5, "Selecting, Recruiting and Retaining Personnel." In *The Supply Management Leadership Process,* Volume 4, McGraw Hill, Burr Ridge, IL, 2000.

Giunipero, L., and R.B. Handfield. "Purchasing Education Training II." CAPS Research, Tempe, AZ, 2004.

GLOBE: Global Leadership and Organizational Behavior Effectiveness Research Project Home Page, www.thunderbird.edu/wwwfiles.ms/globe/

Kramer, R.J. "Developing Global Leaders." The Conference Board, Working Group Report, December 2005.

Ready, D.A., and J.A. Conger. "How to Fill the Talent Gap." Joint study by *MIT Sloan Management Review* and *The Wall Street Journal,* September 2007.

Siegfried, M. "Filling the Leadership Void." *Inside Supply Management,* April 2007, pp. 22–5.

**Chapter 11**

Flynn, A.E., and S. Farney. Chapter 8, "Performance Tracking and Improvement." In *The Supply Management Leadership Process.* National Association of Purchasing Management, Inc., Tempe, AZ, 2000.

Flynn, A., M.L. Harding, C.S. Lallatin, H.M. Pohlig and S.R. Sturzl, (Eds.). *ISM Glossary of Key Supply Management Terms,* Fourth Edition. Institute for Supply Management, Tempe, AZ, 2006.

**Chapter 12**

Carter, C.R., and M.M. Jennings. "Purchasing's Contribution to the Socially Responsible Management of the Supply Chain." CAPS Research, 2000.

Flynn, A., M.L. Harding, C.S. Lallatin, H.M. Pohlig and S.R. Sturzl, (Eds.). *ISM Glossary of Key Supply Management Terms,* Fourth Edition. Institute for Supply Management, Tempe, AZ, 2006.

# Index

## B



## C

## D



## E

## F

## G



## H

## M

## N

## Q



## R

## S

## T

## U



## V

## W



## X



## Y



## Z